THE ROADS
WE HAVE TRAVELED

THE ROADS WE HAVE TRAVELED

Volume 2

RICHARD L. WHITE

Copyright © 2020 by Richard L. White.

Library of Congress Control Number:		2020911388
ISBN:	Hardcover	978-1-9845-8424-3
	Softcover	978-1-9845-8423-6
	eBook	978-1-9845-8422-9

All rights reserved. No part of this book may be reproduced or transmitted in any form or by any means, electronic or mechanical, including photocopying, recording, or by any information storage and retrieval system, without permission in writing from the copyright owner.

Any people depicted in stock imagery provided by Getty Images are models, and such images are being used for illustrative purposes only.
Certain stock imagery © Getty Images.

Print information available on the last page.

Rev. date: 06/18/2020

To order additional copies of this book, contact:
Xlibris
1-888-795-4274
www.Xlibris.com
Orders@Xlibris.com
815246

THE ROADS WE HAVE TRAVELED: VOLUME 2: 2009-2019

Dedication

This book is dedicated to my primary traveling companion, my dear wife Kerstin

And to Janine, Lisa, and Windy

Cover Photo

August 2017: At a pub in Bowness, England in the Lake District near Windemere Lake. Charles Dickens raised a glass here.

August 2017: Pub in Bowness, England in the Lake District near Windemere Lake. Charles Dickens raised a glass here.

Introduction

In preparation for Volume 2 of *The Roads We Have Traveled*, I looked back at my introduction to Volume 1, which was published in 2009. At age 59, I reflected on my two distinct lives: my first 19 years, when I never boarded a plane and traveled no further than Virginia to the south, Pennsylvania to the west, and New Hampshire to the north; and 1970 to 2009, those years of personal growth, discovery, marriage, fatherhood, parenting, job transitions, and my developing career. And, of course, in the midst of all this *life* there was the constant travel.

This year I turn 70. This second collection of travelogues from April 6, 2009 until December 30, 2019—the very end of the decade—does not encompass as many life changes as the previous four decades, but it does present an unmistakable theme or thread. In essence, it's the story of Kerstin and me opening our arms to the world and connecting with the people and places that mean the most to us. There are numerous trips to Kerstin's native country, Germany (14 in all), to visit her father, mother, relatives, and friends. There are domestic trips to our favorite places for nature and relaxation: southeastern New Hampshire (4 trips), the Adirondacks in New York State (3 trips), the Delaware Seacoast (3 trips), the Amish Country of southeastern Pennsylvania (numerous trips from 2013 to 2015), and Colorado (2 trips). There are graduation trips to Miami, Montreal, and Nashville. There was my professional trip to Israel. We also enjoyed *real getaways* to Mexico, Alaska, Ireland, and Switzerland. And, in November 2019, we made a solemn pilgrimage to Denmark in search of Kerstin's grandmother, who tragically perished in a refugee camp there in October 1945.

Among our happiest travels were those involving our children, Janine, Lisa, and Windy. All are working in the field of education—currently, Janine for a start-up university in London; Windy as a 6th-grade history teacher at a charter school in Brooklyn; and Lisa as a program manager and researcher in support of pre-school education initiatives in San Mateo, California. In normal times, we travel regularly to their exciting locales in the Lauriston village in East London, the

Glendale section of Queens, and the Haight-Ashbury section of San Francisco.

Of course, these are not normal times. During the coronavirus pandemic, we have had to resort to WhatsApp and Zoom family meetings and birthday celebrations. One benefit of the pandemic is that it has inspired and motivated Kerstin and me to explore the natural beauties of southeastern New Hampshire—the stunning coast, the peaceful, pine-needled trails, and the pristine glacier lakes. We often see more wildlife than people on our walks and hikes. It seems fitting that during our last out-of-state trip in early March before the governor's stay-at-home order, I paused and reflected at Henry David Thoreau's Walden Pond and gravesite in Concord, Massachusetts. We feel the spirit of Thoreau every time we look out our back door and see the herons, ospreys, and eagles swooping along the Exeter River.

Our wish is that Kerstin and I will soon travel again to familiar places to visit our children, relatives, and friends. We will also open our arms and imaginations to new places, now that we are mostly retired. One thing is for sure: there will always be *more roads to travel.*

Exeter, New Hampshire
May 2020

Chapter 1

MEXICO

April 6-11, 2009

"Every morning looking east, the villagers would have seen the sun rising out of the sparkling sea"

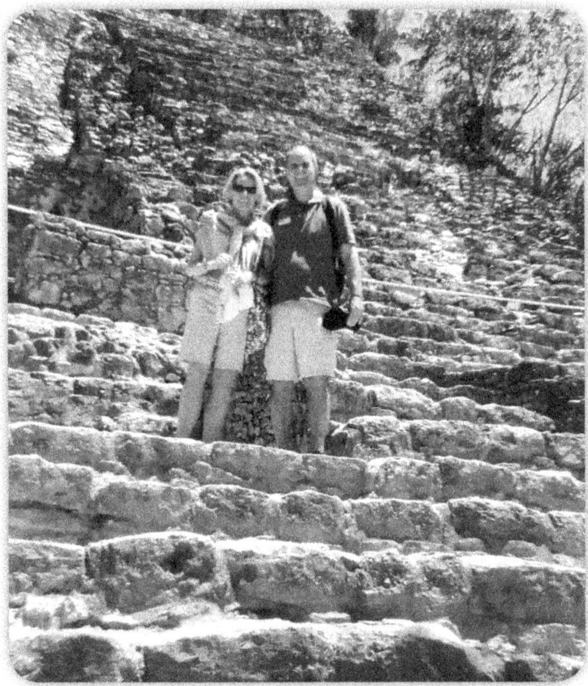

Mayan Ruins at Coba, Riviera Maya, Mexico

Tuesday, April 7

Kersti and I are lounging under an umbrella-like cabana on the Riviera Maya south of Cancun. The sun is shining through thin, hazy clouds, and a steady ocean breeze is keeping us comfortable.

What a contrast to yesterday morning! Norbert picked us up on a cool Monday morning around 8:00, just as the first drops of rain were falling. By the time we boarded the plane for our 10:30 flight to Cancun, the rain was falling steadily, and soon it turned into a pounding thunderstorm, which closed the airport and resulted in a three-hour wait on the tarmac. The time passed quickly enough, as we watched "The Express," the inspiring story of Ernie Davis, the acclaimed Syracuse running back, the first African-American to win the Heisman Trophy in the early sixties. He was diagnosed with leukemia at the age of 22 and died a year later. I remember what a sad day that was. These stories of young heroes overcoming racial bias are very moving to me.

We finally arrived at the Santos de Caracol resort, about half an hour south of the airport, around 6:30 PM. It's a sprawling compound, consisting of about 60 three-story, tastefully designed units. Our room is very spacious with a king-size bed and very firm mattress, a living room area, and a big Jacuzzi in the middle. By the time we went in search of a buffet for dinner, it was dark. We stopped at the first place offering food, an open-air snack bar adjacent to the small "town center" with shops and an open bar. The food was fast and satisfactory—spicy beans, fresh guacamole, diced onions, and a beef stew consumed with plastic utensils. Only after dinner did we discover several nice restaurants, where we will dine this week. We found our way to the beach and lay there for awhile, watching the thin clouds play with the nearly full moon. We grew a little chilly and returned to our apartment around 10:00 by our watches—9:00 Mexican time.

We slept well in our big bed. This morning in the daylight, we found a shorter route to the breakfast buffet. Expecting to hear mostly American accents, we were pleasantly surprised to hear French, German, and a Scandinavian language.

Wednesday, April 8

This was a spectacular day with a perfect blue sky and a brisk, cooling wind. I was reminded of my days in New Hampshire with Jim Harris and Ross Creagan in late August 1971. At noon, we took the bus to the nearby small coastal city of Playa del Carmen. We leisurely strolled along Avenida Quinta (Fifth Avenue), consisting of endless small shops selling Mexican blankets, pottery, scarves, and trinkets for the tourists. So many shop owners lined the streets, calling us "amigos" and inviting us in to take a look. We finally found a nice pottery store and bought some small pieces for Janine, Lisa, Eric, Laurie, and Kersti. Later, Kersti bought a small cupboard shelf for her sand tray, and I bought her a Mayan jewel design for a necklace. At each block along Avenida Quinta, Kersti and I peered toward the ocean, amazed at the light and darker shades of turquoise.

Thursday, April 9

On Eric's 16th birthday, the first that we did not celebrate with him in person, we rose at 6:30 and joined the first wave of breakfasters at 7:00—everyone who was leaving Sandoz Caracol on a bus tour. We headed south at 8:30—half an hour later than our scheduled departure because a California family of five was tired from their outing the previous day. I was a little skeptical at first, but we wound up having a nice conversation with the laid-back dad, probably a doctor, and his wife, a native of the Philippines. The air felt warmer than yesterday, and some puffy clouds decorated the blue sky.

Our tour guide was Hernan, a crusty, gold-toothed man, probably in his early sixties, who had the distinct look of a native Mayan. Our first stop was Tulum, the only known Mayan site on the Mexican Caribbean coast. "Tulum" means "fortress" in Mayan, and its original name is said to be "Zama" or "daybreak." Both are apt, descriptive names, though I like the image of the day "breaking" to the east, across the waters of the Caribbean, in olden times. Tulum was a protected city with three walls of 10-16 feet, bordering a cliff of about 40 feet. Every morning looking east, villagers would have seen the sun rising out of the sparkling sea. As Hernan explained, most of the buildings at Tulum date from the Post Classic period in Mayan history—1200 to 1450 A.D. Within the city of perhaps 100 buildings are three surviving prominent structures. The first is the Castillo, the largest building with a broad staircase leading to a temple, where human sacrifices may have occurred. Archaelogically, the most interesting building is the Temple of the Frescoes, completed about 1450. Finally, there is the Temple of the Diving God. According to our guidebook, Baedecker's *Mexico, 1987*, "in the niche above the entrance is a stucco figure of the Diving God, who is depicted with wings on his arms and shoulders and a bird's tail. There are various interpretations of this divinity, who appears so frequently at Tulum—as a bee flying down, as the evening star on the sun at its setting, as lightning. Practically nothing is left of the painting on the main façade of the temple and the wall of the interior."

Our favorite part of the visit was walking along the pathways at the top of the cliff. We had spectacular views of the curving coastline and the Mayan ruins. Despite the crowds of tourists, we gained a good feeling of what life was like in the days when Tulum was a bustling Mayan center.

Our next stop was Coba, about 50 kilometers inland from Tulum. It is one of the largest Mayan sites, dating from the Classic Period (600-900 A.D.). Amazingly, it was not "discovered" until 1891 by an Austrian archaeologist, Toebert Mayer. It covered a large area of 27 square miles. The two most impressive structures were the "Iglesia" (Church), a pyramid-like structure which is 80 feet high, with nine terraces leading to a small temple, and "El Castillo" (The Castle), which is 138 feet high. The two structures are about 2 kilometers apart, and to traverse the hot, dusty, wooded pathways, we took rickshaws along with Hernan and two British ladies who were on our tour. El Castillo looked formidable, but lots of people were climbing it, so one of the Brits and I climbed the 120 steps of uneven stones. I stayed close to the stairs, climbing like a four-legged animal. Hernan said the government may close this site to tourists next year, so I'm glad I did it. He promised a "magnificent" view of the four lakes making up the Coba region, but it was not that impressive. Looking back down to the ground was more thrilling.

After a late lunch at the poolside of a nearby distinctive hotel with a historic Mayan theme, we drove back to the coast to a beautiful beach near Tulum called "El Paraiso" (The Paradise). Tropical trees provided shade on the beach, and the wind was whipping through the leaves.

The sand was almost pure white, fine, soft, and gentle to the touch. We returned to our resort around 6:30, a full 10 hours after we departed.

For dinner, we enjoyed our best meal and atmosphere of the entire week: a delicious three-course meal at the Riviera restaurant, overlooking the beach and the full moon, which poured down streaks of light on the water as it rose in the sky.

Friday, April 10

Today is Good Friday, but there was no religious observance or slowdown in the pace of activity at the resort. This was the warmest day of the week, even as we sat on the beach in the morning beneath mostly cloudy skies. We read and relaxed after our all-day excursion on Thursday. I was racing through Malcolm Gladwell's bestseller, *The Outliers*, while Kersti was getting into the book I had finished earlier in the week, *The Day John Died,* by Christopher Andersen, about JFK Jr. The April sun burned through the clouds early in the afternoon, and our skin turned red in a few spots despite taking just one afternoon walk. We took three swims, climbing up twice on soft, slippery rocks like beached whales. The water was comfortable and clear, but we had to be careful not to step on occasional rocks. We finally returned to our room after 6:00, wishing we could extend our stay by just another day or two.

Saturday, April 11

We just returned from our final glimpse of the beach and stroll through the compound. I was sweating when we came back into our air-conditioned, comfortable room—this feels like it will be the hottest and most humid day of the week. With the sides of Kersti's legs "beet red" and my stomach feeling a little queasy, it is now time to go.

If our trip to Mexico in January 1988 left us feeling doubtful about the pleasures of vacationing in Mexico, this visit reconciled us completely to the country and the people. Maybe we were a little too adventurous last time, too often seeking the roads and destinations "not taken." "All inclusive" gets my vote. Next time—and there may well be a return trip to Mexico in the future—we may rent a car and do some more things on our own, but a resort—for comfort, tasty and reliable food, and convenience—is the way to go.

Now we will take our final walk to the open reception area and board the Olympus van for our return trip to the airport and our flight home.

Adiós, Mexico. ¡Hasta la vista!

Chapter 2

ISRAEL

May 21-28, 2009

"We sped through the dry countryside with the sun pouring down on us, curving our way through some hilly terrain until we approached Jerusalem"

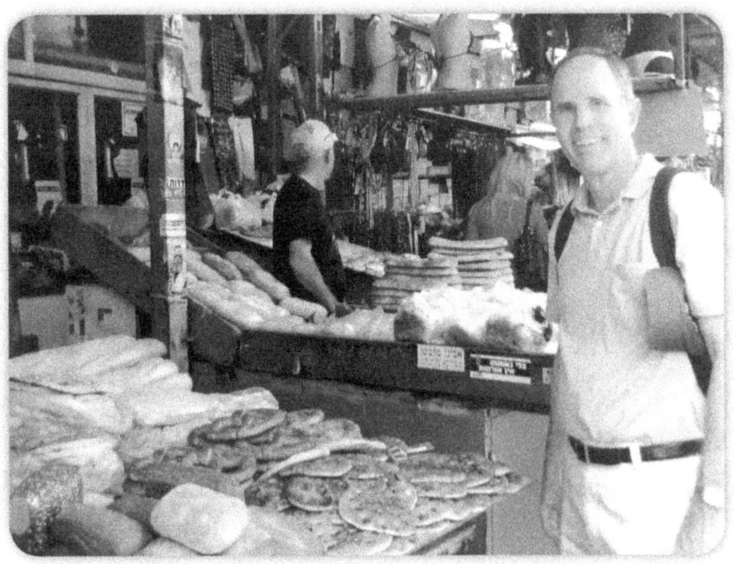

Market in Tel Aviv, Israel

Friday, May 22: Jerusalem

I just curled into my bed at the Prima Royale Hotel on Medeke Street, not far from the old city of Jerusalem. Tiredness is beginning to overcome me, even though it is only 3:30 PM "body time"—a seven-hour difference.

Yesterday's busy day at Rutgers is still resonating. Lisa graduated from Rutgers for the second time in two days. At the university commencement on Wednesday, Lisa represented Rutgers College. The weather was glorious on both days with brilliant sunshine streaming down through the leafy trees of Vorhees Mall, the central quad on the College Avenue Campus. On Thursday in the hour before we lined up to march from Old Queens to the quad, Eric and I were dismantling her bed and loading the mattress and accessories into the car. As I did last year, I marched with the 2,000 students, faculty, and staff and sat on the assembled stage, waiting for Lisa's name to be called so I could congratulate her with a big hug.

We celebrated with a delicious dinner at a festive Greek restaurant in Highland Park. The Papathomases were also there. Norbert and I ordered early, enabling us to finish relatively quickly so Norbert could drop me off at the airport for my 10:50 PM flight. I arrived at the airport around 8:00, allowing the extra hour for the double than normal security checks for the flight to Tel Aviv.

I thought the flight would be 11 hours, but it was a little less than 10. We followed the same route as we do when we fly to Germany, passing over London and Paris before tilting southward across Rome, Athens, Cyprus, and into Tel Aviv. It really helped that the passengers complied with the captain's request to keep the shades down because of the bright sunshine from early morning on. I began reading J.R. Moehringer's memoir, *The Tender Bar*, watched two films, *Paris, J'Taime* and Woody Allen's classic, *Annie Hall,* from the mid-seventies. On my right, I spoke with a Jewish woman in her sixties from Seattle, who was visiting her son, daughter-in-law, and three small grandchildren, living in a very observant and traditional Jewish community close to Jerusalem. It was Friday afternoon, and he would not have been able to drive to pick up his mom if there had been delays and it was after sundown. On my left was a neurophysicist who was born in Lithuania in 1937, moved to Moscow in 1934, survived the Stalin, Krushchev and Breshnev years, and moved to Israel in 1973. He moved to the U.S. (Seattle area) in 1978 and became a citizen. His was an interesting story of identity and cultural connection. For him, Israel felt like coming home, something he could not say about any other place on earth. He gave me a brief lesson in Hebrew before the plane landed.

Jerusalem, the ancient city claimed as the spiritual home of Jews, Muslims, and Christians, is located east of Tel Aviv at the border of the West Bank, which was seized by Israel from Jordan in the Six-Day War in 1967. Today, it is self-governed by the Fattah faction of the Palestinians. My driver spoke no English and just some broken Spanish, so that was our only mode of communication. We sped through the dry countryside with the sun pouring down on us, curving our way through some hilly terrain until we approached Jerusalem. It is built on a series of hills. It is a beautiful, clean city consisting of many sandstone-colored buildings, which blend so well into the natural landscape. Around 8:00, the other 14 members of our career services group returned from their walking tour of the old city, including the stations of the cross on the Via Dolorosa, where Jesus took some of his final steps before crucifixion. I'm sorry I missed that tour, but Aaron Goldberg, the trip coordinator, said he would take me back during the shopping mission later in the week.

Saturday, May 23: Masada and the Dead Sea

(Our Meeting Day 27 Years Ago)

This was a fun and full day, and dinner at a restaurant still awaits us. After a continental breakfast on the outside patio of our hotel, we boarded a bus and headed east through the Palestinian-controlled West Bank to the northern tip of the Dead Sea. We drove the entire 67-kilometer length of the sea to Masada, gazing across to the mountains of Jordan rising on the other side. The Dead Sea is the lowest point on earth. It is below sea level, and the daily intense radiation and limited rainfall contribute to the loss of one meter of the sea every year. Given its extremely dry, rarely replenished condition (only two inches of rain a year), I expected the sea to have a brownish, brackish hue, like the sandstone that dominates the region and the country. But it was bright blue as we drove along the coastal route.

Our first stop was Masada, the fortress built by King Herod around the time of Jesus, and conquered by the Romans around 70 A.D. The Jews who were occupying the fort decided to kill their wives, children, and themselves rather than surrender to the Romans. They chose honorable death over imprisonment or slavery. It is possible to walk up a steep, rocky path to the Masada remains, but we traversed the mountain in a large gondola, holding over 50 people. We toured the fortress, peering into a storage area, walking through Roman baths, and looking out on several Roman campsites.

After lunch, we drove to a Dead Sea beach area, the only one that I saw. After putting on our bathing suits, we boarded large wagons, and a tractor pulled us close to the beach and water. Most of our group braved the hard, salty beach leading into the water, but once we reached a depth of three or more feet, we flopped on our backs and floated like rubber duckies. The Dead Sea has 10 times the buoyancy of the normal ocean, and thus we floated and couldn't really swim. The water was extremely salty, and when I a speck of salt water jumped up into my eye, I could hardly open it, and I couldn't rub it with my salty hands! All in all, it was a fun and memorable experience.

We returned to Jerusalem for a quick visit to the Old City. Our tour guide, Ya-el, took me on a personal tour of the Church of the Holy Sepulchre, the site where Jesus is believed to have been buried after his crucifixion and raised from the dead. The first church on this site was built in 326 A.D. We witnessed some Greek Orthodox Christians performing a Saturday afternoon ritual with a procession, incense, and chants. We then walked along a part of the Via Dolorosa, observing several of the stations of the cross. Later, Ya-el took me up to the roof of an Austrian church where she pointed out the Mount of Olives, where Jesus was arrested the night before his crucifixion, the golden dome of a famous mosque, and the double domes of the Church of the Holy Sepulchre. Before my personal tour, Ya-el took several members of our group to an authentic pottery shop, where I bought some hand-painted pottery for Kersti and the girls. Overall, the city feels extremely safe with people of all races and religions blending together peacefully.

Sunday, May 24: Jerusalem

Yesterday was "Shabat," the Jewish Sabath, but our group maintained our rapid pace. Sunday in Israel is like Monday in the U.S., although we did not venture out of the city, and it was a much more evenly-paced day.

In the morning, we drove to Mount Scopus, home of Israel's top university, Hebrew University. When it opened in 1925, Israel was not yet a state and under the control of the British and its so-called British Mandate. But early on, the university had a vision and invited Albert Einstein onto its first board of governors. He came to the university for its opening ceremony. Today, it is a beautifully landscaped, spacious institution with 24,000 students. It has a spectacular 360° view of Jerusalem. We were the guess of the Rothberg International School, which attracts 2,000 students a year from 50 countries. The most interesting part of the visit was the discussion between an Israeli professor and his Israeli—Palestinian co-researcher. They discussed the complexity of the Israeli-Palestinian problem, and I gained more clarity into the challenge of the economic gulf that exists between the Palestinian and Israeli geography. I also enjoyed my chat with an American graduate student from Florida, who is not Jewish, but came here with her now ex-boyfriend, and received a temporary visa and work permit based on her relationship at the time. She is graduating this summer and wants to stay in Israel, but may be asked to leave when she seeks the renewal of her temporary resident status in August. It would be a different story if she were Jewish.

After lunch in the student cafeteria, we toured Belazel, an art institute on the same grounds as Hebrew University. We joined an architectural class that was touring a Scottish church, built in the late 1920s after the British "liberation" of Jerusalem during World War I. We concluded the day with a visit to the Israeli Holocaust Museum. It was a powerful and moving exhibit, detailing the atrocities in each of the European countries. In the triangular-shaped museum, we kept crisscrossing the hallway, as we gradually moved our way from the darkened depths to the sunny, hopeful conclusion and a view overlooking the Holy City.

After a nighttime tour of the city with Ya-el, including a glimpse at the traditional site of the Last Supper, my friend, Joe Dupont from Brandeis University, and I strolled through the quaint German part of the city. It felt a little like Beacon Hill in Boston. We enjoyed some traditional Middle Eastern food—a generous portion of hummus and skewers of lamb—while several others opted for an Italian restaurant.

Monday, May 25, Memorial Day: Jerusalem to Tel Aviv

Today was another full, 12-hour day. After breakfast, we boarded our bus for our trip to Tel Aviv. Soon after departing from Jerusalem, we left the hilly topography and dry terrain behind, replaced by wide flat fields of crops. Tel Aviv is a busy, bustling city, which is much less clean than Jerusalem.

Our first stop was a high tech company that employs five interns. They are sponsored at their work site by Career Israel, an agency whose representative addressed us along with two interns and their supervisor. Then we drove to a poor part of the city to a small social service agency, which provides assistance to illegal immigrants from the Philippines, Sri Lanka, and Africa. Four interns from four countries—the U.S. England, Canada, and Uruguay—described their experiences and plans. We ate a delicious typical Israeli lunch consisting of tapa-like appetizers—small plates of mushrooms, eggplant, shredded carrots, chickpeas, and hummus—followed by skewers of tender chicken and beef. I finally started using one phrase of Hebrew—*tobá rabá* or "thank you very much" followed by *shalom*—"goodbye" and "peace" as well as "hello."

Continuing our whirlwind tour, we next traveled north of the city to IDC, Israel's only private university. It was founded in 1994 with an expressed mission of helping and serving the state of Israel. It focuses on programs such as counterterrorism, conflict resolution, computer science, psychology, and business. The vice president gave an impassioned overview of the school and its mission and then took us on a personal tour. Although his speech and actions were overtly militaristic and aggressive, I was impressed by his genuine affection for the students and faculty whom we encountered on the tour, including his "favorite" students from Ethiopia, Jews who were rescued from turmoil and poverty a few years ago by the Israelis. Of course, his action of putting his arm around one Ethiopian female and stroking her hair would not be acceptable at an American institution.

Our final stop of the day was our favorite: the ancient port of Jaffa, just to the south of Tel Aviv. Jaffa was cited in the Bible several times; it was the site from which Jonah sailed and returned after his encounter with the whale. Peter came here after the crucifixion of Christ and raised a young woman, Tabitha, from the dead. Jaffa was the entry point to the Holy Land in the eighteenth and nineteenth centuries, before the port was deemed too small. Tel Aviv, which was founded just 100 years ago this year, has far surpassed Jaffa in size and importance.

A German archeologist, who has spent the last 15-20 years conducting digs in Jaffa, took us on a fascinating tour of one outdoor dig, which revealed some Egyptian hieroglyphics from the King Ramses era, and an indoor-outdoor excavation of a nineteen-century French hospital built atop the grounds of a fort and moat built during the Crusades. The archeologist described the delicate relationship between the excavation and an investor's plans to convert the old hospital to a luxury hotel. As it turns out, the old fort and moat will be part of the grounds of the hotel, and it should be quite an attraction, quite good for business.

We finally arrived at our nearby beachfront hotel at 8:00, and Joe and I, still stuffed from our big, late lunch, decided to call it a night. I snacked on an apple and orange in my room.

Tuesday, May 26: Tel Aviv

Throughout the trip, I have been awakened by the morning sun without the benefit of a wake-up call. Most mornings the bus left promptly at 8:30, meaning I came down for breakfast around 7:45, and this morning was no exception. We drove to south Tel Aviv, one of the poorer areas of the city, and visited a school where young American Jews volunteer. The coordinator of the program that brings students to this school is Sara, a 2001 Rutgers graduate. She told me that she moved to Israel and became a citizen after meeting her future husband, an Israeli, in a summer camp. She told me she misses her hometown of Ridgewood and even New Brunswick. All the students we met at this school and throughout our time in Israel spoke highly of their sponsoring organizations, the culture, and people, and the meaningful work they were doing. The same was true of the two additional stops we made in the late morning at a social service agency and early afternoon at a school.

We have been going at quite a pace, and finally we got a break with three hours of free time in the afternoon. Joe and I strolled to the market, where I found an authentic Tel Aviv soccer jersey for Eric. We swung down to the boulevard along the beach, and walked most of the way back to the hotel along the beach. We then put on our bathing suits—mine was still heavy with salt and not yet dry from my dip in the Dead Sea on Saturday. We arrived at a wide, beautiful, not crowded beach in about 10 minutes. We waded into the clean, warm ocean waters—probably in the mid-70s. We swam for awhile and then returned to the hotel for a shower and a team meeting at 5:30.

The evening highlight was attending a VIP reception and annual gala of MASA. MASA (accent on the second "a"), which means "journey" in Hebrew, works with about 160 nonprofit organizations in Israel, which arrange five- to ten-month volunteer assignments and cultural and historical tours for about 8,000 Jewish students a year from about 50 countries. We had heard that Prime Minister Netanyahu, who just last week had his first meeting in Washington with President Obama, would address the crowd of perhaps 2,000, mostly young volunteers. Sure enough, shortly after we were seated, "Bibi" appeared with his security entourage. In his distinctive, forceful voice, he spoke about the importance of the Israeli state and the role of MASA in building students' appreciation for this Jewish "homeland." At one point, a student yelled out, "Two states!," referring to Israel and Palestine, but the prime minister ignored that and kept on talking. He was followed by the Israeli finance minister, who was even more adamant in appealing to the young people to pursue *aliya* or citizenship. We listened to about four loud songs by an unappealing, mid-level Israel rock star, Moshe or "Mosh," before we were mercifully allowed to leave to catch our bus back to the hotel. Our hosts, Aaron and Fredda, both criticized Netanyahu and the finance minister for their pressure tactics in trying to get MASA students to stay and become citizens. Ya-el also expressed her disapproval of the heavy-handed tactics and tone of the prime minister.

Wednesday, May 27: Tel Aviv

I am sitting in the Tel Aviv Airport at 10:15 PM, waiting for our departure at 11:50—almost the beginning of a new and very long day. It has been a full and enjoyable final day in Israel. This morning we traveled to a school an hour north of the city that offers intensive instruction in Arabic. We also learned about the ancient common roots of Arabic and Hebrew (just compare *shalom* to *salam*) and the influence of Hebrew on Arabic since Israeli statehood in 1948. After lunch in the school cafeteria—which we shared with about 200 Israeli soldiers who are studying to gain admission to universities as part of their pending transition from the army— drove to a small town operated largely by Israeli-Arabs. We heard from the deputy mayor, the student interns who are teaching English in the town, and later an elderly Palestinian, who told us about life during the pre-1948 British rule. Some small, cute children scampered about, demonstrating the carefree, curious nature of all young children around the world. The Palestinian also invited us into a nearby, dim, smoke-filled room, where several of the men of the town were idling away another afternoon.

Our final stop was a total contrast: a high-tech company on the 34th floor of one of Tel Aviv's tallest buildings. The company specializes in water system security from an integrated standpoint, combining prevention, detection, maintenance, and solutions. We had a magnificent view of this large, modern city on the eastern coast of the Mediterranean.

We ate a final tasty dinner at a restaurant at the port, and I enjoyed chatting with Rebecca, an intern from the University of Michigan who was completing a 10-month internship. I'm not quite sure where she has been working—she may be teaching English at a school—because we mostly talked about her two years as a Teach for America volunteer in the Bronx, her boyfriend in Springfield, New Jersey, and her uncertain plans for the future—MSW or Psy.D.

This is the first time I have flown west, leaving when it is dark, flying through the entire night in the dark, and landing with the first faint light of dawn. It will be a long night and a very long day tomorrow.

This has been a marvelous trip—full of new places, new impressions, and a deeper admiration for this country and its people. In just 60 years, it has built a modern, progressive, proud country in the desert. In defense of its people, homeland, and faith, it has stumbled at times and made some wrong choices in its treatment of the Palestinians, but overall I am leaving with great respect for the nation and people of Israel.

It seems fitting to close this experience with an excerpt from Psalm 122, a "Song of Praise and Prayer for Jerusalem":

1. I was glad when they said to me,
   "Let us go to the house of the Lord!"
2. Our feet are standing within your gate,
   O Jerusalem
3. Jerusalem—built as a city that is bound firmly together.
4. To it the tribes go up, the tribe of the Lord, as we decreed for Israel to give thanks to the name of the Lord
5. For there the thrones for judgment were set up, the thrones of the house of David
6. Pray for the peace of Jerusalem: "May they prosper who love you.
7. Peace be within your walls."

Chapter 3

SURF CITY, NEW JERSEY

August 8-15, 2009

"We returned to the beach for our favorite time of the day, when the beach clears out and the sun and sand turn golden"

Monday, August 10

After our family vacation in the Azores in August 2007, I wondered if we would ever find the time as a family of five to vacation together. But in late June, during a Sunday day trip to Surf City to visit Anja and her house full of kids, we realized that we would all be in New Jersey the second week of August, so we rented a house at 254 15th Street in Surf City on the bay side. We seized our narrow window of opportunity between summer and fall activities. Lisa returned from her month in Spain on July 29; Kersti ended her summer job at Sage Day on July 31; Janine concluded her human rights fellowship in New York on August 4; and Eric would not begin his soccer camp at the high school until August 17.

We had a very leisurely departure around 12:30 with Eric behind the wheel, me in the front seat, and Kersti and cousin Dave in the middle seats. Pete had brought Dave and Cordelia down from New Hampshire on Friday to visit Grammy at King James, where she is recuperating from her broken hip. As we were leaving Madison, we swung by King James to wish Grammy a happy 91st birthday one day early. She was sitting outside in the August sunshine and was happy to be surrounded by two sons, her daughter-in-law, and all five grandchildren.

Eric was steady behind the wheel, and our unintended detour from the Parkway to the Turnpike and Route 18 before the Raritan bridge and tolls enabled us to avoid miles of congestion on the Parkway. We arrived around 3:30 and were on the beach in less than half an hour.

Our two-story house is about a six-minute walk from the beach and a two-minute walk to the bay. The highlights of the house are the spacious master bedroom, the bar and den area upstairs, and the deck with a nice view of the bay. The kitchen is small and in need of an upgrade, but overall the place is comfortable.

After an unseasonably cool and rainy summer of 2009, this week has been very hot with today's temperature soaring into the 90s. After morning rain on Sunday, today was bright and sunny from dawn to dusk. Kersti, Lisa, and I took an early morning bike ride to 69th Street in Harvey Cedars, where we rented a house about five years ago. We enjoyed the Surf City bike paths, which are as wide as the car lanes. Our rapid movement from the teen-numbered streets to the sixties created a breeze, but we still were sweating when we returned to the house by 9:30. We spent a few hours on the beach, but it was too hot in the afternoon, and we retreated to the air-conditioned comfort of the house.

Dave adds a nice dimension to the family with his easy-going manner. Eric and he are getting along well, and I am confident that they—as well as the girls—will remain close as cousins for many years to come, despite the distance.

Friday, August 14

Thirteen years ago today, after our visit to Middlebury, Vermont during our vacation at Lake Dunmore, we received the call from Mom that Dad had died at King James around 10:00 AM. Mom is at King James today. Janine was 10, Lisa 9, and Eric 3. I remember so vividly the quiet, deliberate, sad moments of packing the car and traveling home, then pulling into the driveway on Dellwood Avenue in Chatham to see Mom in her familiar place in the lighted kitchen window.

Tuesday was our best day of the week. It was the perfect beach day with a steady sea breeze and low humidity. Kersti and I set up our compound early in the now familiar location at the swimming site near the 16th Street entrance. The water was refreshing, and the morning waves and tide manageable, with low tide arriving by late afternoon. We were nicely settled into our routine. I was reading Nathaniel Philbrick's *Mayflower*, the story of the voyage and the first 50 years of the Plymouth Colony, which Pete loaned me. Kersti was reading a classic sandplay book, Janine Anita Daimant's *The Red Tent*, Dave *Three Cups of* Tea for school, and Eric *The Fight Club* for school. Around 1:00, we began our trek back to the cottage for lunch, walking down 16th Street and crossing LBI Boulevard and Central Avenue before turning left onto Sunset Street. Kersti and I made a run to the Shop Rite in Mannahawkin on the mainland, but returned to the beach for our favorite time of the day, when the beach clears out and the sun and sand turn golden. That evening we had a late dinner on the deck with a sushi takeout and a rice-curry dish.

On Wednesday morning, Kersti and I rode our bikes along Barnegat Boulevard toward the Surf City-Barnegat border. We paused to look at the small bridge connecting LBI and Cedar Bonnet Island and the large bridge reaching to the mainland. In the early morning, the bay side of the island was quiet, and we could hear the peaceful, lapping sound of the water. The sky was a solid gray, and the humidity was back in full force. The raindrops began falling by mid-morning, and it rained most of the day. Lisa was not feeling well, but she rallied and joined Kersti, Janine, and me for a matinee showing of "Julie and Julia," the amusing and entertaining story of the famous TV chef, Julia Child, and her dedicated pupil (whom she never meets), Julia Powell.

Thursday was another cloudy day, but the rain held off. In the morning, I inflated the bike tires, and Janine, Kersti, and I road about seven miles to Barnegat Lighthouse at the northern tip of the island. Janine led the way, and after awhile we lost her—or she lost us. We thought we would meet her at the lighthouse, where swarms of people were gathering because of the cloudy weather, but we did not connect. Kersti and I kept a steady pace, heading north from Surf City through North Beach, Harvey Cedars, Loveladies, and Barnegat Light, then back again. On the return trip, we found a road along the bay with tall, reed-like vegetation completely blocking our view of the bay. The wind rustled the reeds, and I was reminded of the narrow roads of Cornwall close to the Atlantic coast.

In the afternoon, Norbert, Nellie, Nellie's friend Kelly, and Daniel visited on their way home from Williamsburg. Despite the cool breeze and gray skies, we trekked off to the beach, and watched Janine, Eric, Dave, Daniel, Nellie, and Kelly frolic in the challenging, pounding surf. The lifeguards were still there, and the kids had them all to themselves. We had an early dinner of cheeseburgers, prepared by Eric on the grill, stir-fried veggies from the Rutgers farm, and salad on the deck—all 10 of us. Our visitors lingered after dinner, not wanting to leave, but they reluctantly departed around 8:30. The kids drove to Beach Haven for ice cream, and Kersti and I took a stroll to the bay and beach. The sky was clearing up, and I immediately saw the Big Dipper hanging low and clear in the sky above the bay.

Sunday, August 16

Friday was another glorious late summer day. The crashing surf of Thursday had subsided, but in its place we found swarms of small jellyfish babies. You could see the white cluster swirling in the waves, and feel them entering and leaving the ocean. They were tiny and harmless—about the size of a lentil bean—but a few stuck to the skin and hair. I had never seen anything like this before in all my years of going to the shore.

We were all in a little funk, knowing that our vacation was coming to an end. Dave helped me put the storage compartment on top of the car. Around dinnertime, Eric's friends, Danny Wasky and Kyle Flanagan, joined us. We lingered at the beach until it was nearly empty. While the boys were playing football and soccer on the beach, Kersti, Janine, Lisa, and I hurried to the bay side to catch the sun sinking toward the western horizon. We watched the big orange ball dip lower and lower before being swallowed up by the mainland. For dinner we had pizza and baked ziti on the deck. The stars were out by the time we finished.

On Saturday morning, after most things were packed, Kersti and I took our final bike ride to the small harbor at North 3rd, 2nd, and 1st Streets. We are thinking about renting a Swiss-style chalet at the corner of 1st Street. It's a much longer walk to the beach, but watching the setting sun each day over the bay would be a special treat. We may just rent for a week next summer, not knowing what our schedules will be, and then see who can join us.

Kersti, Janine, and I headed home a little after 11:00. We encountered some slow traffic on the first 15 miles heading north, where they are expanding the Parkway from two to three lanes, but it was smooth sailing after that. Lisa and the four boys spent the morning at the beach, sunning, swimming, and avoiding the badge checker, but they were done with the beach and on the road themselves by 1:30. We arrived at 2:30 to our excited pets, Peaches, Misty, and Cinnamon, who were glad that we were home.

As I write this early on Sunday morning, the sights and sounds of the sea and the bay remain with me.

Chapter 4

GERMANY

August 20-27, 2009

"We had a spectacular view of the Rhein in all directions: west toward St. Goar, north toward Hessen and the abandoned Ehrenfels Castle, and east toward the Mauseturm and Bingen"

Calv, Germany—Visit to Hermann Hesse's home and museum

Saturday, August 21

It's a beautiful late summer evening in Bingen. Kersti and I just walked through the streets overlooking the Rhein on our way back from *Kaffee und Kuchen* at Bärbel's and Ansgar's. The colors are so sharp in the clear air of late afternoon.

It was such a relief to leave hot, hazy, and humid Madison on Thursday afternoon. Kersti and I enjoyed sitting in the middle seats of the van, while Eric drove and Janine helped him navigate. We flew a comfortable Continental 767 with ample leg room, leaving on time and arriving about 20 minutes early. It was so good to see Vati and Mutti waiting eagerly for us at the airport. We drove back to Bingen in Vati's new brown VW Golf under cloudy skies with intermittent showers.

After our short night, our first day in Bingen was long but leisurely. After lunch, Kersti and I walked along the Nahe to the Rhein, and then explored the new walkways along the Rhein that had been constructed for last year's major outdoor garden show in Bingen—the *Landesgartenschau.* I especially enjoyed the "before and after" impressions—photos of the previous run-down sites juxtaposed to framed, live views of the same sites. Later, the sun came out, and Vati, Mutti, Kersti, and I visited several gardens on the Rhein that had also been created for the flower show.

We made it through the day without napping, finally sliding beneath the comforters around 10:00 PM. We were tired, but didn't realize how tired we were until we woke up this morning and looked at the clock: 11:30 AM! I can't ever remember sleeping for 13 hours. I raised the shades to a sunny, comfortable day. After a quick breakfast (Mutti was disappointed that we didn't have time for my "Saturday egg"), we drove to Vati's favorite Italian restaurant for an easy, tasty lunch of salad and pizza.

Tonight we're looking forward to our visit and dinner with Gabi and Wolfgang.

Monday, August 24

As I explained to Mutti in German, yesterday was a "top 10" day with blue skies, a pleasant breeze, and warm sunshine. After a restless night, we rose for an early breakfast, and we were on the road around 8:45, heading south toward the *Schwarzwald* (Black Forest). Vati handled the morning drive somewhat erratically, sometimes jerking the wheel and the car back into the lane, but we arrived at our destination, Calw (pronounced "Calf") around 11:30. This was the birthplace and boyhood home of the German novelist, Hermann Hesse, one of my favorite authors, along with Thomas Wolfe and D.H. Lawrence, during my college years. I was captivated by the stories of his youthful protagonists' search for the meaning of life and their struggles and reflections on the relationships between art and life, formal education and experience, men and women, and parents and children. We met Mutti's cousin, Irmgard, and her husband Albert, who had taken the train from Karlsruhe. Calw is a beautiful, typical Black Forest town with a square decorated by old Tudor buildings, a church, and town hall. Almost immediately, we discovered a plaque at number 6 *Markstrasse* (Market Street), indicating the birthplace of Hesse on July 2, 1877. After lunch (lamb chops for me, five full-headed trouts for the others), we strolled to the Hesse museum, located in a former schoolhouse from the 1870s. We spent about two hours, walking from room to room, exploring different aspects of Hesse's life: his early years as the son of Christian missionaries, his troubled relationship with his father, his early writings, his three wives, and three sons, his opposition to both wars, his discovery of painting, his work with Jung, his Nobel Prize in 1946, his long-time home in Switzerland, and his death on August 9, 1962. The many photos of Hesse, a tall, thin, bespectacled, scholarly-looking man, and the narratives, paintings, and excerpts from his writings and letters brought him to life. I especially enjoyed the pictures of Hesse when he was three, his naked pictures with his sons, the photo skiing with Thomas Mann, and the photo with his sympathetic look in his eighties. With reverence, I touched the wicker chair where he wrote in his house in Switzerland. Later in the afternoon, after *Kaffee und Kuchen,* we stood at Hesse's favorite spot in town, the bridge above the Nagold River. A life-size bronze statue of Hesse with his kind, curious, wise look, stands nearby.

Nearby Calw is the small town of Störnberg, where Mutti spent six months in a cure house, recovering from tuberculosis from May to November 1963. We walked through the park, which she still remembers as the site of her daily strolls, breathing in the good air of the Schwarzwald. We were searching for the house where she stayed. We thought it might have been torn down, having yielded its land to all the new construction, but we finally found it. I was reminded of our search for her girlhood house in Poland in 2005 and the house where they stayed in Scheidegg in December 1963 when they visited Kersti—just one month after Mutti was declared healed and headed home to Worms.

Kersti drove the entire way home. We stopped for dinner outdoors in a *Biergarten* on a quiet, tree-lined street in Karlsruhe. It was dark by the time we parked the car at 9:45. Walking to the apartment, I looked up and saw the same Big Dipper that I had last seen two weeks ago above the beach in Surf City.

Wednesday, August 26

It is late afternoon, and in just a few hours, the sun will set on our six days in Germany.

On Tuesday, we drove to Bibertal to visit Rosi and Hans. It was a pleasing, familiar visit. We arrived around 11:00; ate a "*zweites Frühstuck*" (second breakfast) on the outdoor lower patio; toured their impressive flower and vegetable gardens; had a delicious four-course meal; and then drove to some nearby locales for a walk—a lake and a former castle perched high on a hill, surrounded by neat homes with colorful flowers. It now serves as a church conference center and youth hostel. We dodged the intermittent rain on our walk, but it rained most of the way home, this time with me behind the wheel.

Late this morning, we drove across the Nahe to Bingerbrück, and then up into the Bingerwald. Growing up, Kersti and the family made many weekend treks to the woods for hiking throughout the year and her first skiing lessons when there was enough snow. The air was brisk and clear in the higher elevation—about 600 meters or 1800 feet—and we felt the warm sun on our faces. We ate lunch outside at a popular restaurant; my *Wiener Schnitzel* with a cream sauce and mushrooms rivaled the dish that I had ordered when we had dinner with Gabi and Wolfgang. After lunch, Mutti, Kersti, and I set off on a fairly brisk walk through the fields to a spot where we had a partial view of the Rhein, leaving Vati behind…but he hobbled his way toward us. We returned to the car and descended through the thick woods, stopping at a clearing with a spectacular view of the Rhein in all directions: west toward St.

Goar, north toward Hessen and the abandoned Ehrenfels Castle, and east toward the Mäuseturm and Bingen.

Vati and Mutti droped us off in Kempten, and we joined Connie and Klaus for *Kaffee* (we actually drank cup after cup of Connie's delicious herbal tea from her garden) and *Kuchen* (plum tart and cheesecake). Connie's husband, a doctor with the German army, will be heading to Afghanistan in September for a one-month assignment. After a walk with Connie's dog, King, Connie dropped us at the Rhein for our final stroll and film. Almost immediately after starting our walk, the sole of my left loafer came lose, reminding me of Mom's shoe incident from late July, except that I did not fall. I hobbled my way along the walkway, alternating between my broken shoe and bare feet on grassy stretches. While Kersti visited the Bingen Museum, I found a sturdy vine, tied it around my shoe, and was able to arrive back at the apartment, walking nearly at my normal pace.

Thursday, August 27

Even with the windows closed, the late summer cricket chorus chirps loudly outside our window. It's a little after 10:00 PM in Madison (already 4:00 AM in Bingen), and the Dr. Sieglitz Strasse crew will soon be back at work on the road-widening project.

This was a long but successful day of travel. After our final breakfast of *Brötchen,* bread, honey, jam, and cheese (Kersti threw in an egg for some extra energy), we departed for the airport at 8:30. It felt cool when we first walked outside, but as we drove toward Mainz and on to the airport, a haze settled upon the fields. It was going to be a sunny, hot day in southern Germany. The plane was late in arriving and then had a technical matter to resolve, so we did not leave until 1:30—more than two hours late. But the eight hour and 20 minute flight went smoothly, aided by our books, Derek Bok's *Our Underachieving Colleges*, and Martha Beck's memoir, *Expecting Adam.* We landed at 3:30, just 90 minutes late, moved briskly through customs, retrieved our suitcase, and met a smiling Janine with the van. It felt good to be together again and enjoy a family dinner on the deck.

Chapter 5

NEW HAMPSHIRE

July 9-12, 2010

"In that moment of departure, I felt something familiar and touching"

July 9: Yardley, PA to Madison, NJ to Enfield, NH

On a sunny, steamy summer morning, Donna and Lou set out from their home in Yardley for the first leg of their trip. Kersti and I were still busy preparing for the refinishing of the floors in three bedrooms upstairs and the hallway and living room downstairs. After consolidating our luggage, cooler, and miscellaneous items in our Honda CRV—including the perfect birthday present, a treasure chest to hold all our mementos and memorabilia—we hit the road around 11:00 and began the familiar trek north, which Lou and I had done numerous times during our Dartmouth days.

We made good time, crossing the Tappan Zee Bridge and then pausing for a picnic lunch at a nice rest stop just north of the Connecticut border on Route 684. The day turned cloudy, and it felt like rain might be on its way. We continued into Massachusetts and then Vermont, stopping at a beautiful new rest facility that looked and felt like a ski chalet. Despite the lack of rain in the New York area, the hills and woods of Vermont were green and lush. We exited Route 91 at the junction with 89, then crossed the Connecticut River for the first time into New Hampshire and took Exit 17 for Enfield Village just a few miles down the highway.

We pulled into our bed and breakfast property a little before 5:00 and immediately were struck by the bright, beautiful, colorful gardens surrounding the main house. We met our innkeepers, Al and Nancy, who were warm and welcoming. Nancy told us that the house dated from 1793 and that most of the floors were original. The rooms were spacious and comfortable with views of the garden and a lake in the distance.

After quickly settling in, we took our first trip into Hanover. On the south side of the town and campus, everything felt familiar and hardly changed. We ate dinner at an Italian restaurant, and then strolled through the moist summer air—an unfamiliar feeling—across the green and then down a surprisingly subdued Fraternity Row. We passed Beta, where Lou lived his senior year, but he decided not to go in and challenge the brothers to the original version of beer pong, which is so much better than the one they play today. Rounding the corner onto Occom Ridge Road, we peered in to the old Pi Lamba Phi house, where I spent my final year. The structure has been completely renovated and modernized, but I was pleased that it was alive with students—women undergraduates—who were enjoying Friday night. Most likely, it's a sorority now, but clearly still part of the college. We passed the Dartmouth Outing Club, but didn't make it as far down as Occom Pond before returning to the car for the drive back to Enfield Village.

Saturday, July 10: Cornish, NH and Windsor, VT

We could hear the rain on the roof early Saturday morning, and it continued throughout most of the morning. Normally, Nancy serves summer breakfasts on the porch that stretches for two long sides of the house, but the rain shifted the breakfast indoors to the dining room. There we enjoyed the company of family members representing three states who were heading off to a large family reunion later that day in Cornish. The 70-something parents, David and Pat, were originally from Maine, but are currently living in Minnesota. They were joined by their two daughters, one from Minnesota and the other from Colorado, and their granddaughter, Emily. David is a retired researcher and plant manager in the animal care division of Boeringer Ingelheim, the German company located close to Bingen. Nancy served a delicious fruit compote, homemade blueberry scones, and a spinach and onion omelet.

Given the showery conditions, we decided to visit the historic home of Augustus St. Gaudens, most likely America's greatest sculptor ever, though he is not that well known. Born in Ireland in 1848, he and his family moved to Boston when he was six months old and soon after to New York City. He rose to prominence as a sculptor of Civil War heroes, including Abraham Lincoln, Admiral David Farragut, General William Sherman, and Colonel Robert Shaw and his brigade of black soldiers from Massachusetts. We watched a compelling film of St. Guadens' life and work, took a tour of the house where he lived and worked for the last 20 years of his life, and marveled at some of his original works and reproductions. The emotions carved into the faces of his subjects were powerful and expressive.

After a "tailgate" lunch in the parking lot, we drove across the country's longest surviving and utilized covered bridge to Windsor, Vermont, birthplace of the state in 1777 when the constitution was signed and ratified. For their afternoon activity, Kersti and Donna chose to walk through a maze within an attraction called the Path of Life. They got lost and panicked a bit, plowing their way through a hedge to escape the maze. Meanwhile, Lou and I drove into town for a beer and the last half of the Germany-Uruguay match for third place in this year's World Cup in South Africa. We both enjoyed a pint of Long Trail Ale, a local Vermont beer, as we watched a 3-2 comeback win for the boys from Deutschland. We returned to Hanover for dinner at Murphy's Pub on Main Street.

Sunday, July 11: Lake Mascoma and Hanover

The sun was pouring into our rooms when we lifted the shades on Sunday morning. Nancy served another hearty country breakfast on the porch to the four of us plus David and Pat, fresh from their all-day family reunion. There was fresh mixed fruit, scones, and a leek omelet. The air was comfortable in the early morning, but as we walked briskly along the Rail Trail, which winds around the long, narrow Lake Mascoma for 23 miles, we felt the humidity creep back in. We strolled for a couple of miles along the pine-needled path, drinking our water as we gazed out on the calm, clean lake. Lou told us about his high school and freshman year diving career, including the time he hit his head on the diving board during a freshman meet and wound up in Dick's House, the college infirmary, for a few days.

Our next stop was the small beach and swimming area at Mascoma Lake, just a mile from the center of town. Kersti, Lou, and I waded and then dove into the warm lake waters, then swam out to the raft, where Lou demonstrated a dive with a minimal splash—well, a bit more splash than 40 years ago. We then sat in the shade and munched on cheese, bread, fruit, nuts, and crackers accompanied by glasses of Pinot Grigio wine.

Since we were so close to the house, we returned and watched the final game of the 2010 World Cup between Holland and Spain. After two hours, it was still 0-0 in a game that did not generate much excitement or many chances to score. Facing at least 30 minutes of overtime plus the possibility of penalty kicks to determine the winner, we turned off the set (Spain later scored the lone goal with just a few minutes left in overtime) and set off for Hanover to rent a canoe. With Lou paddling in the bow and I in the stern, and Kersti and Donna seated in between, we rowed north through the late afternoon sunshine. Being on the water did not cool us off. We passed occasional river houses, but most of the time on both the Vermont and New Hampshire sides, we gazed at evergreens. On our way back, I looked up the steep, forested hill on the New Hampshire side, trying to catch a glimpse of my old porch at Pi Lamb, where I spent many hours reading and editing my thesis during the warmer days of the fall of 1971 and spring of 1972. But it was impossible to identify the house. After returning our canoe to the boathouse, we were not yet done with our Dartmouth sports day. We drove to the tennis court on Wheelock Street, and Lou and I did some good hitting on green clay courts. Tired and sweaty, we drove back to our house for quick showers, and then returned to the green in Lebanon for a tasty Italian dinner at Tres Tomatoes. We toasted Lou in the final hours of his personal decade.

The sky was clear when we returned to Enfield Village. After everyone went upstairs, I tiptoed out of the house and across the street to a dark lot with an unoccupied home and gazed upward at the sky. The Big Dipper was immediately visible and so were the millions of stars comprising the dense, swirling Milky Way. I had not seen a sky like this since 2007, when Rocky Pacheco took us up on a hill in the Azores to gaze at the stars.

Monday, July 12: Enfield Village to Madison and Yardley

We celebrated Lou's 60th birthday with a card, a written tribute, a rendition of "Happy Birthday" (Nancy and Al chimed in), and six candles atop a blueberry coffee cake that Nancy had baked for the occasion. Lou was in his usual spunky mood and felt good that he was 60 and in good health and spirits, just as I felt when I had transitioned into my sixties two weeks earlier. We lingered, not wanting our long weekend in New Hampshire to come to an end, but we finally packed and departed around 10:00.

We had said goodbye to Hanover twice before, but we decided to return one more time. Nancy had served her scones in a beautiful, rustic wooden bowl with pointy edges and smooth wood grains. She said it was on loan from a wood craftsman who lived just outside Hanover. She recommended that we pay him a visit on our way to Route 91. Heading up the hill from Hanover, and after a few bends in the road, we came to Dustin Coates' property, which was littered with tree trunks, stumps, and limbs in various stages of weathering. Dustin, who is about 50, and his Aunt Judy, who is not much older, invited us into his showroom, and he explained in detail the process of selecting, curing, and turning the wood to create bowls, utensils, and plates that are works of art. He's a true New Hampshire artisan. Donna bought a ladle and Kerstin a small bowl, which fits in the palm of her hand.

On a warm, sunny day that reminded me of my last day at Dartmouth in June 1972, we headed down the hill from the center of Hanover and across the river into Vermont. I was wondering if 38 years after graduation it would still be possible to see the steeple of Baker Library poking up above the trees. At first I noticed the tall smoke stack but no steeple, and I thought the years of growth had finally obscured it, but then I glimpsed it, the most visible symbol of the college. Lou and I are both fond of the college and enjoy returning to it, but we have moved on with our lives and don't dwell too much on what we had there. But in that moment of departure, I felt something familiar and touching.

We stopped just twice on our way home—once for a restroom and picnic at Salinger's apple farm on a country road, shortly after passing into New York State, and a second time to fill up at the Hess station in Boonton. We made very good time and pulled into our driveway on Vinton Road a little before 5:00. We said goodbye to our dear friends, and they completed the final leg to Yardley.

Chapter 6

CANADA AND ALASKA

July 30-August 13, 2010

"Alta Lake gave us the gift of one of the most beautiful and peaceful moments of our entire trip: the cool, clear lake water, cool to the touch, the brilliant, warm late afternoon sunshine, the lush green grass, and the ever-present mountains rising in the background"

Glacier Bay, Alaska

July 30: Madison to Vancouver

On the 20th anniversary of my first day at Rutgers, Kersti suddenly opened her eyes at 3:57 AM—a minute before the alarm was set to go off. We swung into action and scurried about for the next 75 minutes, including her repacking of one big suitcase into a smaller suitcase and carry-on bag. By 5:15, we were ready to go. Eric's friend, Danny Wasky, drove us to the airport, and we arrived as the first faint light of morning was visible.

Our flight to Vancouver was filled with spectacular views of the northern United States and southern Canada. Within the first two hours, we flew over three or four of the Great Lakes: Erie or Ontario, and probably Huron and Superior. The lakes stretched to the horizon, the blue-green waters glistening in the brilliant sunshine. Then came hundreds of miles of cultivated fields and farmlands, a beautiful patchwork of quilts. Then, all of a sudden, the flat topography became jagged and hilly, and we were peering down on the magnificent Rocky Mountains. At first they were dry, brown, and sharp-edged, and later snow-capped and lush with occasional pristine blue lakes nestled among the peaks. As we approached Vancouver and began our descent, it almost seemed as if we were driving alongside the peaks.

Anja, Daniel, Nellie, Rich, Kersti, and I collected our bags and arranged to ride into the city in a stretch limo. We opened up the windows and enjoyed our first fresh air in weeks. We arrived at our Best Western Hotel on Drake Street around 1:00, and our rooms were ready. Kerstin and I dropped off our things, and then headed on foot to the waterfront area where we will pick up our cruise ship tomorrow. We shared a falafel by the water, looking across to the mountains rising out of the sea.

Returning to the hotel, we decided to take the "Big Bus" tour of the city. The highlights were Stanley Park, which we remembered from our visit in 2000, Granville Island, and Gastown, where we had dinner 10 years ago. We only got off the bus once to pick up a free ice cream cone in Gastown.

After a tasty dinner at White Spot, the restaurant connected to the Best Western, Kersti, Nellie, and I strolled on the promenade along the beach. The sun was still bright at 7:00; the lifeguard was still in his chair; and many Vancouverites were biking, roller blading, and walking on this glorious summer evening.

Saturday, July 31: Vancouver to Somewhere on the Inner Passage, British Columbia

It's a little after 10:00 on Saturday night, and the last faint light of the day has finally faded away. We're nestled in our cabin, heading north from Vancouver. Kerstin and I greeted another beautiful, comfortable day with a long walk along the beaches of Vancouver: English Bay Beach and all the way to Second Beach in Stanley Park. We stopped at a stone Inuit sculpture, a gift to the people of Vancouver from the people of the Northwest Territories in the far north of Canada, above the Yukon and straddling the Arctic Circle. The sculpture, in six blocks of granite, vaguely resembling the feet, body, arms, and head of a human, signifies peace and reconciliation. Along the way, we met Nellie, who was taking a jog along the winding beachfront path.

Around 11:30, we jumped into two taxis for the quick ride to our cruise ship. We were very impressed by how well the cruise officials and U.S. customs people processed two shiploads of people: likely close to 5,000 in all. We walked on board our massive, 10-deck ship, the *Zuiderdam*, named after a small coastal town in Holland and registered in Rotterdam. We immediately took the elevator to the 9th deck for an outdoor buffet lunch beside one of the pools. A little later, our "staterooms" were ready, and we checked into a small, but comfortable room with a firm queen-sized bed and even a small couch. Outside our window we had a view of the water and coastline beyond one of the big orange lifeboats. During the afternoon, we continued to snack at the buffet, oriented ourselves to the ship, played some tennis and basketball with Nellie and Danny, rested on our beds, and participated in the mandatory emergency drill. Tired of the loud music, smoky grill, and casual meals, Kersti and I opted for fine dining in one of the dining rooms, joining a traveling couple from Alberta and two bell-playing sisters from Indianapolis. After dinner, Kersti and I strolled around the upper deck one final time, and at 9:30 orange and red tints were still visible in the western sky.

Sunday, August 1: Inside Passage

We continued our northward journey. We awoke to pelting rain and thick gray skies. After breakfast, we listened to Captain Werner Timmers, a Dutch native, tell a small group about how he became a ship's captain. He was asked how he spends his vacation or at least the six months that he is not at sea: he admitted that he relaxes in his cabin in the North Carolina woods, away from the water and people. Later in the morning, the intense summer sun burned through the clouds, and we were treated on both sides of the ship to mile after mile of pristine woodlands, sometimes rising into craggy mountains. There were no towns, no houses, only occasional small fishing boats. We saw the spout of a humpback whale, then a break of the surface and the top of its tail as it dove downward. By later in the day, the fog rolled back in as we entered the open ocean. After dinner, we enjoyed a music and dance show, featuring Broadway and popular hits.

Monday, August 2: Tracy Arm and Juneau, Alaska

The morning fog lifted quickly, and we entered a fjord known as Tracy Arm. Captain Timmers opened the bow on our deck, the fourth deck, and several hundred passengers marveled at the lush, steep mountainsides, the snow-peaked mountains, thin curving waterfalls, and clean green water. We saw several humpback whale spouts, brief breaches and dives, but searched in vain for bears on the occasional beaches.

Close to 1:30 PM—an hour ahead of schedule—we arrived in Juneau, Alaska's capital. While everyone else took the helicopter ride to the Mendenhall Glacier, I opted to explore the historical aspects of the state capital, so far from the two major cities of Alaska, Anchorage and Fairbanks, and accessible only by plane or boat. I took a tour of the state capital building, visiting the senate and house chambers because the legislature is only in session from January to March. Next, I visited the governor's mansion, currently occupied by Governor Parnell, who took over for Sarah Palin when she resigned in 2009. I don't know if the governor was home, but his dog was wandering around the yard.

My next stop was the Alaska State Museum. I had only 20 minutes, but enjoyed the Indian artifacts from many centuries, a beautiful exhibit of photographs of Alaska, and historical documents, photos, and memorabilia. Finally, I briefly stopped at St. Thomas Russian Orthodox Church, built in 1893 with the familiar Russian "onion steeple" against the mountain backdrop.

The glacier delegation arrived 10 minutes before I did. We still had five hours before departure, so Nellie, Kersti, and I made the steep climb toward 8th and Gold Streets on route to Perseverance Trail, the most popular hike in Juneau. We passed colorful houses, some painted in two colors, many with pretty, multi-colored flowers. We paused to look back down, and saw how far we had climbed. Some have called it the "San Francisco of the north country." The topography leveled out, and we discovered a trail to Mt. Robert, a steep, slightly muddy trail through thick, almost tropical woods. We hiked it for just five minutes, before turning back and heading along the "flume trail," mostly consisting of wooden planks on railroad ties and a final winding stretch to the town below. Throughout the walk, we heard the constant rush of water below.

Tired, we worked our way back to the ship for a later dinner prior to our 10:00 PM departure for Skagway.

Thursday, August 3: Skagway, Alaska

We woke early, around 6:00 AM, and opened the curtains to glimpse Skagway, the northernmost point on the Taiya Inlet, which reaches up from the Lynn Canal. The town derives its name from the Tligit word for "strong wind." In 1896, the Klondike Gold Rush began when gold was discovered at Dawson Creek in the Yukon Territories, and Skagway became a boomtown—the destination for would-be miners coming from Seattle, San Francisco, and Vancouver to strike it rich. They still had 580 more miles to go after Skagway through treacherous, mountainous terrain. Of the 100,000 would-be miners who set out, only a third made it to Dawson Creek, and only about 500 in all ever made money from mining gold. All this is captured in the Gold Rush

National Historical Site, our first stop of the morning. We went on a tour of the four-block-wide, 20-block long town, which has been largely restored by the Park Service—21 buildings in all. The ranger told us about the infamous swindler, "Soapy" Smith, who cheated aspiring or returning miners out of money through various tricks and scams. He was finally confronted by Frank Reid, a Skagway official, who shot Soapy dead, but Frank sustained a wound from Soapy's gun that led to his death 12 days later. Frank has the bigger tombstone in the local cemetery, and Soapy's grave is technically outside the graveyard, but Soapy is better remembered.

We returned to the ship for lunch, then hastened back to the train depot in time for the 12:45 train ride to White Pass, elevation 2,685 feet. It was a spectacular ride, climbing and winding along mountain passes, crossing the gushing Skagway River, sometimes looking down at 1,000-foot vertical drops. The tour guide remarked that this was the clearest day of the summer, and we were able to admire several snow-capped mountains normally shrouded in low clouds. We saw a wooden bridge that had been abandoned in 1969 for safety reasons, and the narrow pathway that the miners had traversed in 1898. Passing briefly into British Columbia at the 20-mile mark, we flipped the train seats and then traded seats with the passengers opposite us, so they could enjoy the same magnificent vistas on the way down.

After returning to town, Kersti and I walked to Broadway and 7th and spent an enjoyable hour at the Skagway Museum. We were especially captivated by the photography of Michael Klensch, a local photographer who takes amazing photos of the Alaskan sky at night, especially when the northern lights are on fire. We later picked up a signed book of his best work, and the storeowner said that Michael was his neighbor and worked as a border guard during the day. We strolled through the busy but calm shopping district, stopping at several stores with tasteful, artistic items. We bought an attractive Alaska tray for ourselves, wind chimes for the girls, and an Alaska print for Eric. As we approached the ship, we saw a seal frolicking in the water. At one point, it swam up a wide spout of gushing water, only to tumble back into the bay as if on a water slide.

Wednesday, August 4: Glacier Bay

Throughout the night, our ship continued south from Skagway and then turned west and northwest into Icy Strait at the mouth or Glacier Bay. A national park since the 1970s, the bay, which was covered by ice as late as 200 years ago, is 65 miles long and 2-10 miles wide. As we awoke, the ship was entirely shrouded in fog, and a light rain was falling. The early-morning whale watch was called off. We had an early breakfast and then attended a moving presentation by Lee, a native Tlinglit Indian who works for a company that promotes native cultures. He gave a personal account of how the Christian missionaries and American officials made a concerted effort to force the natives to assimilate by destroying the "pagan" art and forcing them to learn and speak English. Today, only those elders over 65 years old—about 15,000 of 65,000 natives—still speak the language. Lee ended on an encouraging note that the natives now see opportunity in developing eco-tourism for visitors who want to experience the native life and culture not only in museums, but outdoors where on the sacred natural ground and sea.

Nature provided the most wonderful, amazing gift for us today. The fog persisted until mid-morning, but then, as if in a fairytale, the gates of fog parted on both sides of the ship, revealing majestic, gleaming mountains, some rising from the water to more than 12,000 feet. At the end of Tarr Inlet, our reward awaited us: the massive Margerie Glacier, just a fraction of what it once was, but still a powerful, jagged force of nature. The ship slowly turned around twice, so we had close-up views of the rocky peaks, the white, blue, and black ice, and the mountain rising in back. Next we visited the Johns Hopkins Inset: while the glacier was much smaller than Margerie, it left behind even more spectacular vistas, the green water, high snowy peaks, and the cloudless blue sky. A short time later, the clouds and fog rolled back in, shutting the door on the most beautiful scenery of our entire trip.

We rested later in the afternoon and read our books: David Remnick's *The Bridge*, about President Obama's rise to prominence, and *Two Old Women*, an Alaskan legend of betrayal, courage, and survival by Velma Wallis. After dinner, we attended a magic and comedy show and then called it a day. It is still daylight as I write this, but the fog is thick and the ship's foghorn sounds periodically in the night.

Thursday, August 5: Ketchikan, Alaska

We pulled into the small port of Ketchikan, our last stop in Alaska, around 11:00 this morning. The Alaska guidebook had forewarned us about the frequency and likelihood of rain in Ketchikan: some 220 days and 160 inches of rain each year! But once again, our luck held out, and the sun poured down through a bright blue sky the entire day.

While Anja, Rich, and the kids headed off to a wildlife adventure tour by plane, hoping to see bears (they only saw a small herd of mountain goats), Kersti and I took the local bus 10 miles north to Totem Bight State Park. It was a beautiful park with a pathway winding through a dense rainforest leading to a clearing adjacent to the sea where 14 reproductions of totem poles stood along with a clan house. We studied the meanings, symbols, and stories conveyed by each totem pole, most of which featured eagles or ravens, the two most powerful and central mythical symbols of the local Indian tribes. Other symbols included bears, beavers, thunderbirds, and people. Fields of tall purple flowers swayed in the breeze, and we even heard the sound of children wading in the chilly Alaskan waters at a nearby beach.

We hopped on the bus back into town, but missed the next bus to the well-publicized Saxman Indian Village, just 2.5 miles south of Ketchikan. We began walking, then hailed a cab to take us the rest of the way. We were expecting a village with a vibrant clan house, Indian dancers, and woodworkers, but the clan house was locked, the woodworkers were not welcoming, and there was not even a brochure providing descriptions of the nearly 20 totem poles. Two figures were of particular interest, appearing atop two tall poles: Abraham Lincoln, an admired figure, and William Seward, who bought Alaska from Russian in 1867 for $7 million. In contrast to Lincoln, Seward is not revered by the natives and is depicted in a drab black suit with a sad expression sitting on a potty. We picked up the bus for the return trip. We strolled through Creek Street, where prostitutes once set up their parlors for the weary miners and seamen, and of course we ran into Anja and her gang. Today the small shops of Creek Street are situated above an inland waterway.

After dinner, we stood outside and watched our ship pull away from Ketchikan. We were the last of four cruise ships to leave. At the end of September, the ships will leave until late spring rolls around again.

Friday, August 6: Southbound toward Vancouver

For all the spectacular vistas we encountered throughout our cruise, this day was the opposite—a day of fog, rain, and gusty wind. The predicted late-day clearing and Orca whale sightings never occurred. I attended an interesting morning lecture by our tour guide, Ron, on Alaska (most interesting fact: it has 3 million lakes) and an evening comedy show, which was quite good, but the rest of the day we read, walked a mile around the ship on deck three, and enjoyed our final delicious meals. The entertainment highlight was the Alert Bay Tumpeteer, Jerry, who sped up in his small boat beside the massive ship, which shut off its engines, and played "O Canada," "The Star-Spangled Banner," and "God Save the Queen" on his trumpet. He has a website: alertbaytrumpeteer.com.

Saturday, August 7: Vancouver to Harrison/Hot Springs, B.C.

The ship passed under Vancouver's Lions Gate Bridge around 6:15 AM and docked just 20 minutes later. We were up by 5:00 and pulled the curtain open on a gray, rainy day. How fortunate we were that the rain held off until our final day and night of travel.

Disembarking from a cruise ship is like passing through a busy international airport. There were lines at the gangway, lines at Canadian customs, lines waiting to pick up our luggage, and lines waiting to board buses for the airport. But just as we experienced throughout our cruise experience with Holland America, everything was extremely well planned, organized, and executed. We arrived at Vancouver Airport around 9:30, less than two hours after exiting the ship.

We picked up our black Suzuki SUV at Enterprise, which was a shuttle ride away from the airport, and drove east about 80 miles to Harrison/Hot Springs. It's a small beach community at the foot of the 40-mile long Harrison Lake. On both sides of the narrow lake, steep mountains—topped by Mount Cheam (two syllables) at about 7,000 feet—lined with fir trees, some growing on solid granite cliffs, rise from the shores. The rain ended by late afternoon, but low clouds and mist continued to float through the mountains. Kersti and I had a very tasty dinner at a lakeside Swiss restaurant. My "Swiss" *Bratwurst,* carmelized onions, creamed corn and carrots, *Sauerkraut,* and potatoes tasted just like a meal from Mutti's kitchen in Bingen.

Sunday, August 8: Harrison/Hot Springs

The weather remained cool and cloudy, but there was no more rain. In the morning, Kerstin and I took a path around the other side of the lake, passing a pool of water that smelled of sulphur and was very warm to the touch. We were reminded of our *cuzido,* Rocky's stew cooked in the underground hot springs in the Azores. Shortly beyond, a metal fence blocked our passage, so we took another route back through the steep rainforest of ferns, stumps, and moist vegetation. We crossed bridges and thin streams before returning to the hotel.

After lunch at our favorite deli, we met Anja, Nellie, and Daniel and headed east on foot along Hot Springs Road. At first, we picked up the trail toward Campbell Lake, but after one stretch of a 35° grade pathway with loose gravel, we turned back and discovered a flat trail that wound its way through tall grasses. We saw a few snakes dart across the path on our way back to the beach.

The highlight of the day was the kickoff of the 2010 *Wiehlertreffen.* We mingled before dinner and at dinner with Mutti's cousin, Onkel Heinz, and his wife, Edelgard; Mutti's other cousin, Marianna, who will stay with us later in the month; and new family members, mostly from the Vancouver area. It's a much smaller group than we had in

Oberwesel in 2005—about 60 in all—and thus more intimate and relaxing. We met Heinz's daughter, Bärbel (Barb) Peters, her husband Mel, daughter Kyla, and Kyla's four-month old daughter, Jaida. We were very interested to learn from Barb about a second Wiebe-Wiehler connection: Edelgard's sister, Thea, married Vati's Uncle Gerhart. Unfortunately, they had a bitter divorce, and Gerhart's son, Hartmut, has not been in contact with his Onkel Hans-Hermann, even though he lives in the Frankfurt area. Barb is a close friend of Hartmut, so future contact may be in the offing.

Hartmut did indeed visit Vati in August 2015.

Monday, August 9: Harrison/Hot Springs; Grammy's 92nd Birthday

The light rain continued all day on Monday, but it did not dampen the spirits of the Wiehler clan. After breakfast, we gathered in the community hall—a far cry from the ceremonial and media coverage of our trip to Elblag (Elbing), Poland in 2005—for a family meeting, highlighted by a presentation by Stefan Wiehler, a 44-year-old journalist living in Berlin, on the impact of the fall of the Berlin Wall in October 1989. It was an interesting, impressionistic talk from the perspective of a young, aspiring journalist who moved from Munich to Berlin in early 1990.

Kersti and I returned to our room and had a good long chat with Eric and Lisa. We then broke up into groups. Kersti joined Marianna and several others on a trip to a nearby botanical garden, while Nellie, Daniel, Anja, and I joined about 20 others on a rain forest hike. We retraced our steps from yesterday morning as far as the fence just beyond the hot spring, then turned left and took a steep, winding path upwards perhaps 200 meters (600 feet) into the Harrison Lake rain forest. The light rain was the perfect complement: I debuted my blue rain jacket and pulled my hood up tight. We traversed some rocky, muddy, rooted terrain, then walked along a fairly level, pine-needled path before our steep descent to an uninhabited cover and beach. We chatted for awhile on the beach, figuring out a few more family ties while Daniel and a couple of younger boys from Vancouver or Calgary climbed along a rocky part of the coastline and skipped stones in the light green tinted water. We returned to the hotel without Daniel and his friends, but they managed to find their way back along a different route. We're off to the community center at 5:00 for an early dinner and talent show.

As it turned out, there was no talent show, but one of the clan, George Bartel from nearby Agassiz (brother of the event organizer, Fred Bartel), showed the video of his special moment on February 7, 2010, when he carried the Olympic torch on its way to Vancouver, just five days before its arrival in Vancouver to begin the Winter Olympics.

Tuesday, August 10: Harrison/Hot Springs, Chilliwack, Agassiz

After our buffet breakfast at the hotel, we walked to the community church for a moving Mennonite church service, led by Dorothy Kirkpatrick, another of our many second cousins, once or twice removed. The sun was struggling to break through the cloud cover. We prayed for the family gathered together in Western Canada, for family members not present (Mutti was on our mind and Heinz's mind), for our ancestors, our children, and those yet to come. We prayed for the land, water, and sky that nourish our lives on this earth.

Heinz then invited Kersti, Anja, and me to join him and Edelgard for lunch and a trip to their home in Chilliwack. Heinz's sight and reflexes are not what they once were, so he did not hesitate to turn the keys over to me. We took the back roads, stopping by the cemetery where their infant boy is buried; he died after only four days of life in 1955. We also passed the 26-acre dairy farm that Heinz bought in 1951 for just $10,000. He worked the farm, producing milk from his herd of 16 cows, until he sold it in 1991 for $200,000. We stopped for a sandwich at Tim Horton's in the center of bustling Chilliwack, visited the Mennonite Central Committee thrift shop where Edelgard volunteers; drove past their former residential home that we had visited during our 1999 family vacation; and finally arrived at their condo adjacent to their current Mennonite church. It's an attractive, compact home with big windows welcoming lots of sunlight surrounded by beautiful, colorful flowers, blessed by the frequent rain and comfortable temperatures of the region.

Our final family meal took place at the federal agricultural station where Heinz's daughter, Heidi, works. Heinz also worked at the station for 26 years. We enjoyed burgers on the grill and coleslaw and potato salad that Kerstin and Anja had helped prepare on Monday night. We took some special family portraits—Wiehlers, Wiebes, and Whites—standing on some big logs from a giant tree that had recently been taken down. After Heidi gave us a quick tour of her lab, we looked up above the building and gazed a Mount Cheam, which had a reddish glow against the backdrop of the dark gray, nearly nighttime sky.

Wednesday, August 11: Harrison/ Hot Springs to Whistler, B.C.

This morning was the farewell breakfast for the 2010 *Wiehlertreffen.* When it came time to say goodbye to Heinz, both Kersti and Anja wept, and tears came to Heinz's and my eyes. He and Edelgard are dear relatives, and it is not certain that we will see them again. Overall, it was an enjoyable and meaningful family gathering, which generated new relationships and connections. We are looking forward to Hattingen in the Ruhr Valley of Germany in 2015. *(The 2015 gathering actually took place in the northern town of Plön. See Chapter 20.)*

The morning was sunny and warm with low clouds and a gentle haze hanging over Mt. Cheam and the adjacent mountains. We grew warm, walking on the gravel path around the swimming lagoon. We returned to the hotel, fetched our rental car, loaded it up, filled the gas tank, and headed west toward Vancouver.

A little after 1:00 PM, we arrived in Surrey at Barb's and Mel's home. We munched on fresh veggies, fruit, pate, crackers, and cheese, while Daniel played with their 13-year-old Jack Russell terrier, Oliver. Later, Kyla arrived with Jaida, the youngest member of the Wiehler clan. Barb and Mel are so warm and welcoming, and we feel a close bond to our Canadian second cousins. They will be our first point of contact next time we come to Vancouver, and we hope to see them if they visit New York.

Around 3:00, we continued our journey, heading west on Highway 1 and then north on Highway 99 along one of the inland western coasts of Canada. During the next hour and a half, we saw some scenery that rivaled some of the best vistas of the cruise. Rounding mountain passes, we gazed out on the sparkling blue ocean. Halfway to Whistler, we stopped at Shannon Falls and cast our sights hundreds of feet upward at the tallest waterfall we have ever seen. It cascaded down the sheer granite wall, worn smooth through the millennia, then gushed through rock beds before entering a small river at the base. North of Shannon Falls, we passed the Squamish ski resort, and then it was on to Whistler. We ate dinner at a decent Greek restaurant and then wandered around the loud, busy village, the place to be seen. The crowds and loud music made us long for the quiet comforts and companionship of the cruise and the *Wiehlertreffen.*

Thursday, August 12: Whistler

We experienced the best of Whistler on our final full day of the vacation. The solid gray sky around 9:00 was not promising, but the hot summer sun began to burn through the cloud-locked sky by mid-morning. Kersti and I strolled through the central village and along main roads to the Aboriginal Centre, but after purchasing a dream catcher in the gift shop, we decided that this was a day to spend outside rather than inside. We found a shortcut along the gushing green Fitzsimmons Creek, passing teenage boys and even five-year-olds racing their bikes on age-appropriate dirt tracks, complete with moguls and ramps. We packed a picnic lunch—German *Schwarzbrot* and Havarti cheese—and headed to the gondolas. The sun was shining brightly by then, and there was a long line, but it moved quickly. We lifted off into the sky in our six-person gondola, passing above the dare devil mountain bikers, high above tall pines and rock formations. We reached about 1,600 meters—nearly 4,800 feet—but we weren't done yet. After our sandwich and apple, we hiked along a winding path to our next destination: the Whistler summit around 2,100 meters (6,300 feet). This time, we hopped aboard a ski lift. We passed over a deep ravine and then appeared to be heading for a collision with a solid rock cliff—Kersti's eyes were shut tight—but we lofted above it and came in for a safe landing.

The return trip—traveling down rather than up—was less intimidating, as was our next destination: Whistler's companion peak, Blackcomb Mountain. As we boarded the large, modern red gondolas with a capacity of 28 passengers, we gazed across a wide valley to Blackcomb Peak. At 4.4 kilometers (about 2.5 miles), it is the longest unsupported suspension cable car route in the world. At first, we arched lower, but beyond the midpoint of the valley, we began climbing, crossing Fitzsimmons Creek far below before landing at Rendezvous Lodge. We looked west toward two of the largest peaks in the Whistler area, Mount Currie at 8,000 feet and Inscoop Mountain, just slightly less. We treated ourselves to a locally made pistachio gelatto, and Kersti sipped on a green tea for a little energy lift. For the next hour, we walked along the narrow Alpine Trail, past pine trees, mountain brush, and pretty purple, yellow, and white flowers. And every time we glanced outward, we saw the majestic snow-capped mountains. About halfway around the mountain, we peered out at the two highest p3aks in the region: Castle Mountain at nearly 8,500 feet and Davidson Mountain, just slightly lower. The two highest peaks were linked by a glacier. Swinging back toward Rendezvous Lodge, we actually climbed up and along some very rocky terrain. At one point, I couldn't help myself from stepping off the trail and grabbing some snow to make a snowball in August! Then it was homeward bound, back across the valley in the red gondola—Kersti had a quick glimpse of a bear—and then our descent back to Whistler Village. Blending in with the sprawling crowd, we watched mountain bikers from around the world do their spins and tricks on a big-screen TV. Admittedly, it was pretty cool when they crashed.

We topped off our day at Whistler with a quick drive to two lakes that we had admired from high above: Green Lake with its distinct green tint and the deep, dark blue Alta Lake. Some pesky flies chased us away from Green Lake, but Alta Lake gave us the gift of one of the most beautiful and peaceful moments of our entire trip: the cool, clear lake water, cool to the touch, the brilliant, warm late afternoon sunshine, the lush green grass, and the ever-present mountains rising in the background. We walked along Valley Trail and were reminded of Cranberry Lake on a bright September afternoon, when the motor boats are silent and the only sounds are the birds, lapping waters, and cool breeze dancing through the still-green leaves.

Friday, August 13: Whistler to Madison

It is still bright as we sail above the clouds around 8:45 PM Eastern time. Just about 75 minutes until touchdown. Our two wonderful weeks in Canada and Alaska are coming to an end, but the memories will remain for a long time to come.

Early morning in Whistler was sunny and brisk, a harbinger of beautiful late September days at home. Everyone was up and ready to go promptly with 9:00 as our projected time of departure. The clock said 8:58 when I turned the ignition key. (Good job, Anja, Nellie, and Daniel!) The drive south on 99 was more spectacular than the trip north on Wednesday because of the clear sky. We drove by a continuous string of snow-capped mountains on both sides. Closer to Vancouver, the coastal waters reappeared along with a thin haze. After exiting the highway, we drove through the city. Two landmarks brought our trip full circle: driving over the Lions Gates Bridge, which we had sailed under on July 31; and passing by our Best Western Hotel on Drake Street. Finding the Enterprise rental agency was challenging, but we pulled in around 11:45 in plenty of time for our 2:00 flight on Air Canada. The only glitch was that our "Beautiful British Columbia" license plates are not so beautiful—in fact, they were gone, probably stolen while the car lay idle in the parking lot of the Executive Hotel in Harrison or in the Listel garage at Whistler. We were not charged for them.

Now the sun has set in the western sky behind us. We are flying into nighttime, through thin clouds, beginning our descent to our East Coast home.

Chapter 7

GERMANY

April 10-18, 2011

"We felt again Hildegard's presence, as she walked these quiet grounds, listening to the chirping birds, praying and mediating her way closer to God"

Tuesday, April 12

The early morning sun has turned to a steady rain as I look out from the 4th-story window of our apartment in Bingen. We were greeted yesterday by glorious sunshine, the first real dose of spring after the long, cold winter.

After Norbert—"ol' reliable"—dropped us at Newark Airport on Sunday evening, we had a smooth, on-time flight. Kersti slept for a few hours, strewn across my lap, while I watched a 1969 classic, "Easy Rider," about the tragic search for a tolerant, peaceful America, and the fairly recent British film, "An Education," starring Carey Mulligan as a schoolgirl who has an affair with an older, married (as she finds out at the end) man. The first streaks of daylight appeared at 6:30 new time, and the sun was shining when we touched down.

For the first time, we took the train from Frankfurt to Bingen with a change of trains in Mainz. The train sped through lush fields with newly blooming flowers. We left Vati some messages, but he did not receive them, so we walked across the Nahe from Bingerbrück to the apartment. The Idsteins had a key, so we were able to enter the apartment and settle in before Vati's return from his errands and Mutti's from her rehab for her new knee. Vati was doing much better with his oxygen, a new lease on life, and Mutti was in excellent spirits. We enjoyed a German sausage and Mutti's carrot soup for lunch.

After *Kaffe und Kuchen*, Kersti and I walked down to the Rhein and met Vati and Mutti at the ferry. It was warm enough to peel off my sweater. People were outside, sunning, strolling, and sipping coffee in the café. The trains and boats were moving up and down the river. After dinner, when darkness had settled over the Rhein Valley, we took a final stroll down the street toward Budesheim, and the breeze was still soft and springlike. We stayed awake until 10:00, then indulged in an 11-hour sleep.

The rain has stopped, blue sky has pushed the clouds away, and the sun is pouring down again. It looks like a nice day for Eric and his friend, Zeev, to travel to Germany.

Wednesday, April 13

This morning, there is not a cloud in the sky as I look outside from my window seat. The apartment is quiet. Mutti is at rehab; Vati, Kersti, and Eric are at the bank in Bingerbrück; and Zeev is catching up on some sleep.

Yesterday, we were running late as usual, having a leisurely buffet lunch at the Rochusberg, and we missed Eric and Zeev's arrival both in Bingerbrück and Dr. Sieglitz Strasse. Kersti and I walked quickly through the woods, bundling up as a protection against the wind, along the streets leading to the cemetery and *Gymnasium* (high school), down the steps and around the bend to find Eric and Zeev waiting eagerly. They had flown in from London, and Eric successfully navigated their way from the airport to Bingen. They had spent four good days in London, staying with Zeev's aunt and attending a Premier League soccer match between Chelsea and Wiggin (Chelsea won 1-0).

George drove down from Cologne, where he is working three days a week, to join us for a celebration of Eric" 18th birthday at Calamari, Vati's favorite Italian restaurant. George was tired after a long day of work, and we really appreciated his effort to drive to Bingen to see us. He was in good spirits and, as usual, dreaming about travel, retirement, and his olive grove in Italy.

Friday, April 15

The rain has held off the last two days, but they have been cool with intermittent clouds and temperatures in the mid-50s. On Thursday, Vati treated us to a tasty lunch at the Rheinblick Hotel with a stunning view of the Enrenfels Castle and Mäuseturm. We finished in time to make the 1:00 passenger ferry to Rüdesheim. A cool wind was blowing off the water, so we stepped downstairs and looked out the window virtually at water level. We puttered along the Bingen side of the river, then crossed to Rüdesheim in between busy barges, freight ships, tankers, and cruise ships.

From the Rüdesheim train station, we picked up a cab and headed through the busy town and then up the hill and through the sleeping vineyards to the Abbey of St. Hildegard, overlooking the village of Eibingen. It appears to be centuries old in the Romanesque style with its turrets and dark brown stone facades. But it was actually built early in the 20th century, opening in 1904. The link to Hildegard (1098-1179) is the land, the site, and the magnificent view of the Rhine. In 1150, Hildegard came to the juncture of the Rhine and Nahe Rivers, a place called Rupertsberg, to establish her first monastery. We have a direct view of the site, which is today Bingerbrück, from our balcony. A few years later, as more and more women gathered around her, Hildegard bought the former Augustinian monastery at Eibingen. Throughout most of her remaining years, she crossed the Rhine twice a week to visit her sisters.

Sitting at a bench, we gazed upon the Rhein as Hildegard must have so many times during her visits to Eibingen. We could clearly see the Rochuskappelle rising above the woods, the spire of St. Martin's Church, and the Burg Klopp, which shielded us from a view of the Dr. Sieglitz Strasse apartment. Kersti sketched the scene in her sketchbook, and I sketched the abbey while she shopped in the gift shop. Later, we visited the church, highlighted by a large round painting of Jesus in the apse and bronze depictions of five key moments in Hildegard's life. Outside in the courtyard, we paused to admire a statue of a petite, spiritual Hildegard with her eyes closed, praying, meditating, contemplating and sharing her love of God with all who entered into her presence.

About half a mile below the abbey lay the parish church of St. Hildegard. Rather than taking the roundabout roads that wind through the vineyards, we walked through rows of vineyards, across grassy knolls most filled with blooming dandelions. We opened a gate at the back of the church, which lies on the foundation of the original convent. On the altar, we found a shrine to Hildegard, a gold coffin that contains her bones, hair, and heart. Every September 17—the day of her death in 1179—the shrine is carried during a parade through the streets of Eibingen.

We continued our walk into Rüdesheim, stopping for tea at a restaurant in the famous *Drosselgasse*, featuring small shops on a thin alleyway, filled with throngs of tourists from the many buses and cruise ships that stop there.

We took the 5:00 PM car ferry back across the Rhein to Bingen, and spent a delightful hour and a half with Bärbel and Jonas Bourneman. We first saw Bärbel when she was walking her dog, Savannah. From Bärbel's house, we had a magnificent view of the abbey.

It was cool but still light when we returned home and then slowly, steadily walked down the street to the Schlossberg restaurant, where we enjoyed a late dinner with Vati and Mutti.

Today we had the ideal complement to our visit to Eibingen yesterday—the Hildegard von Bingen Museum. Located in the original Bingen electrical works brick building built in 1898, the museum describes the life and journey of Hildegard with models, writings, narratives, and even ruins from her convents at Disibodenberg and Ruptertsberg. We felt her presence throughout our trip, and during this afternoon's *Kaffee und Kuchen*, looked across the Nahe to the place where she first settled in Bingen.

Sunday, April 17

It's Sunday evening, and our suitcases lie on the bed nearby, packed for our flight home tomorrow.

Yesterday, we crossed the Rhein again, accompanied this time by Vati, Mutti, and their brown VW Golf. We drove just a few miles north to the idyllic "wine village" of Johannesberg. It was past noon, so we enjoyed a delicious meal at the restaurant outside of town in a secluded, wooded area. Some people were dining outside, but the day was still cool and more cloudy than sunny, so we selected a table in the glass-enclosed winter garden. My curry chicken dish was the best of the trip. After lunch, we drove to the Johannesberg Castle in Geisenheim, which had been the home of the famous Metternich family, which played a key role in European politics after the fall of Napoleon. The broad yellow castle stands in front of a gated community of buildings, where the well to do still live today. In front of the castle, one looks out on endless vineyards. This is precisely where I stood in October 2005 during my Fulbright trip to Germany. It was the last day of the harvest, the fields were golden yellow, and the young workers in the back of the trucks were laughing, carousing, and celebrating. Looking across the Rhein, I could see Bingen and the Rochuskapelle, but I had not realized six years ago how close we were to Bingen and Rüdesheim. Later, we visited the church that adjoins the castle.

Gabi and Wolfgqang joined us on Saturday night for our second dinner at the Schlossberg restaurant. They are always lively and fun.

Today we completed our "Hildegard pilgrimage" by driving to Disibodenberg, the site of the monastery that she entered in 1112 at the age of 14. The ruins of the monastery, which later evolved into a convent, lie on a wooded hillside overlooking the town of Odernberg and the Glan River. To reach the ruins, we walked along a fairly steep path past grazing sheep with young lambs. The first ruins appeared, and then more and more structures, perhaps 20 in all, including chapels, a large community hall, a bakery, a kitchen, men's quarters, and women's quarters. We felt again Hildegard's presence, as she walked these quiet grounds, listening to the chirping birds, praying and mediating her way closer to God. One woman passed us wearing no shoes, feeling the cool earth as Hildegard felt it centuries ago. I ran my hand along the mortar that was mixed and dried so many years ago and picked up a stone, perhaps a part of a building, which had been there when

Hildegard walked these grounds. It was brittle with age, and I easily snapped it in two.

On the return trip, we drove for miles along the Nahe. I imagined Hildegard, following the path along the Nahe to the point where it flowed into the Rhein. That is where she established the convent at Rupertsberg in 1150. We stopped on that site in Bingerbruck on the way home. We could not see the two rivers, because of modern construction, but it must have been a glorious view over 800 years ago.

After our final *Kaffee and Kuchen*, Kersti and I visited Connie and Klaus, who has grown into a tall, handsome young man studying French, English, and Spanish. Afterwards, we drove to the Rochuskapelle and walked along the grounds toward the Rhein, hoping for a glimpse of the Eibingen Abbey that was as spectacular as that of the Rochuskapelle from Eibingen—but we were disappointed that the trees were blocking almost every view. But driving home from the Rochusberg, we looked out one more time to that very special place above Rüdesheim. Our journey was complete.

Chapter 8

SOUTHERN ADIRONDACKS, NEW YORK

July 21-30, 2011

"We spent the remainder of the afternoon in the shade of the backyard at the Orendata, gazing at the leaves of the tall trees dancing in the wind and the ripples twisting on the lake"

Friday, July 22: Madison to Northville, NY

Nearly 40 years ago—I must have been about 13 or 14—we had a family vacation atBlue Mountain Lake in the central Adirondacks. Yesterday, on a sweltering July afternoon and after a busy partial day at work, we drove to the Village of Northville on the Great Sacandaga (Indian for "land of waving grass") Lake in the southern Adirondacks. We rented a one-bedroom suite from a nice young couple, Michele and Mike, artisans from Alfred University and owners of the complex. Michele is a potter and Mike a woodworker. Ten years ago, they bought a dilapidated "camp," as New Englanders call their lake places, consisting of several cabins and a motel-style lodge, and began renovating all the facilities. The result is the new "Orendaga," a Mohawk phrase meaning "wind over water."

When we first arrived just past 7:00 PM, we noticed that there is just a sliver of a lake view from our porch. Then we entered our lodging, and were almost stunned by a blast of trapped heat and humidity on a day when the temperature in New Jersey topped 100 degrees. We quickly dropped our things and headed into the quaint, New England-style town of Northville for dinner at the Timeless Tavern. We had a tasty meal of haddock and chicken cordon blue, interrupted when Kersti lifted the small salad dressing tray, knocking over her glass of seltzer and shattering the glass! The waitress, Kate, was very accommodating and moved us to an adjacent table. It was the very same table where we would sit on our two later visits to the tavern.

We knew it would be a long, restless night without AC. We put the futon mattress on the floor under the ceiling fan in the living space with our own small fan aimed our way, and managed to have a decent night's sleep. Today is still hot but less humid, and next week the nighttime temperatures will dip into the 50s. Is it too soon to call it a "harbinger" of fall?

We took an early morning bike ride along Seven Springs Road, at one point stopping with a wide view of the lake and drinking in the refreshing breeze blowing off the lake and through the swaying pines. These were moments of utter peace and relaxation.

Now we're heading down to the lake to take a ride in the two-person kayak.

Saturday, July 24

Today was the third consecutive day of high humidity and 90°+ heat. We woke early after another restless night, this time sleeping in the bedroom. Some early morning clouds quickly burned off, so we knew it would be another hot one. Michele was watering some of her hundreds of plants around the property, and we asked her for some hiking suggestions. She told us about the Hope Falls hiking trail, featuring three waterfalls in the nearby town of Hope. We packed a picnic lunch and set out on our adventure. The entire trail—more than two miles in each direction—paralleled the gently rolling Tennent Creek. Our pine-needled path took us through rising terrain. We could hear the stream almost all the entire way. After a mile or so, we came upon the first waterfall, which had carved a swimming hole and sandy beach. The waterfall was not high, but perfectly landscaped, cascading over big boulders beneath tall overhanging pines. We waded into the cool mountain water, thinking at the time that this would be the extent of our swimming activity. We continued on to the second waterfall, which was more impressive than the first, and then quickly on to the third, which, just as Michele had told us, was the most spectacular of all with its deep pool and multi-layers of rock and pulsating water. I was wearing my red bathing suit under my shorts, so I was ready to jump in. Kersti had decided not to wear or bring her bathing suit, but without a soul in sight—we had not seen a single person on the trail—she stripped off her bra and panties and slid down a slippery rock into the chilly water! I slid right in with her. We swam for just a minute and then retreated to a sunny rock where we marveled at this beautiful, peaceful, solitary place. Kersti jumped back in and had a longer swim on the sunny side of the pool. Then we enjoyed our picnic lunch in this perfect place.

Late in the afternoon, we drove on the Route 30 toward Amsterdam in search of a T-Mobile connection. On the way back to Northville, we took the coastal route through Mayfield and Northampton, and we enjoyed some beautiful views of the Great Sacandaga Lake. We ate dinner outdoors at a pub, looking across the arm of the lake to the town of Northville.

Yesterday we met a nice young couple from Toronto, Robin and Eli and their children, Sam (4) and Reese (2). At one point, we were chatting about our three, and Kersti mentioned that Eric was going to college in Canada. She asked where and we told her, "Concordia." "Great school," she replied. "I went there and loved it!"

Monday, July 25

Finally, the intense heat wave broke last night. We went to bed with just a sheet as a cover and the windows wide open, but by early morning we had closed the windows and pulled the blanket back up onto the bed and all the way to our chins.

Yesterday morning, we took a bike ride along the Great Sacandaga Lake on Route 152 in Northampton, retracing our route by car on Saturday. The sun glistened on the water in the early morning. We spontaneously headed down a "Dead End" road and found a house for sale, a beautiful modern four-bedroom house at the end of the street overlooking the lake. We parked our bikes and walked into the backyard, convinced that no one was there, but we retreated when we saw a towel hanging on the deck railing. We picked up a flyer—$650,000—lower than I suspected. Something to think about.

Around 11:30 AM, Susan Riback and her friend Marco pulled into the Orendaga in Susan's light blue Honda with Marco at the wheel. They had driven over from Marco's "camp"—in reality a permanent trailer—in nearby Edinburg, just five minutes away. Marco took us on a tour of the area where he spends many weekends, then across the lake for a drive north on the eastern side. We made turkey sandwiches and ate at the picnic table, and with time running out, I persuaded Susan to take what may be her only lake swim of the summer. After Susan and Marco left, Kersti and I took a swim and a ride in the rowboat, but not for long because of the loud, creaky oars. Getting in and out of the small beach, we had to traipse through a leafy, but not overly murky bottom.

The day remained hot despite the intermittent clouds, and we kept the funs running all day. After another tasty dinner at the Timeless Tavern in town, we strolled along Skiff Road at sunset, looking across the lake at an open stretch to the silhouetted low mountains of the southern Adirondacks. We felt our first chill in the air. We complimented a lady who was weeding her colorful flower garden. "Thank you," she said to us. "It's been too darn hot to do it before evening!"

I just finished a riveting novel about the Nazi regime and Holocaust, *Those Who Save Us* by Jenna Blum, with its multiple perspectives and impacts on contemporary Germans and Jews as well as the second generation. I will recommend it for the 2012 Rutgers Honors Colloquium. Now I am reading Jeannette Walls' memoir, *The Glass Castle*, and also reviewing Lauren Groff's *The Monsters of Templeton*, this fall's honors' book, prior to our visit to Cooperstown on Friday.

Tuesday, July 26: Northville to Blue Mountain Lake

Only occasional showers were predicted for Tuesday, but it poured a good part of the day and during our trip north on Route 30 to the Central Adirondacks. The flowers at Orendaga and the entire parched region were refreshed by the rain, which was heavy at times. It was the perfect day to take a break from swimming, hiking, biking, and boating. We drove through Wells (Algonquin Lake), Speculator (Lake Pleasant), which offered a nicely landscaped public park by the lake, Indian Lake, and finally Blue Mountain Lake. I kept searching for some signs of recognition and familiarity as we approached and later drove around part of the lake. I vaguely recall a cottage that we had to walk down some fairly steep steps leading to our lakefront cottage and even more steps to the lake.

The highlight of the day was the Adirondack Museum in Blue Mountain Lake. It opened in 1957, so it's possible that we visited in 1964 or 1965, but again I had no recollection. It was raining when we arrived and cool even with our rain jackets. We toured all 20 buildings or exhibits, featuring an A.J. Tait art exhibit, non-power and power boats, a camp exhibit, a one-room schoolhouse, an introductory film (we were the only two people in the small theater), transportation, logging, a fire tower (which we climbed), and much more. It was an intimate introduction to the history, life, and culture of the Adirondacks. At the café, we enjoyed a magnificent overview of the tranquil lake with its picturesque islands, only one of which was inhabited. After leaving the museum, we drove further north to Long Lake, which was a pretty mountain village on two sides of the lake. We stopped for a soft ice cream and ate it in the car, as the rain poured down.

Wednesday, July 27

(Morning)

It's our last full day in Northville and the Adirondacks—and the most beautiful day of all. Yesterday, we set off on our most vigorous hike, a 1,500-foot vertical climb to the top of Hadley Mountain at a height of 2,675 feet. It was a perfect day for hiking, cool with large puffy clouds, vying with the sun and blue sky. We got off to an inauspicious start—twice. First, for the second straight day, we had to return to our cottage after traveling about five miles down the road to a historic covered bridge, built in 1879, to fetch Kersti's hiking boots. Then, after arriving at the Hadley Mountain trail and checking our backpack, we realized we had left our picnic lunch in the cabin! Fortunately, not far from the trail in the sprawling, endless town of Day, we found a country store and picked up some deli sandwiches, chips, and even a pack of peanut M&M's. Then it was on to our hike. It was a demanding ascent. We climbed up steep, rocky terrain interspersed by long smooth slabs of granite. We paused a number of times to catch our breath, take some sips of water, and wipe our brows. About three quarters of the way up, we came to a meadow and followed a more level path before the final push along rocky terrain.

The views at the top were well worth our toil. Despite the thick clouds and windy, threatening weather, we had a spectacular view of the Great Sacandaga Lake with its twisting raised northern arm leading to its large mid-section. All around we marveled at the green immensity of it all. After our tasty lunch, we had one more ascent to make—about 50 more steps to the top of the Hadley Fire Tower. We felt our first few drops of rain and began heading down, at times through a steady rain.

As we continued north on North Shore Drive, the rain stopped, the sky cleared, and the sun poured down on the glistening water. We had almost continual views of the lake from the road. At Conklingville, we came to the 60-foot high dam, which created the lake after the severe flooding of Albany and Troy in the late 1920s. We crossed the dam and continued south on South Shore Drive, still hugging the coast. We were surprised to see signs welcoming us to Day, just as we had on the other side. Was the town on both sides of the river? Then it all made sense: when they flooded the Sacandaga Valley to create the lake, they had sacrificed houses, farms, and roads that crisscrossed the valley and even reinterred a number of graves on higher ground. Marco had told us that to this day divers explore old homesteads that rest at the bottom of the lake.

We spent the remainder of the afternoon in the shade of the backyard at the Orendaga, gazing at the leaves of the tall trees dancing in the wind and the ripples twisting on the lake. It was a little too chilly to swim, but refreshingly so.

(Evening)

This time, Kersti remembered her hiking shoes, and we remembered to take our lunch. We drove just a few miles out of town on Hope Falls Road, but not to the falls trail. We took a different trail toward Bennett Lake. It was a moderate hike of just 1.5 miles, slightly uphill, sometimes along the rocky bed of a dried-up stream, while at other times on level forest paths. The lake was small and pristine. We paused to eat an early lunch, sitting on a log in the warm sunshine. We then set out toward our next designation, Middle Lake, another 1.6 miles away, but we decided to turn around after traversing a muddy part of the trail. The woods felt moist and tropical, almost like a rain forest.

We returned to town, stopping at the Red Barn, which consisted of two barns and three or four small cottages, filled with "antiques"—more accurately, lots of typical, useless garage sale items. We didn't see anything worth buying. We returned to the shade of the Orendaga lawn and ate the rest of our lunch. Time was passing deliciously slowly. Kersti took a quick swim, and then we kayaked the entire length of Northville Lake, traveling underneath the overpass on which we had walked our first night in town. On our return, we had the wind at our backs and sometimes let the wind and the currents take us where they wanted. For dinner, we enjoyed our third and last meal at the Timeless Tavern, and watched the setting sun from our bike ride along Skiff Road.

Thursday, July 28

This morning we said goodbye to our home of the last week at the Ornedaga in Northville. We had our final breakfast on the porch in front of our "cabin" on a cool summer morning that required a sweater. We took our last stroll along Skiff, taking pictures of the cool lake in early morning.

We left around 10:30 AM, heading southwest toward Johnstown, where Elizabeth Cady Stanton and Louisa May Alcott lived and worked on women's suffrage in the 1870s, and Canjaharie, site of the Arkell Art Museum and Beech Nut Gum factory for many years. We enjoyed the American and regional artists, including Homer, Inness, and Sargent, and learning about Mr. Arkell, CEO of Beech Nut and a patron of the arts and community. We continued along Route 5 west, following the Mohawk River, and discovered by accident an Indian museum and shrine to Kateri, a young Mohawk native who converted to Christianity in 1676 at the age of 11 and was designated as "blessed" by the Catholic Church. She died of a disease when she was just 21 years old.

We arrived in Herkimer at the Bellinger Rose Bed & Breakfast around 2:30 PM. We were greeted by the hosts, Leon and Chris, and stepped into Victorian England. It's an ornate, flowery place, not quite our preferred style, but comfortable and friendly.

After depositing our things, we were back on the road to visit my friend, Scott Brown, interim dean of students at Colgate University in Hamilton, New York. Scott took us on a tour of the beautiful, spacious campus on a hill, at times driving on sidewalks and hoping that the president would not see him. He then treated us to a drink and appetizers at the elegant Colgate Inn, and even drove us to his home a few miles up the hill, where we found about 10 people of all ages—his wife, Ann Marie, two of his three children, and four members of a family visiting from Switzerland. Scott is an energetic, lively, funny fellow with whom I collaborated on a number of college consulting visits, and I always enjoy catching up with him.

Kersti and I concluded our visit to Colgate with a tasty dinner at a Mexican restaurant and a walk around the town green.

Friday, July 29: Cooperstown

After our first "country breakfast" of the trip—two eggs, wheat toast, raisin toast, mixed fruit, and tea—we headed to Cooperstown, 26 miles south of Herkimer. I was curious about the town, since this fall I will be teaching *Monsters of Templeton*, the novel by Lauren Groff based on her experience growing up in Cooperstown. We decided to take the lake route, and about nine miles from the town, we glimpsed the northern tip of Ostego Lake and followed it all the way. While not as wide as the Great Sacandaga Lake, it was a beautiful lake, largely undeveloped on its eastern side. The road closely followed the jutting western shoreline. Just outside of town, we saw the impressive Fenimore Art Museum on our left and the Farmers' Museum on the right. Just a mile beyond, we came to Main Street, which was already bustling with shoppers and Hall of Fame visitors. After parking outside of town, we took the trolley back to the Hall of Fame. Kerstin walked around town and visited the library while I spent two hours reliving the history of baseball. I especially enjoyed the Babe Ruth exhibit, the history of the World Series winners since the early 1900s, the Negro League exhibit, and of course the plaques enshrining just 1% of the 15,000 players who have worn a Major League Baseball uniform.

I met Kersti outside around 12:15 PM, and we jumped on the trolley for the Fenimore Art Museum. There, overlooking the lake on the spacious grounds, we ate our final picnic under a tree as a light shower passed by. The museum featured several memorable exhibits: Edward Hopper's sketches and paintings, the photographer Nikolas Murray's photos of his lover, the Mexican artist Frida, patriotic paintings, twentieth-century American trends, and, of course, the Hudson River artists.

Our final stop was just across the street at the Farmers' Museum. The rain had stopped, and the air had turned muggy, but the complex of 25 buildings was very inviting. We stepped back in time to the 1840s, visiting a pharmacy, general store, blacksmith's shop, a spinner/ seamstress at home, barnyards, a tavern, and a Methodist church—all original buildings that had been moved to the museum in recent years. We met practitioners in 19th century attire, demonstrating their skills and specialties.

Tired by 5:00, we drove back into town for an early dinner at a tavern/inn, and then returned to Herkimer, this time driving by Canadarago Lake, which we followed for about five miles.

Postscript

Rather than connecting with 90 East to the Thruway South, we took the leisurely route home on Saturday., We drove back through Cooperstown and then on to Oneonta along hilly, winding roads on a bright sunny morning. We paused in Oneonta to visit Wally's college, Hartwick, high on the hill atop the town, and also the nearby campus of SUNY-Oneonta, where Debbie Leshem, the mother of Eric's good friend Zeev, went to college. Not yet wanting to bid farewell to our mountain vacation, we charted a route through the northern Catskills. There were some scenic moments, but as we approached the Thruway, we saw more and more stores and billboards on the side of the road. We picked up the Thruway at Kingston and arrived home around 6:00 PM to find Peaches eager to see us. After nine days alone, Misty and Cinnamon were a little wary of us, but quickly warmed up.

Chapter 9

GERMANY

March 28 – April 7, 2012

"Time seemed to be standing still. I was reminded of a museum, which captures the reality and tenor of daily life of one now gone, but who lives through his art"

Thursday, March 29

What a first full day in Germany it has been! Planning for our whirlwind, emergency trip began mid-morning on Wednesday, when Kersti received a call from Mutti that Vati was declining and now attached to a respirator. We acted and reacted immediately. Eric made arrangements to fly from Montreal to join us in Newark. Lisa took the train home from New York, but then had to drive to Highland Park to pick up her clothes and passport. Janine took the train out from New York, but had to drive back to her apartment on 109th Street to pick up her passport and unwashed laundry. Fortunately, I had a Rutgers alumni program at Morgan Stanley in Short Hills and returned home by 11:00 AM. Kersti and I booked our flights, packed, and made arrangements for the pets, and I handled matters at work via email and phone. Laurie Silverstein picked us up a little after 5:00 PM, and after a brief scare—Eric was originally on another flight, which he missed, and was initially waiting at another terminal—we departed on a Lufthansa jet around 8:30 PM.

It was a bumpy flight, but we landed safely in Munich around 10:30 this morning. Our "delegation" included the five of us plus Anja and Nellie. We met George, who took Kersti, Lisa, and me, while Anja and the others followed in a rented car. Southeast of Munich, we encountered our first glimpses of the lower Alps, still snow covered and magnificently rising from the rolling green valleys with their farm villages and *Zwiebelturm* (onion tower) churches.

We arrived in Bad Reichenhall around 1:30 PM and found Mutti sitting outside on the patio of her apartment, sunning herself in the warm air. After a lunch of fresh *Brötchen* and cheese, we walked to the clinic to visit Vati. Mutti took us in to visit Vati in pairs: Kersti and me, Janine and Nellie, and Eric and Lisa. George and Anja visited later after returning the rental car. We found Vati lying immobile, hooked up to multiple tubes, his eyes closed and unresponsive. We saw his foot sticking out from the covers, and it look bluish. We talked to him and touched him; his skin was cool. The doctor, whom Mutti nicknamed *der kleiner Artz* (the little doctor), pulled us aside and said things did not look good. We all came out crying, fearful that we would lose Vati and regretting that he might never know that we were there for him.

Then an "angel" appeared: a grief counselor named Christine. She attended to our immediate needs, giving us sparkling water for our thirst and Tempos for our tears. A bit later, without telling the doctor or nurse in the closely guarded intensive care unit, she summoned us all to Vati's bedside to say a prayer. Suddenly, he opened his eyes. I think Lisa was in his immediate line of sight. He was a bit startled and confused at our presence; but he heard us; he saw us; and he knew we were there with and for him. He could not speak, but a tear fell down his cheek as he raised his hand to wave. We talked to him, rubbed his skin, and kissed his forehead. We recited the Lord's Prayer in German and English. He was not alone.

Later, the doctor reprimanded Christine, but she had joined us in saving Vati's life. As we were checking in to the comfortable Vital Bayern Hotel, just 200 meters from Mutti's apartment, Christine rode by on her bike. We thanked her again for everything she had done for our family.

That evening, Patrick and Dirk joined us for a tasty buffet dinner at the hotel.

Saturday, March 31

Whereas on Thursday, we felt we were on the verge of losing Vati, yesterday and today he improved dramatically. On Friday, the respirator, which was enabling him to breathe, was removed, and he began breathing on his own with the help of an oxygen mask. Kersti and I visited in the afternoon, and he was responsive and conversant, though his words were muffled and his sentences short. By this morning, he was eating muesli, fed to him by Mutti. He is still frail and visibly tired, and the future remains uncertain, but we are elated that he is still with us.

During the past two days, in between visits to the hospital, we enjoyed buffet breakfasts and dinners at the hotel. We had *Käsebrot* lunches at Mutti's apartment and walked through the *"Kur"* town of Bad Reichenhall. Swen joined us after taking the train from Berne, Switzerland, where he is studying architecture. After *Kaffee und Kuchen* at the most popular coffee shop in town, Kersti and I walked through a park past the tall wooden racks of twigs with salt water flowing downward, like raindrops, generating a salty scent to the surrounding air.

Swen joined us for dinner at Vati's and Mutti's favorite Italian restaurant, just off the *Fussgängerzone*, the pedestrian shopping zone.

Sunday, April 1—Palm Sunday

Today we went to the mountains. We opened the curtain to a solid blue sky with the sun pouring down on the white-peaked mountains. It had snowed during the night, and I scraped together enough snow to throw a few snowballs, but the dusting quickly disappeared. During the morning, everyone visited Vati, who was reportedly stable, while I took care of my email and updated my internship course at Rutgers. Around 1:00 in two waves, Anja drove us to the nearby town of Kirchberg, where we boarded a gondola to the *Bergstation*, 1583 meters high. We took a brief hike across the mountain to an alpine lodge, where we sat outside in the brilliant spring sunshine and ate our sandwiches (prepared during breakfast at the hotel), and indulged in *Apfel Strudel* and apple cake with mounds of fresh whipped cream. Then Lisa and I set off on a 148-meter climb to the Hochschlegel peak along a winding path in the snow. Sometimes, our steps crashed through the underlying crust of snow. With our hearts beating hard, we reached the summit. Kersti soon followed. We looked around, almost 360°, at the magnificent Alps, glistening in the early April afternoon sunshine.

Returning to Bad Reichenhall, Mutti and I stopped at the hospital and found Vati in the best shape since our arrival. He no longer needed a mask; instead, the oxygen was being delivered via tubes attached to his nose. A bland, unappealing dinner arrived—dark German bread, two slices of ham, and shredded celery salad. Mutti buttered the bread, placed the ham on top, and then cut it into small pieces. Vati was able to eat by himself and sip his cup of black tea. We talked about my job, our neighbors, and of course the mountains. I lifted my feet and showed Vati that a part of him had just visited the mountains—in his shiny black hiking boots.

Thursday, April 3

The alarm rocked us out of a restless sleep at 4:45 this morning. The birds were already chirping loudly, but it was still cool and dark when we climbed into Vati's brown metallic VW Golf and departed from the hotel at 5:30. Originally, Janine, Lisa, and Eric were scheduled to fly home on Saturday, but Vati's stable condition and the demands of their studies and work prompted them to fly home four days early.

We could not even see the faint outline of the mountains until about halfway to Munich Airport. First, they loomed like dark, solid silhouettes, and then the snowy ravines appeared, giving the mountains texture and life. A cold, pelting rain began to fall, and the day did not look promising.

We arrived on time around 7:30 and dropped them off for their 9:30 flight to Newark. I recalled dropping them at Newark Airport in 1998 when they were 12, 11, and 5—adventurous young children then, experienced adult travelers now. I will see Janine and Lisa on Saturday and Eric just two weeks from Friday when I pick him up with his friend Josh to begin their summer break from college.

Kersti and I headed east toward Burghausen on the Austrian border. Our destinations were Stammham, where Erich Horndasch lived, and Marktl, where he painted the ceiling and walls and created a cloth mural for the Catholic Church in town. Driving toward Stammham, we quickly recognized his distinctive yellow stone house, probably dating from the 1800s. Both Erich and his wife Barbara died two years ago, just a few months apart. We pulled into the long natural driveway under an arch and into the courtyard where Eric and I had had a catch in 2003. A man named Herr Göttin came outside from the apartment adjoining the main house to see what we wanted. Kersti explained her relationship to the artist and asked if we could visit the house. Somewhat reluctantly, he opened the heavy wooden main door, and we walked inside to a cold, musty house, but one that almost seemed lived in. Time seemed to be standing still. I was reminded of a museum, which captures the reality and tenor of the daily life of one now gone but who lives on through his art. There were several pairs of Erich's shoes close to the entrance; two suitcases ready to be packed; an unopened phone bill; a black-and-white framed photo of Barbara and Erich, happy and holding hands, probably from the 1960s; and his vast library of books on all four walls. Upstairs, we noticed cans of paints and brushes and piles of paintings, several of which had fallen to the floor. Erich's spirit and artistry were still very present.

We drove into the center of Stammham and visited the gravesite of Erich and Barbara. They lie beneath a light, modest headstone, acknowledging his legacy as a church artist. Freshly planted flowers decorated the front of the headstone, which was engraved with a view of Jerusalem, the holy city, which had witnessed Christ's triumphal entry, the tragedy of his crucifixion, and the glory of his resurrection.

We now felt we were on a mission, trying to figure out how Erich's paintings, drawings, and religious artifacts in his house could be collected and preserved. We asked at the tourist office in Marktl. The lady had never heard of Erich, but said she would inquire and get back to us. Just outside the office, we saw a plaque commemorating the house where Pope Benedict was born in 1938.

We continued on to Burghausen, just 11 kilometers east of Marktl. The town was also influenced by Erich, who helped determine the orange, green, blue, and yellow pastel colors of the row houses in the main square, dating from the Renaissance period. We walked across the bridge over the Salach River, which flows southwest through Bad Reichenhall, and entered Austria for just a few minutes. We looked back to admire Burghausen's 1000-meter castle complex, the longest in Europe.

After a light, tasty lunch of *Brotsuppe*—a beef broth with sauteed onions and croutons—we drove up to the castle. As the sun warmed and brightened the day, we walked along a cobble-stoned street past old stone houses where people still live today. The complex, which was completed by 1387, was the home of Bavarian princes and their relatives. There were homes, a bakery, a military fortress, and even a prison. The views were spectacular on both sides. By the time we returned to our car, we needed to strip off our coasts. We drove the final leg to Bad Reichenhall in about an hour, enjoying the mountains just thinly shrouded in the late afternoon haze.

Thursday, April 5

Yesterday was a major step forward in Vati's recovery: he was moved from intensive care to the regular hospital wing. We visited in the late afternoon. He now has a private room with a balcony and a panoramic view of the Predigstuhl Mountain, which we visited on Palm Sunday. Vati was feeling a little agitated because of a new oxygen machine and the effects of some medication, but his snappiness was in some ways a good sign.

Saturday, April 7

I'm sitting in a Lufthansa plane in row 30 with Anja and Nellie about 20 rows back. It's a rainy, chilly Easter weekend in Munich. Yesterday, George picked us up in Bad Reichenhall after a moving goodbye to Vati. He continues to make progress and is now able to get out of bed and walk to the bathroom on his own.

Friday was cool and cloudy, and on our drive on the Autobahn toward Munich, the mountains were covered by low-lying clouds. About 20 miles from Eglharting, George left the highway and took the back roads through quaint Bavarian towns connected by lush green, rolling pastures. In several towns, we saw a tall mast, painted in light blue and depicting village scenes and personalities—the baker, the butcher, the woodsman, the farmer, and so on. George explained that each Bavarian town has one. This is a ritual that goes back centuries: the townsmen—only the men—identify the tallest tree in the nearby woods, cut it, prepare it, and erect it every 10 or so years with great fanfare. In the nearby town of Zorneding, where Nellie and Anja spent the night, George and I studied the statue of "Mad" Ludwig II, a tribute to the men of Zorneding who fought and died in Bavaria's 1866 war against Prussia and Germany's 1870-71 victory over France.

George's house was in disarray, as he and Sonny are deliberately and scientifically packing for their move to Italy at the end of April. But Sonny still prepared a tasty Italian tomato sauce on spaghetti and a salad that looked like the Italian flag. After dinner, we watched George's slide show of their visit to Syria a few years ago. I caught up on a big chunk of my email on George's laptop, and then lay down on the mattress in Dirk's old room. It was chilly, so I put on my Northface fleece and socks to get warm under the thick comforter.

I wish Vati and Mutti well in the coming weeks and look forward to Kersti's return on Wednesday evening.

Chapter 10

AMISH COUNTRY

March-November 2013

"We began to observe signs of Amish homesteads—parked buggies, lines of washed clothes, flapping in the morning breeze, and no signs of cars or power-driven tractors"

"Especially for Kerstin, with her Mennonite roots and her descent from many generations of farming forebears, it felt like coming home. It was home"

March 1-2

In the middle of this long, cold winter, Kersti received an invitation to participate in an eight-week sandplay training program close to Lancaster, Pennsylvania, in the heart of the Amish country. She hesitated at first, concerned about the distance and the long-term commitment, but she decided to go for it—for the experience, the adventure, the deep learning, and a new community of practitioners.

On Friday, March 1, I rode down to Rutgers with Janine's former "Butler's"* roommate, Krista Kohlmann, to my office in exile, located in the Administrative Services Building III off of Route 1 in New Brunswick. I was no longer counting the months or even weeks until my departure from Rutgers—it was now days, with March looming large on the calendar. I had been fortunate to spend my final two months in the Academic Scheduling Office within a group of kind, supportive, collegial, and sympathetic colleagues, and I wanted to introduce Kersti to some of them. But my building was so remote from the campus and so hard to find that she was running late after a few frustrating turnarounds on Route 1 South and North. We said a hurried hello to Maria St. George and then jumped into the car, heading south on Route 1. It was a cloudy, chilly first day of March. *(*Butler's was the name of the variety store above which Janine and her roommates lived.)*

We made good time, but on this day before springing the clocks ahead, the darkness still fell early. By the time we reached Route 30 west toward Lancaster, the daylight was beginning to fade. We followed our directions through the small towns of Christiana and Atglen, across a one-lane bridge, and along a country rode to Gabriel's Hill Bed & Breakfast at 432 Noble Road. We drove up a winding, bumpy, pot-holed dirt road, surprised to pass pens with several donkeys, goats, and chickens, and even more astounded to receive a hearty greeting from a guy with a patch over his eye. Were we in a theme park, being welcomed by a pirate? No, it was only our friendly innkeeper, Rick, who apologized for his eye; he was recovering from a recent procedure. We entered the quaint house, passing three or four cats on the porch, and met Rick's wife, Rosie, who was also very warm and welcoming. They showed us to our room on the first floor, a small but comfortable room with a good mattress, and then gave us the lay of the land for dinner. Rosie drew a small map to "Dutch Haven," which she recommended for its buffet breakfasts, lunches, and dinners. (Its actual name was Dutch Way, but we liked the sound of "haven.") It was just a few miles away. We were impressed by the number of cars in the parking lot and the number of Amish people who were eating there. We skipped the full-course, meat-and-potatoes buffet, opting for the soup and salad menu. On the way home, we stopped for a brief walk in the small town of Atglen and saw several horse-drawn Amish buggies driving through town with gas-powered safety lights. We also saw a small corner café in the center of town.

We slept fairly well, but we were awakened early in the morning by the rooster, which cockle-doodle-dooed at regular intervals from the first trace of light. We also heard the clippety-clop of a few early buggies passing by. Rick and Rosie cooked up a hearty breakfast of thick buckwheat pancakes, sausage, and eggs. We were joined at breakfast by Doty from Pittsburgh, who said she was also in town for the sandplay workshop.

The workshop was at facilitator Betty Jackson's house, just a 10-minute ride from the B&B. The day was brightening, and we drove along winding roads, up and down small hills, admiring the wide-open cultivated fields and properties. We passed more buggies along the way. We began to observe signs of Amish homesteads—parked buggies, for sure, but also lines of washed clothes, flapping in the morning breeze, large propane tanks, and no signs of cars or power-driven tractors. Betty's house was standing alone in a wide open area with a magnificent tall evergreen standing in front as a landmark.

While Kersti participated in her first of eight workshops this year, I returned to the B&B to pack up and then relax in the sitting area. Rick gave me Internet access, so I took care of my email, and I later read some magazines and a book. At noon, I returned to Betty's house and picked up Kersti. The skies had turned gray and threatening, and a chilly breeze was blowing across the fields. We had packed a fair amount of food the previous day, and so we had a picnic lunch in the car in the parking lots of a nearby Mennonite church. We took a quick walk through the church cemetery and later along the path in back of Betty's house, returning in time for the afternoon session.

The trip home went much faster than our route the previous day. We took 30 East and then 202 North past Doylestown and New Hope all the way to the Somerville circle. We only stopped for gas and managed to get home in a little more than two and a half hours.

April 5-7

Now free of work and my Rutgers ordeal, other than the legal proceedings, we were able to leave directly from Madison shortly after walking Peaches and eating lunch. It was a beautiful early spring day with the forsythia and some daffodils in bloom. We encountered some backups on 202 around Lahaska and Norristown, but still made decent time.

Our destination this month was Bird In Hand, Pennsylvania, just east of Lancaster. Kathy Shoaf had recommended it for its quaintness and quilts. We had selected Greystone Manor B&B based on its appealing description and pictures. As we drove through Intercourse and into Bird In Hand, we didn't find much quaintness, and the quilt shops were all shut down at 5:00 PM. After checking in, we decided to take advantage of the extra hour of light and drove to Aaron & Jessica's

Buggy Rides. After a wait, a guy who did not look Amish—no brimmed hat or black clothes—welcomed us into the front of the buggy with the other passengers in back. We took the four-mile "Cookie Ride," which included a stop at an Amish farm for cookies and other homemade products. Our driver was a feisty 80-year-old Mennonite, who never drove a car, and told us that he rides his bike 8 or 10 miles each way to get to his job at the buggy business. He kept slapping the slow-moving horse but to little avail. We had a Pennsylvania-Dutch-style dinner on the premises of the buggy place and then returned to the B&B.

We had been promised a quiet room, but our room overlooked a fairly busy roadway, leading west toward Lancaster. We were also close to the railroad and occasionally heard a freight train passing through town. The more pleasing sound was that of the Amish buggies up early on Saturday morning.

I dropped Kersti at Betty's house for her second sandplay session and then drove northwest toward Lancaster, passing through about 15 miles of wide-open, scenic farmland. Entering the city, I found many brick row houses, reminiscent of parts of Philadelphia, Easton, and Bethlehem. I parked on a tree-lined street and walked into the central square of the city, visiting a small historical art gallery with several Peale and Stuart paintings of historical figures. I mentioned to the attending lady that I was interested in visiting Wheatland, home of our 15th president, James Buchanan. She recommended that I go immediately, because the last tour was starting at 11:00. I was there in just 10 minutes. Wheatland is in a residential part of west Lancaster. The tour was conducted by the director of the foundation that oversees Wheatland and other historical sites in Lancaster. It was a personal, in-depth tour with only about eight people in attendance. We learned about Buchanan's precociousness (he was asked to leave Dickinson College because he was often showing up his professors with his knowledge), his bulk (he was probably the third heaviest president after Taft and Cleveland), his distinction of being the only bachelor president (his niece served as first lady), and his frustration at not being able to resolve the differences that led to the Civil War (it broke out just a month after he left office).

After the tour, I returned to the center of the city and visited Buchanan's gravesite. After lunch—a burger and an ice cream at the downtown McDonald's—I visited another small art gallery and the indoor farmer's market, which was just wrapping up business. At 4:45, I picked up Kersti after another meaningful workshop. We returned to Bird In Hand at the tail end of its own Saturday market, but again we were too late to visit any quilt shops in town. For dinner, we had another Pennsylvania-Dutch meal in town, sitting next to a young Amish couple, probably in their early twenties and already caring for three small children. The children were noticeably polite and well behaved.

As part of our ongoing 30th-anniversary celebration, we extended our stay until Sunday afternoon. As we were planning our Sunday activities, we received a text from our dog walker, Devin Koep, that Peaches had escaped from the house and bolted down the street. We texted back and forth for awhile, until Devin reported that after looking all over the neighborhood, he had returned to the house to find Peaches safe and sound. (I later found out that our neighbor, Susan Penders, had found Peaches and, with help from her children, had lured Peaches on to her deck with a treat.)

We considered visiting an Amish compound called the Amish Experience, but when we pulled into a mall parking lot and found it scrunched next to a much more formidable Target, we decided to look elsewhere for an Amish farm. We saw a Panera in the same lot, so we ate a quick lunch, and then drove to an attraction appropriately called "The Amish Farm." This package was just right. We had a personalized tour from a college student, who was not Amish himself, but was very familiar with the Amish way of life, clothing, and history. Later we wandered around the grounds, enjoying the animals, including some sleepy baby pigs, which were curled together in the hay for warmth on a blustery day, and some skittish baby chicks, who could not stand still. We also stopped by the one-room school, an Amish house, and a store. We considered staying for the afternoon, but we grew tired and felt the pull of home.

May 3-4

I am writing this installment in the shade of a tree on Betty's property on our fifth consecutive "top 10" day of the year. We left yesterday at mid-morning so we would have time to tour Longwood Gardens in Kennett Square, just north of the Delaware border. What a feast for the eyes we found! Many varieties of tulips were still in bloom: tulips of all colors, some taller than small children, some looking like they were made of crepe paper. It was a sea of multi-colors, bathed in sunlight! We walked along a wooded pathway, past Pierre Dupont's magnificently designed fountains, through the conservatory that was so much more expansive than the one at the New York Botanical Garden, through the children's garden, and finally to the Idea Garden with its multiple colors and patterns.

We were just half an hour from Christiana. Driving north on Route 41, we were pleased that we had grasped the lay of the land as we wound our way back to Gabriel's Hill.

(At this point at 4:30 on Saturday afternoon, Kersti came out of Betty's house and rejoined me for the trip home. I recounted the rest of the story back in Madison.)

Rick, no longer sporting his eye patch, gave us another hearty welcome. This time we checked into a room on the third floor, which was actually a suite, consisting of the main room, a corridor with two single beds, and the bathroom. Several of the screened windows had stinkbugs, and I took care of about 15 in all. Rick gave us some suggestions for dinner, and we wound up at Four Brothers, another Pennsylvania-Dutch family-style restaurant on Route 30 westbound. It was nearly dark when we drove back through Atglen, where I checked the time of the library opening Saturday morning: 9:00 AM. We were sad when we noticed that the corner café was dark with a sign that simply said CLOSED.

We returned to the inn in time to watch the second to last installment of "Fashion Star." We were thrilled that our friend, Daniel Silverstein, son of Laurie and Jim, emerged at the end of the show as one of the three finalists. He is only 24 and already a brilliant, creative, and artistic fashion designer. Daniel came up a bit short the following week, but it was still a great run and will help him to launch his career.

Our night was a bit restless—it was chilly, then warm, then chilly, and of course the rooster greeted us early in the morning. Breakfast felt like déjà vu—once again Rick served buckwheat pancakes, and our breakfast companion was Doty. After breakfast, I dropped Kersti at Betty's house and then headed back to Atglen to the library. On the street, people were setting up tables for a community garage sale. I spent the morning at the library, working on responses to the interrogatories prepared by Rutgers' lawyer in our wrongful termination lawsuit. It was not fun work, and I was not sure if I was properly saving my comments on my flashdrive. Nevertheless, I felt a part of the community, as young and old, including some Amish folks, came in, asking questions of the librarian, including the location of the book sale. I drove back to meet Kersti for lunch. We sat at a round table in Betty's front yard and chatted with several of her sandplay colleagues. After lunch, we took a walk into the wooded area in back of Betty's house, arriving at a bridge spanning a stream. Three young people were camping there and stoking a fire. Kersti returned for the afternoon session, while I settled under another of Betty's tall trees in the shade. The hours passed quickly, as I completed my responses to a second set of lawyers' questions and then began my Amish Country travelogue.

We were not in a hurry on the way home. We noticed a sign for a covered bridge not far from the inn. We drove through it and then strolled along a quiet road in a wooded area. We stopped for dinner at an upscale Italian restaurant in Buckingham, close to Doylestown, before taking our final leg of the trip, arriving home around 9:00 PM.

June 7-8

I'm sitting in the car in the small town of Atglen in the heart of the Amish country. A young Amish man wearing his distinctive hat and work clothes just passed by on a scooter. Kersti is at her sandplay workshop about 15 minutes from here. It is totally peaceful. The window is open, and a slight breeze ruffles the early summer leaves, now a deeper green than a few weeks ago. Most of the morning, I was working on my driving tour of Madison, writing in longhand (as I am this chapter), preferring this to the tapping of my laptop in the nearby Atglen public library. Next to me is a historical marker that reads: "Atglen: Named from Its Location in North Valley." Midway through the morning, I grew tired, reclined my seat, and took a nap.

This is our fourth trip in four months to the Amish country. It's Kersti's final sandplay training session in the first of four series—16 total sessions, continuing through the fall of 2014. This time, the weather, the preparations for our departure, and our sightseeing were all different from the three previous trips. It rained all day. It was raining when I walked up Vinton Road and Academy Road to my new office at Drew (I began on Monday, June 4), and it was still raining on my walk home. Kersti was not even packed when I arrived. We finally left about 1:45 PM, nearly two hours later than we had originally planned. The heavy rain continued all the way to our Clarion Hotel in Strasburg. It finally stopped after our dinner at the Olive Garden off of Route 30.

We drove back to Strasburg on Route 896 South, stopping in a quaint, red brick town. We felt we had entered the 18th century. The numerous antique shops and old-fashioned stores contributed to the special ambiance. We passed an Evangelical Lutheran church, a direct link to the old country.

The "historic inn" in which we were staying was on "Historic Drive," but neither the inn nor the drive felt historic. A youth group and bikers midway on their journey from Philadelphia to Harrisburg gave the pool and spacious grounds a resort-like feel. Inside, the room was clean and comfortable, but the mattress of our full-size bed (we had requested a queen) was spongy, and I had a short night. The breakfast this morning was more plentiful than expected with scrambled eggs and waffles, but it felt like "anywhere U.S.A." We are planning to return to Innkeeper Rick in September.

I am enjoying this day of relaxation and reflection with no computers or home chores. I did have a good conversation with Janine, who is coming home this evening. I did a lot of thinking and writing—about my Rutgers situation (chapter 6 of my saga), my Madison driving tour (I'm not sure if I will ever offer this in the future; maybe it will be ready to go when we are ready to leave Madison), this travelogue (installment four of our Amish country travels; will we make it to 16?), and thoughts about our family, our parents, our siblings, and our dear children.

Now I will take a walk and then dip into John Cunningham's history of Drew, *University in the Forest* for the first time since the fall of 1979 during my first stint at Drew.

September 6-7

After a summer off, we resumed our monthly visits on the weekend after Labor Day. We were not at all in a rush and left after walking Peaches and eating lunch, around 1:30 PM. It was a relaxing drive on a sunny, comfortable day. With the cooler weather and memories of Rick's and Rosie's hospitality, we were ready once again for the rustic delights of Gabriel's Hill B&B. The rocky, curling driveway was bumpier than ever, but we made it to the parking area at the top of the hill. I sat for a moment on the back porch, and four cats immediately came up and vied for a spot on my lap. Rick was out picking up some things for the weekend, so Rosie greeted us warmly. We dropped our things in the room and then headed out to find a place to eat. Remembering our visit to Strasburg in June, we headed west toward the town, catching a glimpse of four or five hot air balloons that were soaring overhead. The Iron Hill Inn looked appealing, and several couples were sitting outside in the late afternoon sun, so we decided to eat there. It took awhile to be served, but we enjoyed what will likely be our last outdoor dinner of the season.

Loud male voices woke us up around 6:45 AM. We learned that Jerry and his wife, old friends of Rick, had driven down from their dairy farm in the Rochester area to check out some farm equipment. They were chatting away, unconcerned that some guests might be hoping to sleep in on Saturday morning. Jerry and his wife, along with Doty, joined us for breakfast, and Jerry asked a bunch of questions about sandplay.

After dropping Kersti off at Betty's, I picked up Route 41 South toward Delaware. My cousin, Bonnie Miles, had emailed me earlier in the week that she was planning to visit her mom, Aunt Peggy, at Cokesbury Village, her assisted-living facility in Hockessin, just across the border from Pennsylvania. Our bed and breakfast and Cokesbury were only 22 miles apart. I arrived on time to find Bonnie and her friend, Laura, waiting in the reception area. They were in town for their 50th high school reunion. We walked to Peggy's room and were welcomed by Peggy and her 98-year-old "boyfriend," Jim Stewart, Harry's former boss at Dupont. Peggy is suffering from Alzheimer's; she looked a little plumper than I remember; and her curly hair was thinner; but her voice was strong and familiar.

"Who are you?" she asked when I walked in.

"I'm Dick, your sister Jean's middle son," I replied.

"Oh," she said, acting as if she understood but not really getting it.

She did demonstrate that she had good recall of the past. I brought along my album of old Wallace and White family pictures, and when I pointed to a formal photo of Don around age 15, she said, "That's my father." She especially enjoyed the photo of Don, Helen, Jean, and herself in formal attire on their way south to visit colleges in 1934, the photo of her as a new bride in 1944, and the 1944 Christmas card, featuring Harry and the hand-written message, "A boy at last!"

We had a tasty lunch in the dining facility. This is where Peggy amused us with her constant questions. On several occasions, she again asked me who I was and who Laura was. Laura explained that she was Bonnie's friend from high school and the stable where they rode horses. Peggy then asked if we had children.

"Two," Laura replied.

"Three," I added.

"So you have five children?"

"But with different partners."

Peggy never quite got it. As we were enjoying a bowl of ice cream, she asked Bonnie and me,

"How do you know each other?"

"We're cousins," we each replied. She nodded and had another bite of ice cream.

We dropped Peggy off for her afternoon nap and strolled out to our cars. It was so good to see Bonnie and Peggy. I hope Lynne can arrange her next visit during one of our visits to the Amish country this fall.

I drove back to Betty's house, arriving around 4:00 PM. We headed home just past 5:00, stopping only for gas in Flemington. It was another powerful and meaningful workshop for Kersti, and an enjoyable day for me with Bonnie and Peggy in Delaware.

October 3-6

It's a damp, foggy Sunday morning, and I am sitting in a cottage on a Mennonite working farm, owned by Lisa and Brian Harnish. Kersti is at her third day of sandplay training, just two miles down Georgetown Road. What a joy it has been these past days. In spite of the hot and humid weather, which felt more like August than October, we felt closer than ever to this special place and land. Our cottage—clean, spacious, and delightfully rustic—felt like home. Lisa is kind and soft spoken, and the breakfasts, which she carried over each morning from the main house, were delicious and gluten free for Kersti. Usually, she was accompanied by two-year-old Leah, holding on to her mom's skirt or being carried by five-year-old Peter.

We arrived on Thursday afternoon, just after touring the oldest building still standing in Lancaster County, the Hans Herr house. Hans was the earliest Mennonite settler in what is today Willow Street, PA, south of Lancaster. The house was actually built by Hans' son, Christian, in 1719, and Christian's name and the date are still visible above the main entrance. We went on a personal tour with an energetic lady, a Mennonite and a Herr descendant. The house provided a cool break from the muggy outdoors. Our tour guide described some of the German innovations in contrast to typical English colonial homes, such as the central stove and chimney arrangement, which kept the heat centralized and the kitchen safer. We paused at the main meeting room with rows of benches for Sunday services in the home. We then climbed the steep steps to the wide-open second floor, where the children slept. Some 80% of the flooring and walls are original. Our last stop was the underground cellar, cool even in the summer, where perishables were stored year round.

When we walked into our cottage, we immediately felt a kinship to the Hans Herr house, especially the wooden doors leading to the upstairs bedroom and cellar, the brass handles and latches, the open fire place, the candles in each window, the long kitchen table, the steep winding staircase to the bedroom, and the five beds, including a small white frame bed for a baby or toddler.

On Friday morning, eight-year-old Nathan offered to take Peaches and me on a hike around the property, and ten-year-old Seth joined us later on his bike. Nathan pointed out the fields of corn that had already been harvested and those that remained. Across the fields, he showed me the next-door farm and homestead where his grandparents live. He kept picking up grasshoppers, closely observing their antennae and bulging eyes. The boys are home schooled by Lisa, and I kept thinking what a rich learning environment the farm provides.

The cottage was cozy, cool, and comfortable, and I had Internet access, and thus the hours passed quickly on Friday afternoon. I am rereading *Uncle Tom's Cabin* in a location not far from the Maryland and Delaware borders where the Underground Railroad was active. Appropriately, just across the main room is a 19th-century school desk with a wooden writing surface and brass legs and supports. A white Raggedly-Ann type doll and a black one are sitting there side by side, learning together.

On Friday evening, we drove about 20 miles south to Kennett Square, a picturesque, historical town not far from Brandywine Battlefield, site of the largest battle in the Revolutionary War. We had dinner at an Italian restaurant next to a wine and cheese festival. There was a party atmosphere on a warm Friday evening in October, but our service was slow and the food so so. We were glad to return to our farm, passing a number of Amish buggies with their flashing red lights.

On Friday afternoon, when I was picking up Kersti, I met one of the husbands named Richard. He is from Holland and is married to Kersti's new sandplay colleague, Ruth Castellano. They live in Oceanport, New Jersey, close to Sandy Hook. Richard told me about a nearby trail he had discovered called Wolf's Hollow Country Park. This became Peaches' and my destination on Saturday morning, before it got too warm. We first walked along a stream on a wide stretch of mown grass. At one point, there is a concrete section over which the water passes, perhaps an inch or two deep. I crossed each way on big flat stones, to keep my shoes dry, but Peaches proudly paraded right through the water. Over the next hour, we walked through a short wooded trail and then back into the sunshine, passing rolling farmlands and fields everywhere we looked. There was not a soul in sight. We paused a few times in the shade of large trees, feeling a close connection to the land. On our way back, Peaches was thirsty, so we stopped at the water spill, and Peaches drank long and deep. On our way back to the parking area, we jumped across the stream, Peaches first and me following.

After Saturday's all-day session, I drove back to the park, and we took the walk to the water spill. It began to rain, and thus we had an at-home country dinner, consisting of smoked chicken legs that we had bought from a local Amish farmer, a big salad, and some leftovers. Peaches gobbled down the chicken skin, and the solid gray barn kitty—Sox or Boots (reminiscent of Lynx)—climbed up on me on the porch to enjoy some chicken skin and dog bits from Peaches' bag. The Calico brother or sister (reminiscent of Freckles) is also very snuggly. The other day it caught a mouse and was toying with it in the grass.

This cottage has given us a very special feeling the last four days. Especially for Kersti, with her Mennonite roots and her descent from many generations of farming forebears, it felt like coming home. It was home.

November 1-3: Christiana and Millersville

Last night, we changed the clocks, setting them back an hour, and it seemed in that same moment, we were changing seasons. We went from late summer-like weather on Friday and Saturday to a cool, blustery Sunday morning, suggestive of late fall. I am sitting in our Mennonite cottage, no longer with the heat from the wood stove warming the place, but with brilliant sun pouring in. Peaches spent the cool night in the dusty basement, but now is in the car, which I moved early this morning so the sun could warm up the car and Peaches.

On Friday afternoon, we took the 78/29/100/113 route once again to Route 30, enjoying the bright day and still some glimpses of color. I settled in while Kersti drove over to Betty's house for her supervision with the visiting sandplay specialist, David, from North Carolina. We had a tasty dinner at Four Brothers Diner on Route 30 in Gap. We complimented the waitress and chef on their gluten-free menu, and even bought a six-pack of rolls from the personable chef, a native of Egypt. On the way home, we stopped at a gift shop, and Kersti found an Amish buggy, family, and lighthouses for her sandplay collection. We even picked up some free pumpkins next to a sign, FREE PUMPKINS—YES, REALLY FREE. Our night was a bit restless, and midway through we kicked off the comforter.

Saturday featured a change of scenery: a visit to Millersville University in Millersville, about half an hour west of Christiana. I dropped Kersti off at the conference center and took Peaches for a walk across an attractive, nicely landscaped campus. I was drawn by the sound of the band, practicing around the sports complex. I asked a faculty-looking local if there was a football game scheduled, and he said he didn't know. On the way back to the parking lot, I stopped and watched the Millersville women's rugby team and thought of Lisa, our one college "varsity" athlete during her year at Lehigh.

I settled into the back seat of the car and worked for a while on a crossword puzzle. One moment, I looked up and saw a group of people passing by on a campus tour, led by two women in their cheerleader uniforms. I popped out of the car and joined the tour. Although childless, I didn't seem to stand out, and I gradually worked my way up to the front of the group to ask questions. The two students were cordial and approachable, but they obviously were not as well trained as other student tour guides whom we have seen. For example, they did not walk backwards; when they addressed the group or answered questions, they often were facing forward; and their knowledge of the university seemed based solely on their personal experiences. I asked about enrollment, and they weren't sure—they thought about 12,000-14,000. Given their attire, I asked if there was a game, and they said yes, at noon against Kutztown. The one perky cheerleader, who reminded me of Lis, said she didn't think Kutztown was very good, and thus she was hopeful for a victory. The tour—which, I came to realize, consisted primarily of high school football prospects and their parents—ended around 11:00 at the stadium, so our tour guides could "go to work."

It was a perfect afternoon for football, but it was soon apparent that Millersville—despite their snappy black uniforms with yellow trim—was no match for Kutztown. I left at noon with the score 31-0 and later read that the final was 45-9. Millersville is now 1-8 on the season.

Kersti joined me around 4:45 PM, and we strolled through the nice parts of campus, circling two small ponds. We took 741 East toward Strasburg, stopping first for a stroll around the Hans Herr house grounds in the town of Willow Street. We walked over to the Indian long house, but it was closed for the evening. It was almost dark when we stopped at the Iron Horse Inn, where we had eaten outdoors in October. It was crowded, so we had a small table in the corner adjacent to the bar. I had a burger and Kersti French onion soup and a salad. We walked along the main street into the heart of town, and Kersti picked up some delicious almond butter at a country store.

Our host, Lisa Harnish, is as sweet and accommodating as ever. It appears to give her great pleasure to see how much we are enjoying ourselves in her cottage. She is sensitive to Kersti's dietary restrictions. Yesterday, she served two varieties of pumpkin bread and this morning a gluten-free delicious blueberry-egg based casserole. We only ate half the dish and packed the rest to take home.

Last night, after dark with the temperature falling and the wind picking up, Lisa stopped by to ask us about the timing of our Sunday morning breakfast. We chatted about her upbringing—she is one of 13 children—and gluten-free recipes—she recommended the online site, Elena's Pantry. I told her how much we enjoyed coming to the cottage and the farm. "We've been married 30 years," I explained, "and we have traveled to lots of different destinations in the U.S. and Europe.

But this is the first place ever that we have returned to." It is a very special place.

I brought my mitt to have a catch with Seth and Nathan, but we didn't have time. We'll find the time in the spring. I left on the table a Little League baseball and four Penn tennis balls, numbered 1 for Seth, 2 for Nathan, 3 for Peter, and 4 for Leah.

Day Trips to Christiana

We took day trips to Betty's for Kersti's individual sandplay sessions on the following dates: October 21, October 27, November 22, November 27, December 6, December 15, and December 22.

Peaches always came with us. During the comfortable autumn days, I sometimes took her for a walk at Wolf's Hollow Park. But usually I just sat in the car and read or napped in Betty's long gravel driveway. On two occasions, it started snowing, and in the darkness of late afternoon, it grew chilly in the car. Usually, we drove home after the sessions, but once we stopped for a delicious Mediterranean meal at the Olive Tree restaurant in Lionsville, close to Downingtown. Our new regular route, taking 78, 29/100, 113, 30, and 10 is so much more comfortable than our original trips via 202.

Chapter 11

FLORIDA

April 12-17, 2013

"The cruise was marvelous, the sights and bay breeze perfect as the late afternoon yielded to night"

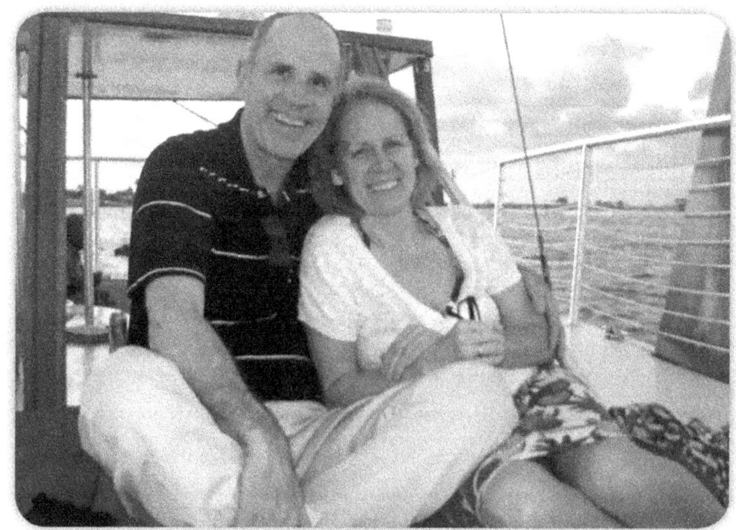

Miami, Florida—30th wedding anniversary gift from Lisa

Tuesday, April 16 (Pete's 60th Birthday)

After a long, chilly winter and cool early spring, we flew to the tropics on Thursday evening, April 12. Originally, we were scheduled to fly at 8:30 PM and arrive at 11:30, but we moved up our flight to 6:00 so that we would not have to arrive at our apartment past midnight. Of course, because of stormy weather on the East Coast, we had a change of gate and a delay of an hour, but we finally took off. Our United flight was unexpectedly bumpy, but we landed safely around 10:00 and quickly met Lisa. A 20-minute drive brought us to Coconut Grove, a lush residential, trendy area in the southwest quadrant of Miami. We entered our apartment complex, took the elevator to the third floor, and walked into a spacious, clean apartment, which we had rented through Airbnb. As it turned out, it was close to midnight when we clicked off the lights.

On Saturday, Lisa met us after our early swim in the pool and breakfast, and we strolled through the heart of Coconut Grove. It was mostly sunny, but clouds were swirling above, and it was quite muggy. We walked along McFarlane Street to a short boardwalk—no more than 50 feet—overlooking the Bay of Biscayne. We passed a park where they were setting up a two-day food festival, "Taste of the Grove." A stroll along Main Highway (really Main "Street," not at all a highway) brought us to Barnacle Historic State Park. We walked along an old buggy trail to Miami's oldest house, built by a 19th-century commodore from New York, overlooking the bay. A sea grape tree—known as the "everything tree" for its multiple uses—caught my attention for its broad, flat green leaves and reddish leaves that had fallen. Throughout the Grove, I was surprised to see so many leaves on the ground so early in the spring. In a shed, two craftsmen were working on wooden boats the old-fashioned way, boring and sanding.

We arrived at the bustling Peacock Restaurant on McFarlane Street as a storm was approaching and made the right call to sit inside rather than under the large canopy outside. Midway through our Greek and salmon salads, a torrential rain poured down. Only a fine rain was falling when we departed with just a five-minute walk in front of us. But two short blocks from our apartment, the skies again opened wide. We sought shelter under awnings on opposite sides of the street. Kersti and Lisa were laughing, because I was situated just in front of a Victoria's Secret model. The rain was not letting up, so we ran through the downpour and puddles, getting totally but enjoyably soaked.

The sun came out soon after, and Lisa drove us to the University of Miami to her office in the Flipsie Building on Route 1. It's nice to think that my last office at Rutgers and her office for the next four years are on the same road, though separated by over a thousand miles. The Psychology Department is located in a modern commercial building on the fringe of the campus. Lisa shares a small, windowless office with Irina, Janine's undergraduate roommate at Rutgers, and one other part-time student researcher. We met Casey and Tracy, two of her closest colleagues, who were working on Saturday afternoon. Later we drove over to the main part of campus and walked through the student center. We wondered how students could study seriously in such a resort-like environment.

On Saturday night, we accompanied Lisa to her spring graduate student party at the home of one of her statistics professors. The highlight of the evening was the first-year student skit. A number of students paired up, making fun of the graduate-student and first-year experiences. Lisa and a colleague played ditzy Miami girls who got a "boob job" in an effort to get ahead. Later, Lis on the guitar accompanied soloist Matt in a rendition of a popular Green Day song. We enjoyed meeting Lisa's great group of friends in the program. I particularly liked the former Northwestern tight end, Josh, and had a long chat with him.

On Sunday afternoon, we drove across the Rickenbacker Bridge to Virginia Key and then a smaller bridge to Key Biscayne. We parked at the South Beach of Brandon State Park and had a picnic lunch underneath a palm tree. We swam in the Atlantic, but it felt much more like a bay with shallow waters, some seaweed underfoot, and no waves. I napped for awhile, sometimes glancing up at the swaying palm branches and leaves, which I thought were protecting me from the sun, but I wound up with a red chest and shoulders by the time we left around 4:30 PM.

Now the rush was on to get to the sunset cruise, Lisa's gift to us for our 30th anniversary. We quickly showered and dressed, and then drove to the dock from which Lisa and Janine had taken their cruise in January. Wrong dock. We raced to the correct location, confirmed that we were at the right spot, and then sought some fast food. At an adjacent hotel, Lisa and Kersti picked up some sushi rolls. I was content with the basic hor d'oeuvres and beers on board the catamaran. The cruise was marvelous, the sights and bay breeze perfect as the late afternoon yielded to night. We glimpsed the sun setting over the city and marveled at the mansions of the rich and famous on Star Island: Elizabeth Taylor, Leonardo DiCaprio, Sylvester Stallone, Oprah

Winfrey, and Madonna, were among the most prominent homeowners. Lisa befriended a sweet, precocious eight-year-old girl and her family from Fairfield, Connecticut.

Lisa took Monday off from work, and after some stats homework, we picked her up and drove south on Route 1. Our destination was Key Largo. The references to Key Largo in song (Jimmy Buffet and the Beach Boys), in film (Humphrey Bogart's film of the same name), and conversation (Lisa's roommate Trish and our friend Jim Silverstein both scuba dive there and rave about it) built our expectations. We stopped for lunch at a local place on the off-the-beaten-track Route 905 South called Alabama Jack's. The country music was live and the atmosphere local, despite license plates displayed from throughout the U.S., Canada, Central America, and the Caribbean. We then drove over a roller coaster-like bridge from Dade into Monroe County and Key Largo. We passed by Everglades-like terrain and wondered if we would see any crocodiles. Back on Route 1, we stopped at the information center and asked the lady where we could find the village of Key Largo with nice restaurants and quaint shops. "There are shops and restaurants all along Route 1," she replied. "In the old days, the residents would meet at the post office for news of what was going on." We did not ask where the post office was. She did recommend John Pennekamp Coral Reef State Park, just three miles south. We spent a relaxing afternoon there. Kersti and Lisa swam at one of the beaches, though the "beach" and swimming area were hardened with coral. We walked along the boardwalk of the Mangrove Trail, and later I enjoyed the shaded, wood-chipped Wild Tamarind Trail. Hot and tired, we decided not to explore Key Largo any further, and headed back north.

We had a special 30th anniversary and 26th birthday dinner at Bouchon, an upscale French restaurant on McFarlane Street. We felt like we were in France in the 1920s or 1930s, almost expecting Hemingway or Fitzgerald to pop in for a drink. We had delicious dishes: chicken fricassee with mushroom risotto, a scallop salad, and lamb chops (not quite up to the standard of the other two). The evening weather was more comfortable, as we walked back through the quiet streets.

Wednesday, April 17

On our final full day in Miami on Tuesday, Lisa picked us up after her morning class, and we drove across the McArthur Bridge to South Beach. It was a bright sunny day with a solid blue sky, a mild breeze, and no threat of rain. We strolled along Lincoln Road Mall, joining the thousands of shoppers and people watchers. Lisa took us to an "Argentinian" restaurant where she had eaten twice before—it turned out to be Cuban—and after a tasty lunch, we drove to the 13th Street parking garage close to the beach. Kersti and Lisa enjoyed a delicious swim in turquoise waters on a wide, white sandy beach, while I plopped down in Lisa's beach chair under a big palm tree to read Thomas Costain's 1952 best-selling novel, *The Silver Chalice.* On the return trip to the Grove, we navigated our way into Little Havana. In the commercial district, I felt like we were in a Central or South American country. We were trying to find the monuments to the Cuban freedom fighters who died in the invasion of the Bay of Pigs in April 1961, located at 8th Street (Calle Ocho) and 13th Avenue. We were ready to give up, but Lisa persisted, and we discovered a tree-lined mini-park with a number of monuments. There must have been close to 100 names of those who had sacrificed their lives for freedom. On the ride home, Lisa took us through a more upscale residential area that still had a Latino flavor.

Lisa and Kersti were planning to spend the evening at one of Lisa's yoga studios—she even pointed them out on the way home—but they were tired, so we settled for a home-cooked stir-fry dinner of chicken, sausage, rice, broccoli, and my leftover sauce from the night before. We packed a bag of leftover cans and items from our fridge for Lisa, and then took a final stroll through Coco Walk. Lis picked out a custom-made frozen-yogurt treat with a few toppings. The evening was comfortable. Lisa then drove her car up the ramp from the underground garage one final time. She stepped out of the car, gave us both a big hug and words of thanks, and drove off on Virginia Street toward her apartment.

Now we are on board American Airlines flight 692 to Newark—fortunately. We arrived at the airport with plenty of time to spare—about two hours—and wound up needing every extra minute. When we checked in at the kiosk, we received an unusual message: "We believe in being early too. Check-in for your flight will begin 23 ½ hours prior to departure. Please visit us again at that time." We glanced at our e-ticket, and the date of our return flight was Thursday, April 18, not Wednesday the 17th! We explained the situation to one of the reservation agents, Maria, and the news on all fronts was not good. She told us:

(a) the cost of changing tickets the same day was $150 per person
(b) our original 1:15 flight was totally full
(c) we could be booked on the 6:50 flight to Newark, arriving close to 10:00
(d) we could take the 3:00 flight to LaGuardia or one other flight to JFK

Kersti and I even considered checking into an airport motel, but we quickly decided to pay the extra $300 to get home today. I asked about stand-by, and that must have been the magic word, because all of a sudden Maria perked up with some good news: four seats had just become available on stand by, and there was a good chance we could get on the 1:15 flight. She even printed out some seatless boarding passes for us. The TSA baggage check line was short, but it moved so much more slowly than in Newark. It may have been related to the recent furlough of TSA agents and air traffic controllers, or the Boston Marathon bombing of Monday afternoon. We finally got through, took the sky train to terminal D, and rushed to gate D10. The flight was delayed until 2:10, but when our full names were called, we felt a deep sense of relief and good fortune.

Chapter 12

NORTHERN ADIRONDACKS

August 24-31, 2013

"On the way back, Peaches was unable to climb some steep, irregular railroad-log steps, so I lifted her up into Eric's outstretched arms. No complaints or yelps from Peaches"

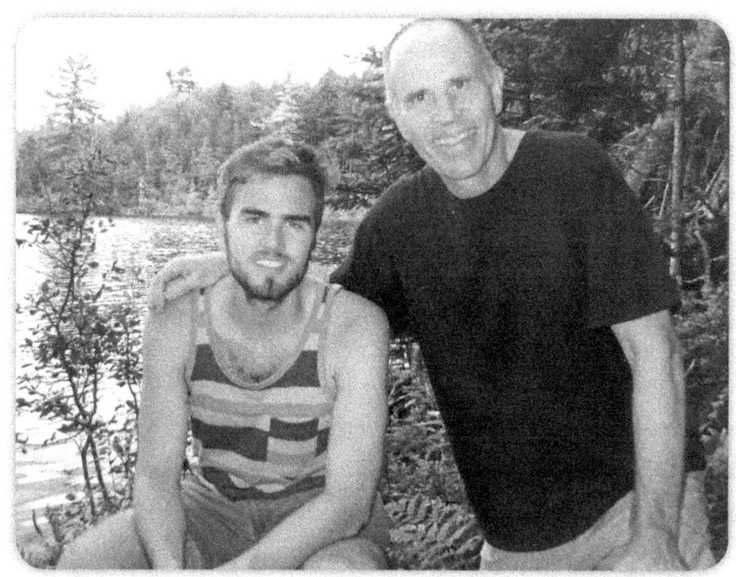

Mountain View Lake, Northern Adirondacks, New York

Monday, August 26, Mountain View Lake, New York

It's a cool, breezy morning in the northern Adirondacks. After a beautiful weekend with comfortable temperatures, blue skies, and patchy clouds, I heard the rain pattering on the roof of our log cabin last night. We're sitting on our screened-in porch at mid-morning, looking down the steep slope to the lake, where the wind is creating ripples in the water. We took a canoe ride after dinner our first evening and two more yesterday—including one when I broke my paddle while stroking the water, a first—but today with the wind creating a current, we would struggle against the wind.

This is an utterly peaceful place. Our "camp," as they say in upstate New York and New England, is a few miles from the village of Belmont, consisting merely of Belly's restaurant and a church. It is about 15 miles from Malone, the seat of Franklin County. We cannot see another house to the left or right on the lake. Our cottage is set back from a rocky dirt road. When we arrived on Saturday around 5:00 PM—having left Madison at 9:30 AM—we were welcomed by the friendly owner, Doug Johnson. He owns the camp next door, a substantial house that we observed from the lake. He grew up in Malone and came here with his family as a boy. He bought this property only last year from the Beck family and continued the tradition of renting it from late May until September. The cabin is dim, even on sunny days, since we are surrounded by a canopy of tall trees, but there are so many places to sit, enjoy, and bond with the woods—in front looking out on the lawn and uncultivated gardens, on the porch, on the narrow deck in front of the porch, and on the deck at the lake after descending along a narrow path. Last night after our canoe ride and while it was still light, we made a fire in the fire pit and watched it burn and crackle until the first drops of rain chased us away.

Peaches came with us for the first time. She was very excited and anxious when we first arrived, prancing through the cottage, sniffing, and exploring. But she has now settled into her familiar crate and the slow pace of life here. Yesterday, we took her on an excursion to nearby High Falls. It was a beautiful, not-too-strenuous walk along the pine-needled Big Salmon River, which flows west to Malone. Sometimes we heard the gush of water, believing we were close to the falls, and at other times the sound grew distant. Often we crossed bridges consisting of two railroad ties. Peaches initially, instinctively stepped toward the sometimes muddy gully, but I kept jerking her onto the bridge, and she seemed to get the hang of it. We encountered one broken tie, which had fallen into the mud, but even Peaches managed to negotiate the "one lane" bridge. At the end of our hike, at a rocky ledge, we were treated to a view of the rushing currents—not a narrow stream of water falling from on high, but currents spilling loudly and powerfully over the rock bed.

Because of my freak accident on Sunday, August 11, when the pot of spaghetti with the jagged top fell out of the fridge and attacked my left foot during dinner with the Silversteins, our hiking has been more limited that we had wished. My seven stitches were taken out last Friday, but I am still walking gingerly, flat footed to minimize the normal arching movement of the foot, though with hardly any pain. I hope we can do some more serious hiking later in the week.

Tuesday, August 27

We're just back from a small, narrow "public" beach at nearby Indian Lake, where Kersti took her first swim of the vacation. Unlike the murky waters of Mountain View Lake, there was a sandy, slightly pebbled swimming area adjacent to a 4H camp. A light rain was falling, and we put the heat on in the car for the 10-minute ride back to our cottage.

Despite the clouds, which hung low in the sky all day, we had a full Monday away from our camp. We drove west to Duane Centerand then picked up Route 30 South, backtracking from the final leg of our trip on Saturday. In about 15 miles, we arrived at the "VIC"—the Visitor's Interpretive Center—a nature center and preserve, which was established by the state of New York in 1990 and transferred to Paul Smith's College in 2011. Students from the college are actively involved in the care and maintenance of more than 10 trails, which wind through pine forests, meadows, and marshlands. We took a mile-long trail, the Barnum Brook loop, which had great views of the marshes that signal the end of the "high peaks" of the Adirondacks and the beginning of the plateau leading into southern Quebec. Later, we drove to the 2.5-mile loop around Black Pond and began the walk, but we returned to the car, not wanting to aggravate my foot. We'll add this to our activity list for Wednesday with Eric. We did see a "lean to," which Kersti several times called a "lean on."

Our next stop was Paul Smith's College. We passed small residence halls, most featuring dark brown Adirondacks-style boarding, some probably housing no more than 30 students. We gazed out on Lower Saint Regis Lake from the central green and imagined the beauty of this campus in all four seasons. The campus was coming alive with students, greeting and hugging each other after their summer vacations. These students—and this setting in the north country that attracts, holds, and molds them—are connected to both the land and their community, studying culinary arts, the environment, forestry, and hospitality. On our way further east toward Saranac Lake, we saw more evidence of the college's commitment to community, including the donation of a playground in nearby Brighton.

We strolled through the downtown shopping district in Saranac Lake, stopped at the original Trudeau lab, now a museum (it was closed), and then drove outside of town to the Trudeau Institute. We visited once again the statue of an elderly, frail Edward Trudeau, sculpted by Gutzon Borglum, creator of Mount Rushmore in South Dakota. Trudeau looked sadder than we remembered, embracing the pain and world weariness of his TB patients and his own battle with the disease.

On the way home, close to Paul Smith's, we followed a sign for White Pine Camp, site of President Coolidge's summer White House, but the camp was closed until next summer. Tours are available only on Wednesday and Saturday.

We ate dinner on the porch, listening to the soothing sounds of a steady rain.

Thursday, August 29

I'm sitting in the car with the windows wide open, while Eric and Kersti take a swim in Indian Lake at the small sandy beach. On Wednesday, during Eric's one full day at the cottage, we took a two-hour canoe ride across Mountain View Lake, through a narrow channel, and into Indian Lake. Shortly after entering the lake, we came ashore on a sand bar that stretched out into the lake. Eric calmly stepped out of the front of the canoe and pushed us afloat. The sand bar was actually an auspicious sign of a lake without the reeds, lilies, and marshy muck of Mountain View Lake. After landing at the small beach, we swam out into the cool lake, and could still stand on the sandy bottom, even when Eric and Kersti swam over to the float at the 4H camp.

After a late lunch at the cabin, we drove with Peaches and headed to the VIC to complete the loop around Black Pond that we had started on Monday. It was a beautiful, scenic, comfortable hike with views of the pond from almost every vantage point. It was already around 5:00 when we continued on to Saranac Lake on Route 86 East, continuing through busy Lake Placid toward Whiteface Mountain. Late in the afternoon, in the heart of the high peaks, we marveled at the various shades of mountain silhouettes: black, gray, and brown. However, when we arrived at the mountain tollbooth, we discovered that the road to the summit closed at 5:30. We had an enjoyable outdoor dinner at the pub portion of the Hungry Trout Inn, overlooking a gushing stream. We took a peek at the Whiteface Ski Resort and glimpsed how steep the Olympic slopes were. Driving back into Lake Placid, we saw the ski jumps looming high above the tree line with the silhouetted mountains in the background.

Beyond Saranac Lake on 86 West, then north on 30, and finally east again toward Mountain View, we may have encountered a total of five cars in a 25-mile trip. It's a quiet, almost desolate region in late summer.

Eric's two-day visit began on Tuesday, when we met him in Montreal. Driving into Canada at a small border crossing just north of Malone, we encountered an agent who glumly responded to my "Bonjour" with a heavily Quebecfois-accented question about where we were coming from. Driving along 138 East, we passed wide farmlands punctuated by small towns. Our GPS lady put us off track—she was having a bad day—and the trip grew a little more complicated, so we switched to English. We didn't spend long at Eric's apartment before we were back on the road, this time staying on 138 West and avoiding 30.

At U.S. Customs, there was just one car in front of me, so I crept up around a small bend so I could see when that car was moving on. When we arrived at the booth, the smart aleck agent scolded me for not stopping at the light that I had not seen and waiting for it to turn green. I apologized and then answered his questions: no, we had no firearms or alcohol in the car; I forgot that we had just bought a bottle of sparkling cider, assuming it was non-alcoholic. I then briefly explained our purpose in picking up Eric. With no cars behind us and little to do at the Trout River border crossing on a Tuesday evening in late August, his next step was to detain us! He ushered us into the waiting area, had us fill out a customs card—we reported $16 in purchases—and then summoned his partner to conduct a thorough search of our car. It all felt excessive and intrusive under the watchful eyes of a half-smiling picture of President Obama. Ten minutes later, he entered the room, holding a plastic bag of brown capsules.

"What are these?" he asked pointedly.

"Vitamins from my doctor," Eric calmly responded.

"From a prescription?" he asked.

"No," Eric replied.

"In the future, keep them in their original bottle," he advised. "You can go now."

Friday, August 30

Our time with Eric was short but special. We enjoyed dinner on the porch on Tuesday evening, our outdoor dinner in Lake Placid on Wednesday, breakfasts down by the water, and quick lunches on the cabin deck. We savored the sparkling cider that we had "smuggled" across the border—not too sweet and similar to champagne—on Wednesday evening after dusk as we gazed upward at the glittering Milky Way.

Our Thursday morning hike to High Falls along the Salmon River was even better the second time, because Eric led us down to the bottom, where we looked up at the gushing, splashing, foaming torrents. On the way back, Peaches was unable to climb some steep, irregular railroad-log steps, so I lifted her up into Eric's outstretched arms. No complaints or yelps from Peaches.

Our dinner in Montreal on Thursday evening was an unexpected treat. Walking along Rue St. Urbain, Eric wanted to discretely show us Burger de Ville, the restaurant where he works, without being noticed by his boss, a native of Egypt. But there he was, standing outside for a smoke. He spotted Eric and invited us in for a complimentary dinner—a deluxe burger, chicken salad, and ribs. (It's pretty easy to figure out who had what.) We dropped Eric off, exchanged warm hugs, and headed back to Mountain View Lake

Saturday, August 31: Blue Mountain Lake

We departed from our cabin around 9:30 AM after a final breakfast on the porch and a clean sweep of the cottage. On the road to Route 30, the first sprinkle of rain touched our windshield. I had been talking all week about the nature trail in Duane Center and proceeded to take a solo five-minute walk along a promising, pine-needled path. The rain grew steadier as we passed Paul Smith's College and continued south, rather than turning east on 86 to Saranac Lake, as we had done three times during the week. The community of Tupper Lake was disappointing after all we had heard—more honkytonk than rustic—but Long Lake, which we had visited two years ago, had scenic delights, a sandy beach, and appealing lakefront cabins along Route 30.

Our final full day on Friday was dedicated to the mountains. It was a mostly sunny, comfortable day. First, we tried to climb a mountain—Azure Mountain, west of Duane Center and south of St. Regis Falls. We stopped in the town of St. Regis Falls to ask for directions, and spoke with a personable lady who was strolling to the small post office with her grandson and 10-year-old ailing beagle, Max.

> The lady gave us directions and then added, "My dad, who died a few years ago at 81, was the long-time and last fire warden at the Azure (she pronounced it "Asher") Mountain fire tower. He hiked up for the last time at the age of 80."
>
> "Is it steep?" Kerstin asked.
>
> "Not bad," she replied.

We traveled for seven miles off of 458, four of them on a dusty, rocky road, and parked our car. At first, the path was wide and the incline was slight, but then we started climbing steadily upward. We paused often to catch our breath, trying to pace ourselves. Peaches was showing no signs of tiredness. It is hard to image a 1,000-foot vertical climb; three football fields seemed manageable.

But about two-thirds of the way there, we decided to turn back. We descended quietly with Kersti out in front. We didn't say much. I kept thinking about our vigorous climb to the Hadley Mountain fire tower two years ago, and about the 80-year-old man who made the climb. But we had made the right decision to turn back.

Still eager for a view from a mountaintop and with a mix of blue and white above, we decided to return to Lake Placid and Whiteface Mountain. We drove up the winding, worn, and bumpy road to the parking area, pausing at "miradors" (as Rocky would say), overlooking wide stretches of evergreens. At the parking area, we began to climb the snakelike staircase with uneven stone steps, and with the wind picking up, we opted for the elevator. This was an interesting experience in its own right. We had to walk perhaps 200 meters into the mountain along a chilly, dank corridor and then take an elevator ascending some 27 stories to the summit. Atop Whiteface at 4,865 feet, we had a spectacular view of Lake Placid, which is adjacent to several interlocking lakes, and could even see Lake Champlain in the distance. One of the information stands said that Montreal is visible on a clear day.

The trip to the summit had consumed more gas than I had anticipated, so we headed down the mountain with a range of only 19 miles. I knew there was no gas station before Lake Placid, some 10 miles away. I watched the mileage indicator closely, and it still read 8 miles when we pulled into a Mobil station.

It was dark by the time we returned to the cabin to prepare and eat dinner, pack and spend our final night at Mountain View Lake.

As we approached Blue Mountain Lake on our drive back to New Jersey, Kersti asked if we could stop at the Adirondacks Museum gift shop. She purchased two miniature canoes, a miniature Adirondack chair, and a children's book about the seasons of the moons in Indian cultures. We continued south, stopping a few times, passing through one of the fiercest thunderstorms ever, and arriving back at 34 Vinton Road around 7:00 PM.

Chapter 13

VERMONT

December 28, 2013 – January 5, 2014

"I walked Peaches through a small pine forest down to the river... She loves to romp and nuzzle her nose in the soft snow."

"We saw the Green Mountains turn a brilliant, lucent pink in the setting sun for a few minutes before turning into dark silhouettes."

Ski Vacation with the Pachecos in Hancock, Vermont

Tuesday, December 31, 2013

On Saturday, we embarked on our first full family vacation since visiting the Azores with the Pachecos in the summer of 2008. For the first time, however, we ventured in two cars, packed tightly with ski equipment, bags of food, boxes of water, Nellie, and Peaches. Kersti and I drove in the Honda CVR, while the four young adults drove in my new Jetta with Eric at the wheel. On the drive north, Kersti and I enjoyed two CDs with 42 of my favorite songs of all time, which Eric had compiled for Christmas. Despite the early snowfalls in the Northeast, we did not see the ground solidly covered by snow until we were off the Thruway and entering the Green Mountains of Vermont.

We made good time and were on target to arrive in about five hours when, in the small town of Rochester, just about five miles from our destination in Hancock, we were pulled over for speeding by a burly Vermont state policeman in an unmarked pickup-truck-like vehicle. I did not see any signs; I knew I was not going that fast; but he told me I was going 48 in a zone that had been 40 and then became 30. He apologized for taking about half an hour to write me up. I asked if he could just give us a warning, given that we were visitors to the state, but he said he had to give me the ticket. The cost: $150. I paid close attention to the couple of signs on the final leg of the trip on the outskirts of Hancock, most of them indicating 50 mph.

The next challenge was finding our farmhouse. We entered the center of Hancock, consisting of an inn, a general store, and a non-functioning gas pump, continuing further west on Route 100 as we looked for No. 2362. Before we knew it, we were in the next town of Granville, so we turned around and headed back to Hancock, where Kersti asked the innkeeper if he could help. This time, we found it. We drove up an unplowed driveway and stopped in front of rundown steps and a door in need of a couple of coats of paint. After some wangling, we managed to retrieve the key from the lockbox, and then entered a chilly, musty den area. When Kersti raised the toilet seat for the first time, she found a dead mouse floating in the water. But our mood soon brightened as we discovered a spacious kitchen, dining area and living room, two bedrooms downstairs, and three more bedrooms upstairs, one in a dormitory style, sleeping three or four people.

A little later, the kids arrived and began unloading their stuff. All of a sudden, Peaches darted through the open door! She headed toward town along an icy, winding, dangerous state highway with no sense of her surroundings. Eric ran as fast as he could after Peaches, followed by

Janine and me, while Lisa and Nellie took off in the CRV. Fortunately, Lisa and Nellie spotted her and, when Peaches stopped to pee, Nellie clipped her leash back on. They drove back to the house, picking up Janine and me along the way.

After this inauspicious start, we finally caught our breath and began the traditional process of settling in. We all figured out our sleeping arrangements, but Kersti and I encountered one more snag: the kerosene heaters in our master bedroom and the downstairs den were not working. We later found out from Betsy, the landlady who was comfortably situated somewhere in Florida, that the outdoor kerosene tank had been stolen. It took until Monday for the local caretaker named Chet to install a new tank, restoring comfort to both rooms.

The Pachecos—Rocky, Anita, Alissa, and Michael—arrived around dinnertime, and they enjoyed our sliced grilled chicken dish. Rocky also opened the first of four bottles of red wine that evening. For the next three days, we were treated to breakfast and dinner specials from the man we also affectionately know as "Chef Zeca," his boyhood nickname in the Azores. All we did was help with the consumption and the cleanup.

Sunday was our skiing "warm up" day, when Janine and Kersti tried out their new skis and boots, Lisa her new boots, and I my waxed and refurbished skis. We drove over to the Middlebury Snow Bowl, a modest but enjoyable slope just 15 minutes from our house. Only one lift was working, so we were treated to half-price tickets of just $25. We must have taken close to 20 runs, roughly a buck a ride. The more experienced skiers in the group were not so happy, but Kersti and I enjoyed the same five-minute run on nicely packed powder with virtually no wait at the lift. It began snowing by mid-afternoon, and that added another fun dimension to our outing. The winding roads heading home from the Bowl were covered by snow, and we saw a car spin out. We took it easy and arrived home safely to a delicious black bean and chicken casserole prepared by Rocky.

On Sunday night, we played a fun game that Michael had brought along, "Man Bites Dog." It consists of cards—funny and suggestive nouns, verbs, and adjectives with various point totals from 0 to 50—and the object is to create newspaper headlines that can be improbable, outlandish, and hilarious, but must be syntactically correct. We were enjoying the game so much, that we decided to add to the 100 cards contained in the original game. A little after 9:00, the lights flickered, but held. Then they flickered again, just as Eric was walking into the dining area from the kitchen, and the house was plunged into darkness. Rocky said, "Eric, what did you do?" But it wasn't Eric—it was the icy snow that had disrupted the power lines and led to a complete power outage. We regrouped; gathered flashlights and phones; and—why not?— carried on with the task at hand, creating new cards for Man Bites Dog.

Rocky slipped away to his room, pulled the comforter off his bed, draped it over his head, and reintroduced himself as the pope, even though he looked more like a clansman. Offering the sign of the cross, he asked Eric, Janine, and Nellie to confess their sins. Eric grabbed Rocky in a mock display of disrespect and drove the imposter Pope away. In all seriousness, this was an eerily familiar experience, reminding us of our days without power in the aftermath of Hurricane Sandy in late October and early November 2012.

Cold, frustrated, and wired, not tired, we all climbed into our beds, not knowing when power would return. It did around 3:00 AM, when all the lights that had not been turned off before bedtime, blazed back on, waking us up and ensuring a short, restless night of sleep.

On Monday, we headed to Sugarbush, which is adjacent to Warren, about half an hour away, for a full day of skiing. With Alissa joining our skiing group, Rocky took Eric and her in his car. The sun was shining, but with the temperature in the teens, the roads were fairly icy. We felt the wind and cold as we huddled in the cattle cart for the ride from the parking lot to the lodge. We invited ourselves into a conference room, just after an out-of-town businessman was concluding a conference call, and we made it our place for storage, lunch, and meetings. As we were putting on our boots, a mom who had just returned from the slopes said, "It's like sheets of ice out there." I decided to take a run with Kersti and Alissa, but found the conditions not to my liking, and traded in my pass for a day later in the week. Kersti patiently served as

Alissa's ski instructor for most of the morning, riding up the lift to the "bunny" slopes a number of times. Janine, Lisa, Nellie, and Eric came down from the highest peaks around 1:30, saying that the conditions were a bit better higher up, but still icy. I borrowed Eric's coat for one more run, which was still icy. On the way up on the lift, the cold slapped me in the face, bringing icy tears to my eyes.

On Monday evening, Rocky produced another delicious casserole with Italian sausage, brown rice pasta, spinach, and various seasonings. Around 9:00, cousin Dave and Max, his good friend from elementary school in Hampton, New Hampshire, pulled into our snowy driveway in Max's customized sleeper van. The boys were the center of attention for the next couple of hours. Dave told us about his fall semester at Peking University, while Max described his job as a photographer and cinematographer of skiers and skiing competitions. We marveled at how Max manages to live in the moment. Example: I invited him to stay over, but when I asked him what his plans were for the night, he said he didn't know if would stay with us or head to Burlington, about an hour and a half away. Even when we said goodnight, he gave us a "just in case" farewell hug. In the morning when we looked out, his van was gone.

This morning, the skiers headed back to Sugarbush. The Pachecos packed up and departed, and as they drove off, they shouted across a field where Kersti and I were creating cross-country trails, which had been started by Michael on Monday. Rocky rolled down the window and shouted his farewell, which echoed across the snowy field. We built up quite a sweat in the bright sunshine. During the afternoon, we drove to Middlebury, ate lunch at a cozy café, restocked our food supplies at Shaw's, visited with Laurie Silverstein's brother, Bart, at the food store that he owns and operates, and then returned to the farmhouse to prepare for New Year's Eve.

It doesn't feel like a special night, but ends are always followed by beginnings. That is the reassuring cycle of life. It will be a better year for us all. I am confident of that.

Thursday, January 2, 2014

Just like New Year's Eve, New Year's Day felt very ordinary, in part because there was no TV, no ball drop at midnight, no Rose Parade, and no bowl games. Dave joined Nellie and our family of four for another day of skiing at Sugarbush. Under a brilliant blue sky, I expanded and solidified my cross- country track, taking two runs. Afterwards, I walked Peaches through a small pine forest down to the river, most likely the Mad River, which was still flowing despite the frigid temperatures. She loves to romp and nuzzle her nose in the soft snow.

After our spaghetti and garlic bread dinner, Max returned to pick up Dave for the drive back to New Hampshire. Dave was eager to hit the road on the eve of his 21st birthday, but Max lingered, enjoying the main course, salad, and dessert and then several games of Bananagram and Man Bites Dog. It was close to 9:30 PM -when they finally bid us farewell. We very much enjoyed Dave's time with us, and we are happy that Eric and he have developed a close bond as cousins.

Today we stayed close to Hancock, enjoying an old-fashioned New England blizzard. It was not exactly a monstrous storm, but close to a foot of powdery snow fell all day with the temperature hovering close to 0°. I ventured out this morning to take one complete run of my cross-country track, concerned that today's snowfall would bury it. It was still clearly visible by late morning, but I'm not sure if it will still be discernible in the coming days. Returning to the house, I was preparing to take Peaches for a walk, when the door blew open, and out she dashed for the third time since Saturday. She must be attracted to houses, because she again wound up in front of a house similar to our farm house about a third of a mile toward town. I called her; she raced back and forth in front of me; and then stopped and accepted my collar hold.

After lunch, the five of us plus Peaches and Nellie in the trunk drove to Texas Falls, just a few miles outside of Hancock on Route 125 West. The falls are modest in height, just 35 feet, but the view from the bridge spanning the White River is spectacular. About half the river was frozen in large chunks of white ice. We then began hiking along a nature trail through pristine, untouched snow. Hundreds of pine trees were decorated by the freshly fallen snow. The trail wound higher and lower, across short bridges where we flicked the snow off the railings. Several times I stopped and listened to the sounds of the woods in winter, but there was only silence. At one spot, Janine fell backwards into the soft snow and created an angel, just as Lisa and she used to do when they were small girls. Approaching the final leg of the loop, we listened again and could hear the pulsing sound of the waterfall. It was a memorable hike, one that we will need to do again in the other seasons.

The snow was still falling as we drove to Rochester, just five miles east of Hancock. We stopped for gas and a few groceries, and then enjoyed hot drinks and a cookie in Sandy's used bookstore and coffee shop. It was fun browsing around and looking at books in multiple categories, stacked in small rooms and corners of the shop. We chatted with the owner's husband, who was seated with his four-year-old son, whom Lisa befriended. The man asked where we were from, and we told him New Jersey. "You are pretty chill for people from New Jersey," he told us.

It felt good to return to our warm farmhouse. Eric took the lead on dinner, preparing delicious lemon-garlic-balsamic chicken, while Janine prepared mashed potatoes.

Tuesday, January 7: Back Home in Madison

I am sitting at Eric's desk, looking out on the coldest landscape in two decades in much of the country. I just returned from walking Peaches. The temperature is just 5^0F with a wind chill of -11^0.

On Friday, January 3, we all spent our final day of skiing at Sugarbush. We got an early start, and found the actual temperature at the base of the mountain to be -9^0F with colder temperatures at the higher elevations. The young foursome seemed undaunted by the frigid conditions and skied without a break until around 1:00 PM. Kersti and I sought relief after a few runs, including several "difficult" trails. I made a run after Kersti went in, managing to ski down the deceptively named "Sleeper" trail, which had lots of trees and almost seemed like skiing through the woods. By the time Eric came in for lunch, his face was red and his reddish beard icy.

Kersti, Nellie, and I departed for Burlington at 2:30 so Nellie could pick up the 4:30 bus to New York. We dropped her off at the Megabus stop on the University of Vermont campus. Fortunately, she was able to wait in a small lounge in the historic Old Mill Building, which houses the English and political science departments. The bus was delayed by about two hours, so Nellie did not arrive home until 2:00 AM Saturday morning after being picked up by Norbert at the Port Authority bus terminal in New York. She was expecting to leave for Nashville later that morning, but her new car delivery was delayed because of Friday's snowstorm, and she didn't make it to Nashville until Tuesday.

On the way home, Kersti and I saw the most unbelievable sunset. Driving east on 89, we saw the Green Mountains turn a brilliant, lucent pink in the setting sun for a few minutes before turning into dark silhouettes.

After picking up the kids, we drove to Warren to fetch Peaches, who had spent most of the day at a doggie day care. It was like her first day of school. If only she could talk!

Saturday was Janine's 28th birthday, and we kicked off the celebration with a brunch after the kids slept in. In the afternoon, we drove to Warren, where we had hot drinks and a cold walk through town and across a covered bridge. Later, we drove to Waitsfield, a quaint town with a number of Vermont specialty shops. After dropping off Peaches, we headed back to Rochester for a delicious dinner at the School Street Bistro. For most of the evening, we had a private room at a round table in front of the toasty electric fire. The kids each enjoyed a couple of hot ciders spiked with bourbon.

We devoted Saturday night and Sunday morning to packing and cleaning the farmhouse. My initial aim was to head north to Montreal with Eric around 8:00. We managed to climb into the Jetta around 8:30—not a bad start. But as we were approaching Waitsfield, we received a call from Lisa, asking if we had the keys to the CRV. Sure enough; they were in my pocket. So we returned to Hancock one more time to hand off the keys. But of course there was another hitch—after our brief stop in Waitsfield to locate the keys, the driver's door would not close; it wouldn't latch; it was like a limp door, attached to the car, but frozen and non-functional. We had to get going, so I took off my belt, looped it into the car door, and held it tightly across Eric's lap as he drove and shifted. A few times, the car started beeping steadily, so I had to pull tighter. We needed gas, so I filled the tank at a Citgo near Sugarbush, and, thank goodness, in those few minutes the door thawed and closed. That latching sound was a sweet one. We did not open the door again until our arrival in Montreal—actually, our arrival at the duty-free store just south of the border, where I bought a bottle of Jagermeister for Eric.

With Eric behind the wheel, we made excellent time to Montreal—about 2 hours and 45 minutes, 25 minutes less than what Mapquest had predicted. We quickly unpacked—the final blooper of the morning was that Eric's ski boots and helmet were heading to New Jersey in the CRV; my misake; but at least Eric was back home. We hugged goodbye in front of his apartment on Rue Esplanade, and I headed south on the final leg of the journey.

Despite the rain and slow driving conditions between Albany and New Paltz, I made good time and arrived home in 6 hours and 4 minutes, taking just three short stops for gas and two breaths of fresh air. When I arrived, I was pleased that Kersti and Lisa had shoveled the driveway and were off picking up a roasted chicken and salads from Whole Foods. We unloaded everything in the kitchen, and the house felt in disarray, but then we paused for a tasty dinner. It felt good to be home.

Postscript

The following July, I wrote the following ode to commemorate our winter vacation in Vermont. The participants included the Whites (December 27-January 4), the Pachecos (December 27-30), Nellie (December 27-January 2), and Dave (December 29-31).

"A Vermont Winter Tale"

We arrived late on a Saturday afternoon
With a speeding ticket in hand from a state police goon
It took awhile to find our farm house
And we discovered in the toilet a floating dead mouse
The den was noticeably dim, cool, and musty
But the kitchen was spacious and not at all dusty
The White kids and Nellie arrived after us
And all of a sudden in the unpacking fuss
Peaches darted out and ran toward town
Until Lisa and Nellie tracked her down
We settled into our rooms upstairs
Leaving downstairs bedrooms for the two Pacheco pairs
The Pacheos arrived, bringing food and wine
After four bottles of red, we were feeling so fine
We ate and drank well during our days together
And stayed toasty inside despite the brutally cold weather
We alternated games and had plenty of laughs
The skiers rested their tired calves
Michael's crazy headline game kept our heads spinning
And the Bananagram word game was all about fun…no winning
One night when we were playing our games
The power went out, so we summoned some flames
To navigate our way through our quaint farmhouse
Hoping not to step on an errant mouse
All of a sudden a sheeted figure appeared
Was it a ghost or the Abomindable Snowman, we feared?
The figure spoke grandly, offering a blessing
It was Pope Rocky, no longer were we guessing
Cousin Dave joined us for two days of skiing
He's always chill and excels at just being
We rang in the new year on the thirty-first

And imbibed champagne to quench our thirst
We stayed until the 4th for Janine's special day
Then reluctantly packed and were on our way
Dick dropped off Eric in cold Montreal
While the girls tied up, locked the door, and said, "Folks, that's all!"

(How refreshing to write about the coldest days of the winter on this muggy July day!)

Chapter 14

AMISH COUNTRY 2014

"Rising and falling with the topography, the road winds ahead like a ribbon, bordered by fields, ponds, and large Amish farms"

Christiana, Pennsylvania—With Socks and Boots at the Mennonite farm

March 7-9

Following nearly weekly day trips to Christiana, PA for Kersti's sandplay sessions with Betty Jackson in January and February, we set off on Friday, March 7 for a one-night stay in our Mennonite cottage on the Harnishes' working farm. We wound up extending our stay to two nights and a good part of day three.

Saturday provided a real taste of spring after this long, cold, snowy winter. The temperature reached the mid-50s under mostly sunny skies. Around noontime, I took Peaches for a walk at Wolf's Hollow Park. We walked along the asphalt trail, crossed the still frozen stream, and then returned along a sunny slope where the snow was giving way to brown leaves and grass. Throughout the afternoon, I worked on taxes in the cozy cottage, still feeding the woodburning stove throughout the day and both nights. At 5:00, I picked up Kersti at Betty's and had a nice chat with Ruth Castellano's husband, Richard, from Holland. We returned to Four Brothers Diner on Route 30 in Gap for the second straight night, attracted by the friendly servers and four-course "senior" dinners.

The sunsets on Friday and Saturday night were spectacular. On Friday, we marveled at the rich dark pink hue of the western sky, while on Saturday, the sun was a brilliant orange-red ball hanging low in the sky before dipping beneath and tree and meadow lines.

We had a revealing chat with Lisa Harnish this morning, as she was collecting our breakfast dishes. She said that the Amish, despite their widely perceived reputation as quiet, dignified, peaceful people, actually suffer from a troubling amount of sexual and emotional abuse. She added that they believe deeply in God and God's will, even in the face of the tragedy, such as the murder of the Amish schoolgirls in October 2006, which occurred within five miles of here. However, they do not encourage close, personal relationships with Jesus.

Today, Sunday, a biting wind has swept away yesterday's spring harbinger, despite the brilliant sunshine. We will have a warm lunch in the cottage after Kersti's 12:00 session, and then head home, certain to arrive in the daylight because of last night's "spring ahead."

April 4-7

We headed to our familiar home away from home in the Amish country early Thursday afternoon after my half-day at Drew. It was a delightfully warm spring day. Picking up Route 100 south toward Downingtown, Kersti started jotting down the names of all the streets that were particularly descriptive of a place, nature, a profession, a rural activity, or a farm or wild animal. We came up with a list of 27 street names. Here they are approximately in order, north to south, left to right:

<u>Route 100:</u>

Indian Creek Road *Batman Road* *Schoolhouse Road* *Tollgate Road*
Old Homestead Lane *Creamery Road Huff's* *Church Road* *Church Hill Rd.*
Nannygoat Hill Road *Dairy Lane* *Mill Street* *Church Street*
Pigeon Creek Road *Flowing Springs Road* *Timber Drive* *Horseshoe Trail*
Conestoga Road *Birch Run Road* *Blackhorse Road* *Graphite Mine Rd.*

<u>Route 113</u>:

Eagleview Boulevard

<u>Between Route 10 and Georgetown Road in Christiana</u>:

Highland Road *Fallowfield Road* *Wolf's Hollow Drive* *Old Forge Rd.*
Creek Road *White Oak Road*

As we have come to expect, we had another meaningful conversation with Lisa. She was born in northern Ontario to Mennonite missionaries and spent her first eight years there, before returning to Downingtown, Pennsylvania, her father's hometown. While in Canada, her parents adopted two "First Nation" brothers, who eventually returned to their reservation, but remain in touch with Lisa to this day. Remarking on the size of her birth family, Lisa joked, "My parents had two children when they went to Canada, but when they returned to Downingtown, they had ten!" Lisa's Canadian roots are undoubtedly the source of her curiosity about and interest in the world beyond this Mennonite farm community.

We enjoyed another tasty dinner at our favorite local restaurant, Four Brothers, in Gap. Following our soup and salad courses, Kersti had chicken breast with mushrooms, onions, and green peppers, and I had eggplant parmesan.

The cabin was still warm at bedtime, but the day dawned chilly, gray, and blustery, and the weather persisted throughout the day. It was cozy in our cottage with enough heat from the furnace that we did not need to burn wood in the woodburning stove.

In the afternoon, I had some fun with the descriptive street names that we had compiled on our way to the farm and wrote this poem:

"Amish Country"

On our trip last week to the Amish country
Heading south on Route 100 from Allentown to Downingtown
(After waving heartily to Mr. Allen and Mr. Downing along the way)
We flung open a treasure box of images and names
And let our imaginations run wild
We met Indians patiently fishing on Indian Creek Road
Can you believe we glimpsed Batman soaring aloft above Batman Road?
We passed the one-room red schoolhouse on Schoolhouse Road
Paid a modest toll on Tollgate Road
Stopped for piping hot chicken soup on Old Homestead Lane
Picked up some farm-fresh butter on Creamery Lane
Said our prayers—and of course greeted Mr. Huff
On Huff's Church Road and Church Hill Road
Herded the goats on Nannygoat Hill Road
Skimmed off the cream atop the milk bottle on Dairy Lane
Paused to listen to the magic of the spinning mill on Mill Street
Witnessed pigeons bathing in the stream on Pigeon Creek Road
Or were they taking a ride with the tide on Flowing Springs Road?
We noticed that row after row of timber on Timber Drive
Saw scattered horseshoes from last summer on Horseshoe Trail
The dust was kicked up by the wagons heading west on Conestoga Road
And tall white birches scampered along Birch Run Road
We marveled at the elegant, fleeting horses on Blackhorse Road
Exhausted miners, their lunch pails hanging low, were heading home on Graphite Mine Road
We soared high above the landscape, sharing the view with the eagles on Eagleview Road
Felt the pulse of our Scottish blood on Highland Road
Blessed the sleeping fields on Fallowfield Road
Peered in on the sleeping wolves on Wolf's Hollow Drive
Heard the blacksmith's loud hammer on Old Forge Road
Soothed our dusty, tired feet in the creek on Creek Road
Rode the wind through the trees on White Oak Road
Then turned right onto Georgetown Road

Made a quick left into our Mennonite farm
Entered our cozy cottage
Which our host Lisa calls Spruce Edge

Saturday dawned bright and sunny, but the blustery winds continued to blow across the still dormant cornfields. There are very few trees to buffet the relentless wind. I dropped Kersti off this morning around quarter to nine, and then took Peaches for a walk close to the Mt. Pleasant Methodist Church on Bartville Road. We always pass it on our way to Wolf's Hollow Park and Route 10. We walked down a fairly steep road, enjoying the brilliant sun and lessening wind. An Amish man with a gray beard, probably in his fifties, was on his hands and knees positioning a long rail, almost like a railroad tie, into the ground. He did not acknowledge me when I first walked by, but he gave me a hearty "Good Morning" on the way back. I replied in kind. A woman who was probably his daughter or daughter-in-law was hanging up the wash. Awhile later, sitting discreetly in the car at some distance, I counted 98 hangings of all sizes, dominated by black and dark purple. They undoubtedly were drying quickly in the sun and wind. Peaches and I strolled through the cemetery adjacent to the church, focusing on families and veterans. One mother and father, born in the 1860s, lost their two children at the ages of 7 and 12 in the 1890s. A number of gravesites were identified as Civil War, World War I, or World War II veterans.

At 12:30, I met cousin Lynne at the Dutch-Way restaurant in Gap. She left Columbus early this morning for the drive to Hockessin to visit Aunt Peggy. It's an eight-hour trek, and she does it about every other month. We ate a bowl of chili and a garden salad and caught up on family matters, focusing primarily on the Whites, Ayres, and Bernarts. I shared with her our "breaking news" about our move this summer. She said she was pondering her retirement from the American Cancer Society, and was thinking about moving to the Raleigh or Charlotte area later this year. She knew nothing about my Rutgers ordeal and was outraged at how Rutgers had treated me. It was a fun, leisurely, engaging lunch of two hours, and we will do it again during one of our fall trips to the Amish Country.

On Saturday afternoon, I put the finishing touches on my 2013 taxes and successfully submitted my 1040 electronically for the first time. I picked up Kersti a little after 5:00 PM, and she said she was returning to Betty for a 7:00 individual session, so we headed back to Dutch-Way—the supermarket this time—to pick up some broiled chicken legs and beef vegetable soup. On the way to and from Gap, we drove along White Oak Road, a short cut between our cottage and Noble Road. It takes less than five minutes, but it's my favorite passage through the heart of the Amish country. Rising and falling with the topography, the road winds ahead like a ribbon, bordered by fields, ponds, and large Amish farms. At the top of the hill close to Noble Road, we paused to admire at least 50 brown cows and some baby cows milling close to the road in the late afternoon sunshine—a marked contrast to the dirty, mean-looking black cows penned in on the Harnish farm.

We enjoyed a tasty dinner of heat ups, before Kersti headed back to Betty's. After her return, we decided to try to get out of our commitment to move to a condo at Madison Commons and instead to consider a small house on Hamilton Street in Madison. We'll see what happens in the next day or two.

Sunday was sunny and warmer with diminished winds. We awoke after a restless night to the sounds of chirping birds. After Kersti's final session with Betty at 10:00, we ate lunch in our cottage and set out for home in the early afternoon.

May 2-4

It's Sunday morning in the cottage, and I am wrapping up our final stay of the spring while Kersti has her final sandplay session with Betty. The weather has been cool for the middle of spring, with occasional showers, but comfortable enough for Peaches to spend the long weekend in the car—her home away from home.

We arrived in the warm sunshine on Friday afternoon after my unusual half-day of work on Friday morning. Kersti drove most of the way. We brought along some tennis rackets, balls, and bats that our kids had used, and I was happy that Lisa accepted the equipment on behalf of her kids. I helped her deliver the equipment to their garage, and a short time later when I looked out, Nathan and Peter were already playing tennis against the garage door. It's nice to know that our old equipment will have a new life on this Mennonite farm.

We returned to the Dutch-Way restaurant, where we had had our very first meal in the area in March 2013. The chili and vegetable beef soup were tasty, and the salads fresh and plentiful. That evening, we curled up on the two-seat sofa and watched "Philomena" with Judy Dench, the story of an Irish woman in search of her young son who had been taken away from her because she had borne him out of wedlock.

On a sunny Saturday morning, after dropping off Kersti at Betty's, Peaches and I took what is becoming our favorite walk along White Oak Road. It is right around the corner from the farm, beginning at Bartville Road. We walked along the winding road with its lifts and dips and constant vistas of farm compounds, fields, and grazing cattle. At the bottom of a big hill, we paused to watch a mother and her young colt or foal. Whenever she moved, the young horse moved with her, always remaining by her side.

Soon Peaches and I were off in the direction of Lancaster to visit two of the area's historical sites. Boehm's Chapel in Willow Street is the oldest Methodist church in Pennsylvania and the fourth oldest in the U.S. It was built in 1791 by the Reverend Martin Boehm, himself an itinerant pastor, who settled here and was buried here. Francis Asbury preached here on his travels west. The chapel looks out on a peaceful valley, now sparkling green in the springtime. Unfortunately, a Methodist youth group, probably from nearby Lititz, was assembled outside the chapel and then lingered inside while I ate my ham and cheese sandwich. I was hoping to get a closer look, and would have enjoyed listening to the lecture of their leader, but there was no sign of their departure. So I headed north into Lancaster. I stopped at the Lancaster Art Museum, which is housed in a Georgian-style brick home on North Lime Street. I was expecting more traditional art from the region, but instead found American contemporary "pop" art, including works by Andy Warhol, Roy Lichtenstein, Robert Indiana (the "LOVE" artist), and Peter Max, whose patriotic pieces were colorful and stunning.

The highlight of the return trip was discovering the beginning of White Oak Road just five miles south of Strasburg on 896. It's a continuation of the brief stretch between Bartville Road and Noble Road—not quite as panoramic or hilly—but with its pastoral scenes, infrequent cars, and Amish of all ages working or playing outside. I was treated to the heart of the Amish Country. Kersti and I took the same route back to Strasburg for dinner at the Iron Horse Inn in the brilliant sunshine, but showers were falling and dusk was approaching for our return trip.

Lisa gave us two more cartons of eggs at breakfast. She was wearing a dress and her prayer cap for Sunday services at the Bartville Mennonite Church. Her gentleness, kindness, and hospitality, in addition to her delicious, plentiful, and gluten-free breakfasts, make this cottage and this connection very special. We'll see Brian, the children, and Lisa in September.

May 25-26

During our many trips to the Amish country during the past year and a half, we have encountered a wide range of weather in the different seasons. These two days—Sunday and Memorial Day Monday—were the most glorious days yet. They followed torrential rains on Friday and Saturday, so when we set out around 9:45 on Sunday morning, the road ahead felt promising. We were hoping to stop for a roadside picnic, but seemed to have bad luck with the lights and the plodding church drivers, and we arrived at Betty's with just a minute to spare for the first of Kersti's three sandplay sessions at 1:00 PM. I parked in the shade off of Betty's driveway and decided to stay put. I set up a folding chair in the sunshine with Peaches' leash securely fastened under one of the legs, and enjoyed my chicken sandwich. The sun was usually either too hot or not warm enough, but at the right moments felt deliciously "schoen warm." I worked on my crossroad puzzle and read Dan Balz's *Collision 2012: Obama vs. Romney and the Future of American Elections.*

In between sessions, we returned to our farm cottage and met Lisa as we were unloading. She eagerly accepted three hockey sticks from our garage clear out. Kersti and I walked Peaches along the trail—wide enough for pick-up trucks and tractors—leading to the woods, which Seth had originally taken me on during our first visit last fall. It seems like much longer ago when we first came to the farm. Back at the cottage, Seth and Nathan invited me to have a catch. I had brought my mitt, hoping they would ask me. I haven't thrown, caught, or hit a ball in about three years—ever since Eric went away—but my instincts were still pretty sharp. Later I hit some balls to the boys, a mix of grounders and fly balls, several of which nearly plunked our car. At 11 and 9 years old, Seth and Nathan are very good ballplayers. I later had a long chat with Lisa about home schooling, baseball, and the challenges of parenting at all ages.

It was nearly 7:00 PM when we headed out along our now familiar back roads along White Oak and Lower Valley and then through Christiana to Route 41 and then 30 West. Everyone seemed to be outside in the late afternoon sun, the Amish boys and girls on their farms, and the "city" kids on their porches and small front yards. Our dinner at Four Brothers was not quite up to expectations, so we will scout around for other restaurants when we come back in the fall. On the return route, it was still light enough around 8:30 to enjoy the landscape and the outside play.

Memorial Day breakfast arrived at 8:15 with Nathan lending his mom a hand. Lisa asked about veterans in our family, and I said that Mom and Dad had met in the Navy during the war followed by their marriage in 1946 and the arrival of three boys between 1947 and 1953. Lisa remarked, "Your mom should have tried for one more." I turned to Nathan and said, "You must be glad you have a little sister." Shaking his head, he replied, "I wish I had another brother, but I guess Leah is better than nothing!"

We still had an hour of free time, so we returned to the fields and walked along a marked trail deep into the woods. This land—"Penn's woods"—must have been largely like this area before the English and German settlers arrived and began clearing it. All of a sudden, Kersti's ears perked up: she thought she heard running water. We pushed through a tangle of thin, young trees and discovered a stream. It was shallow and crystal clear, and Peaches happily jumped in and took a long drink.

Kersti is now at her last session. We will depart afterwards and probably stake our chairs at the side of the road for a picnic lunch. The forecast is for the low 80s at home, so we may conclude this Memorial Day with our first swim of the season at the Madison Community Pool.

(Note: I am writing this note on a cool, windy, rainy Saturday morning, the first of November. I can't believe this is my first entry in the "Amish Country 2014" travelogue since May 26. So much has happened since May. Fortunately, I can turn to Lisa Harnish's visitors' log to reconstruct our visits during the past six months.)

June 21-22 *(my log entry)*

"What a treat to spend the summer solstice at the farm and cottage, our "home away from home." After dinner at the Iron Horse in Strasburg—where it was comfortable enough to eat outside—we drove home along the scenic White Oak Road. When we arrived, the western sky was ablaze in shades of orange and pink. We get such a restful and peaceful feeling when we come here, especially now that we are in the midst of selling and constantly staging our house in Madison, New Jersey. Every aspect of the life here brings us joy: talking with Lisa, savoring her delicious and creative breakfasts, and watching and hearing the children playing outdoors at all hours. Looking forward to next time."

(Note: Kersti and Janine made the next two visits with Kersti providing the log entries in late August and early September.)

August 25-26 *(Kersti's log entry)*

"Thanks again for a delicious breakfast and peaceful stay at your cottage. My daughter and I enjoyed our special time together. We always feel rejuvenated when we come here.

Looking forward to being back in 2 weeks for a longer relaxing weekend. Sending you many blessings."

September 5-7 *(Kersti's log entry)*

"You keep coming up with new delicious gluten-free surprises for us. We continue loving your cottage in all seasons. We will be back mid-October. All the best and THANKS again."

October 10-11 *(my log entry)*

"For the first time, we got up at 4:30 AM and drove 3 ½ hours to Betty Jackson's all-day sandplay conference at a Christian center in Quarryville. We stayed here Friday night, so Kerstin could attend a few sessions with Betty on Saturday, back at her home just a few miles down Georgetown Road from the cottage.

"Today, the weather is rainy and cool, but Lisa, your plentiful and scrumptious breakfast made our day bright and cheerful. We loved the mini-pastry-free quiches, the pumpkin-cheesecake muffins, and the scone with your homemade apricot jelly! You make every visit a special one. See you the last weekend in October."

While Kersti was attending her session at the Christian center, I took Peaches for a few walks, read, and did my email by the fireside, since it was cool enough for a staff member to start a fire. Betty had an extra seat at the lunch table for her group, so she invited me to join them. That evening, we drove to the Iron Horse Inn in Strasburg and enjoyed the deluxe Strasburger. On Saturday, we returned to Strasburg to visit the toy train museum, especially enjoying some of the German models from the early 20th century.

October 31-November 1

We left our new home at 6 Beechwood Drive in Convent Station around 8:45 AM on a mostly sunny, comfortable Halloween Day. As we sped along 78 West to the sounds of Enya, we noticed that the fall colors had become muted, even though many leaves were still on the trees. The reds and oranges had yielded to mostly shades of gold. We arrived at the cottage in three hours and had a quick lunch before Kersti drove to Betty's for her private sandplay session. She returned at 1:30, and we had the entire afternoon stretching before us. We took Peaches for a vigorous one-hour hike through the woods and across the meadow at Wolf's Hollow Park; I had previously done this alone and on separate occasions with Janine and Eric. We kept up a good pace, unzipping our jackets and breaking a sweat.

Our next stop was Zook's Quilt and Craft Shop in Strasburg. We wanted to exchange the quilt that we had ordered over the summer and I had picked up on October 31. It was a beautiful quilt, but it seemed to be a king size, and we only needed a queen size for our guest bedroom. Mary measured the quilt and even summoned her husband, Amos, from the back room to join in the discussion, though she was quite curt with him. We realized that the original quilt was indeed a queen-size quilt, but it was draping on the floor because our bed does not have a box spring. We found a more desirable pattern, and Mary said it would be finished in two to three months.

We drove over to Gap, picked up some food items at the Dutch-Way, and had a leisurely, early soup-and-salad buffet dinner at the Dutch-Way restaurant, which still affectionately called "Dutch Haven." It was dark by the time we departed and wound our way back to the cottage along Upper Valley Road and White Oak Road.

I will be here all day and into the night, since Kersti has her workshop until 5:00 PM and then a group consultation until 8:00 or 9:00. This is a milestone, the final of Betty's 12 workshops during the past year and a half. The first one was on a chilly weekend in March 2013, just days before my departure from Rutgers. We will head home afterwards to be in our toasty home and bed during what is forecasted to be a raw, blustery day.

Lisa keeps raising the bar with her breakfasts. This morning she served a spinach-sausage-egg casserole, yogurt with strawberries, six plain scones, and four large maple-walnut scones. She even provided plastic containers to take the leftovers home.

We invited her to come stay with us, whenever she is ready to visit New York City, and she may think about it in the spring. After all her hospitality and delicious breakfasts during the past year, it would be joy to welcome Lisa and her children to our home and show them some of the sights of New York.

Even though Betty's formal program is at an end, I have no doubt that we will return to the cottage in the future.

Chapter 15

FLORIDA

March 21-26, 2014

"The gator sniffed the kernals, recognized them as food, and opened its massive, powerful jaws with 80 teeth—40 on the top and 40 on the bottom—to swallow the small caramel popcorn along with a sizeable swamp-water cocktail"

Monday, March 24

For the third straight day, we are enjoying the poolside at Lisa's apartment complex in Coral Gables. The southwestern-style, two-story buildings are shaded by swaying palm, fern, and orchid trees. After an early afternoon rain shower, the sky is blue with only a few wisps of clouds, though the air is warm and muggy. The swim will feel good.

We escaped our cold, snowy, seemingly endless winter on Friday, the second day of spring. The alarm sounded early—at 3:50 AM—and our old reliable airport shuttler, Norbert, was as punctual as ever at 4:30. There was a brief snag at the TSA checkpoint—they asked about the gluten-free zucchini-chocolate cake, perhaps suspecting that we were hiding something illegal inside—but let us proceed.

Our flight was delayed for an hour because the ground crew broke some equipment as the plane was backing out of the gate, so after a journey of 50 feet, we were towed back into the gate for the repair. Once aloft, the time in the air was only two and a half hours. We took a cab directly to Lisa's apartment. Our driver was a Haitian native, who said she had left Haiti some years ago and had lived in Montreal, New York, and finally Miami. I told her that these were the current residences of our three children. This seemed to make her day and also gave us a lift.

Lisa joined us just before noon and showed us her nice apartment, which she shares with her University of Miami colleague, Casey. We stopped at Whole Foods for lunch, then dropped Lisa off at her apartment before heading on to our rental at 744 Biltmore Way at the intersection with Anderson Road. Turning right onto Coral Way off of Red Road, we drove along a magnificent thoroughfare, lined by exquisite houses and properties and framed by a canopy of huge, overarching fig trees. They look like giant hairy tarantulas with their tentacles spreading out in all directions and interlocking.

Our apartment is on the edge of the residential and business areas. It is spartan but spacious with a small living room, a sunny den-like area, and even an outdoor private patio. The kitchen is narrow but adequate, and the mattress is firm. We walked around the neighborhood and discovered that we were only a five-minute walk from the famous Venetian Pool, created in the 1920s by George Merrick (1886-1942), the Gables' visionary, but it feels much more like an ancient Roman spa. Also nearby is the original Biltmore Hotel, which stretches skyward for 15 stories topped by a tower.

We enjoyed a tasty dinner at a local restaurant called Whisk. The baked Brussels sprouts sprinkled with parmesan cheese appetizer was a real treat. After dinner, we took our first trip to the largest local supermarket, Publix, for breakfast and lunch items.

On Saturday morning, Kersti and I took an early morning walk along Coral Way and visited the grounds of George Merrick's boyhood house, now a museum. We picked up Lisa and then headed northwest to the Ikea store in Sunrise, Florida, where she picked out a new mattress after flopping on a number of prospects. It was a roll-up mattress, so it fit easily into the half-folded-down back seat of Lisa's Jetta, her "silver dolphin." Tired after our shopping mission, we had some quiet time at our apartment before retiring to Publix to pick up supplies for our evening barbecue. As the daylight faded to dusk, I managed to light the old-fashioned grill with briquettes and lighter fluid. Lisa prepared five foil-wrapped bundles of veggie—red and green peppers, broccoli, onions, mushrooms, and carrots—topped with feta cheese. We complemented the grilled veggies with hot dogs, sausages, turkey burgers, and hamburgers. We were joined by a number of Lisa's colleagues and friends—roommate Casey from Minnesota, Mark and Danny from California, Brian from Massachusetts, and Christina from New Jersey and Stephanie from California, who are after-school teachers working for City Year in Homestead. Everyone's warmth, collegiality, compelling work, fun spirit, and commitment to helping people are very impressive. Working in their midst, Lisa is in a very good place.

Sunday was a full day. For our early-morning walk, Kersti and I traversed a good portion of the Granada Golf Course, another Merrick creation in the 1920s. It was already warm and humid. We picked up Lisa and headed to her yoga studio for a 75-minute session with her teacher, Janet. I began sweating in the warm, packed room, but overall it was a relaxing, empowering experience. We ate a good lunch at Lime, a Mexican restaurant next to the studio, and then headed northwest to Weston for an airboat ride in the Everglades at Sawgrass Recreation Park. Guided by the steady hand of the bearded, Hemingwayesque "Captain Gerald," we powered through the sawgrass, which our captain warned us not to touch because it could cut our fingers like a saw. We stopped twice and observed two alligators, which Gerald recognized. They both lingered by the side of our idle boat, undaunted by this now familiar incursion into their habitat. One passenger was munching on some Cracker Jack and threw a few pieces into the murky water: the gator sniffed the kernals, recognized them as food, and opened its massive, powerful jaws with 80 teeth—40 on the top and 40 on the bottom—to swallow the small caramel popcorn along with a sizeable swamp-water cocktail. After our excursion, we toured the Sawgrass zoo and saw more gators, large turtles, pigs, snakes, panthers, and a bobcat.

We enjoyed a second night at the grill, eating our leftover meat and a fresh batch of vegetables.

Today, it was back to work for Lisa, but she kindly offered to ride her bike to school—just a 10-minute ride—so we could use her car. The day dawned cloudy, and we decided it was a good day to drive west on Route 41 to the Indian village at the Miccosukee Reservation. After driving through congested West Miami, with its distinct Latino atmosphere, we were suddenly in the Everglades on both sides of the highway. Kersti actually saw one gator and a few egrets as we drove by. The village was nicely arranged with old dugout canoes, hand-made tools, and lady artisans demonstrating their crafts. We joined an early tour with Marcela and a bunch of Indians from India. At one point one of them asked, "So why are you called 'Indians?'" Another member of the tour explained that Columbus thought he had arrived in India. These modern-day Indians were loud and talking while Marcela was trying to give her explanations, so we decided to take a later tour.

The museum captured the tribe's heritage and its sacred Everglades homeland with photos, displays, and artifacts. We were especially moved by the brilliant, colorful, provocative paintings of Stephen Tiger (1949-2006). After munching on deep-fried pumpkin bread and dough right out of the pan, we joined the 12:00 tour. We met the artisans, including Jamie, a pretty mother of six, two of whom were already at work on their crafts. As the tour concluded, we took our seats in the small outdoor theater for the gator show. Carlos pulled two large gators by the tail up onto the sandy stage and proceeded to entertain the audience with "tricks of the trade"—sticking his hand in the gator's mouth before its loud snap, going nose to nose, and holding its mouth closed with his chin while he pretended to tie the mouth with imaginary string—the way they have captured gators in the wild for many generations. Later, I passed on the chance to hold a baby gator, about a year old and two feet long, beginning its growth spurt of about a foot a year for its first 10 years.

We picnicked at one of the other airboat establishments and, sure enough, saw one more gator lurking in the water beside the dock, with just its eyes and the top of its head peering out over the water. Kersti said she had seen enough gators over the past two days, but she did find a cute, small hand-carved specimen to bring back to her sand play collection.

That evening, we enjoyed Cuban cuisine at Hungry Harry's with Lisa's mentor, Darryl Greenfield, and his wife, Eva. Eva told us about her Hungarian heritage, her first year in Homberg, Germany, and her upbringing in Cleveland. Daryl provided details on the history of the developmental psychology doctoral program at the University of Miami and current projects, including Lisa's research into the benefits of early bilingualism. Darryl and Eva were both full of praise for Lisa as a dedicated graduate student and a kind, likable colleague.

Now, I am going to jump into our private pool for a swim. Only a couple of workers, chatting away in Spanish, are in the pool area.

Tuesday, March 25

We are back at Lisa's pool for our final swim on a bright, humid afternoon. After a pounding, seemingly all-night rain, thick gray skies, early-morning showers, and a forecast for an 80% chance of rain at 1:00 PM, we thought the day would be a wash out. We did want to see and touch the ocean at least once, and so we set out without our hats and my sunglasses, driving north on Routes 1 and 95. On the way, we stopped at two of Merrick's cultural villages, the Southern Colonial Village close to the Biltmore with its magnificent columns and colonial and Greek mansions. Just off of Route 1, we stopped at the French Normandy Village, consisting of four rows of attached houses, amply decorated by roses and lilacs. We felt we were in an old French village outside Paris.

Our next stop was South Beach. We parked, appropriately enough, on Meridian Avenue, about 6 or 7 blocks from the beach. The beach had only a few people strolling about, including an Indian family: the dad was trying to coax his shivering son into the chilly water, while the mom was building a small castle and decorating it with shells. Kersti and I took off our shoes and walked along the shoreline for about half a mile. The sun began to struggle to break through, and then it chased away the clouds. We had a tasty early lunch at Finnegan's Irish pub on Ocean Drive, just across the street from the swaying palm trees: a spaghetti Alfredo dish for me and Portobello mushrooms for Kersti.

After a brief stop at our apartment, I dropped Kersti at Lisa's place so she could cool off at the pool, while I drove to two more villages on Lisa's side of Route 1: the Dutch-South African Village, whose massive homes overlooked the Coral Gables waterway, and the French Country

Village, providing the flavor of 18th century French life among the well-to-do. Now it's time again to jump into the pool for my final dip.

Wednesday, March 26

Now just half an hour from landing, we are peering down on a shock to our warm-weather senses: the snow-covered fields of southern New Jersey. Our final delightful evening with Lisa, dining at an outdoor Greek restaurant in downtown Miami, feels like it happened much more than 15 hours and 1,500 miles ago. But we carry our memories with us, including the walk around our Coral Gables neighborhood last night around 9:30 with the wind picking up but with the temperature still comfortable. Our time with Lisa and our five days in Coral Gables are still resonating.

Chapter 16

ADIRONDACKS: BLUE MOUNTAIN LAKE

August 28 – September 1, 2014

"Sitting atop the large warm rock, we felt a deep sense of peace and reverence for nature and the land. It was the moment we will remember most fondly from our vacation"

Monday, September 1, Labor Day

I'm sitting in a rocking chair on the porch at Hemlock Hall, looking down the terraced grassy slopes to the cool waters of Blue Mountain Lake, framed like a "V" by the tall pines. Puffy clouds decorate the blue sky and a steady breeze keeps the air comfortable. Janine and Kersti just went down to the dock, and Peaches is resting in her usual spot in the car.

Last night while sleeping, we turned the calendar to a new month and a preview of a new season. Day five of our Adirondacks vacation gave us a taste of late summer and early fall—the cool early morning, the first leaves yielding their green to red, yellow, and orange, the rapid warm up and afternoon humidity during our hike. It was a day of endings and beginnings, experiencing both the most memorable highlight of our trip and the long ride home.

We did not leave 6 Beechwood Drive until 7:00 PM on Thursday because of our busy workdays at Drew and Sanctuary of Hope, and Janine's and my trip to 148th St. off of Frederick Douglass Blvd. to dismantle her bed and load up a desk, chair, dresser, and miscellaneous items. It was the definitive conclusion to Janine's time in New York—at least for the foreseeable future. We headed north on the New York Thruway (I87) with Peaches occupying her back "cabin," and continued on the "Northway" above Albany to Exit 23/North Creek. Our final leg was driving west on 28 to the intersection with Route 30 at Blue Mountain Lake. Hemlock Hall was just about a mile west on Route 30, then down a dark country road bordered by a steep slope to the left not far from the water's edge. The "HH" compound, consisting of an old-fashioned lodge, cabins, and a motel, was quiet when we arrived close to midnight. The friendly (at the outset) owner, Paul, had waited up for us and extended a warm greeting. He showed us around the living and dining areas, focusing our attention on three plates with the thickest, tallest, meatiest, fatiest sandwiches we have ever seen or tried to eat—quarter-inch thick slices of homemade white bread enveloping thick slabs of corned beef—leftovers from dinner. We only managed to consume about a quarter of our "midnight snack," leaving some on the plates (more than a polite token) and bagging the rest for Peaches for her next day's breakfast, lunch, and dinner. We proceeded upstairs to our so-called "Gold" room, which did not quite meet the "gold standard": between Janine's rickety cot and our full-sized bed, there was little room to maneuver. The walls and ceiling were covered with an odd hard plastic material that was peeling in places. We also had to negotiate a public bathroom with a number of second-floor guests. But the room and floor were cozy and quaint in their own way.

Around 7:30 Friday morning, we were rudely awakened by loud vacuum cleaners, the loud voices of the HH crew, and the clinking sound of tables being set for about 50 guests. At 8:00, we heard the first breakfast bell, rung about 20 times, followed by the final bell at 8:30, summoning everyone to breakfast—camp style. We joined a family of seven—a grandmother and grandfather from Michigan; their daughter, son-in-law, and granddaughter from Arizona; and their son and daughter-in-law from Missouri. We learned about the rich history of the place, which the grandma had initially visited with her family in 1944. Her story was the first of several we heard of families and generations coming here year after year. Meanwhile, we indulged in a plentiful country breakfast of steel-cut oatmeal, crispy bacon from a plate piled high, homemade white and wheat toast, eggs to order, and pancakes. We had the exact same breakfast for the next four mornings, varying only the style of eggs and skipping the ritual on Sunday because of our early departure for Montreal.

After breakfast, we drove just a mile or so up the road past the Adirondack Museum to the Blue Mountain trailhead. Janine and Peaches took the lead on hiking the two-mile trail with an 1800-foot climb. Kersti and I wore our fleeces at first, but peeled them off as we ascended the rocky, sometimes rooted, often challenging terrain. About halfway up, breathing heavily, we paused; Kersti ate a sandwich to boost her energy, but decided not to go on. I persisted, giving my legs, heart, and mind a vigorous workout. I arrived at the summit in about two hours and was eating my turkey sandwich when Janine and Peaches appeared from another lookout. The day was partly sunny, and we had a decent view on the ground and a more expansive one from the fire tower. While Janine and I climbed the tower, Peaches, while tied to a tree, entertained several young children. The descent was easy by comparison. I was pleased to get the hardest hike out of the way on our first full day.

We had an enjoyable dinner at a table of seven people—all from New Jersey and all from towns beginning in "M"—Morristown (including a young grandfather named Herbert), his daughter, Christina, and granddaughter, Sophie (Mendham), and Bonnie and Walt from Medford in southern Jersey (they also have a summer place at the shore in Margate). Bonnie had heavy eye shadow and squinty eyes, and she made fun of Walt's fishing—or rather, his lack of catches—after he left the table for some early evening fishing. Herb's wife, Hildegard, was deceased, but she had brought up Christina bilingually, and she had lived near Ludwigshafen as a lawyer for BASF for several years. So we all had a lot in common. We enjoyed the "Friday special"—ham, haddock, green beans, scalloped potatoes, and strawberry short cake for dessert.

After dinner, while Janine and I were playing Trivial Pursuit ("boomer edition," 1980-2001; Janine beat me) in the sitting area, Paul approached us with a scowl on his face. He asked, "Do you have a dog?" We said we did and were confining the dog to the car. But Janine had taken Peaches down to the beach during our afternoon swim, and she had "peed" in the sand. Paul told us emphatically that a guest had reported a pee and a "poo" that had not been picked up. We asserted that the latter was not true, but he had the last word: "Dogs and other pets are not allowed on ***my*** property!" We assured him that Peaches would remain in the car. We were relieved that Paul was not evicting us from the premises.

We broke Saturday into two hikes: Cooney Mountain in the morning and Buttermilk Falls in the afternoon. Herb had recommended Cooney Mountain, located 11 miles west of Long Lake off of Route 30. It was a two-mile round trip, moderately difficult, with great, expansive views of nearby lakes and the countrywide from the summit. The sun was pouring down, the wind was whipping, and we were reminded of Cadillac Mountain on Mt. Desert Island—minus the ocean view. We had the mountain all to ourselves for a short time, before waves of hikers arrived and disturbed our reflective mood.

Buttermilk Falls is about midway between Blue Mountain Lake and Long Lake. The falls were modest, cascading about 40 feet along the Rasquet River. In some ways, the mile-long hike along the river was more stimulating, winding along pine-needle paths and occasionally through moist terrain. We chatted with some students from Kalamazoo College, who were at the midpoint of a 16-day canoe excursion from Blue Mountain Lake through Long Lake and eventually to Tupper Lake. They had to carry their canoes around the falls and all the way to the continuation point, I believe on Eaton Lake.

Saturday night at Hemlock Hall is the weekly turkey feast with stuffing, gravy, mashed potatoes, cranberry sauce, and chocolate cake and ice cream for dessert. The highlight was our conversation with a spunky and sprightly lady who has been living in Long Lake for the last 68 years—ever since she was a newlywed. When she explained that she had recently come to Hemlock Hall for her 90th birthday celebration, Kersti and I exclaimed, virtually in unison, "You're 90?" She told us that life in the Blue Mountain Lake area had changed little in all the years, except for the decline in the school-age population and school enrollment.

After dinner, we wandered down to the dock and took our only canoe ride across the lake and around one of the large islands, returning to the dock when it was nearly dark and the crescent moon was hanging brightly in the sky.

We rose early on Sunday morning to a cool day and wet grounds. For breakfast, the kitchen staff gave us some buttered toast along with a backpack loaded with big sandwiches and thermoses of tea and water. This was compensation for not serving dinner on Sunday night. We headed north on 30, then east to Newcomb (the site where Teddy Roosevelt learned that he was president after McKinley's assassination) and then to the Northway at exit 29/North Hudson. We sailed through the border, where I announced to the Canadian official that we were three people (with passports) and a dog (rabies certificate). It was Peaches' first international trip. We made good time, arriving in showery but mild Montreal in about 3 ½ hours. We checked out Eric's apartment at 5804 Rue de Saint Vallier, close to the intersection of St. Denis and Rosemont Avenues, said hello to roommates, Adam and Kai, and delivered a stand lamp, bag of goodies from Trader Joe's, some decorative lights, and a few other items. Unfortunately, with all the commotion prior to the trip, we had forgotten to bring a soccer ball, night table, night lamp, towels, and an area rug. We had a delicious lunch at Salmigondis, a restaurant at 6896 Rue Saint-Dominique in "Petite Italie," and then wandered through the open-air market where Eric bought a large basil plant and Kersti some specialty cheeses. We hung around Eric's apartment for a while, and then bade him farewell and extended best wishes for the fall semester, beginning on Tuesday.

On the way home, we enjoyed a picnic dinner at our favorite rest stop, High Peaks, between exists 30 and 29. From an overlook in Newcomb, we observed the highest of them all, Mt. Marcy, shrouded in the low clouds.

And so the circle comes around on our Adirondacks vacation. Monday's hike was just a short walk or drive from Hemlock Hall to the Castle Rock trailhead. Janine set off at her own pace with Peaches, while Kersti and I took a .3 mile alternate trail to a small, private, sandy beach on the lake. Kersti swam refreshingly in the cool morning water.

We then headed toward the Castle Rock summit, a distance of two miles with a 450-foot elevation, traversing rooted paths, some fairly steep, and then climbing up rocky slabs of granite. Kersti grew dizzy close to the summit, and decided not to continue after glimpsing the last leg—a step climb of rocky outcrops and gnarled roots. It looked intimidating, even dangerous. She said I should go ahead, and at the summit, I found Janine and Peaches waiting, summoning me to take in the vista. It was one of the most beautiful panoramas I have even seen: the whole of Blue Mountain Lake with its long and small islands, Blue Mountain rising to the left, the blue sky meeting the clear water beneath puffy clouds, the dark green woods below firing up their first dabs of fall color. Sitting atop the large warm rock, we felt a deep sense of peace and reverence for nature and the land. It was the moment we will remember most fondly from our vacation.

Now the time has come to clear our room, pack the car, listen for the last 6:00 dinner call, enjoy our last dinner (Monday night is "roast beef night," though Kerstin and Janine made it "vegetarian night"), and then head south, hoping to be late enough to avoid the Labor Day, end-of-summer traffic.

Postscript

The traffic was light; Janine drove to the rest stop just below Albany; I delivered us to Beechwood Drive around 11:45 PM. We were glad to be entering our new home.

Chapter 17

GERMANY AND SWITZERLAND

September 19 – October 4, 2014

"Just as we were passing by Stuttgart, it started to rain, and then Norbert appeared again as a brilliant rainbow, one of his special calling cards"

Near Lauterbrunnen, Switzerland—Jungfrau Mountain at "The Top of Europe"

Tuesday, September 29: Munster

It's early morning in Munster in the north of Germany. We're staying in the home of Marrianne and Michael Ulrich. We met Marianne at the *Wiehlertreffen* in 2005 in Oberwesel, Germany. She is the second cousin of Mutti and part of the Mennonite clan that fled from West Prussia in the spring of 1945 when she was just seven or eight years old. The light of day is now pouring into this room with wood paneling all around, including the ceiling. I hear an owl or mourning dove hooting. The heat is on, taking the chill out of the air. The shelves in this room and throughout the house are filled with books, notebooks, photos, miniatures, and mementos—clutter for some, but collectively all these things create a powerful sense of German *Gemutlichkeit*. This feels like a warm, welcoming German home.

Anja picked up Kersti, Janine, and me around 4:30 on Friday afternoon, September 19 for the trip to the airport. It was the first time in a long time that Norbert was not at the helm of the shuttle. We had a smooth, relatively quick flight, aided by our ability to completely stretch out our legs at the emergency exit and beside our distinguished companion: a 6' 7" professional basketball player from Minnesota named Amber Dvorak. She was heading to Prague for her first season in the Czech women's league. It was her first trip to Europe, indeed her first time outside the U.S. She was as sweet as she was tall: curious, courteous, playful, polite, and chatty. She told us that her mom welcomes up to four adults at a time into their home through a Minnesota foster care program, and it's clear from where Amber gets her evident compassion for people.

After landing in Frankfurt and taking a bus to the terminal, we picked up our car—a white stick-shift diesel Fiat from Hertz and drove to Bretzenheim, a village that is part of Mainz and home to Gabi and Wolfgang for over 20 years. As always, they were so excited to see us. We sat down and enjoyed a tasty German brunch. The weather was warm and muggy. We lugged our suitcases up to the 3rd floor and settled into a cozy loft with slanted roofs on both sides of the room. We banged our heads a few times. They had a bottle of water, glasses, and a small plate of fruit waiting for us.

Around 5:00 PM, we dropped off Janine at Eva Guha's apartment in the city. It was good to see Eva, who was her usual perky, still girlish self. We strolled along the Rhein, and all of a sudden a bright, magnificent rainbow and a faint companion rainbow arched over the river and city. Norbert was welcoming us to Germany.

Kersti and I returned to an empty apartment, because Gabi, Wolfgang, and Wolfgang's brother Ulrich had walked to the stadium to see Mainz take on Dortmund in an early-season Bundesliga matchup. Gabi left behind a potato soup, salad, and a big dish of *Zwiebelkuchen* (potato tart). Around 9:00, after an hour or so of lightning flashes, the skies opened up and the rain poured down, drenching, as we suspected, the three soccer fans and thousands of their compatriots. But Gabi and Wolfgang were absolutely joyous, because Mainz had defeated Dortmund for the first time ever, 2-0. They elatedly and proudly hung up their bright red Mainz shirts to dry overnight.

Sunday dawned cloudy and cool with rain on the way. After breakfast, we set off on our mission of reconciliation and healing to Bingen. We warmly greeted Mutti outside in back of the apartment complex and then took the elevator to the 3rd floor, where Vati, dressed in his Sunday best, was waiting for us. We cordially shook hands and then sat down in the living room, where he delivered a letter of apology to Kersti. She remained strong, composed, and empowered during this initial exchange and throughout the day. We ate a buffet-style lunch in the Hildegard-inspired restaurant at the Rochusberg, while a steady rain fell outside. After lunch, Kersti, Janine, and I strolled around the grounds and the church atop the hill. We returned to the apartment for *Kaffee und Kuchen*—Mutti's delicious *Käsekuchen* and a Lüning fruit tart—before departing. There were still wounds, scars, and difficult memories, and we remained far from a return to "normal" with no plans to stay over any time soon, but the healing had begun.

We had an enjoyable Sunday evening in Mainz, featuring a plentiful dinner from a Greek take-out restaurant, and photos and memories of Gabi and Wolfgang's trip to the U.S. and Canada in August and September 1982. They met Kersti in Los Angeles at the end of her cross-country Aven bus tour, drove up to San Francisco, and then spent two weeks with us in Bernardsville, including our five-day odyssey to New Hampshire, Montreal, Quebec City, and Boston in a "Rent a Wreck" vehicle. Gabi and Wolfgang kept us refreshed with a special beer from Dortmund and Greek anise schnapps from the restaurant.

On Monday, we packed our suitcases and bags and headed off on the next leg of our journey to Biebertal, Rosi's and Hans' home close to Giessen. We were concerned about Rosi, because she is now suffering from Alzheimer's. She seemed alert during most of our visit, though her blue eyes seemed deeper set than usual, and occasionally she turned to Hans to remember things. At times, he seemed to carry the conversation to compensate for her. Hans produced a delicious gourmet dinner, starting with sweet cantaloupe followed by tender veal cutlets, noodles, and green beans. The sun came out in between rain showers, so Rosi, Kersti, Janine, and I took a walk in the neighborhood before returning to the house for K&K and our departure soon after.

Two and a half hours later, around 7:00 PM, we pulled into Michael and Marianne's driveway and entered this cozy home.

Wednesday, September 24: Munster; Opa Bruno's and Daniel's Birthdays

We spent a delightful early fall day in Munster yesterday with our knowledgeable tour guide, Marianne. We took a brief self-guided tour of the *Friedenhalle* (Hall of Peace) in the *Rathaus* (town hall). On October 24, 1648, a peace treaty was signed in this room after five years of negotiations by representatives from Germany, Holland, France, Sweden, and Spain, ending the 30 Years' War. We walked around the two major religious structures in the city, the church with the tall spires and the Munster *Dom* (cathedral). The air was brisk and the sun felt good. The city has the distinct feel of northern Germany, reminding me of Gdansk, especially in the *Füssgängerzone* (pedestrian zone). It was warm enough to have lunch outside at the bistro at the new art museum.

At 4:00 PM, Kersti and I met with Martin Richter, a local publisher, to discuss the publication of her book about her childhood trauma in Scheidegg and her healing as an adult. Kersti was encouraged at first and almost ready to sign up, but decided not to rush it. It will be published at the right time and by the right publisher in German and English. We returned to the house at 5:00 after being picked up by Marianne. Janine and I had a hurried bite of cake on the patio and then departed for Osnabrück, about half an hour north of Munster. We strolled through the 18th century *Schloss*, the main building in the university, with its distinct yellow color shining in the soft light of late afternoon. We waked through the *Altstadt* (old city), and the vibe of the city was better than I suspected based on Janine's mixed experience there in the fall of 2008 and winter of 2009. Janine shared her story with me once again, including her weekend visit to Marianne and Michael, who helped her determine that it was the right decision to leave Osnabrück that spring. Later, we drove past her apartment. It was already dark when we headed back to Munster for our final delightful evening with Marianne and Michael.

Friday, September 26: Beatenberg, Switzerland

I am gazing out from the 3rd-floor balcony of our hotel onto the majestic Alps and three snow-covered peaks in particular: Escher (3,970 meters), Mőnch (4,099 meters), and Jungfrau (4,158 meters, one of the five tallest of the Swiss Alps). A thin layer of clouds is covering the peaks, but the sky above is a solid blue. A thick white shroud covers the lower ridges of mountains and further below, the steep green fields, decorated by chalets, are bathed in the late afternoon sunlight. Some young people—students at the theological school that is housed here—are playing volleyball just below. Two wind sailors are floating through the sky.

We departed from Munster around 10:00 on Wednesday morning, heading south toward the Stuttgart area. Our first stop was Karlsruhe for *K&K* with Albert and Irmgard. Irmgard was really on a roll, speaking almost non-stop about silly things happening in her neighborhood. By 5:45 PM, we were on the Autobahn again for the final leg of the trip. On our way to Esslingen, just as we were passing by Stuttgart, it started to rain, and then Norbert appeared again as a brilliant rainbow, his special calling cards.

That evening, we had dinner with Detlef, his wife Ute, father Kurt, mother Gelinde, and brother Michael at a pub in their hometown of Esslingen, a short distance from Stuttgart. It was an evening of good food, drink, conversation, and memories of Norbert. At dinner, we shared stories and memories of Norbert, while feasting on Swabian specialties. Back at Detlef and Ute's apartment, we flipped through his photo albums of his trips to the U.S. to visit Norbert in 1978 and 1982, when Kersti and I became part of Norbert's inner circle. We had no idea that Detlef was an artist; a number of his paintings were hung in the hallway outside the apartment.

Detlef, Ute, and their daughter Hannah were all gone by 7:30 Thursday morning, so we enjoyed the comfort and privacy of the apartment until our departure just past noon. The trip to Beatenberg took longer than we anticipated. We arrived just in the nick of time at 7:25 PM for the buffet dinner before the closing of the *Speisesaal* (dining hall) at 7:30.

With Kersti's sandplay conference beginning in the late afternoon on Friday, we had the morning and early afternoon free to explore the town and area. We brought some sunglasses and a hat for Kersti at a local shop, and then drove to the nearby Buddhist meditation center. Nothing was stirring at the center; we assumed everyone was meditating. We set off on a hike into the cool woods with the scent of pine in the air, then into an open field after climbing some steep stone and wooden steps. The view across the fields with the mountains in the background reminded me of the final triumphant scene in "The Sound of Music." We found a picnic table and ate lunch. A Swiss family—a young boy and girl and their grandparents—were enjoying a picnic at the next table. After lunch, we split up—Janine headed toward town via another path and Kersti and I back to the car. Janine's route brought her quickly into town: she was nearly back at the hotel when we passed her on the street.

I just stepped out for 20 minutes for a trip to the bank with Kersti to pick up some Swiss francs. The three peaks are now totally clear and pointed.

Saturday, September 27: Beatenberg and Thünersee

Janine and I just returned from an amazing hike in the Swiss Alps. On this warm, clear fall day, we ate breakfast on the deck and then packed our backpacks for our day of hiking. We headed toward the Beatenberg bus station, walking not along the main street but on a parallel wooded path that featured posts with highlights from the life and work of Beatenberg's most famous citizen, Eric von Daniken, a science fiction writer, scientist, and futurist. After half an hour, we arrived at the Niederhorn gondola. There was a big crowd on this beautiful Saturday, but we soon boarded. We were quickly hurtled up the steep mountain, enjoying the shrieks of excitement from a wide-eyed little boy, who reminded us of Eric at three. Arriving at the summit around noon, we looked out on the panorama of the three major mountains and a number of other peaks in the 3,000 to 4,000-meter range. We hiked for about an hour across the mountain, above the tree line and in brilliant sunshine. Before descending, we actually climbed about 100 meters, sometimes on stone steps, at other times along grassy paths. We paused around 1:00 PM for our picnic lunch of meat and cheese sandwiches created at breakfast, always keeping the mountains and the Thünersee in our vistas.

The descent was not an easy one. We really felt it on our feet (Janine was still breaking in her new hiking boots), our knees, and shins. We traversed a variety of walkways: a steep and slippery gravel road; winding wooden and stone stairs with a thin wire railing through a dense forest; open fields of moderate terrain with spectacular views; and for the final leg, a wooded path with aggravating gnarled roots that we felt in our knees. Janine demonstrated her map-reading expertise by choosing a final path that delivered us to the main street in Beatenberg just a few hundred meters from the hotel. We paused in the shade in back of the hotel, gulping water and snacking on pretzels. In all, we hiked for nearly five hours, taking only occasional breaks. I'm perplexed by the sign in town that reads, "Niederhorn: 2 Stunden, 40 Minuten." That seems unlikely, if not impossible for the typical hiker, especially climbing 700-800 meters of difficult terrain.

We spent an enjoyable evening on a dinner cruise on the Thünersee. A bus transported us to Interlaken, where we boarded the boat. We sat at a table with Kersti's new friend, Susanna, and Rudy from Austria. On the deck before dinner, I had a good conversation with Bert Meltzer, the American-Israeli who had given a presentation to the group on his work bringing Israelis, Palestinians, and Bedouins together through sandplay.

Monday, September 29: Beatenberg

After gazing with wonder at the three mountain peaks during our first four days in Beantenberg, we went to the mountain top, dubbed "The Top of Europe," on a perfect Sunday afternoon. We drove to Lauterbrunnen, a short distance from Interlaken, and boarded the Jungfrau train. It began its slow climb, passing deep gorges, thick woods, and panoramas of the steep fields and glaciers. I marveled at the history of the train line, built in the first decade of the 20th century, when the technology was still primitive by today's standards. We changed trains at Kleine Scheidegg, elevation around 2,000 meters, for the final push to the Jungfrau station at around 3,400 meters, the highest railway station in Europe. The concluding stretch was a 7-kilometer-long tunnel, which culminated in an underground station. We walked through a long, cool tunnel and then outside into winter in early fall. The wind was whipping as we walked 360 degrees around a grid, admiring the massive Mőnch and Jungfrau Mountains up close and the glaciers stretching far into the distance. We befriended a young man (probably in his early 30s) from Dubai, originally from the Pakistani part of Kashmir, who had sat adjacent to us when we first boarded the train in Lauterbrunnen. He took a number of pictures of us and we of him. Then we walked outside.

We were only there for an hour and a half, and then crammed our way into the packed 5:45 PM train, the last departure of the day. My Kashmiri companion and I were standing at first, and then we were directed to some fold-down seats in the space between cars. We talked about present-day conflicts: India and Pakistan in Kashmir; Israel and Palestine; and the current threat of terrorism and I.S.I.S. in Syria and Iraq. Janine, Kersti, and I left the train at Wengen, a mountain town, and ate dinner at a restaurant with a clear view of Jungfrau. We first sat at a table outside, and watched the white mountain assume hints of pink before turning dark at dusk. It grew cool outside, so we resettled at a table inside.

Tuesday, September 30: Beatenberg

It's our final evening in Beatenberg. Monday was our fourth straight beautiful day. Janine set off on hikes halfway up the Niederhorn and later halfway down to the lake, while Kersti and I relaxed at the hotel most of the day, in some ways simply "chillin'" from the hectic pace of our first 10 days in Europe. Toward 6:00, we walked toward the home of Monica and Dietmar, high above the main street in Beatenberg with spectacular views of the three mountains and Thünersee. Monica and Dietmar are originally from Germany, and they were introduced to us by Sabrina, who is editing both Monica's and Kersti's memoirs. We enjoyed a cheese fondue dinner, featuring small potatoes, wheat bread, apples, and even bananas. Monika is battling cancer, and her memoir tells the story of her difficult life, which includes raising five children on her own and losing one child at the age of three; he died when he was accidentally dropped by one of his siblings.

By the time we walked back to the hotel after dinner, the clouds had rolled in and the stars were no longer visible. When we opened the shade this morning, the grounds were damp from the nighttime rain. We continued with our breakfast routine: boiled eggs, whole wheat bread with jam, cheese, and sliced meat, and the preparation of sandwiches for lunch. Kersti and I came down for breakfast around 8:30, Janine at 9:20 sharp. We decided to head back to Wengen, where we had eaten dinner on Sunday, to buy some typical miniature Swiss houses and chalets for Kersti's sandplay collection. First, we drove to Lauterbrunnen, but we could not find the road to Wengen, despite our maps and GPS. So we drove to nearby Grindelwald, but still did not see a sign. We asked at the train station, and the agent told us that the only way to Wengen was by train. We walked back through town and then descended a winding road past farmhouses, befriending a small black cat that came running up to us. After half an hour, we arrived at the *Gletscherschlucht* (Glacier Ravine), a deep gorge carved by the river, ice, and snow over millions of years.

We then drove back to Lauterbrunnen. Despite the rain, Janine and I decided to hike to Wengen, a rise of about 500 meters from roughly 700 to 1,200. It was strenuous, not because of the terrain—the path was wide and mostly a paved or gravel surface—but rather the steepness. Every time we climbed one stretch and rounded the bend, another one loomed before us. We were breathing heavily, our heads wet from the rain and sweat, but we pressed onward, pausing fairly often to catch our breath or take a sip of water. We made it in about an hour and a half, just what the sign had indicated. We joined Kersti at the shop, where she bought 12 Swiss houses for herself and some friends. Janine and I were pretty soaked, so we warmed up at a pub with drinks, *Apfel Streudel*, and a couple of *Wieners*. Kersti joined us for the descent back to Lauterbrunnen, which only took about 50 minutes and was so much easier on our hearts and lungs. Two thirds of the way down, through the clouds, we saw the chalets of Lauterbrunnen decorating the green hills. It looked just like villages that Kersti's children may build in the sand.

On the way home, we drove through Interlaken and then west along the lake. We paused at a parking place, and Janine and I enjoyed a *Weissbier* and pretzels before heading back to Beatenberg for our final dinner and packing.

Thursday, October 2, Einsiedeln, Zollikon, and Zurich

I'm sitting on a path above the town of Zollikon, overlooking Zurichsee (Lake Zurich). The city of Zurich is just 5 kilometers to the north. The wind is flapping my paper, and the early October sun feels warm on my face. Low clouds are moving in, blocking the view of the sun-peaked Alps to the south.

We're back in Zollikon for Kersti's second of three sandplay sessions with Martin Kalff, son of Dora Kalff, the founder of sandplay therapy. The sessions take place in Dora and Martin's house, an old home with overgrown shrubs covering the front of the property and a roof filled with crumbling tiles. But inside, in the studio where Dora met her clients, the work Kersti is doing is profound, and she is gaining strength and insights from sessions conducted in her native language and integrated with Martin's meditations.

We left Beatenberg yesterday morning at 10:00 for the two-and-a-half hour journey to Zollikon. Beatenberg was totally shrouded in fog when we rounded the bend and took our last glimpse, looking backward. We took the local roads along the east side of the lake. It was raining intermittently, and the gently rolling hills rising above non-descript towns and industrial buildings reminded us that Switzerland is not just the high peaks.

After dropping off Kersti, I sat for an hour by the lake, while Janine was futilely searching for a café for her afternoon coffee, and later I settled on a bench in a small park across from Martin's house. In the small sandbox, I found a toy turtle, which Kersti may add to her collection.

Following Kersti's session, we spent some time in Zurich, waiting for our 8:00 PM dinner at Peter's apartment near the train station. It's a beautiful city, defined by the lake, which stretches out on both sides of a canal. A little before 8:00, we took the elevator directly to Peter's apartment, and he welcomed us with his warm smile and hugs as soon as the door opened. His apartment is spacious and modern with white the dominant theme. He ushered us up to his sizeable deck atop his apartment. It was dark by then, but on sunny days he has good views of the lake and mountains in the distance. Peter whipped up a tasty meal of arugula/parmesan/smoked ham salad, and tortellini with sautéed sage and parmesan cheese. As always, we talked about the family, alternating between laughter and serious concerns.

We returned to Einsiedeln via the highway, shaving a good half hour off the local route, heading away from the city and long after rush hour.

We are staying in a small but clean and comfortable apartment at the Sihlersee on the outskirts of Einsiedeln. One of the photos on the website gave us the impression that we would be directly on the lake, but our apartment is behind one house and up a sharp driveway from the lake. There is no access to the lake; no path by the roadside; and no rowboats or canoes. But it's a picturesque, quiet setting. We're on a working farm, and I am reminded of our Mennonite cottage, except that that cottage is old and spacious, and this apartment is modern and compact.

This morning we walked around Einsiedeln, known for its large, dominating convent and life-size dioramas of Old Testament stories and Christ's story. But the dioramas did not open until noon, and we needed to be on our way by then. We stopped for lunch at a lakeside restaurant just a mile from our apartment. Before arriving in Zollikon, we paused for half an hour in Zurich to meet Janine and her friend from Osnabrück, Nina, by the lake. It was our second and final farewell to Janine, who will be traveling in Switzerland, Germany, and possibly France until her return home on October 13.

Saturday, October 4: Zurich

I'm sitting in row 32 of a United plane, one row behind Kersti. We are awaiting takeoff on our flight to Newark.

Our last full day in Europe included a quick return trip to Germany. We drove to Konstanz for the long-awaited meeting with Kersti's current book editor, Sabrina. Konstanz was cool and gray on this holiday celebrating German reunification. Awaiting Sabrina's arrival, we kept looking at faces. I spotted a young woman, thinking she was too young to be Sabrina, but I remarked to Kersti, "Is that Sabrina?"

Just then she turned to us, and we greeted each other. Kersti later found out that Sabrina was born in 1988, so she is a year younger than Lisa. She has been a big help to Kersti with the German version of her book. Kersti and Sabrina headed off to a café, while I strolled to the small harbor on the Bodensee, passing an accordion player. Once again, Norbert was with us. Konstanz was not the clean, sunny city that I remember from April 2007, when we visited Janine during her semester abroad.

Around noontime, we returned to Switzerland and drove to Zollikon for Kersti's final session with Martin. It was scheduled for one and a half hours, but lasted for two and a quarter. I waited in the small park across the street and found a small plastic turtle beside my bench. We drove into Einsideln for dinner at a kebab restaurant and then back to our apartment for packing.

We got up this morning at 5:15 and were on the road to the airport at 6:15, half an hour earlier than we had planned.

Postscript

It was a seemingly quick flight, aided by the four films that I watched: "Heaven Is Real" (a moving Christian film based on a true story), "In Secret" (based on a Zola novel), "Gravity," and "Labor Day." We arrived half an hour early on a warm, cloudy Saturday, and Steve Wells met us on the arrivals level and shuttled to our new home in Convent Station.

Chapter 18

MONTREAL

November 2010 to September 2016

"That beautiful spring morning, we had a nice hike with his friend, Amy, up the hill to Mont Royal and took in the view of the city"

Montreal, Quebec, Canada—Windy's graduation from McGill

(Written in 2015, 2016, and 2020)

2010

Eric's college years in Montreal brought us to this North America-European city on numerous occasions. It's worth remembering that Eric's first-ever trip to Montreal took place in July 1993, when he was just three months old. On that vacation, we spent six days at Mont

Tremblant, an hour and a half northwest of Montreal, and visited the city on two occasions.

Our initial college-focused trip was part of our tour of northern campuses in November 2010, during Eric's senior year at Madison High School. Taking advantage of the annual New Jersey teacher's convention the first week of the month, we visited Concordia University, which had originally been recommended to Eric by a professor during a yearbook-related workshop at Columbia University. At Concordia, we took the bus tour from the Loyola Campus to the downtown campus. We only glanced quickly and casually at McGill. The next day we headed south on Route 89, crisscrossing Vermont on our way to Pete's house in Rye on the New Hampshire coast. It rained heavily during most of the trip. On day three, we took the UNH tour (it was still pouring), and the focus was clearly on the hockey arena, athletics, workout facilities, the on-campus train station, and the spiffy residence halls rather than academics. The following day, we drove to Boston and took the BU and Northeastern tours before heading home.

Eric's college decision came down to Rutgers and Concordia, and he chose Concordia in part because he was accepted directly into the journalism program. A more compelling reason was his desire to get out of New Jersey and experience a different place and culture during his college years.

2011

On June 14, 2011, we drove to Montreal so Eric could attend Concordia's orientation program on the 15th. We returned home the following day. Our full day in Montreal was sunny and warm, and while Eric was attending his program, Kersti and I strolled around the Loyola Campus, especially admiring the large statue of a "First Nation" chief or warrior.

August 2011 was a momentous month. A day after his return from his travels to England, Germany, and Holland with his friend, Zeev Leshem, Eric told us that he was gay. We thanked him for his honesty and courage and told him how much we loved and supported him. A few weeks later, we packed our Honda CRV and drove on Saturday morning, August 27 to Concordia to help Eric settle into his single room in the Jesuit Residence Hall. We had heard reports of Superstorm Irene working its way up the East Coast, but the weather was perfect on Saturday for the move in. On Sunday, however, the rain and wind were relentless, and by mid-afternoon the power went out in much of the city. We were in a café at the time, trying to order tea and coffee, but to no avail. We had decided to stay an extra day for the parents' barbecue on Sunday, but that was also canceled. We said goodbye to Eric and then struggled mightily in the pouring rain to find our way back to our motel close to the airport.

Monday was beautiful, and we set out anticipating a 6 to 7 hour drive. But it wasn't until around 1:00 AM—15 hours later—that we pulled into our driveway in Madison, having endured lengthy traffic jams and forced exits on the Thruway and even on a number of back roads that were closed because of the torrential rain from Irene. One benefit of our long and winding drive home was our first visit to Saranac Lake, home of Dr. Trudeau's TB lab and sanatorium.

Canadians celebrate their Thanksgiving during the first weekend of October, and with his classes canceled for Friday and Monday, we arranged for Eric to come home. I believe it was the first time he took the four to five-hour bus ride from Montreal to Albany, where we picked him up at the bus depot. The drive to and from Albany was manageable, about two hours and 15 minutes each way.

On November 5-7, we visited Eric to see how he was doing. He had adjusted well to college life. I recall our chat one afternoon at a café in the central city. He said that his journalism classes were fine, though intellectually limiting. Eric explained, "I want to study religion and sociology and culture and history and literature!" With this assertion, he planted the seed for transferring to McGill. He applied during the spring semester, based on a strong fall semester at Concordia, and he was accepted for the fall of 2012. On Saturday, we visited the Basilica Notre Dame and witnessed a demonstration by Montreal's "Occupy" group, which was inspired by the Occupy Wall Street movement protesting wage and gender inequality. On Sunday morning, we picked up a bunch of bagels at the famous St. Viateur bagel shop at 1127 Mont-Royal East.

In December, I was invited to conduct a three-day review of the McGill career services office known as CaPS—Career and Planning Service. We drove up on Monday, December 15 and back home on Friday the 19th. I had met CaPS' director, Gregg Blachford, through the National Career Services Directors' Benchmarking Group; I attended conferences every January from 2002 until 2011, usually on member college campuses. I was at the career center Monday through Thursday, and McGill graciously extended our stay by a day so Eric could complete his final exam. Three highlights—actually lowlights—of our time in Montreal were Kersti's disappointment in the so-called Christmas village and craft fair, which consisted of no more than a few tables; the bitter cold and biting wind; and my nasty fall, slipping on ice and hitting the back of my head after walking out of the Brown Student Services Building at 3600 McTavish Street. We did not leave Montreal until after 5:00 PM, joined by Eric's friend Liz from Madison and a Concordia friend from Basking Ridge. It was another long and late trip, but we were happy that Eric was back home for the holidays.

2012

Eric's classes started shortly after New Year's Day, so we probably took him to Albany to pick up the bus. For spring break, which took place the last week of February—hardly feeling like spring—he flew to Miami to spend some time with Lisa and enjoy a respite from the Montreal winter.

Eric was done with his spring semester by the third week of April, and I picked him up on Friday, April 20 along with his new friend, Josh. It was quite a marathon drive for me, since I had been in Storrs, Connecticut since Wednesday afternoon to conduct an external review of the UConn career center with my colleagues Scott Brown from Colgate and Pamela Gardner from the University of Vermont. I believe the trip to Montreal took about five hours followed by the long trip home. Josh spent about 10 days with us. Eric and Josh visited the city a few times and hung out with Zeev and Raz Leshem and Sam Triolo.

In late August, we returned to Montreal to help Eric settle into his new university and his first off-campus apartment on Rue St. Urbain in the section of the city called "The Plateau," not far from the McGill Campus. Eric was rooming with Josh and two other friends. We had an enjoyable dinner one evening with Josh's parents.

That fall, Eric did not come home for Canadian Thanksgiving in early October, and because he had classes on American Thanksgiving, he decided to skip that too. This led to one of the most memorable "shocks of our lives." While I was cooking the stuffing, Kersti wandered into Eric's room to drop off some laundry, noticed a lump in Eric's bed, probably a pillow stuffed underneath the covers…but then something moved…a head of thick hair…and she screamed, "It's Eric!" It was so good to have him home along with Janine from New York and Lisa from her first semester in Miami. The following Sunday afternoon may have been the one time we dropped Eric at a roadside bus stop in Ridgewood, where he picked up the bus for Albany and Montreal.

2013

Eric returned home for his spring break in late February, utilizing the Albany bus station on both ends.

Eric moved again in May to an apartment at 5145 Avenue de L' Esplanade, close to the big park. He roomed with Liz, Martha, and one other person. The apartment was on the second floor, accessed by a steep, worn, and winding staircase. In the back, it had a balcony where Eric and his friends set up a small grill and grew some fresh herbs before the cold weather arrived.

Around the middle of August, Eric returned to Montreal for his 3rd year of college and 2nd year at McGill. Travelling lightly, he may have once again taken the bus from Albany. On Saturday, August 24, we packed our car and Peaches, and headed to Mountainview, New York in the northern Adirondacks, not far from Malone. We drove the "back way" via the tiny Trout River border station to Montreal on Tuesday the 27th to pick up Eric, and he spent three days and two nights with us before we drove him back. On our return trip into the U.S., we nearly caused a border incident. *(See Chapter 13 for details about the incident and Eric's time with us.)*

Unable to match the incredible Thanksgiving surprise of 2012, Eric decided to stay put in late November 2013. So just a few days before Thanksgiving, we decided on our own spontaneous act: driving to Montreal on Friday, November 23 to deliver some fresh turkey and all the trimmings. We stayed in L'Hotel in the vicinity of Vieux Montreal on 262 St. Jacques Ouest. The hotel featured 120 contemporary and popular art works from Lichtenstein, Miro, Warhol, Chagall, and Botero. We had a delicious dinner with Josh at Vieux-Port Steakhouse at 39 Saint-Paul Est. We drove back home on Sunday.

2014

My next trip to Montreal was a brief one—to drop off Eric after our ski vacation in Hancock, Vermont. *(See Chapter 13 for details.)* On January 6, I wrote to Eric, "I made it home in 6 hours and 4 minutes…When you don't have to stop to pee, you make really good time."

Eric spent his spring break in Montreal, relaxing and hanging out with friends. He concluded his spring semester in late April. On Saturday and Sunday, May 7 and 8, we drove to Montreal to help Eric move his things from his apartment at 5145 Avenue de L' Esplanade into a storage facility on a narrow street not far from his new place. His roommate, Adam (later Parker and ultimately Eve), arranged to move Eric's things into their new apartment at 5803 Rue de St. Vallier across from the Rosemont metro and close to Little Italy. Eric described it as a "cozy, light-filled, 4-bedroom apartment in a nice old building."

Eric came home with us for 11 days before heading to Berlin on May 19. He was planning to spend the entire summer there, but Norbert died suddenly and tragically on July 21. Eric came home on August 1 to attend Norbert's memorial service on August 7. Four days later, we moved into our new home at 6 Beechwood Drive.

In mid-August, we dropped Eric in Albany for his trip to Montreal to begin his fourth year. On Sunday, August 31, during our mini-vacation at Hemlock Hall at Blue Mountain Lake in the Adirondacks, Kersti, Janine, and I drove to Montreal for lunch and a visit with Eric in his new apartment. We drove nearly four hours each way, heading north on Route 30 to Malone and then northeast toward Montreal.

Eric came home for Thanksgiving and Christmas, but headed back to Montreal to celebrate the new year with friends.

2015

During a seven-week stretch in May and June, we made three trips to Montreal, all associated with the conclusion of Eric's college career.

After submitting his final research paper and then chilling for a few days, Eric came home on April 27. He spent some time with Janine in Manhattan and Nellie in Brooklyn, where she was wrapping up her spring semester at "Belmont East." We drove him back on Thursday, May 7 and returned home on Friday. That beautiful spring morning, we had a nice hike with his friend, Amy, up the hill to Mont Royal and took in the view of the city.

Eric decided to skip the formal graduation ceremony, but we drove to Montreal on Sunday, May 31 to celebrate his achievement. On Monday, we had a special lunch at a Korean restaurant not far from Concordia's Loyola Campus. We then headed back to McGill to attend a history department reception. We spoke with several professors, including his "Cold War" professor, and also chatted with Eric's Madison High and McGill classmate, Ryan Byrne, and his parents.

On June 14, Eric wrote about his annual change of address and his plans to spend the next year in Montreal. "It's a 3-bedroom place that's pretty spacious for a total of $800 a month. It's a bit dingy but we're looking forward to painting and making it a home. It's on Belanger and de Normanville, a few blocks north and east from my current place."

On Friday, June 19, Kersti, Janine, and I drove to Montreal in our CRV packed with our travel bags, Peaches, and food and drink for Eric's graduation picnic and party on Saturday. Lisa flew in from Chicago on

Thursday to join the festivities. We were joined by our friends, Gregg and David, along with a bunch of Eric's friends from Concordia and McGill. Eric managed to get a small barbecue going, and we enjoyed chicken sausages, hot dogs, snacks, salads, beer, woodchuck cider, and champagne. It was a beautiful afternoon and evening—the last day of spring and a harbinger of the summer in Montreal.

A few days later, I wrote to Eric, "Thanks so much for hosting our memorable weekend in Montreal. The party in the park is still resonating with us: the delicious food, the 'top 10' weather, your skilled grilling, your great friends, and the five of us, together again." Eric responded, "Thanks so much for your kind, thoughtful note. The visit worked out so well, and I had such a wonderful time with family and friends. Thanks so much for being my dad and always being so supportive, caring, and present. I wouldn't be where I am today without you and all your encouragement and understanding. You and Mom are of course my first teachers, and have taught me so much about how to be in this world. I am so thankful for both of you! And Janine and Lisa as well, of course."

On Sunday, we enjoyed brunch outside at a restaurant some blocks from Eric's apartment before heading home.

Eric came home on August 17 for a brief visit before heading back to Montreal on August 24. On September 15, he wrote that he was promoted to supervisor at the vegan restaurant where he was working.

On Friday, November 13, Eric, Adam, and two other friends rented a car and came down to New York for a long weekend in Brooklyn, where they were attending the annual gay film festival. Eric and his friends joined Kersti, Janine, Janine's friend Liza, and me for dinner at a cozy, informal Italian restaurant close to the Bowery in lower Manhattan.

All three children were out of the country for Thanksgiving—Janine and Lisa in Germany for Omi's 80th birthday and Eric in Montreal—so it was our smallest and quietest Thanksgiving ever with only Mom and Cynthia joining us for a turkey breast.

Eric came home for Christmas on Wednesday, December 23. Lisa picked him up in Albany. The following Sunday, Kersti and I packed the CRV and drove to New Hampshire to visit Pete and Cordelia. Pete served a complete tasty leftover turkey dinner. On Monday the 28th, Kersti, Cordelia, and I drove to Barnstead to a lakefront cottage. Our three *Kinder* drove the Jetta, arriving close to 10:00 PM. On New Year's Eve day, we drove in two cars to Brattleboro, Vermont, where we dropped Eric and the Jetta for the long New Year's weekend with his friends, Sam and Dom. We then dropped the girls at their yoga retreat in Stockbridge, Massachusetts before completing the final leg of our journey.

That night, lounging in bed at midnight, we watched the countdown on the computer and then clinked our champagne glasses filled with chilled lemon-lime seltzer. On Sunday, Eric picked up the girls for the return trip to New York, where they spent the night before Janine's 30th birthday. Her birthday was eventful, beginning with the towing and later retrieval of the Jetta, highlighted by our lunch at the famous Red Rooster on 125th Street in Harlem, and concluding with Lisa's departure for the airport, Eric's for the Port Authority for the long bus ride to Montreal (he eventually walked into his apartment around 3:00 AM), and Kersti's and my drives back to Convent Station in the CRV and Jetta.

2016

Windy spent their final night in Montreal on September 18. Kersti and I drove up from Blue Mountain Lake on the morning of September 19, loaded up the car, and drove home that evening, encountering some car problems around New Paltz. *(See Chapter 28 for details.)*

Chapter 19

AMISH COUNTRY, PENNSYLVANIA

2015

"She found 12-year-old Seth chatting away with me about baseball, chickens, the local butcher, home schooling, and their anticipated trip to New York City in September"

Kersti made three solo trips to the Amish country in January and February, staying at our farm cottage. She wrote the following entries in the log.

January 18-19

Spending a night at your cottage is a wonderful and very refreshing start for the new year. Always time to pause and step back to appreciate the bigger things in life like your warm hospitality and delicious gluten-free breakfasts. Thank you so much. Cannot wait to come back soon.

January 30-February 1

Your cabin has become my writing retreat. I am leaving nourished in body, mind, and spirit. Thanks again for your warm and caring hospitality. Will be back soon.

February 13-15

The woodstove was burning and the wind howling during some of the coldest nights of the winter. The cottage was comfortable and warm, and the delicious breakfasts nurturing. I enjoyed my sand play supervision group, just down the road. Thanks again, Lisa, for making your cottage available to me. I am looking forward to my next peaceful retreat in the Amish Country.

March 7-8

Kersti and I arrived this afternoon after attending Aunt Peggy's memorial service in Wilmington, Delaware. Our delegation drove from Madison in two cars: Pete, Kerstin, Mom, and Cynthia in Pete's car, and Wally and I in our Honda. It was a simple service, highlighted by Lynne's reflections and memories and our reconnections with family members during the reception.

Driving north on Route 41, the sun was shining brightly across the snow-covered fields, and we felt the first hint of spring in the air. It's still light as I look toward the western sky close to 6:00. We give back the hour tonight that we gained last October during our stay in the cottage, so it will be even brighter at this time tomorrow.

May 15-16

After a busy morning of horseback riding for Kersti and my attendance at a surprise retirement party at Fairleigh Dickinson University for the long-time career services director, Valerie Adams, we hopped in the car with Peaches and our bags of food, clothes, egg cartons, and Amish quilts, and headed to the Amish country. We stopped briefly in Bernardsville to drop off some checks for Anja, filled our gas tank at our usual Exit 7 stop on Route 78, and made good time. We drove directly to Strasburg, eagerly anticipating our "Strasburgers" at the Iron Horse Inn, but when we pulled into the parking lot, there were no cars and a sign posted that it was "Closed." In front, we saw another sign that the inn was for sale. We drove less than a mile into the main intersection in town, and sat down at the local deli for some tasty cheeseburgers with fried onions supplemented by a cup of vegetable soup and sweet potato fries. Kersti also picked up jars of fresh almond butter and peanut butter.

We arrived at our cottage around 6:30 PM and were greeted by Lisa, Peter, Leah, and their frenetic dog, Jewels. She frantically sniffed and stood up to get Peaches' attention, but Peaches just stood there impassively and disinterestedly. What a canine contrast! We're fortunate that we have the calm type of pet. We quickly settled in, took Peaches for a walk after Lisa corralled Jewels, and then Kersti headed off for her 7:00 session with Betty. When she returned around 8:30, she found 12-year-old Seth chatting away with me about baseball, chickens, the local butcher, home schooling, and their anticipated trip to New York City in September.

The weather was hard to fathom, fluctuating between early and late spring. Mugginess and showers were predicted for the Morristown area on Saturday morning, but it's comfortable and breezy here this morning. We took our favorite walk along White Oak Road, before Kersti headed off for her first session with Betty, and I drove to Strasburg to try to return the two quilts that just don't fit into our current home décor. The elderly Amish lady was adamant that we could exchange quilts, but never get a refund. So I'll see if we can sell them on Ebay or elsewhere.

Kersti has one more session this afternoon, and then we will head home, arriving before the daylight gives way to darkness.

Chapter 20

GERMANY AND POLAND

July 10 - August 13, 2015 (KW); July 16 – August 6 (RW)

"We left with a deep sense of reconciliation and understanding between the Polish, German, and American peoples"

Zelicowo, Poland—Visiting Mutti's girlhood home in Petershagen, West Prussia

When searching for photos for Volume 2 of "The Roads We Have Traveled" in May 2020, I came upon a series of photos from the 2015 Wiehlertreffen, which took place in Plön in northern Germany. The trip also included visits to Mutti in Bingen, Onkel Walter and Tante Helga in Bremerhaven, Mutti's childhood homestead in Petershagen (Zelicowo), Poland, and Berlin. I realized, however, that the original travelogue was missing. I searched for it on various computers and flashdrives, but to no avail. Fortunately, my 2014-2015 scrapbook (Scrapbook #11) offered our three-week agenda and numerous other brochures, invoices, and mementos, enabling me to reconstruct the events, interactions, excursions, and feelings. Kersti and Lisa also provided some memories.

Friday, July 10 (KW) and Thursday, July 16 (RW) – Wednesday, July 22: Bingen

On Friday, July 10, I drove Kersti to Newark Airport to begin our summer vacation in Europe. Her United flight left early at 1:00 PM and included a stop in Washington, DC before her scheduled arrival in Frankfurt at 5:20 AM Saturday morning. Wolfgang picked her up at the airport, and she stayed with Gabi and Wolf at their home in Bretzenheim/Mainz from Saturday until Monday. She then took the train to Bingen, settling in to a *Ferienwohnung* (vacation apartment) at Pfarrer-Heberer-Strasse 16, hosted by Herr and Christiane Winter. Vati was in declining health, and Kersti was not comfortable staying with Vati and Mutti at Dr. Sieglitz Strassse. Nevertheless, she visited them every day, often joining them for a meal.

I took the very same flight from Newark to DC to Frankfurt on Thursday, July 16, arriving on Friday the 17th. I managed to take the 5:52 AM train to Bingen. Kersti and I stayed in Bingen from Friday until the following Wednesday, engaged in our familiar Bingen activities: shopping for food, shoes, and clothes, ice cream at Rialto, walks along the Rhein, some meals at our apartment, some with Vati and Mutti, and others in town at the *Biergarten*, Chinese restaurant, Calimero, or one of the small *Döner* restaurants.

Wednesday, July 22 – Friday, July 24: Bremerhaven

On Wednesday, July 22, we picked up our VW Golf car rental in Ingelheim around 9:00 AM and drove back to Bingen to collect our things and say goodbye to Vati and Mutti. Mutti wished that she could travel with us to the *Wiehlertreffen*, but she did not want to leave Vati alone, even with Daniela.

Our trip to Bremerhaven to visit Onkel Walter and Tante Helga took more than six hours and covered about 550 kilometers (340 miles). We arrived around dinnertime. I remember sitting in their beautiful, colorful, mid-summer garden before a tasty dinner. On Thursday, Walter and Helga took us to the port of Bremerhaven on the North Sea. It is one of the largest in Germany, especially for passenger traffic. Walter showed us the Deutsches Schiffahrts Museum (German Maritime Museum) with several ships on display outside the museum. It's a great and proud landmark for him, having spent his career in the German Navy. We spent the evenings looking at old family photos and slides and reminiscing about the old days.

Friday, July 24 – Sunday, July 26: Wiehlertreffen in Plön

After breakfast on Friday morning, we bid farewell to Walter and Helga and headed northeast toward Plön and the Plönersee. The distance was not great—about 180 kilometers (110 miles)—but the entire trip was on the one or two-lane back roads of northern Germany, and our travel time was about three and a half hours.

We checked in to a *Jugendherberge* (youth hostel) just after the *Wiehlertreffen* registration desk opened at 2:00 PM. During the afternoon, we began mingling with attendees, focused especially on those with codes approximating the **1.8.11.2.2** codes on our badges.

1 – 1st generation; 1st born; Heinrich Wiehler (1826-1889) and Katharina Stobbe (1823-1910)

8 - 2nd generation; 8th born; Jacob Wiehler (1864-1941) and Margarete Pauls (1866-193

11 –3rd generation; 11th born; Bruno Wiehler (1902-1990) and Elisabeth Neufeld (1909-1945)

2 - 4th generation; 2nd born; Anneliese Wiehler (1935-) and Hans-Hermann Wiebe (1932-2016)

2 - 5th generation; 2nd born; Kerstin Wiebe (1959-) and Richard White (1950-)

Later in the afternoon, we dropped off the car in nearby Kiel, timing it so that we could meet Lisa, arriving on the train from Hamburg. Lisa had begun her European vacation with her flight from Miami to Frankfurt on July 18-19. She spent her first few days in Bingen, visiting Omi, and in Stuttgart, visiting her ex-boyfriend Daniel Arndt and "cousins" Detlef and Frank Schindler. On Friday, July 24, she took the early train from Stuttgart to Hamburg, winding up in a raucous and celebratory train car in the midst of a bachelor party! After our rendezvous in Kiel, we took a taxi back to Plön.

The *Wiehlertreffen* plenary session commenced at 8:00 on Friday evening. Second cousins Margarethe von Rhein and Kirsten Back were among the greeters. On several occasions, we launched into the rather kitchy but catchy "Wir Sind Wiehler" family song. Kerstin announced to the group that she would be presenting her book at a session the next morning.

On Saturday at 9:00 AM, Kersti presented *Das Mädchen auf dem Zauberberg*, her story about her childhood recovery from TB, to a gathering of about 10 people, including an elderly professor who asked some pointed questions. She gave a compelling and moving presentation. Before lunch, we gathered outside for the extended family photo, a tradition dating back to the first *Wiehlertreffen* in 1921. During the afternoon, we visited the picturesque town of Plön and took a boat ride on the lake with a group of about 20 Wiehlers. We participated in additional group activities and singing on Saturday night. We concluded the 2015 *Wiehlertreffen* on Sunday with a calm, meaningful *Gottesdienst* (church service), immediately followed by a tense session in which Kersti and I wound up with the Wiehler quilt, tentatively signifying that we would serve as 2020 hosts; Marianne was pushing for a New York/New Jersey/Amish country-based gathering.

Throughout the *Wiehlertreffen*, we spent a fair amount of time with Kersti's second cousins, Barbara Peters, Margarete von Rhein, Brigitte Dochhan, and her brothers Eckhard and Martin Bohnke. Lisa befriended the four Schwab sisters, her third cousins Angelika (1983), Thesia (1985), Olivia (1987), and Tatjana (1990), nieces of Margarete. She also enjoyed hanging out with Brigitte's daughter, Linea (1985).

Sunday, July 26 – Sunday, August 2: Germany and Poland

After lunch on Sunday afternoon around 1:30, we boarded a bus in Plön for the long ride to Frankfurt on the Oder at the Polish border. The journey of 438 kilometers (272 miles) lasted more than six hours, including a stop in Berlin, where we unloaded those who were not continuing the journey to Poland. We stayed that night at the Ramada Hotel.

On Monday, we traveled across western Poland from the Oder at the German border to Poland's northern coast at Gdansk (Danzig), a journey of nearly 480 kilometers (300 miles). We checked in to our Novotel Centrum for the first of two nights and had dinner at the hotel.

On Tuesday, July 28, we explored Gdansk. We first visited an old Mennonite Church and had a brief prayer service. Our next activity was a *Rundfahrt* (tour) of the city by bus and an organ concert at a church at the Oliva section of the city. After a late lunch in a very crowded restaurant on the canal, we took a *Stadtführung* (walking tour) of the *Aldstadt* (old city). The highlight was our visit to the historic St. John's Church, built between 1360 and 1465. In 1559, it fell into the hands of the Protestants, and finally was returned to the Archdiocese of Gdansk in 1991. We had a special dinner at a restaurant founded in 1597 by a Mennonite, Ambrosius Vermollen, and later owned by a Mennonite family, the Bestvaters.

On Wednesday morning, we took the bus to Tiegenhof (Nowy Dwor), where Mutti and Vati attended school. We visited the Werdermuseum and the restored Mennonite cemetery at Heubuden (Stogi), followed by a tour of Marienburg (Malbork) and its famous Malbork Castle Museum, established as early as 1274.

Wednesday afternoon was free, and families were encouraged to set off on their own missions of discovery and remembrance. So we hired a driver to take us to Mutti's girlhood home in Petershagen (Zelicowo). Unfortunately, the driver spoke limited German and English, but when we met the family—whom we had visited with Mutti in July 2005—they remembered our visit and the significance of the home and farm for Mutti and the Wiehler family. We scribbled some dates (such as 1945 and 2005) and acronyms (such as U.S.A.) and drew some maps as our methods of communication. In one photo, Kersti, Lisa, and I are smiling broadly as we stand near the front door, through which young Annelie had passed countless times. In another photo, Lisa and I are beaming in the company of the smiling husband, wife, and another man, perhaps a brother, given the facial resemblance. Lisa was particularly moved by the visit and her vision of her Omi's peaceful life on the farm before the war and the flight. She wrote to me, "I imagined her life on the farm and how she used to walk to school along the river and take care of the animals in the fields. It is hard to believe that this same land was war stricken just months after she spent her most formative years there, and now we were standing on that same land." As in 2005, we left with a deep sense of reconciliation and understanding between the Polish, German, and American peoples.

That evening, we stayed at the Hotel Mlyn on the outskirts of Elbing (Elblag). It was an old mill converted to a quaint hotel and restaurant.

On Thursday, July 30, we traveled from Elbing to Rosengart (Rozgart) to stand solemnly at the grave of Katarina Stobbe Wiehler, matriarch of the Wiehler clan and wife of Heinrich. In the afternoon, we headed to Masuren (Mragowska) on the banks of Spirdingsee. On our way to Masuren, we passed through the old army barracks at Sensburg, where Johannes Wiebe was based and trained, and where Charlotte raised their three children, Hans-Hermann, Walter, and Rosi prior to their flight in the fall of 1944 and winter of 1945. It gave us a strange feeling. Lisa felt the darkness and trauma of the years leading up to the war and the war itself, which claimed the life of Johannes on the Russian front in 1943.

In Masuren in the bright afternoon sunshine, we had a scenic walk into town, where Kersti bought an amber bracelet and earrings. That evening, we stayed at the resort-like Hotel Gotebiewski in Masuren for the first of two nights.

On Friday morning, we visited the Wallfahrstskirche Heiligenlinde and the Wehrkirche St. Georg in Rastenburg (known in Polish as Ketryzn and Rastembork), which was first established in 1329. On a cool, cloudy, showery summer afternoon, we took a horse and cart ride into a local forest, arriving at a river. Our next mode of transportation was a bunch of long dark green flatboats, each operated by a man standing in the stern with a long pole and reaching down to the riverbed to push us forward. Lisa and I were in one boat and Kersti in another. After a round trip of about 45 minutes, we arrived back at our departure point, where a floating fire was ablaze in the middle of the river. Passengers were given long sticks with sausages, and we paused long enough to grill them over the open fire. We were stuffed after one or two sausages, not realizing until a bit later that these were merely our hors d'oeuvres. We disembarked and walked up the embankment to a multi-course buffet dinner laid out on long tables in the *Grillhütte* (dinner hut).

On Saturday, we began the long trek back toward Plön, taking a different route through southwestern Poland and eastern Germany. In the morning, we traveled to the resort city of Neustettin (Szcaecinek). From our Hotel Pojezierze, we took a long walk on the wide boardwalk at the Streitzigsee before an early dinner at the hotel.

We concluded our excursion on Sunday, departing Neustettin at 7:00 AM sharp and arriving back in Plön around 1:30 PM. We hugged and said goodbye to all our Wiehler traveling companions. Looking back on her experience, Lisa shared the following impressions with me: "It was so amazing to me that complete strangers were not really strangers at all, that there were these threads that instantly connected us and always will. This is the beauty of heritage, ancestral ties, and family history."

Sunday, August 2 – Thursday, August 6: Berlin

After our arrival in Plön on Sunday afternoon, Kersti, Lisa, and I stayed on the bus to Berlin, traveling a distance of about 345 kilometers (215 miles). We took a taxi to Bernauer Strasse 115-118 and checked in at the Gastehaus Lazarus. It was a comfortable, *Schwesternheim* (Catholic nuns' home) with guesthouse accommodations.

The guesthouse was directly across the street from where the Berlin Wall had split the city into East and West. Also nearby was an outdoor memorial and museum, describing the wall. It was actually two walls with soldiers stationed at frequent lookout posts, ready to shoot. We read a number of plaques written in German and English, which described the harrowing efforts of East Germans attempting to escape to the West. In all, more than 140 Germans perished in their flight to freedom between 1961 and 1989.

The single biggest and most memorable highlight of our time in Berlin was our Berlin Wall and Cold War bike tour, organized by Fat Tire Bike Tours Company. Monday, August 3 was a sweltering day—close to 100° F—but we were determined to make a go of it. We met our second cousins, Irmgard and Karin Cornelsen (Marianne's nieces), at Alexanderplatz, hopped on our bikes, and headed "across the wall" into East Berlin. We biked along the imposing architecture of the Karl-Mark-Allee and later paused at the East Side Gallery, the Treptower Park Memorial, the Peter Fechter Memorial, and Checkpoint Charlie. We stopped for lunch in Kreuzberg. The most moving and impactful memorial was the Mother Russia Memorial, built shortly after the end of the war. Mother Russia mourns her citizens, soldiers, and children, while celebrating their heroism and patriotism through a number of bas-relief panels.

Another highlight was our tour of the city by boat on the River Spree and the Landwehrkanal. Key sights included the Bundeskanzleramt (Federal Chancellery), the Haus der Kulturen der Welt (House of World Cultures), Museuminsel (Museum Island), the Reichstag mit Glaskuppel (Parliament building with glass dome), the Berliner Dom (Berlin Cathedral), the Fernsehturm (television tower), the Hauptbanhof (main train station), the DDR Museum, the Potsdamer Platz, and the Scholss Chrlottenburg (Palace).

Lisa reflected on her time in Berlin.

> This was my first trip to Berlin. I instantly fell in love, as I had never been to such a cool, metropolitan, international city with such a pace, but was also German. It felt instantly like the familiarity of Germany, with the excitement and pulse of a big city, something I had felt in NYC in the U.S. and Madrid in Spain, but had never experienced in this way in the country that I call my second home.

The days passed quickly as we walked along the streets and through the parks of Berlin. We also got comfortable riding the buses and navigating the subway system. We ate a full German breakfast every morning in the hostel, enjoying the just-baked *Brötchen,* cheeses, muesli, fruits, yogurt, and hard-boiled eggs. We ate most lunches on park benches and most dinners in small bistros or restaurants. Lisa found her preschool friend Lucy on Facebook, and they spent an enjoyable time together at a Vietnamese restaurant. The torrid weather continued throughout our stay. Sleeping at night was challenging.

Lisa left on Thursday morning, August 6. Kersti and I remember waiting for the taxi with her outside the guesthouse. We were all sad to be saying goodbye after our memorable and special time together—bidding farewell not just to each other, but also to the city, German culture, and our summer vacation. Lisa later shared her feelings with us:

> I vividly remember our last full day in Berlin, sitting with you and Mom on the bench in the park, and having an emotional, tender cry. I was so touched by the city, the happiness that I felt there (though I knew there was an element that heightened this because of my vacation and escape from grad school), but nonetheless, I sat there on the bench, watching the people go by, and had the idea that maybe I would live there one day, and start a family. I saw all the happy families and children in the park, and couldn't

> help but think maybe that would be me one day. I left with a heavy heart, as I always do when leaving Germany, but I was prepared for my next adventure.

Lisa flew to Valencia to visit her Spanish *familia* in Ontinyent. She returned to Miami on August 11 after enduring a 24-hour Valencia to Frankfurt to Newark to Miami odyssey. She had plenty of time to reflect, not only on her time in Germany and Spain, but more significantly on her life bi-cultural identity. She wrote in her journal:

> That last day in Berlin, in the park, my heart felt full. I felt it fill as I watched the children play in the park, the families stroll by, splashing in the water, enjoying nature and life together, a central part of German life. I feel the constant pull and sadness when leaving Germany, taking it as a sign of what this place means for me. My conversation with the Turkish taxi driver captures both the challenge and blessing of my dual cultures. He had been living in Germany for 30 plus years. After I briefly described my German and American identities, he responded, 'I have the thought that you feel more German than American, just from the way you are so *sympatisch*...you seem that way.' This meant more to me than he could ever imagine.

That same Thursday morning, just a few hours after we said goodbye to Lisa, Kersti and I took our own taxi to Berlin Tegel Airport. I left Berlin at 12:45 PM, stopped over in Munich, and landed in Newark at 6:35 PM. Meanwhile, Kersti flew to Frankfurt and spent six more days at the Winters' apartment, visiting with Vati and Mutti daily. She flew home on Thursday, August 13. Vati had just one more year to live.

Chapter 21

GERMANY, SWITZERLAND, AND FRANCE

October 29 – November 7, 2015

"This time, Basel turned out to be a real treasure"

Saturday, October 31: Mainz

We arrived on Friday morning in Frankfurt after an uneventful flight. We were met by Wolfgang Scholl, who took us to his condo in Mainz, where Gabi had another delicious German brunch waiting for us. It was a warm and mostly sunny day, and the woods and vineyards displayed brilliant shades of yellow and gold. I was reminded of my time in the Rhein Valley 10 years ago during the final days of my Fulbright experience.

After brunch and a brief rest, we borrowed Gabi's car and drove to the assisted-living facility in Gensingen, where we found Mutti waiting for us in the downstairs reception area. In the midst of our heart-to-heart conversation, Vati appeared, and this upset Kersti, who was not in any mood to speak with him, and so we hurried out of the facility. This would have been a hurtful conclusion to Kersti's meeting with Mutti, and fortunately, Mutti, despite her slow, frail pace, hobbled in pursuit of us. It was chilly, and so we sat in the car to continue our conversation. On a lighter note, we did not know how to drive Gabi's car in reverse, and thus we drove forward and onto the grass and sidewalk and through an open parking space where we were able to park, always facing forward. I returned to the facility to pick up a 100-euro note from Mutti for Kersti's birthday. At one point, Mutti and I walked arm in arm through two rows of old folks, who were listening to a Juniper-like entertainer, and she remarked that it was as if we were getting married. It so happened that October 30 was her 58th wedding anniversary.

We returned to Wolfgang and Gabi's place for *Kaffee* and four varieties of delicious *Kuchen*. It was dark by the time we took a brisk walk, and when we returned, Gabi prepared a "take-out" dinner for us, because we were beginning to fade: a turkey-vegetable-noodle dish, squash soup, salad, and German beer. Wolfgang also said that we could keep the car until Sunday. We then settled in for the night at the Park Inn Hotel in the Bretzlingen section of Mainz, less than a 10-minute drive from Gabi's and Wolfgang's.

Today we traveled across the river from Rheinland Pfalz to Hessen. We crossed to the town of Kaub, and then drove up toward the Kauber Platte, the site of the horse stable and meadows where Kersti had started working with her mentor, Sabine, several months ago. The Epone Quest training builds confidence and dispels fear, as individuals work with, ride, and communicate with the beautiful Arabian horses. Sabine lost her father just six days ago, and thus she was understandably subdued, but she took us into the ring with one four-year-old female, who bonded with us, looking into our eyes and sniffing our hands. Later, two one-year-old fillies did the same. We heated up our lunch in a cottage adjacent to the stable, and we felt a part of the community. On our walk around the field, we stopped at a magnificent lookout above the Rhein and later communed with a few more horses, which seemed as interested in us as we were in them.

On the return trip, we drove north to Rudesheim and then up the hill to Hildegard's abbey, where we bought some things in the gift shop, paused for a cup of tea and coffee, and then sat, prayed, and centered ourselves in the church. The Saturday evening bells were ringing loudly as we drove away, heading toward the ferry for the return trip to Bingen and Mainz.

Monday, November 2: Basel

The darkness is falling upon this city, which Lou Fantin and I visited 33 years ago, during our year of graduate study in England. We took the boat and train from England through France to Basel, where we spent two days before Lou headed south to his relatives in Italy and I north to Freiburg for a visit with my former German girlfriend, Ulrike. I remember Basel as being cold and dark and gray, though Lou and I did manage to meet and hang out with two Danish girls, Susan and Helene, sporting our "high-heel" shoes purchased just hours before.

This time, Basel turned out to be a real treasure. On Sunday morning after Kersti's breakfast with Gudrun, Wolfgang dropped us at the Mainz train station, and after a slight delay, our journey took us just a little over three hours. With our backpacks, suitcases, and two plastic bags of food in tow, we traipsed through a modern part of the city toward the *Altstadt* (old city) and the *Jugendherberge* (youth hostel), feeling very much like college students again. We arrived at the hostel, a four-story building mostly with stark, concrete décor, including the rooms, but through an entire wall of glass, we looked out on old buildings and a ginkgo tree of golden leaves, which became our beacon for the week. After a cafeteria-style dinner at the hostel, we bundled up with our beanies and gloves and took an evening stroll along the Rhein.

We did the same this morning, as the early gray skies quickly turned to blue. It was special to think that Kersti was born on this very river in Worms and lived in Bingen for 15 years after that. We then walked up some steps and arrived at the Münsterplatz, home of the Münster Cathedral, Basel's most famous landmark. The red sandstone church was built between 1019 and 1500 in a Romanesque and Gothic style. Originally, it was a Catholic church, but during the Reformation, it became Protestant. We walked around the insides, marveling at the large, round stained glass window of Christ, beaming with the eastern morning light. Outside in the square, workers were getting ready for another day of the carnival that had been set up for the next three weeks.

We read for a good part of the afternoon: Kersti was reading a German memoir of two lifelong friends, one who became a nun, the other a journalist; and I was reading another Pearl Buck novel of India, *Mandala*, her last novel. We broke up the afternoon with one more walk along the Rhein, kicking up the yellow and golden leaves as we sought the warming afternoon sun. We watched the small, old ferry delivering passengers to and from the other side of the river, operating through a pulley system that stretched across the river.

Wednesday, November 4

Our days in Basel pass by somewhat predictably, but enjoyably. They are defined by our meals and sleeping hours. On Tuesday morning, after a restless night, we slept until 9:15 and nearly missed our morning breakfast. We rushed downstairs to assemble our trays: Sugar Smacks cereal for me, gluten-free oatmeal brought from home for Kersti, yogurt, mixed fruit, fruit juice, bread and jam, tea, and cocoa. We also discreetly prepare cheese sandwiches (mine with ham and gluten-filled bread) for lunch. Kersti has created her own large plates of salad at the hostel twice for lunch, while I munched on my sandwiches.

Tuesday was mostly sunny, and after breakfast we hopped on the No. 3 Burgfelder *Grenze* (border) tram at our regular St. Alban *Tor* (Gate) stop. We twisted our way through the busy streets, past the Splenator *Tor*, one of the oldest and largest city gates in Europe, to the end of the line. We were close to the French border, and I wanted to walk across, but Kersti was battling a bug, so we got back on the tram and returned to our starting point.

It was dark when we returned to the tram for our evening outing. We took it just a few stops to the Barfüsserplatz, the tram hub of the city. Despite the cool evening, there were throngs of people enjoying the mid-fall festival with rides and booths offering candies and nuts. We walked up a cobblestone street toward the Münsterplatz and marveled at the Ferris wheel, many stories high, and another ride that flung riders through the air, flags whipping behind them. They must have imagined crashing into the cathedral tower as they circled 'round and 'round. Leaving the busy square, we walked past row homes and small old shops, selling crafts, jewelry, antiques, and old furnishings. One old building boasted: "Erbaut 1411." And then we saw one that was even older: 1290. It was warm in our room when we returned, despite the barren gray concrete walls.

Saturday, November 7: Kerstin's 56th Birthday

I'm sitting on a bench overlooking the Rhein with my summer jacket unzipped, the sky a deep blue, and the warm November sun glistening on the water. A Viking River Cruise ship is boarding and preparing to continue its way either downstream toward Holland or upstream toward Konstanz and the Bodensee. This morning, after our "birthday breakfast in Basel" at the hostel, Kersti and I took the tram a few stops, picked up some Swiss francs, and then leisurely strolled to her sandplay conference in the Heuwage section of the city. The conference was the catalyst for our coming to Basel, but our week here has been filled with so much more: the sights, sounds, art, and nature—the ever-present Rhein—of this very special and quintessential European city, at the crossroads of Switzerland, Germany, and France. After dropping Kersti off, I was curious what I would find at the final stop on the St. Louis Grenze line. So I hopped aboard the 36 to Barfüsserplatz, waited just a few minutes, and then took the No. 11. It paralleled the Rhein, and I noticed the park at the St. Johanns Tor stop, where I am now sitting. At the border, I walked only about 100 meters, and I was in France in a small border city. The day was warming, so I took off my jacket and stuffed it in my backpack. I passed a full range of shops, keying on the French, Spanish, Japanese, and Chinese restaurants and pondering a special birthday dinner for Kersti in France. Young men and women on bikes sped past in the bike lane, and grandmothers and mothers were strolling with their young ones. In these moments, I knew why Kersti and I were always drawn to this country, its people, and its language. On my way back, when I saw the "Rue du Rhin" street sign, I followed it to the left, hoping to glimpse the Rhein from the shores of France, but apartment buildings and clustered trees blocked the view.

Thursday and Friday—along with today—were the most beautiful days of our trip, and we spent most of the days inside art museums and outside in the warm city. On Thursday, we took the tram across the river to the Tinguely Museum. We had seen numerous signs on the trams, asking the question, "*Ist alles Kunst*?" (Is everything art?) The main exhibit in the Tinguely answered this question with an emphastic "YES"…or perhaps a curious, questioning "maybe." The exhibit displayed the creative, iconoclastic, ground-breaking, challenging, colorful, fantastic, linguistic, real, and surreal art of the French-Swiss artist, Ben Gautier, born in 1932. We were amazed at the number and variety of his art works, clearly in the thousands, ranging from words and phrases on small canvases, to black and white videos and photos of his weird performance art, to sculptures of everyday objects pasted and painted together, to the recreation of his second-hand record store in Nice from 1958 to 1973. The brochure describes Ben's work and philosophy as follows:

> "The franco-Swiss artist, living in Nice, signs everything (*Je signe tous*")—and in doing so comments, with his images and actions, on the world as a whole. With his observations that "Art is useless," and "I'm the most important," Ben Vautier has quite deliberately confused and provoked with such and similar statements for almost sixty years, but, just as frequently he also thereby prompts reflection. His linguistic images deal with a broad spectrum, from self-reflection as artist, through postmodern art theories, to ethnology and religion...Ben consistently pursued the assumption that a work of art does not reveal itself by its physical nature but only by its signature."

He himself set up the 30 or so rooms comprising the exhibit and provided insightful video commentaries in English, French, and German.

The Tinguely is named after Jean Tinguely (1925-1991), a native of Basel, who created ingenious mechanical sculptures and artistic machines in the Dada tradition, which were on display in the museum (we were too tired to observe them) and more prominently in a square close to the Barfüsserplatz.

Walking out into the warm sunshine, we had a picnic lunch on the still green grass, now decorated by yellow and gold leaves. We then walked along the Rhein promenade all the way to the Mittlere Rheinbrücke. Spontaneously, we decided to visit Germany, so we took the No. 16 Weil am Rhein bus. We had visions of sitting outside in a small German cafe, sipping on tea and coffee followed by a tasty German dinner. But after passing through the Novartis and BASF campuses, we crossed the border into a large train station within no sight of a town. As we circled around on a small track that reminded me of a kids' choo-choo train and returned to Switzerland, I remarked to Kersti, "That was our shortest visit ever to Germany!"

Wednesday evening, we took a break from the decent, but not memorable, youth hostel dinner scene and joined the fair crowd for a giant *Weisswurst* and tray of fries. After navigating our way through the crowd, we relished the quietude and the reverence of the streets and buildings of the *Altstadt.*

Thursday was another museum day, though this one was literally a stone's throw from the hostel. The Museum für Gegenwartskunst, which is part of the famous Kunstmuseum Basel, was offering an exhibit of some of the best and most famous works from its parent museum, which is closed for renovations this year. We took our time, admiring some 70 works from Cezanne (around 1870) to Gerhard Richter (around 1970). Both chronologically and stylistically, the exhibit portrayed the major developments in European art during these 100 years of social, historical, and artistic change. We listened to the audio descriptions of a number of works, including some by Degas, Cezanne, Renoir, Monet, Van Gogh, and Picasso. This was an exposure to great art in just the right dose in terms of works and depth of interpretations.

In the afternoon, we took a trial run at finding the site of Kersti's sandplay conference. It's good that we did, since the instructions were not clear, and we needed an extra walk around one block before we found the location. After dinner at the hostel, we began packing for the trip home on Sunday.

In my homemade birthday card for Kersti, I wrote the following:

> "We will always remember this as your birthday week in Basel, a magical Swiss city on the Rhein close to the French and German borders. We arrived on Sunday and throughout the week, we enjoyed strolls on the Rhein and through the Altstadt, rides on the streetcar by day and night, traditional and post-modern art at the museums, and glimpses from our youth hostel room of the golden ginkgo tree, our beacon.
>
> We will also remember your birthday for what might have been: just a few early morning hours together prior to your

> sandplay workshop and my solitary train ride to Zurich for my flight home. You were to spend the next week on your own in Zurich and Burghausen.
>
> But after your sandplay workshop, I will be here for you, just as always. I will pick you up, enjoy a birthday dinner in Switzerland, France, or Germany, and then take you home, back to our Morristown cottage on Sunday morning. You are also taking me home—which is wherever you are."

Thursday, November 12, Morristown: Postcript

When I pulled into the No. 6 tram stop at Holbein Strasse just past 4:00 on Saturday afternoon, I saw Kersti waiting for me. We got back on the tram and took it all the way to another nondescript German border (Riehen Grenze), getting off several stops before at the Fondation Beyer. It was too late to visit the art gallery and the current Gauguin exhibit, but it was warm enough to sit outside for a tea and cider as the sun sank lower in the sky. By the time we were walking around the grounds, the western sky had turned a brilliant deep pink. We walked from there to a Mongolian restaurant for Kersti's birthday dinner. We created several tasty dishes, which were cooked right in front of us.

We got up at 5:30 the following morning, and had the early-bird breakfast before our final stroll up the hill to the St. Alban Tor tram stop. There we began our day-long journey, switching trams once, then taking the inner-city train from Basel to Zurich, a smaller train to the airport, and finally the plane to Newark. We spent most of the eight and a half hours watching films, including "Far from the Madding Crowd," "Still Alice," and "Little Boy." As we were waiting to pick up our bags in Newark, a cute little bag-sniffing beagle got a whiff of my hostel-prepared sandwiches, and we had to go through an extra check of our bags.

It was warm, sunny, and breezy when we stepped outside the terminal, and Daniel, continuing the Schindler shuttle tradition, picked us up in a timely fashion and brought us back home to our little cottage.

Chapter 22

NEW HAMPSHIRE

December 27-31, 2015

"Our drive across southern New Hampshire on Route 9 was scenic as we passed snow-covered fields, forests, and even some small mountains"

Wednesday, December 30: Barnstead, NH

I'm looking out on snow-covered Locke Lake from our lakefront cottage. It's actually closer to a ski lodge with three levels and a large open family room than a traditional New England "camp." We came here after failing to find a rustic cabin in Vermont. Just an hour and 15 minutes from Pete in Rye and Cordelia in Exeter, Kersti and I decided on this place for our four-day getaway between Christmas and New Year's.

Given our proximity to Rye, Kersti and I drove up Sunday afternoon in the Jetta to spend the evening with Pete and Cordelia. Pete had a complete leftover turkey dinner waiting for us, including turkey, stuffing, mashed potatoes and turnip, cranberry sauce, coleslaw, mashed squash, and apple and pumpkin pies for dessert.

It was blustery and cold on Monday morning, but the sun was pouring down. We drove with Cordelia to Rye Beach, and we walked for a short distance while Cordelia stood at the water's edge and looked out to sea. We then headed inland to Exeter, stopping at Cordelia's apartment and walking through her quaint town. Our next stop was Living Innovations outside of Portsmouth, where we talked to one of the representatives, Jessica, about residential options and daily support for Cordelia. Afterwards, We stopped for a quick visit to Pete's office, the New England Innovation Center, in downtown Portsmouth.

Cordelia was enjoying her outing with her aunt and uncle and also was eager to see her three cousins all together for the first time since 2010. We invited her to join us overnight in Barnstead, and she accepted. So we drove back to Exeter, stopping for lunch at a Mexican restaurant, before packing Cordelia's bag for the trip. The reality of leaving her familiar apartment suddenly struck her, and she had second thoughts, but eventually settled down in the back seat of our car. We headed northwest on 101, then west on 4 to 28 North, arriving just after 4:00 PM at our chalet-style house.

We prepared a dinner of broccoli rabe, rice pilaf, Rocky's Azorean sausage, salad, and Rocky's homemade red wine, but we had to wait until around 10:00 PM for the arrival of our second wave of family in the Honda CRV: our three kids plus Peaches. Kersti and I opted for the small downstairs bedroom; we set up the air mattress in the same room for Cordelia; Eric took the master bedroom with Jacuzzi downstairs; and the girls shared an upstairs bedroom.

The air was bracing and brisk—our first taste of winter after a mild fall. I had a restless night. The heat came on at regular intervals, loud forced air that reminded me of our heating system on Vinton Road—only much louder. I was also awakened by what sounded like rain on the roof. But when Kersti pulled open the curtains in the morning, she exclaimed, "It's a winter wonderland!" Only a few inches had fallen in the night, but the lake was covered, and we needed to shovel a path to the driveway and tracks for our cars to back into the snow-covered street.

We had a leisurely day inside and outside the cottage. Peaches was happy to frolic in the snow during her morning walk, and we took strolls in various groups throughout this cold, raw day. The sky remained a solid gray. Kersti drove to the Hannaford supermarket in nearby Alton later in the afternoon to pick up a few things, including some materials to work on a big collage with Cordelia, but that never came to pass. Eric cooked a delicious spaghetti carbonara dish with coconut milk, onions, bacon, and mushrooms, which we all enjoyed, but Cordelia was beginning to struggle with all her worries and burdens from the past year and the challenge of integrating into our family unit of "accomplished" cousins. She complained about Eric's dish, nearly spit out my salad dressing, and said she could not stand all the "organic food." She begged us to take her home that evening, and so we quickly packed her things and headed out on a snowy, icy night to drop her back in Rye at Pete's house.

This morning as I was lounging in bed, reading *Living History,* Hillary Clinton's 2003 autobiography, Eric popped his head into our room and said he wanted to go to the emergency care facility because of his "pink eye" condition. So after a quick breakfast, we headed south on 28 to 4/9/202 west to 393 West to 93 South to the medical facility close to the state capitol. The doctor prescribed an antibiotic ointment, and while Eric was picking it up at a local pharmacy, I strolled over to the capitol building and looked at some Civil War flags and portraits of famous legislators and military leaders from the state. My great-great grandfather, Alexander McRobbie, was part of a New Hampshire regiment that fought at Gettysburg, where he perished on the second day of the largest and most decisive battle of the war.

Back in Barnstead, Janine and Peaches took a two-hour walk around the lake. Kersti and I took a shorter walk and watched three turkeys strut up to the front door of a home and then across the driveway and into the backyard. Lis took a nap, and Eric took a bath. All part of our family time together. It has been one of those getaways that has seemed much longer than the mere 44 hours (and counting) that we have been together.

Saturday, January 2: Christiana, PA

I conclude our New Hampshire travelogue, sitting in the back seat of the CRV with Peaches behind me in the trunk, looking out on the wide fields of Betty Jackson's farm in the Amish country. Kersti is inside, engaged in her first of three sandplay sessions. Soon she will join me for lunch in the car. It is a chilly but bright and sunny day, and it is warm in the car.

Back in Barnstead on Wednesday afternoon, Janine and Kersti drove to Lake Winnipesaukee to explore the area, while Lisa and Eric rested, and I wrote the first installment of this travelogue. For dinner, we "threw in the kitchen sink" and created a first-of-its-kind chorizo-bean-mushroom-rice dish. Sitting around the octagonal table, we realized it was the first time we had eaten dinner together this holiday season, just the five of us. We toasted the old year and the new one that awaited us just around the bend.

Thursday morning was our travel day, but with our cheriout at noon, we were in no hurry to depart. For the first time since Monday, the sun appeared, warming the day and causing the trees to shimmer with the melting ice and snow. We finally figured out what to pack in which car and who would be riding in each car. Our two-car caravan remained intact for just a few miles before the Jetta with Janine behind the wheel veered off from Route 28 on the way to Concord. Our drive across southern New Hampshire on Route 9 was scenic as we passed snow-covered fields, forests, and even some small mountains, We dropped Eric off in Brattleboro, Vermont to spend New Year's Eve and the weekend with his Madison friends, Sam and Dom, and then reloaded the CRV with the girls and their bags for the next leg of the trip, the drive to Stockbridge, Massachusetts. With the trunk area stuffed with belongings, Peaches snuggled in the back seat between the girls. It was dark by the time we arrived at the Kripalu yoga retreat for a quick drop off and "Happy New Year" exchange.

We set out in search of 90 West toward the New York Thruway. Although it was only 5:15 PM, we were hungry, so we pulled into the first restaurant we spotted, the Shaker Mill Grill. We enjoyed the pub-like atmosphere on this New Year's Eve, mostly in the company of lively regulars. We were back on the road by 6:00, and it was smooth sailing the rest of the way, arriving back home around 8:45 PM. We unpacked and managed to stay up until just past midnight, sitting in bed, watching the second-by-second countdown on the computer, and then raising a toast with champagne glasses and some bubbly lemon-lime seltzer. It was our quiet welcome to another new year.

Chapter 23

GERMANY AND IRELAND

May 12-23, 2016

"As we ascended, we saw sheep grazing freely and turned around to glimpse the most magnificent scenery of the entire trip: Ireland in all its hilly, green, spacious splendor with the sun pouring down from the blue sky with puffy clouds"

Tuesday, May 17, Bingen

It's our final morning in Germany. These five days, all cloudy and cool and more like March than May, have passed in a kind of blur, as we shifted back and forth between Bärbel's home off of Dr. Gebauer Strasse and Dr. Sieglitz Strasse. Sometimes we slept late; sometimes we rose early; and a few times we took afternoon snoozes. Kersti came down with a bad sinus infection and cold. We did not take a single walk along the Nahe or Rhein.

Our relative state of suspension and inactivity was in large part the result of our trip to Germany on Thursday and Friday. It turned out to be a 23-hour, 45-minute door-to-door odyssey. It began routinely enough when Steve Wells promptly picked us up at 4:00 PM, shortly after I dropped off Peaches at the Barrys' house across the street. We were leaving extra early for our 7:30 flight on United because of the daily rush-hour backup where 78 and 24 converge, but we arrived at the airport by 5 o'clock with plenty of time to spare. Around 6:45, the boarding began, and everything was going smoothly until we were told that a lighting issue—the malfunctioning of the "turn on the seat belt" signs—was delaying our departure. We settled back into our seats, expecting a short delay. Then began an ongoing series of reposted departure times: 8:00, 8:30, 9:00, 10:00 PM and then a jump to a brand new day at 2:00 AM! The time passed slowly, especially when we were told that the parts needed to fix the problem were being shipped from another location by ground transportation—not by plane! We observed some of our fellow passengers: the Omi with the hat and stylish scarf who was constantly chatting and smiling and was later tipsy; the German woman who never stopped talking, while her husband hardly said a word; the Americans from Chicago and St. Louis who were annoyed that they were missing their connection to the Viking River cruise in Budapest; and of course the young man with the Pitt sweatshirt who looked just like Eric. Kersti and I both purchased salads for dinner and later bought a variety of small cheeses and snacks with the $44 in vouchers that United gave us. More hours passed and finally, after the pilot had apparently read the guidelines and felt that it was safe to fly the plane, we boarded around 5:30 AM and finally climbed into the sky around 6:30 in the early light of the new day.

The eight-hour flight went smoothly enough. I watched "Concussion," the film about the NFL's efforts to cover up the damage that players sustain from constant blows to the head. Will Smith did a superb job playing the Nigerian doctor who brought this issue to light, and he should have been nominated for an Academy Award. Later I watched half of "The Breakfast Club" with Molly Ringwald and "By the Sea," written and directed by Angelina Jolie and starring Brad Pitt and herself in a story of a shaky marriage during a vacation in southern France. Kersti slept for a few hours, since we had three seats for two; what had originally been a full plane was down to about two thirds.

We touched down around 7:30 PM, sailed through immigration control, fetched our luggage, and hopped on the 8:29 train to Bingen. After a cab ride from the Bingen train station, we walked into the apartment around 9:45—just 15 minutes short of a full 24-hour cycle. We had pizza and salad for dinner and then headed over to Bärbel's for the night.

The days here have passed quickly enough. I reread Hesse's classic novella, *Demian* (1919), which my German professor, Josh Kavaloski was considering for our German course in the fall, but which would have been much too difficult for the students; it is challenging enough in English with its discussions of philosophy and religion. I also studied my German vocabulary from my spring course and began reading Hemingway's *The Sun Also Rises* for the first time since the 1970s. Bärbel's house was spacious and a welcome break from the confinement and clutter of Dr. Sieglitz Strasse, but there was one problem: the heat was either not on at all or turned down low. We were comfortable enough under the covers at night, but with Kersti's cold, we spent our last night at Dr. Sieglitz Strasse. We will pack this morning, and Daniela will drive us to the Hahn Airport for our two-hour flight to Dublin on Ryan Air. For lunch, I will have the final three mini-slices of the original pizza that Daniela ordered for us on Friday evening. As Kersti said, this pizza was like the fish that Jesus kept multiplying to feed the five thousand!

Thursday, May 19, Drogheda, Ireland

We have been in Ireland for just a day and a half, but already it feels that we have been here for a long time. It is probably because of the connections that we made to the rolling green landscape and to the fortresses and abbeys from long ago.

On Tuesday, Daniela drove us to the Hahn Airport, which I always thought was close to Frankfurt, but is on the way to Koblenz. Inside the single terminal, it felt like the downstairs area of a ski lodge with people milling about. When we reached the Ryan Air gate, we began yet another delay, which baffled me, because only about one plane seems to leave or arrive from the Hahn every half hour or so, but we eventually walked out onto the blustery tarmac, climbed the portable stairs, and boarded our no-frills plane and headed west to Dublin. Europe was cloud covered, but we saw some glimpses of the French and English coasts and the Channel. After a long wait to pick up our Renault Clio car at the Sixt rental agency and asking for help on how to access the back seat (handles near the top of the windows), we headed north on the M1 to our bed & breakfast place in Drougheda, arriving around 6:00 PM.

We actually unloaded our luggage twice. Following Kersti's instructions that the B&B was "at the end of the street," we pulled in next to another car, surely that of other guests, and unloaded our suitcases and backpacks. A lady came out of the house, undoubtedly the proprietor to greet us, and I waved from a distance. A man followed—most likely her husband—and I realized with embarrassment that I was waving at guests rather than the owners. They got into their car and at the foot of the driveway, as we stood there with our luggage in hand, the man rolled down the window and told us that the Kinnelon B&B was at the end of the next street. We thanked him, reloaded our stuff, and found our destination.

We were warmly greeted by our hostess Angela, who showed us our comfortable room overlooking the front yard and some cherry trees next door that were just beyond their annual bloom. We asked where we could have dinner, and she recommended the Glenside Motel, just down the road. We had a tasty dinner of pork tenderloin and halibut with the restaurant all to ourselves.

We managed to eat our way through most of the full "Irish breakfast" on Wednesday morning—ham, sausage, some other rounds meat-like things (Irish pudding?), an egg, toast, orange juice, and tea—before politely telling Angela that toast and an egg would be fine for future mornings.

After breakfast, we headed inland through the famous Boyne Valley. According to Fodor's travel guide, "for every wistful schoolchild in Ireland, the River Boyne is a name that resonates with history and adventure." Our first stop was Slane, where we visited Slane Hill, the birthplace of Christianity in Ireland. It was here on this 500-foot tall hill with its panoramic 360-degree views of the Boyne Valley that St. Patrick proclaimed the Christian faith by lighting a fire in defiance of the pagan king. We walked around the ruins of a monastery, the only visitors on this blustery day in May, though several craftsmen were cleaning and restoring gravestones at the adjacent cemetery. Another attraction just west of the town, the 18th-century Slane Castle, was closed for renovations.

Our next stop was Trim on the River Boyne. After lunch, we walked through the ruins of a castle, built by Hugh de Lacy in 1173. It was soon destroyed by fire, and then rebuilt from 1190 to 1220. It is the largest Anglo-Norman fortress in Ireland with an outer wall that is almost 1,500 feet long. It was the site of the filming of the 1994 classic film, *Braveheart.* Later we took a stroll along both sides of the river. We then drove in a roundabout way to the Hill of Tara, the "seat of the high kings of Ireland." Some 5,000 years ago, ancient burial grounds were created here, forming vast circular designs when viewed from high above. The day was clear enough that we could see the mountains of east Galway some 100 miles distant.

Our final stop was the ruins of the Bective Abbey near Killmessan. Again, we were the only visitors. It was built in the 12th century and then closed on the orders of Henry VIII of England in 1536. We were able to walk into the inner courtyard and could imagine the monks praying there in utter silence and solitude broken only by the sounds of the wind and birds. We had a strong sense of the spirituality of this place.

We drove back to our B&B and had dinner at a tapas restaurant and pub at a nearby mall.

Friday Morning, May 20, Drogheda

Yesterday, we drove to Newgrange, site of the 5,000-year-old sanctuary and burial tomb built by early Irish settlers. The cool showers only added to the sense of mystery and a connection to the fertile earth. From the visitor's center, we walked to a small bus depot, drove to the base of the site, and then walked up a way to an enormous grassy mound decorated with white stones. It looked too perfect to have remained like this for five millennia, and indeed our guide Eleanor told us that the site had been renovated and reconstructed in the 1950s and 1960s, using stones that had been part of the sanctuary from years ago. Large boulders weighing many tons and some decorated with spirals and other symbols surrounded the mound. It was an amazing feat that they were transported along the nearby River Boyne, then up the hill on rollers. An archeologist has estimated that it took 80 men four days to move one of the boulders a kilometer from the river to the site. The most special moment was when we entered the narrow passageway into the inner sanctum. We had to crouch and duck and carry our backpacks in front of us. Inside, we marveled at the layered stonework and the demonstration of the light that pours into the passageway on the five days commencing the winter solstice—days that the early Irish celebrated because they signaled the turn of the year toward longer days and renewal.

The weather improved in the afternoon, and we drove to the coast to Bettystown. After a salad at Relish, a lively beachside restaurant, we took a walk on the wide sandy beach, later parking our car there on the firmly packed sand. Beyond the backsides of some local businesses, the town had a preserve with thick grassy dunes. To the north, we saw the curving coast and mountains rising from the sea.

Tired from our early wake up that morning, we took a nap, and then rallied for a delicious Indian dinner at Tamarind and a return trip to the beach for a late stroll as the sun dipped beneath the dunes around 9:15 PM.

Saturday Evening, May 21, Drogheda

The theme of the last two days was the spiritual quest. The weather was promising on Friday morning, and we drove northwest to Old Mellifont Abbey in Tullyallen. This was one of the wealthiest and most influential monastic houses in medieval Ireland, founded by St. Malachy in 1142. It was the sister abbey to Bective, and it was also closed by Henry VIII in the late 1530s. King William III spent the night of June 30, 1690 in the abbey, and the next day defeated James II at the Battle of the Boyne, a significant victory for Protestant England over Catholic Ireland. This was also the site of the first youth hostel established in Ireland in the 1930s.

We continued north to the Monasterboice, featuring the 5th-century Cross of Muiredach, considered by many to be the finest high cross in Ireland with depictions of Bible stories from Adam and Eve to doubting Thomas. The large tower at the center of a still active graveyard was built as a defensive structure.

In spite of a steady rain that started to fall, we decided to take the M1 north and a connecting roadway east to the coastal town of Cardlington, which our hostess Angela highly recommended. It was a quaint town on a peninsula jutting into the Irish Sea with its quaint old shops and narrow streets. The cobblestones that Angela promised turned out to be pavers, but we enjoyed the town atmosphere anyway, even as the rain kept coming. We had a delicious lunch at a family restaurant before strolling out on the pier. We stopped at the tourist office and gift shop, and on a whim, I asked the man about the Proleek Dolmen, which I had seen in one of the brochures. He said it was in Dalback, adjacent to a hotel. He wrote down the name of the hotel—Ballymascanlon House.

We just wanted to get home to feel warm and dry. We were just about to get back on the M1 south, when I noticed a golf club with the name Ballymascanlon. I said to Kersti, "I think that's it!" We drove in; found some rugged Irishmen playing golf in the rain; and saw some other people in fancy wedding attire. It seemed an unlikely setting for an ancient monument. I asked a man, and he said this was the right place and pointed in the right direction. We followed signs in back of old facility buildings and then along a wet grassy path between holes. We finally arrived at the structure: two enormous boulders with a third resting on top, estimated to be some 30 tons. We were able to walk inside and feel the presence of the ancient Irish, who celebrated the lives and deaths of their loved ones. We asked that age-old question: "How did they ever manage to raise that stone on top of the support stones?"

For an evening meal, we had our first pub experience at the Line Kiln in Juliustown, just a short drive from our B&B.

Anticipating another rainy day today, we weren't quite sure where our paths would lead, so we headed back to the Hill of Tara to spend some more time at this spiritual place. The sun came out, and we looked round and round at the Irish landscape. Basking in the warm sunshine, we finally had an outdoor Irish picnic, and I befriended an orange tiger cat, which jumped up on the table and enjoyed some bits of cheese from my sandwich. Later Kersti bought some prints from a local artist, Courtney Davis, and we had a nice chat with his business associate, Sandra. She asked if we had visited the Loughcrew Cairns near Oldcastle, and we said no. She said it's only "20 minutes up the M3" to Kells—not mentioning that it was another 40 minutes west of Kells along a country road. After a few wrong turns, we arrived at a small cafe, asked for directions, and then began our ascent of a tall grassy hill. As we ascended, we saw sheep grazing freely, and turned around to glimpse the most magnificent scenery of the entire trip: Ireland in all its hilly, green, spacious splendor with the sun pouring down from the blue sky with puffy clouds. When we arrived at the summit, about 30 middle-aged women were engaging in a pagan ritual with chants and words of reflection and wisdom. We noticed that the entrance to the underground grotto was open, similar to Newgrange, though a much shorter way. We ducked our heads and entered the inner chamber. There we stretched out our arms and held each other's hands and prayed for peace, healing, and love.

We concluded this very special day with a return trip to the Line Kiln, where I had my first and only Guinness of the trip.

Monday, May 23, Dublin Airport *(on our 34th meeting day anniversary)*

We're sitting at the United gate at Dublin Airport, awaiting the final leg of our journey. The birds were already chirping at the first light of day when the alarm went off at four o'clock this morning after a short, restless night. We crept downstairs and ate a bowl of cereal with fruit that our host Angela had left for us in a small cooler. We then drove to the airport as the day brightened, traveling around one last mini-roundabout just outside the Sixt drop-off site. We had driven a total of 684 km (424 miles) for the trip. It gave me a lot of satisfaction to turn over the keys of the car to the attendant—and a sigh of relief.

Dublin was the focus of Sunday, our final full day in Ireland. Following Angela's suggestion, we drove to Balbriggan, a coastal town about 10 miles south of Drogheda. It was a quiet Sunday morning, and we were able to park at the station before taking a quick walk along the tracks with its glimpse of the small town port. Initially assuming that the southbound train would be on the right track, we stood for a few minutes on platform one, while most passengers gathered on platform two. We then realized that Irish trains travel by the same left-right configuration as Irish cars.

It was a sunny, comfortable day, and the Irish Rail train, which was loud and obviously had been in service for many years, rambled toward Dublin, stopping at every station along the way. To our left, we saw nice vistas of sparkling blue waters and the curving coastline. We entered Dublin, stopping at three of its main stations—Connolly, Tara, and finally Pearse—named for brothers who were leaders of the 1916 Easter Uprising against the British. They were executed shortly after the rebellion was put down. We walked over to Merton Square and picked up our bright yellow, open-air Cityscape tourist bus, embarking on a roundabout route that included the major attractions of the city:

- Christ Church Cathedral
- St. Patrick's Cathedral, where Jonathan Swift served as dean from 1713 until the 1740s
- Dublin Castle, originally built in the 13th century, where Irish presidents are inaugurated and foreign dignitaries are received (Barack and Michelle Obama arrived exactly five years ago today)
- Guinness Brewery (this stop generated the most hopping on and off of the 29 sites)
- Ha-penny Bridge across the River Liffy
- the 378-foot high tower on O'Connell Street
- Aviva Stadium, home to Irish soccer and rugby
- Irish Museum of Modern Art, National Gallery of Ireland, and National Museum of Ireland Natural History—all free for another day
- Phoenix Park, one of the largest city parks in Europe

Our first driver and tour guide provided lots of interesting and funny stories and even belted out an excellent rendition of "Molly Malone." Completing the entire round trip, we jumped off back at

Merton Square. We took a close look at the relaxed, bemused, lounging, elitist Oscar Wilde, just across from the street from his boyhood home. We strolled through the square, stopping to observe the Dublin Dance Festival with plenty of tiny dancers doing their best moves. Dark clouds swirled overhead, and the temperature dropped suddenly, and we settled into Kennedy's, a typical pub, for a cup of hot vegetable soup and warming teas.

(At this point, we began boarding, and I did not return to this travelogue until Tuesday, May 24 when I was back in my Drew office.)

On our bus tour, our lady tour guide had pointed out a small pharmacy, where in the course of Leopold Bloom's very full day on June 16, 2004, as described by James Joyce in *Ulysses,* Leopold stops at this very pharmacy to buy his wife, Mollie, a bar of lemon soap. I noticed the pharmacy diagonally across the street from Kennedy's, and so we crossed the street and lingered in front for a few moments, admiring the Joyce photographs and old editions of his works. Suddenly, an eccentric man in a white pharmacist's smock came outside and beckoned us to come inside. He obviously wanted us to buy the lemon soap for 5 euros or a Joyce novel in English or German. He rambled on for a while, and Kersti got a creepy feeling from his stained brownish teeth, so we excused ourselves and walked back to Pearse to board the 3:15 train back to Bilbraggin.

For our final dinner, we returned to Duende to split a burger and chicken dish. It was nice to be recognized by our server, who dreams of visiting New York. She was touched when I said that we might see her one day in New York, and she said maybe she would arrange that for her 21st birthday. We were surprised that she was only 20—she was very gracious and mature. For our finale, we drove one more time to Bettystown to take a walk on the beach. It was cool and blustery, and we didn't walk for long.

Our flight was only 6 hours and 50 minutes, but we were crammed in back of a full plane with insufficient space in the overhead compartments for our carry-ons, so it was not that comfortable. I enjoyed chatting with a nice young Irishman, a pianist from Trim as we looked down early in the flight on his country and late in the flight on ours. I watched *Bridge of Spies*, the Cold War story of the prisoner exchange for the U2 pilot, Francis Gary Powers, a compelling story with a strong performance by Tom Hanks. Kersti also watched the film, but we landed before she could see the end. Having gone through U.S. customs in Dublin—half an hour before our scheduled 11:30 landing—we sailed through the airport and were outside by 11:45. Michael Pacheco arrived a short time later to drive us back home, and we were both amazed when he realized that he was the one who had taken the photography of 10 Beechwood Drive that went into the slide show that convinced us that this was going to be our new home.

Chapter 24

DELAWARE

June 8-10, 2016

"The beach is not very wide and strewn with seaweed and horseshow crabs, waiting for the tide to come in and take them back into the water"

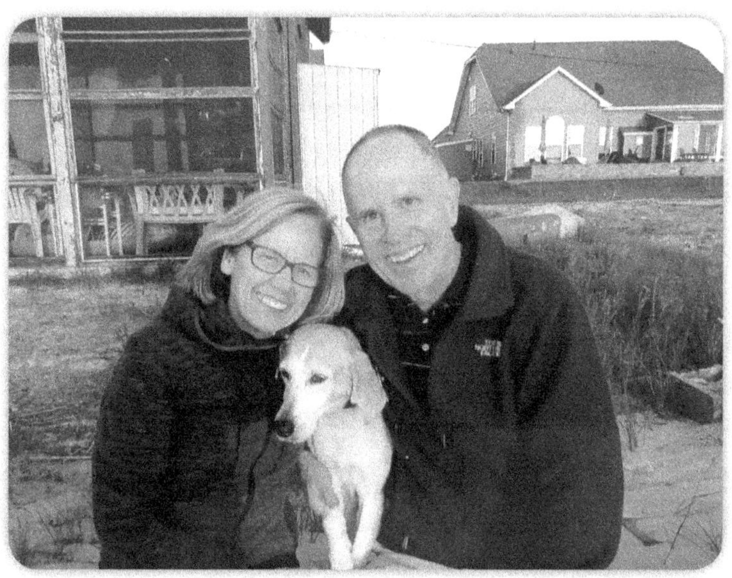

Dagsboro, Delaware—Visiting Jan Wells

Wednesday, June 8

Kersti and I departed around 10:30 AM, a little earlier than expected, because her healer, David, canceled his weekly appointment. We encountered some torrential rain as we headed south on 202 and 31, but it stopped by the time we reached 95. I made the mistake of taking 95 toward Philadelphia rather than 295 toward the Delaware Memorial Bridge, and, as I have often experienced since the early seventies, the traffic around Philly slowed to a crawl. Entering Delaware, we still had two hours ahead of us on Routes 1, 13, and 113 South. At least the sun was shining. After some stop-and-go traffic in congested, commercial, "anywhere U.S.A." northern Delaware, we sped down Route 1 toward beach country. We arrived around 3:30 PM at Jan Wells' beautiful condo in Seagrass Plantation in Dagsboro, situated inland about 20 minutes from Bethany Beach. Jan immediately served up some drinks and snacks, and we caught up on all the family news regarding our three children and her four children and eight (soon to be nine) grandchildren.

As we were bringing some plates and cups in from the outside patio, the door did not close tightly. It swung open a bit, and Peaches raced away. We quickly realized this, but she was already out of sight. Jan immediately alerted her Seagrass community on Facebook. Meanwhile, we jumped in the car and began looking for Peaches, alerting two very friendly and concerned neighbors about our missing dog. Jan heard from one friend, who said she had sighted Peaches close to the exit of the complex about a mile from Jan's. We even drove on the main road outside of Seagrass, hoping to catch a glimpse of Peaches. All the houses look alike, other than some minor customizations, and we wondered how Peaches could possibly find her way back to Jan's. Hungry and resigned to hoping that somehow we would find Peaches before sundown, we headed back to Jan's place. All of a sudden, I spotted Peaches sauntering along the sidewalk in the direction of Jan's across from a heavily wooded area. We called out, "Peaches," and she began to run faster away from us. But then she stopped when she heard Kersti jangling the leash and she came toward us. Just another memorable Peaches adventure! We enjoyed Jan's broiled chicken breasts and salad outdoors, and with Peaches safe and secure in her own little stud, my second Heineken tasted even better than the first!

Thursday, June 9

Thursday was a special day, featuring a trip to the outer banks of Maryland. After breakfast, Jan drove us about 15 miles south to the Maryland border and then a little further east to Assateague National Park. There we utilized Jan's lifelong national park pass to gain access to the park and visitors' center, where we watched an introductory film. We then drove to the protected beach area where the wild horses live year round. Jan stopped a few times where cars were congregated, and visitors were admiring small clusters of the horses. They were gently grazing rather than freely racing, but still it was a marvelous sight. We parked and walked to the beach, setting up our chairs and securing Peaches to one of them. We ate our picnic lunch and basked in the sun with a comfortable breeze blowing. With the sun high in the sky close to the solstice, we only stayed for a few hours. We then drove inland to the small quaint town of Berlin with its brick buildings and small shops that reminded us of a small New England town. Kersti bought an original landscape that now hangs in our living room.

On the way home, we had another special horse experience. Jan had told us about a mother horse and newborn foal, still on spindly legs, not far from her place. We stopped and stood at a fence, close to the mother and daughter, who seemed to enjoy the attention.

It took some effort, but we were finally able to get Jan's grill started for hamburgers for dinner, and we ate another delicious dinner on her patio. After dinner, as it grew dark, Jan lit a fire in her small fire container. We looked up at the sky and could see the sparkling stars of the Milky Way.

During our two days in Delaware, we took a number of walks to the bay, from early in the morning to dusk. A sliver of the bay is visible from Jan's property. The beach is not very wide and strewn with seaweed and horseshow crabs, waiting for the tide to come in and take them back into the water, but the setting is totally calming. We watched the sunset both evenings. Jan made an excellent choice to move here, some four hours from the Morristown area, but well worth the coastal setting, warmer winters, friendly neighborhood, and utter tranquility. We pondered, at least in passing, the possibility of living in a place like this.

Friday, June 10

On Friday morning, Jan drove us to Bethany Beach, where we walked along the boardwalk of this family-friendly resort. We stopped in a toy store, and Kersti bought some sand play items. We returned to Jan's house, packed our things, and headed to Newark, Delaware to pick up Lisa, who was at an early childhood education conference at the University of Delaware. We headed home for Lisa's first visit to our new home, and joined Janine and Eric, who was also visiting for the first time.

Chapter 25

GERMANY

July 22-30, 2016

"I enjoyed a frothy half-liter of Hefe Weizen, and we both savored an anise-accented salad with herbs inspired by Hildegarde of Bingen. There are the moments in Germany that I love the best"

Monday, July 25 and Tuesday, July 26

I have been relaxing in our cool, comfortable apartment in Bingerbrück all afternoon, while Kesti engages with the horses across the river. We did not expect to take a July trip to Germany, but late last week, as Vati's condition deteriorated and we fared that the end was near, we quickly decided on Friday morning to fly to Germany that evening. The Newark flights were extremely expensive, but we found a reasonable one on Singapore Airlines from JFK, so we booked it. We arranged with Daniel Schindler to drive us to Janine's office in Newark, where we met Janine, who had the Jetta because of her early-morning summer program with high school students. It took about two hours to get to JFK on a warm, sunny Friday evening in mid-summer, with the typical stop-and-go traffic on the Belt Parkway, but we arrived with plenty of time to spare.

Unlike our delayed flight to Frankfurt in May, we left and landed on time. Our friend Wolfgang Scholl was waiting for us and took us directly to Dr. Sieglitz Strasse, arriving around 2:30 PM, just in time for Wolfgang to make it to his weekly soccer game in Bingen. Mutti greeted us with warm hugs. Vati was lying on his side in bed, but was able to pull himself up and gave us each a firm handshake. Thus began our routine, which continued most days and consisted of four activities—planning, setting the table, eating, and cleaning up—for four major events: *Frühstuck, Mittagsessen, Kaffe und Kuchen, und*

Abendessen. During each eating routine, we had to witness and endure Vati's labored breathing and Mutti's difficulties chewing, swallowing, and occasionally and spitting out her food. Some things are simpler than in years past: Mutti spends much less time in the kitchen, so the preparations and clean up are much quicker; she is receptive to take-out ideas (pizza from Budesheim on Saturday evening, and salads from the Greek restaurant on Sunday evening); and Daniela arranged for warm packaged meals to arrive from the butcher every day this week.

George's brief, six-hour visit on Saturday and Anja's arrival on Sunday also uplifted Mutti's mood and Vati's engagement. George was able to make his peace with his father. Despite her current battle with Lyme disease, Anja was her usual upbeat self and was a big help with the meals and engaging Vati and Mutti in light conversations. On Monday, Anja and I endeavored to construct a "bottle crate stand holder" (a virtual translation from the German), a concept unknown in the U.S. and probably around the world. The bars were crooked; the screws could not be tightly secured; and this morning we disassembled it. Meanwhile, the three of us, after making sure that Mutti would not interfere, did a major clean up of their storage room in the cellar, delivering several baskets full of empty bottles to the recycling center in town.

Kersti and I took a break from the apartment scene on Monday evening with a stroll on the Rhein and dinner at the *Biergarten.* I enjoyed a frothy half-liter of *Hefe Weizen,* and we both savored an anise-accented salad with herbs inspired by Hildegarde of Bingen. There are the moments in Germany that I love the best.

Friday, July 29

It is a quiet Friday afternoon in Bingen. It is somehow hard to believe that we left a week ago and will be heading home tomorrow. Anja is meeting with her high school friend, Annette; Mutti and Kersti are taking a small "*Mutter-Tochter Asflug*" to the bank; Vati is taking his afternoon nap; the Miele man (whom I originally thought was the doctor) is servicing the dishwasher; and I am updating our week in

Germany. The days blend together, one into another. Anja has done a nice job, preparing, implementing, and cleaning up for the four food events each day. Kersti and I have had time to take walks along the Rhein, the vineyard trail in Bingerbrück, the field high above the Rhein where we discovered the charred dragon log, and the fields close to the Rochusberg. We had another delicious salad at the *Biergarten* on Wednesday evening.

Yesterday, we drove to Biebertal to visit Rosi and Hans. Rosi greeted us warmly and took us for a walk through the garden, but virtually withdrew when Hans arrived and dominated the conversation the rest of the afternoon. He served a prepared meal from the butcher, featuring some grizzly pork, tasty sauerkraut, and potatoes. Then we had sorbet and melon for dessert followed soon after by *Kaffee* (or rather *Tee)* and *Flaumkuchen* (plum tart). Rosi was must engaged when we looked at some old photos from her early twenties, when she had recently met Hans and a life of promise stretched before her. In a private conversation in the kitchen, Hans told Kersti that Rosi was deteriorating rather quickly. She had asked five or six times who was coming, and Hans finally wrote down for her, "Kerstin and Dick." It is sad to see this happening to Kersti's favorite aunt.

Vati continues to rally each day, and thus was are leaving tomorrow on Icelandair. We will be stopping for a 1-hour and 45-minute visit to Rekyavik before arriving in Newark at 7:00. Our combined fare of $2,236 for two one-way tickets stings a bit, but we need to get home to Eric and Peaches before we return here in just two weeks with our trip to Nashville sandwiched in between.

Postscript—Sunday, July 31

We arrived home on Saturday evening around 9:00 PM after a 17-hour door-to-door trip. We said goodbye to Vati and Mutti while they were eating breakfast, reminding them that we would be back in two weeks along with Lisa, Nellie, Eric, and later Janine. Anja dropped us at the Bingerbrück train station, and we took the 9:47 train to the airport. We saw a number of Muslims, possibly refugees, on the train, mostly women with small children. It was our only glimpse of the more than one million refugees who have settled in Germany during the past year.

We stood for an hour and a half in the Icelandair line, before proceeding through security and waiting for another hour at the gate. The flight to Rekyavik (Keklavik) was delayed by about 45 minutes, but we finally were airborne around 2:45. We flew above a thick layer of clouds all the way across Europe, the English Channel, and the tip of northern Scotland, but the sky was clear and blue as we approached Iceland and looked down on the mostly brown, volcanic island. The ocean water was sparkling blue, and we could see the white caps of the Atlantic. We disembarked and wound up spending only 45 minutes in Iceland, before boarding a new plane. Less than an hour into the final leg of our trip, we spotted land once again: Greenland. We looked down on a stunning show of nature: snow-covered fields and mountains, turquoise blue lakes, gigantic glaciers, craggy mountains, and ice floes. We were amazed at the vastness of this pristine continent, an undisturbed work of God and nature, inviting us to bear witness to its beauty and magic. Two hours later, we caught our fist glimpse of North America, Labrador, north of Quebec, but there was no comparison. It looked dark, green, flat, and barren.

We arrived at Newark around 7:25, and Eric picked us up at 8:20 in the pouring rain. At home, he had a surprise waiting for us: a dinner of turkey burgers and roasted regular and sweet potatoes. I added a salad, and we sat down for dinner about a quarter past nine, glad to be home safe and sound and looking forward to a few days' break before we head back to the airport on Thursday evening for our excursion to Nashville to celebrate Nellie's graduation.

Chapter 26

NASHVILLE, TENNESSEE

August 4-7, 2016

"Norbert has definitely been with us during this celebratory weekend in Nashville"

Nashville, Tennessee—Celebrating Nellie's graduation from Belmont University

Saturday, August 6

It is early Saturday morning and quiet in our rented house on the corner of Woodland Street and 15th Street in a residential section of Nashville. Kersti is still sleeping in our downstairs bedroom, and Janine, Lisa, and Eric are upstairs. It does not feel like we are in a city. The owner, Andy Fisher, is an artist and musician, and his wide variety of paintings and styles decorate the walls of the living room and dining room.

Our friend Steve Wells picked up Kersti, Eric, and me Thursday afternoon around 5:30, and we then fetched Janine outside her

Rutgers-Newark office on Bleecker Street on the way to the airport. Our 8:35 PM flight was delayed until nearly 10:00. After sitting around in an atmosphere that was beginning to feel like our overnight airport adventure in May, we had to rush to change gates at the last minute. The airport was extremely cold, so frigid that Kersti bought a "New York City" hoodie. With Nashville one hour behind us, we managed to arrive around 11:15, in time to pick up our car at the Thrifty car rental. It was only a 15-minute drive to our house on Woodland. There we found Lisa huddled in bed, extending her hand and squeezing Kersti's as a welcome.

Friday was Nellie's graduation day at Belmont University. After several waves of fried eggs and toast for breakfast, we walked along the sultry streets to a small cafe for coffees and a shared kale-feta-dried cranberry salad. We then drove to Nellie's temporary apartment on the edge of the Belmont campus, and Nellie greeted us all with her signature big warm hugs. Her friend came to take photos of our various groups on the porch, because of the rain and wet conditions. We drove to a popular lunch place for sandwiches and wraps, then back to the apartment for Nellie to put on her cap and gown.

We walked through the campus to the basketball arena, scurrying at one point as raindrops began to fall. It is an impressive arena, seating perhaps 5,000, and we enjoyed the cool, comfortable air. I was struck by the size of the faculty that marched in and occupied two large sections of the stands: there appeared to be as many faculty as graduates. The board member who spoke mentioned that Belmont has grown more than threefold in the past 20 years from 2,200 students to 7,600 students. Our seats were strategically positioned in the second and third rows directly opposite Nellie's row in the center of the arena, and we made enthusiastic contact with our waving arms and beaming smiles as she marched in and sat down with her classmates. In my view, the speakers cited too many New Testament verses and promoted too much Christianity, though the apparent lack of religious, cultural, and ethnic diversity among the students, faculty, and guests may have minimized any discomfort among non-Christians. Just before summoning the graduates to the stage for their diplomas, the president said that a Belmont tradition is for family and friends to give their graduates a shout out when their name is announced. When "Nellie Maria Schindler" rang out in the arena, we rose and shouted "Go Nellie" with cheers and accolades.

For dinner, we went to The Pharmacy, a German-style pub and beer garden. Unfortunately, because of the lingering showers, we were not able to sit outside, but it was just as well, because it was so muggy and warm. We sat at a long table, five on one side and four on the other, and enjoyed beers, burgers, sausages, and sides. Anja gave a moving toast to Nellie, saying how proud she was of her accomplishments, and also acknowledging Norbert's presence. He has definitely been with us during this celebratory weekend in Nashville. He appeared as the accordion player in one of Andy's Hopper-like paintings. He appeared in the big pine tree outside the living room window. And he was there as I chatted with Nellie on our walk through the campus, and she recalled her first visit to the campus as a junior in high school, accompanied by her dad.

Postcript—August 9 (Mom's 98th Birthday)

I'm back in my Drew office after a busy weekend in Nashville and Monday at Cranberry Lake to celebrate Mom's birthday.

On Saturday afternoon, August 6, we met at the Belmont Mansion around 1:00 for a tour of the home built by Joseph and Adelicia Acklen in 1853. She was soon widowed, but remained one of the wealthiest women in the South from the 1850s until her death in 1887. The mansion was named Belle Monte, describing the beautiful mountain overlooking Nashville, about two miles from the city center. It was not a plantation or working farm, but rather a "party palace." The Acklen plantations, inherited from Adelicia's first husband Isaac Franklin, were located in Louisiana. After her death, it became a girls' school and is now a focal point of the Belmont University campus. Today, it stands as the largest house museum in Tennessee.

We then headed across the street to one of Nellie's favorite bistros for lunch followed by a motor tour of Broadway in downtown Nashville, which was packed with throngs of tourists. The stop-and-go traffic enabled us to observe the people, bars, and shops. We glimpsed a number of the open, multi-seat party vehicles, mostly occupied by groups of bachelorettes, who were well lubricated by mid-afternoon. We considered parking, but the $30 fee for half an hour navigating through wall-to-wall people was not appealing. We headed back to Woodland Street for our cocktail hour, featuring a bottle of champagne and beers. The Schindler clan departed, and the five of us headed over to a Vietnamese restaurant on Fatherland Street for a tasty, authentic dinner. After dinner, we crossed the bridge one final time to drop off the kids close to an outdoor concert that Nellie and Daniel were attending. Kersti and I took a final walk around the neighborhood before calling it a night.

On Sunday morning, Eric left early to begin his journey home with Nellie in her car. Janine, Lisa, Kersti, and I found a nice brunch place called AMOT—short for A Matter of Taste. We still had four hours to spend before arriving at the airport, and given its proximity to the airport, we headed off to The Hermitage—the home of Andrew Jackson. He was the 7th president of the U.S. and the first who had not been a well-do-do politician or landowner from Virginia or Massachusetts. He was orphaned by age 11, fought in the final year of the Revolution at the age of 13, served time as a prisoner of war, became a lawyer, joined the U.S. Army, rose to major general, and led the final victory over the British at the Battle of New Orleans in January 1815. He won the popular vote for president against John Quincy Adams in 1824, but did not receive an electoral majority, and the House gave the presidency to Adams.

Jackson served two terms as president from 1829 to 1837. He is best known, on the positive side, for truly opening the presidency to people of any station in life and for establishing the Democratic Party. On the negative side, he is remembered for owning slaves and forcibly resettling thousands of Native Americans.

Despite the heat, we toured the mansion, which was completed in 1821, the cabin where Andrew and his wife Rachel Donelson lived from 1804-1821 (it later served as a slave quarters), and the garden where Andrew's, Rachel's, and their faithful servant, "Uncle Alfred," are buried. We enjoyed the live tour guides in the mansion and the audio recordings the rest of the way. The inscription on Andrew's tomb only refers to him as "General"; there is no mention of his role as president. Rachel's inscription attests to her character and courage, a lasting response to the scandal that followed her when she eloped with Andrew in the 1790s before she was officially divorced from her first husband. This was one of the best presidential compounds that we have visited, and I liked the emphasis on his life at The Hermitage from 1837 until his death—in the very bed that we observed—in June 1845. We were in good shape time wise, and we dropped off our car and headed over to the Delta counter with plenty of time to spare before our 5:35 PM flight. But when I opened my wallet, I could not find my driver's license. Then it struck me—it was back at The Hermitage where I had deposited it in exchange for our audio units. It was 4:15, and we had less than an hour to boarding. Janine and Lis both jumped into action and ordered me an Uber car. It was there in about eight minutes. I jumped in, and my driver, a Palestinian native from Jerusalem, knew the route well. He told me that his house and property are adjacent to the grounds of The Hermitage. It's a nice thought: this connection between the President and the Palestinian. We made it back to the Delta counter, through security, and to the gate in time for me to move right into the line of people boarding the plane.

We took a 39-minute flight to Atlanta; paused for 45 minutes; and then boarded our plane to Newark for the 101-minute flight. All systems were running smoothly, and the pilot touched down in Newark about half an hour before our scheduled 10:57 landing. Steve was on top of things, and met us shortly after we walked out to the street level and enjoyed a comfortable August evening. We were extra fortunate to arrive on a Sunday evening. By the next morning, the entire worldwide Delta computer system was down. We were glad to be home.

Chapter 27

GERMANY

August 12-29, 2016

"Doing small tasks. Engaging in everyday conversations. Remembering. We are all navigating the terrain of life without Vati"

Bingen, Germany—Lisa departing for Spain

Monday, August 15

It is a quiet Monday morning in Bingen. The late summer weather in Germany has been perfect: we have enjoyed warm, sunny days and cool nights with a waxing moon high above.

It is hard to believe that we arrived less than 48 hours ago. Upon our arrival in Bingen around 12:30 PM on Saturday, August 13, we found Vati lying in the living room on a hospital bed, his mouth arched open as he struggled to breathe, heavily sedated and sleeping. His bed faced the view of the Rhein from the balcony—the view that he had witnessed and reveled in thousands of times. Eric, Lisa, and Nellie were there, having arrived the day before in support of their Omi. It was an unusual scene: life going on, as normal as possible in the *Esszimmer* and *Kucher*, and life slipping away in the *Wohnzimmer*. Mutti even managed to prepare her famous German potato salad for dinner along with sausages, salad, and leftover pizza.

We left around 9:30 on Saturday evening. Kersti gave Vati a kiss, and I patted him on the shoulder and offered him my usual nightly wish: "*Gute Nacht, Vati; schlaf gut.*" We had managed to stay awake until 10:00 PM, so we finally settled into bed in our upstairs apartment in Bingerbrück with a clear view back to Dr. Sieglitz Strasse. The living room light was still on.

Kersti was asleep and I was reading, when my phone rang around 11:00—it was Lisa. My first thought is that Lisa, Eric, and Nellie were locked out and needed me to open the door. Then she uttered the words that we were dreading but expecting: "Opa just died." Kersti and I quickly got dressed and headed back to Dr Sieglitz Strasse to join Mutti along with Eric, Nellie, and Lisa. We hugged and wept and chatted with each other for the next three hours. A doctor arrived to take care of the official death certificate, and a short time later a husband and wife team from the Maessen funeral home arrived. They were very kind and respectful, as they quietly went about their tasks. Kersti and I watched as they gently lifted Vati and put him onto a large black bag on the stretcher. We walked downstairs and said goodbye to Vati as they lifted the stretcher into the back of their van and then drove him down Dr. Sieglitz Strasse for the final time. We watched solemnly until it rounded the bend.

After our long day, we had another short night. I woke up at 9:10 Sunday morning and then roused Kersti at 9:30. We picked up Mutti and went to the funeral home at 10:30 and discussed all the funeral arrangements for the next two hours. We then drove to the Hildegard Forum for a buffet lunch outside. Kersti and I finally had a chance to spend some quiet time together on our walk downhill from the Rochusberg to the apartment.

At 3:00, Mutti's pastors from the Mennonite church in Weierhof arrived, and we proceeded to a small chapel adjacent to the cemetery for a family service. There was Vati, lying in a coffin, dressed in his suit and tie. At last he was sleeping soundly and peacefully. The pastors led us through a brief service, and we shared what we were grateful for. I said, "Vati und Mutti haben mir Kerstin gegeben und später unsere Kinder." We then said our final farewell to Vati. Mutti kissed him and brushed his hair one more time, thanking him for their lifetime together. We left the dim chapel and walked back out into the bright sunshine of late summer.

We concluded our day with a tasty dinner at the Biergarten on the Rhein. Afterwards, the grandchildren walked back across the river to Bingerbrück, while Kersti and I entered the quiet apartment on Dr. Sieglitz Strasse and assisted Mutti as she got ready for bed.

Wednesday, August 17

It's another beautiful, comfortable late summer day in the Rhein Valley. The 5:30 PM bells are tolling in Bingerbrück. I am sitting on the Dr. Sieglitz deck, looking across the Nahe to our apartment and writing this by hand. Janine—who arrived just a few hours ago—joined Kersti and Mutti for their trip into town to stop at Edeka and the flower shop to select flowers for Vati's service a week from today.

After the non-stop weekend of travel, loss, and emotion, today we began to settle into the daily routines of life without Vati. Daniela was off all week after her weekend and previous days and nights of support. Meanwhile, Monday morning brought a steady stream of people to the apartment: the two men who disassembled and took away Vati's hospital bed; the insurance/financial advisor; Pfarrer Carmen Rossol, who planned the service with Kersti; and Vati's massage therapist, who came to treat Vati but quickly transitioned to Mutti when she said that he had died over the weekend. Nellie, Eric, and Lisa went to the natural pool in Bingerbrück on Monday afternoon, before our dinner of *Döner* sandwiches and platters. Monday night was another late one, as we discussed with Lisa how to balance her plans for the service and the family gathering on Wednesday and her trip to Ibiza. Nellie decided to leave this coming Sunday, while Lisa opted to stay through the service and join Nellie on Thursday for their concert. Eric then lay on our bed us to discuss his short-term plans once back in North America.

On Tuesday, the Eric-Lisa-Nellie trio packed their bags for a train ride to Frankfurt Airport and a short flight to Berlin. They will stay at cousin Thomas' place. He and his wife and son Moritz are vacationing in southern France until Friday. After a light dinner, Kersti and I walked most of the length of the Bingen waterfront before turning around. A brisk wind picked up, and we imagined for just a moment what this walk would feel like in the winter months. But the growing chorus of crickets told another story.

Tuesday, August 23

The sun continues to shine brightly during our second week in Germany. It is quiet as I write this, looking out from our apartment in Bingerbrück on the Germania monument across the river that celebrates Germany's triumph over France in the Franco-Prussian War of 1870-71. We had a few showers over the weekend, and it turned cool, but summer will be with us all this week with temperatures in the low to mid-30s (C).

Recent days have taken on a routine quality, but they pass quickly enough. Our time in Germany is not about traveling or visiting relatives or friends. It's all about who is coming and going. It's all about shuttling between Bingen and Bingerbrück and being there for Mutti. Doing small tasks. Engaging in everyday conversations. Remembering. We are all navigating the terrain of life without Vati.

After Lisa, Eric, and Nellie left for Berlin a week ago, Janine arrived on Wednesday, three days earlier than she originally planned. We had spoken several times while she was still in New York, and she felt strongly and rightly that Bingen was where she needed to be. Daniela was able to take the week off, and all four of the grandchildren have joined Kersti and me in comforting and supporting Mutti and even making her laugh. Wednesday was also the day that the announcement of Vati's death appeared in the *Allgemeine Zeitung*, and this was another trigger of the back-and-forth waves of grief and relief that we are all feeling.

We all took turns spending time with Mutti or taking her into town for shopping. This role fell to me on Saturday, August 20. We stopped first at the vegetable store, which Mutti calls the "*Mädels*" after the two sisters who run it. We picked out tomatoes, scallions, red and green lettuce, red and green peppers, potatoes, mushrooms, and eggs. Mutti was happy to introduce me as her "*Americanisher Schviegersohn*." We then continued on to the market, which sets up every Saturday and Wednesday morning at the foot of Burg Klopp. We bought some cakes for *Kaffee und Kuchen*, and chatted with the lady who handles Mutti's taxes. We also bought some honey, flowers, and meat in three separate stops. Mutti ran into her good friend Ingrid, who expressed her condolences and talked about her late husband's friendship with Vati. We stopped back at the *Mädels* to pick up our bags of vegetables, and, as she often is, Frau Krista Mohr was there, chatting away. I enjoyed my time as Mutti's escort into town.

Around 1:00, Kersti and I walked into town to meet her friend Marion and husband Pompei for lunch at the Novo Hotel. They are both doctors and live in New Providence. Kersti met Marion at one of the German ladies' lunches. We were hoping to eat in the *Biergarten*, but the threat of showers and cool temperature kept us inside. We later walked along the Rhein and stopped for *K und K* at the downtown Lüning bakery. All of a sudden, we saw Janine passing by, and invited her in for a cappuccino.

Nellie, Eric, and Lisa arrived from Berlin around 6:00 PM, wrapping up four enjoyable days in Germany's capital with a 5- to 6-hour train ride. We shifted over to Bingerbrück for a typical German dinner of pasta, Mutti's potato salad, my green salad, *Fleischwurst,* and cheese. Mutti was doing well a week after Vati's passing, and was just happy to be with her family and go along with the flow. It grew dark, and we took Mutti back to her apartment, while Nellie and Janine raced into town to buy Nellie some hiking boots before the store closed at 10:00 PM.

On Sunday, Kersti and I drove Nellie to the Hahn Airport for her flight to Valencia. We had encouraged her to move ahead with her trip, that she had been here for Vati when he was still alive and had said goodbye to him at the wake. Vati would have been the first to tell her to go. At the same time, we were happy that Lisa had decided to skip her visit to Valencia and her Spanish family in Ontinyent to be with us at Wednesday's memorial service. She will join Nellie in Ibiza on Thursday.

On Monday morning, Kersti and I did an Edeka run (Mutti is surprisingly agreeable to this) and then prepared a noodle salad (one with corn, one without) and a green salad for Daniela's birthday party at a field and barbecue pit overlooking the Rhein. The morning was cloudy and showery, and we were concerned that we might not be able to enjoy our picnic outside, but the afternoon weather was ideal. We met Daniela's mom, brother, three sons, and assorted friends and relatives. She was very pleased that her "second family" was able to join her for her 38th birthday.

Friday, August 26

Our last day in Germany is probably the hottest of all with the temperature soaring to the mid-30s (high 80s). We just sat down for *Kaffee und Kuchen*, and I told Mutti that it was our last one together until October 6, when she will be with us in Convent Station. Kersti is playing the tape that Rosi, Vati's sister, recorded with their mother, Charlotte (Kersti's Omi) in the 1980s in Worms and Bingen. It is a moving account of Omi's childhood, the loss of her father in World War I at the age of 6, the loss of her husband and father of their three children in 1943, and the harrowing flight from East Prussia to West Germany in 1945.

On Wednesday, we said our public goodbye to Vati. It was a beautiful summer day, which reminded me of the day when we said goodbye to Dad in August 1996. We arrived at the small chapel adjacent to the cemetery around 10:30, just as family members and friends where assembling. We greeted the Ramges (Rosi, Hans, Peter, and Thomas), the Wiebes from Bremerhaven and Köln (Walter, Helga, and Heike), the Wiebes from Italy and München (Hans-Jörg, Patrick, and Dirk) Irmgard and Albert, and others. One member of the Mennonite congregation at Weierhof had a long beard. We recognized another member of the congregation, Gerhard Wieler, from recent *Wiehlertreffens*. Gabi and Wolfgang, Eva and Inge, and Daniela and her mother, also joined us. Just before 11:00, we slowly proceeded into the chapel, passing by a small table with photos of Vati that we had carefully selected: a wedding photo with Vati in his police uniform; Vati, Walter, and Rosi in their 20s and 30s; a bearded Vati laughing in the snow; a young Vati tossing his toddler son in the air; and Vati and Mutti strolling on a snowy afternoon a few years ago. Pfarrer Carmen had prepared the service and homily, but she was not feeling well, so Pfarrer Walter took over for her. Mutti, her three children, and I sat in the first row, and the five grandchildren right behind us. We sang several songs and then listened to the story that Walter told of Vati's life—a life that was at times a struggle, but one that was full and meaningful *trotzdem alles*—in spite of everything. Walter's voice broke and he wiped away a tear as he talked about Vati's annual visits to America—something that Walter now does because of his son and grandchildren in Seattle. Walter was followed by a representative of the *Wasserschutzpolizei* (the water police), who described Vati as a leader and a man of character. We were all moved to see this man standing there in the uniform that Vati proudly wore to and from work for 36 years.

After the service, Mutti slowly led us to the gravesite. A representative of the town carried the urn. Mutti held the arms of Hans Jorg and Walter. At the gravesite, Walter offered a final blessing and then the urn was lowered into the ground. One by one, we then shoveled some earth on top of the urn and scattered some rose petals. It was one more moving goodbye in a series of farewells.

We returned to the chapel and drove to the Rochusberg Forum, less than two miles away. Patrick had by far the coolest car and look: he behind the wheel of his Mercedes convertible, of course with the top down and shades on, Dirk in front, and our girls in the back, smiling, waving, their hair swirling with the wind. We had a private room at the Forum, and with jackets off, ties loosened, and appetites whetted, we began our three-course luncheon. I wound up sitting at a table with Mutti, a relative whom I did not know, Gabi and Wolfgang, and Pfarrer Walter. I assumed that his English was better than my German, and we started out in English, but then he switched to German, and kept going through the second course, telling me all about his son in Seattle, his son's job with the Gates Foundation, and a daughter and another son somewhere in Germany. The funniest moment came after dinner, when Peter appeared in shorts and a black t-shirt. I remarked to Peter, "You are the coolest dude in this place." He replied, tugging his shirt and laughing heartily, "This is my grieving shirt!" Between 3:00 and 4:00, most of the family members and friends left, and a small group sat at an outdoor table to wrap up our successful family gathering.

That evening, while our three children were cooling off at the natural pool in Bingerbrück, Anja, Mutti, Kersti, and I visited the grave to tell Vati that we would be okay and that he could now rest in peace. I left one of the small cards with his picture on top of a "mum" plant that had not yet bloomed.

Thursday was a day of travel and transition. I drove Janine and Eric to the Hahn, leaving at 7:30 AM and pulling back into Henri Miller Strasse in Bingerbrück a little after 9:00. They were flying to Barcelona, Janine to attend Jeanna Occhiogrosso's wedding and Eric to meet up with Nellie before the scene switched to Switzerland. Lisa was the next to leave, departing on the 12:24 train to Mainz and Frankfurt for her flight to Ibiza to join Nellie for a big concert Thursday night. Kersti snapped a picture of Lisa standing on the steps of the train. She took her seat, and we waved as the train pulled out of the station.

On Thursday evening, our remaining foursome drove to Bretzenheim, the section of Mainz where Gabi and Wolfgang live, to join them for dinner at their favorite *Biergarten*. I ordered a *Weizenbier*, only to be told by Wolfgang that the restaurant only served wine. I asked Wolfi for a dry wine, and the bartender poured about half a glass of white wine followed quickly by a half glass of seltzer. We enjoyed typical German food: salad, *Bratwurst*, potatoes, and *Kraut* (cabbage) salad. It was dark by the time we got back on the *Autobahn* and headed home—more than an hour less light than we had in late June.

Today we took the ferry to Rudesheim and drove up to Hildegard's closter. We ate a light lunch and then spent some meditative moments in the cool, sacred, quiet church.

Postscript

On Saturday morning, we ate an early breakfast in Bingerbrück and headed over to Dr. Sieglitz Strasse one final time. Anja and Mutti accompanied us to the station and walked with us to the platform. The forecast was for another hot day, but as we stood waiting for the train, the wind picked up and Mutti shivered. We hugged and said goodbye. It was not a difficult farewell, because she will be joining us in New Jersey in early October. Anja and she slowly walked away. I waved before they rounded the corner, but they did not look back.

Our flight was delayed by 20 minutes, but overall it was smooth. I watched the first chapter of Ken Burns' documentary on Jackie Robinson. We sailed through the new customs wing in Terminal C and were waiting for Steve Wells when he swung by to pick us up and take us home. When we arrived, we realized that we did not have a key, and Janine had locked the door from the garage to the house. But our neighbor Kathy Yamashita was home, and Kersti picked up the key so we could enter the house, greet Peaches, and begin the next chapter at home.

Chapter 28

ADIRONDACKS AND MONTREAL

September 16-19, 2016

"This is a time of great transition for our family, as summer gives way to fall"

Saturday, September 17: Blue Mountain Lake, NY

It is a quiet Saturday evening inside our lakefront cabin. It feels like we have been here for days, but we only arrived yesterday afternoon around 4:00 PM. The main street of the town was abuzz with tourists and vendors selling everything from antiques to artwork to real stuffed animals. It's a four-day bazaar in both Blue Mountain Lake and Indian Lake. Fortunately, our adjoined cabin is in the *back* of a two-story outfitters store and completely quiet at night except for an occasional car.

Yesterday was a beautiful late summer day, and we enjoyed our "cocktail hour" outside our cabin, watching the sparkling waters and Blue Mountain rising in the distance. Two humming birds flitted from flower to flower, and a monarch butterfly wafted through the air. We drove 11 miles to Indian Lake for dinner at a tasty Mexican restaurant. It was dark by the time we drove back, and we had to put on our jackets as the temperature dropped. There are only four more days of summer. Late summer has given way to early fall.

The sun was shining again this morning, and we ate our regular breakfast of toast, tea, and boiled egg outside. Clouds began to roll in by midday, but we didn't mind as we took a fairly strenuous one-mile hike up Mt. Sawyer, midway between Blue Mountain Lake and Indian Lake, and a half-mile hike to Rock Lake along a largely pine-needled path. At the lakefront, as we were sitting on a bench and eating our sandwiches, we were joined by the cutest little red squirrel—not much larger than a chipmunk. He fearlessly jumped up on the bench and appeared to be hungry. I threw half a peanut toward our little friend. He sniffed around, found it, stood on his hind legs to take a quick bite, and then scampered off into the woods. Just as quickly, he returned and repeated this sequence of activities about 10 times! At the Wild Center on Monday, we read about red squirrels, which in the fall gather food for the winter. That is precisely what our little friend was doing.

We returned to the Mexican restaurant for dinner, dodging the occasional light showers. Without a TV or Internet access in our room, we again turned in early.

Sunday, September 18

The sun just set over Blue Mountain Lake. The darkness comes early now. Already this is the last evening of our mini-vacation. The crickets may already know that their days are numbered. Kersti just left to walk to the telephone booth, where she has texting capability. She will send a message to Eric, saying that we are thinking of him on his last night in Montreal.

This is a time of great transition for our family, as summer gives way to fall. Kersti leased her new office on Maple Street in Morristown on September 15; Eric is leaving Montreal on September 19; Janine concludes her job at Rutgers-Newark on September 29; and on October 6, Mutti is taking her first trip to the U.S. since 2007. New journeys and discoveries lie ahead.

We heard the rain last night and expected the day to be a wet one, but it turned out to be warm and mostly sunny—more like summer than fall. After breakfast, we took a canoe out on the lake and paddled for about an hour around several islands and just within sight of Hemlock Hall. It was brisk at first, but we peeled off our fleeces along the way. We then drove north on Route 30, through Long Lake and Tupper Lake, then 3 East to Saranac Lake. We quickly found the Trudeau Institute and the statue of Edward Trudeau. He looked sadder than ever. There were cobwebs on his face and weeds and rows of moss in the plaza honoring him. Kersti admitted that she was no longer as moved as she had been during our two previous visits. We drove down to the edge of Lower Saranac Lake and ate our sandwiches, perched on rocks and basking in the warm sunshine. The wind was blowing, and the cool water splashed against the rocks. A local lady befriended us and told us about the four local lakes: Lower, Middle, and Upper Saranac Lakes and Flower Lake.

We drove into town and picked up some soup and a lamb meatball-couscous dish at a local deli, snacked a bit more at a picnic table on the public grounds of Flower Lake, and then headed back to Tupper Lake. There we enjoyed an afternoon visit to the Wild Center, an interactive celebration of the Adirondacks and the great outdoors. The highlights were the frisky swimming and diving otters; the methodical, curious turtle, which kept extending its surprisingly long neck outside the cage; the eye-level pond, visible from the reception area; the skyline view of the forest; and the three films on the wide screen, two showing the beauties of the Adirondacks and the other a docu-drama of a mother Merganser duck and her 15 babies whom she managed to persuade to exit their nest and plunge into the lake below just a day after they broke through their shells. On the way home, we stopped at Long Lake to partake of its marvelous view of the narrow lake and the mountain silhouettes in the background. We heated up our couscous dish and ate dinner at a picnic table as the sun disappeared behind the gathering clouds.

Postcript

We got an early start on Monday morning, leaving just past eight. We took the back roads east to the Northway, entering at Exit 29. We arrived at Eric's place a little before noon, and he was ready to go. We managed to pack all his belongings into the CRV, and then stopped at a restaurant close to Eric's former Esplanade neighborhood. Our total time in the city was less than two hours. And thus Eric's five years in Montreal came to an end.

I drove to the border, and Kersti picked it up from there. We stopped for gas in Platzburgh and again in Glens Falls. Shortly after leaving Glens Falls, our air conditioning failed, so we simply gave it a break. The air outside was comfortable, so we were fine inside the car with the vent blowing. It was getting dark when Eric said that he was hungry, so we stopped at the Modena rest stop. The engine seemed unusually warm, so I performed the old "open up the hood to cool off the engine" maneuver. It didn't work. When I turned the car back on, the power steering was shot, and I was barely able to crank the wheel and drive about two hundred yards to the gas pumps and Sunoco store. We knew we would not be able to hobble home from there. Kersti called Triple A, and they arranged for a tow truck to pick us up about 45 minutes later. Max the driver took a look under the hood and pulled out a belt that had worn down and was responsible for the air conditioning and power steering. He directed me to drive the car up a steep incline into the back of the truck before he leveled us off. Kersti, Eric, and I then drove the 15 miles back to New Paltz, where we regrouped at a local diner. Fortunately, Janine was home, and she drove the Jetta to meet us. Eric handled the final leg of the trip. We managed to arrive home around 10:30, just two and a half hours after our initial estimate.

On Wednesday afternoon, Eric and I drove to Highland, New York to pick up the repaired car. We had instructed the mechanic not to do a super duper job, and he complied, reminding us to minimize the use of the air conditioning. I drove home without any air. On Saturday, we began looking for a new car.

Chapter 29

FLORIDA

March 21-26, 2017

*"A beaming Lisa, both happy and relieved,
gave her proud mom and dad the biggest hugs
and then embraced all her colleagues"*

Friday, March 24: Miami

On this breezy, sunny Friday morning, so many special moments from yesterday are resonating so clearly and powerfully.

It was Thursday, March 23, the day that Lisa rose to the occasion and defended her thesis with so much confidence, professionalism, and conviction that her advisor, Daryl Greenberg, told an associate that it was one of the best—or *the best*—defenses he had ever witnessed in all his years in academia. We were standing on North Kendall Avenue around 8:15 when Lisa and her roommate Casey rounding the corner to pick us up from our Al oft Hotel. Lisa was grounded and focused, and her tears and concerns from the day before were behind her now. Heading down Route 1 in stop-and-go traffic, Lisa played some comforting tunes, applied lipstick, checked her email, and chattered cheerfully. Arriving at the third floor of Flipse, the psychology building, we sensed how strong Lisa's network was—her cadre of administrative assistants, office mates, and research assistants were all there to support her. One of Lisa's committee members was running late, but Lisa took that totally in stride and even used it to her advantage, saying calmly and confidently, "I think we should begin." She did a superb job presenting her research, findings, and implications, so much so that Education Professor Batya Elbaum opened the discussion portion of the defense, saying, "This is an excellent project. Let's focus on the next steps." The other committee members essentially followed this lead, making a few broad suggestions while commending Lisa for a superb dissertation.

The committee members then assembled in another room to evaluate Lisa's work. Lisa's colleagues lined the hallways, awaiting the inevitable word. Professor Elbaum then emerged and announced with a big smile: "She passed!" A beaming Lisa, both happy and relieved, gave her proud mom and dad the biggest hugs and then embraced all her colleagues. She then popped the champagne, and the cork amazingly flew into the garbage receptacle—a bullseye. We all toasted Lisa with a few sips of champagne and enjoyed the strawberries, blackberries, cake, and cookies from Trader Joes. Lisa stood next to Daryl most of the time, and he was gushing with pride, praising her for pursuing three major lines of inquiry. He said she deserved three Ph.D.s and referred to her as "Dr. Dr. Dr. White." Kersti then told him that in Germany, mentors are called "Doktor Vater," which so beautifully captures the special relationship that he and Lisa forged during the past five years.

Casey joined us for lunch outdoors at the Peacock Garden in Coconut Grove, a popular spot where we had eaten a few years earlier. Afterwards, we took the spectacular drive across the Rickenbacker Bridge from the mainland to Key Biscayne. I was behind the wheel, as Lisa put together her Facebook announcement and pictures from her successful morning. The sun was shining and the deep blue water was sparkling on both sides. We ran into some traffic because of the Miami Tennis Open, but soon arrived at the Silver Sands Beach Resort, which we had booked a few days earlier. We loved the rustic feeling of a seasoned, low-level, bungalo-style complex, the rave review from the lady from Kansas City who has been going there for 20 years, the beautiful pool, and the easy access to the beach and ocean. We took a look at the villa, and quickly upgraded from two individual rooms to the cottage for the week of May 10-17, which will include Lisa's graduation and 30th birthday. We lay on the pool lounge chairs for a while, soaking in the atmosphere, the swaying palm trees, the intermittent sun and clouds, and the significance of Lisa's achievement.

We ran into the usual rush-hour traffic heading back to the Grove, but arrived around 5:00 at one of Lisa's favorite pubs called Town to begin the celebration. It was "free unlimited champagne Thursday for the "ladies night," and the champagne, drinks, dishes, photos, and lively conversation flowed over the next three hours. We were so happy to engage with the core members of Lisa's Miami support system: the administrative assistants, students from the first to fifth years, her faculty friend Julia, and her Educare friend Deborah from Chicago. We took Lisa's car back to the hotel with Kersti behind the wheel, while Lisa spent the night at Julia's place.

Our mini-Florida "vacay" began on Tuesday morning, when our neighbor Cathy Yamashita dropped us off at the airport for our 12:15 flight. It left on time and arrived 20 minutes early. We "ubered" to our Aloft Hotel on at 7600 North Kendall Drive in the Kendall section of Miami, just a little over a mile from Lisa's apartment. After settling in, we took a walk, and suddenly Lisa appeared on her bike! We continued on foot to her apartment, and then she drove us to Black Point Marina and Grill in Cutler Bay. We dined on the deck overlooking the bay, and even caught a fleeting glimpse of a gator that was patrolling the waters in the distance.

We had some ideas for Wednesday—among them the Vizcaya mansion and garden and Crandon Beach on Key Biscayne—but we abandoned them when Lisa arrived in the morning. The enormity of her work and the weight of her defense, just 24 hours ahead, overwhelmed her, so we spent most of the day at or near our hotel. We basked in the sun in the morning and dangled out feet in the cool waters of the pool, while Lis focused on breathing deeply and putting some finishing touches on her presentation. I picked up an order of kee mao tofu from the Siam Dragon Thai restaurant across the street, and we ate it under the canopy at the pool. In the afternoon, Kersti and Lisa ran errands and went for the mani-pedi combo next door to the Thai restaurant. They also picked up a take out from Lisa's favorite Vietnamese restaurant, which we ate in the seating area adjacent to the pool. We took Lisa back to her apartment, where Kersti and she picked out Lisa's outfit for Thursday and sipped tea on the small balcony, while I began a 500-piece puzzle of a small New England harbor scene. We left her, feeling more centered and composed, and then walked back to our hotel along quiet neighborhood streets.

Saturday, March 25: Sarasota

We just ate breakfast with Joan and Wally, overlooking the bay in Sarasota from their sixth-floor condo with a 240° panoramic view. It is cool and cloudy, but the views are splendid. We watch the swooping pelicans, flying high and skimming low over the water, and the "dinky"-like cars skimming across the bridge to the barrier island, reminding me of a motorized car carousel on a Christmas morning 60 years ago. Joan and Wally live in an elegant setting, and they are such gracious and welcoming hosts. The conversation ranges easily from stories of the early days in Madison, when three-year-old Janine and Kristen first met, to the current state of our national politics. Wally is so sharp in his mind and body that it is hard to believe that he will celebrate his 80th birthday on April 13.

We arrived in Saratoga yesterday afternoon after a farewell brunch with Lisa at the Chocolate Fashion on Andalusia Avenue in Coral Gables. As Lisa and I walked toward the car, Kersti captured a special moment as father and daughter Ph.D.s walked arm in arm. Our drive across the state on Alligator Alley and up the coast past Naples and Fort Meyers took a little over four hours. I was expecting scenic overviews of the Gulf Coast, but the landscape was nondescript. We stopped once by a canal to try to spot some gators, but to no avail. For dinner, we took a step back in time and dined at Wally's golf club, the Sara Bay Country Club, famous for a 1926 head-to-head match between golf legends Bobby Jones and Walter Hagen.

Now we're off to a tour of Saratoga with Joan.

Sunday, March 26: Sarasota

We're sitting at the United terminal in the exquisite Sarasota Bradenton Airport, awaiting our flight to Newark. This airport is compact, clean, not busy, walkable (we had only a short walk from the Budget drop off to the terminal), and friendly (everyone is wishing us a good flight).

Joan provided a perfect overview of the city during our one full day in Sarasota. After breakfast, we drove across the bridge to the barrier island and then onto the Lido Key Beach. We took a walk on the wide white-sand beach—all of three minutes. As Joan abruptly announced, "That was the beach." We returned to the compact downtown area and walked through the farmer's market, a Saturday tradition in Sarasota. Joan then took us to the Marie Selby Botanical Gardens, which featured a Marc Chagall (1887-1985) exhibit, consisting of three small paintings and several mosaic reproductions. We walked through a greenhouse with beautiful colored orchids and other lush flowers, and then wound our way along the pathway past a desert landscape, a tropical area, and along the bay. Chagall's messages were sprinkled throughout, most reflecting on the intertwining of love art nature, and colors. Kersti took a photo of one of our favorites:

> *You could wonder for hours what flowers mean, but for me, they're life itself, in all its happy brilliance. We couldn't do without flowers. Flowesr help you forget life's tragedies.*

Wally then joined us for lunch at Lila, a vegan restaurant that served a tasty burrito and lettuce-beet salad.

Back at the apartment, Joan took a mid-afternoon break, while Kersti and I strolled along the bay, pausing several times on benches overlooking the small harbor. While Kersti and Joan prepared dinner, I took my own break, reading a long chapter of Hesse's *Narcissus and Goldmund*, of course in English. Joan brought out a box full of letters that her father had written to his young wife and daughter (Joan's older sister) during his service in the army in Europe in World War II. The conversation kept flowing over dinner, touching on our Pilgrim, East and West Prussian, Armenian, and German-Czech-English heritage (yes, Wally is one-quarter English-Scottish). Wally grilled salmon fillets to perfection, accompanied by Joan's baked asparagus, rice-cooker rice, and leafy salad from the farmer's market. After dinner, Joan drove us to the busy St. Armand's quarter, where the restaurants were filled to capacity and the shops were open late. Walking by a closed deli, we smelled smoke, so Joan did her community service deed of the week and called 911 to summon the fire department. The operator gave her a bit of a hard time, perhaps thinking it was a crank call, but the fire department quickly appeared and discovered a cigarette still alit and smoldering in a portable plant. The friendly fireman carried the plant away to douse the budding fire. Just another exciting Saturday evening in Sarasota!

Now we are flying above northern Florida on our 2 hour and 11 minute flight to Newark, heading from 70° to 40°, from late spring back to late winter, and from days of relaxation and quality time with our daughter and good friends, to our regular weekly routine. It has been a very good trip: a meaningful, memorable, and fun change of pace, scenery, and experience.

Chapter 30

PENNSYLVANIA, DELAWARE, AND VIRGINIA

April 22-24, 2017

"Bill's and Cyndy's favorite sport: not tennis or golf, but rather picking up trash along roadsides, in towns, or wherever they could"

April 22: Pennsylvania and Delaware

Around 8:20 on Saturday morning, I lifted Peaches into the back of our VW Tiguan, since it's a bigger jump than she was used to when we drove the Honda CRV. We left a few minutes later and headed west on our familiar route to the Amish Country: 287 to 78 to PA 100, 113, and 30. Having done this trip over 20 times, we really have our travel time down to the minute. As we entered Route 30 at 10:50, I calculated 32 minutes to Betty Jackson's house, and sure enough, we pulled into her gravel driveway at 11:22 with 8 minutes to spare.

It was rainy and cool, so Peaches and I took only one brief walk before staying warm and dry inside the car, while Kerstin was engaged in her double sand play session inside. I scanned the news on my cell phone, read two *Dartmouth Alumni Magazines*, and also read some pages of Donald Hall's *Seasons at Eagle Pond* (1987), his moving celebration of the seasons in New Hampshire.

In mid-afternoon, we headed southeast toward Newark, Delaware on Route 741 South, avoiding the more congested Wilmington area. We arrived around 4:30 at Jan Wells' place in Dagsboro on the bay, not far from Bethany Beach. We enjoyed Jan's cocktail hour followed by baked chicken, rice, salad, and green beans—except she forgot to serve the beans. Jan is a great conversationalist, and we talked for hours about our families, politics, travel, and plans for our 50th Chatham High School reunions in 2018 and 2019.

April 23: Virginia—Remembering Uncle Bill

The unseasonably cool and damp weather persisted all day Sunday. After breakfast, we prepared some sandwiches for the road, got dressed in our formal attire, and headed south on Route 113 into Maryland's and Virginia's Eastern Shore. It felt like the South as soon as we crossed the border into Virginia and were welcomed by a big "Welcome to Dixieland" sign. We arrived at the Holiday Inn in Exmore at 12:30, expecting to find family members milling about. I told the receptionist that we were joining the Bernart family, and she replied, "They left five minutes ago." But the oldest of the five Bernarts, Will (born in 1957), soon appeared, and he took us upstairs, where we popped into several rooms, meeting his wife Cindi, children Bill and Kate, cousin Chris and Aunt Cyndy. Cyndy looked good for her age (83 in August), but she was barely responsive and did not recognize Kerstin or me. She sometimes does not even know her own children. Doug (the youngest) popped out of a room, and I greeted him with "Hi Matt"—they have a similar look and build—but he identified himself as Doug. We briefly said hello to Doug's three sons (ages about 8 to 14) and greeted Sarah and her husband Steve Barnes. Downstairs we gave a hearty greeting to the cousins representing the two other Wallace families: Lynne Ayres and John Davidson. Lynne had arrived after a two-day drive from Columbus, and John had driven down that morning from his home in Yardley, PA. Matt and his wife Beth appeared and got busy loading coolers of beer and wine into the trunk of their rented car. Matt told me, "I had two assignments getting ready for the memorial service: contact the Whites and take care of the booze."

We followed Matt to the historical Hungar's Episcopal Church in a remote location in Machipongo (formerly Bridgetown), Virginia. It was established in 1623. At 2:00 PM, family members gathered under a tent for a brief internment service, led by the senior and associate pastors. Bill's urn lay on top of a small table. The memorial service in a packed church followed. Will delivered a brief but moving and humorous eulogy, describing Bill's and Cyndy's favorite sport: not tennis or golf, but rather picking up trash along roadsides, in towns, or wherever they could. We immediately thought of Mom and her compulsion to pick up any scrap or object on the ground or floor. Will later told me that the local Virginia road commissioner had put up a big sign, acknowledging Bill's ecological efforts, but the modest man he was, he insisted that it be taken down. The goal was not fame, but rather keeping the land of the Eastern Shore beautiful.

A reception followed in the parish house. The most interesting person we met was the only African American to attend the funeral: Evelyn, the Bernarts' long-time maid. She is probably in her eighties and still feisty and full of memories about helping to raise the five Bernart children, starting in the early sixties. In addition, she somehow managed to raise five children of her own. It was touching how several people, myself included, served Evelyn some small sandwiches, desserts, and a drink after all those years of serving others. She initially said she was hungry, but ate only a few items, telling us, "I'm so busy talking, I lost my appetite!" A little later, Matt gathered some family members in a circle and presented a memento from the Cranberry Lake cottage—one that he had taken with him to Oregon and later Utah, but had now brought back east to give to Wally so it can arrive back home where it belongs. Cyndy showed a little glimmer of recognition and memory when we talked about July 4 swimming races at the community house.

Janine called from London, and we chatted with her in the car, while the reception wound down. Most of the family members returned to the hotel to get changed, but Kerstin and I headed to the historic Eastville Inn for our family dinner. We were the first to arrive, followed shortly by Matt, Beth, and the chilled refreshments. Matt is very interested in family history and recently read *Journey through the Centuries*, providing a correction about Grandpa Wallace's mining experience after graduating from Lehigh in 1913: the mine where he was searching for gold was not in Arizona, but rather near Boulder, Colorado. Matt said that he had persuaded Bill and Cyndy to both provide a specimen of their DNA for a test through the 23 and Me company, and the big surprise is that the Bernart family—which came from the Lorraine area of northeastern France in 1866—was 7.5% Ashkenazi Jew. The Ashkenazi Jews originated in the Middle Ages and populated the Rhine valleys in Germany and northern France, including Worms and Mainz.

The table was set for about 25 people. I sat next to Sarah on my right and Logan, Matt's 28-year-old son, on my left. He is pursuing his master's degree in engineering with a focus on forest products at Oregon State. Like his dad, he is very interested in family history, and he identified us as first cousins, once removed. His 30-year-old brother, Bryan, currently residing in Los Angeles, was sitting across from us. Through the delicious buffet dinner—local asparagus, crab casserole, spinach-strawberry salad, lasagna, and tiramisu for dessert—family members shared their memories of Bill and the family. When the lake cottage was mentioned as a favorite site, I told the group that I had transcribed the lake logs, which often described various young Bernarts falling into and being plucked out of the lake. Kerstin enjoyed her chats with John and Cindi.

It grew dark, and we bid farewell to our cousins and relatives, happy to have renewed old contacts and fostered new ones. On our way north on Route 13, we dropped off Lynne and John at the Holiday Inn, hoping to see them soon again at a more joyous occasion. The roads had very little traffic on a cool, showery Sunday evening, and we made it back to Jan's in about an hour and 40 minutes.

April 24: Delaware to New Jersey

We walked Peaches down to the bay before breakfast on Monday morning. The wind was whipping through the tall grasses, and it felt good when we were back inside. We had a leisurely breakfast on the couch. We were toying with the idea of walking on the Bethany Beach boardwalk or shopping at one of the outlet stores, but we stayed indoors and watched Michael Moore's latest film, *Where to Invade Next,* from late 2015. He focused on so many ideas in education, healthcare, and workers' and criminals' rights that had originated in the U.S., but had taken root in European countries and are now scoffed at here by many people. We ate a quick lunch, and then set out for home, arriving a little after 5:00.

Chapter 31

MIAMI

May 10-17, 2017

"At times we walked arm in arm, happy to be together. We looked upward and saw the Big Dipper, then outward toward the ocean"

Coral Gables, Florida—celebrating Lisa's Ph.D. from the University of Miami

Tuesday, May 16: Key Biscayne; Lisa's 30th Birthday

What a busy, wonderful, memorable week we have had with no time to record my reflections and impressions. I am sitting on the deck of our cottage at the Silver Sands Beach Resort, looking out at the swaying palm trees and the deep blue ocean. The wind is whipping steadily. Kersti is taking a late afternoon stroll on the beach. Our three beautiful children have departed: Janine is at the airport, awaiting her flight to Newark and then to London, and Lisa and Windy are getting ready for a happy hour in downtown Miami to celebrate Lisa's birthday.

We're looking back at a week in which we celebrated the achievements and lives of our children. Of course the focus was on Lisa, but it was also on all of us as a family unit, coming together at this time and place to share memories and refocus our relationships. Just before Lisa's graduation last Thursday, Eric told us that he was increasingly identifying himself as Windy and would preferred to be called Windy. By the end of our time together, we were finding this change to be more comfortable and natural. Throughout the week, the constant sea breeze kept us cool, even on hot days.

Kersti and I arrived at Newark Airport on Wednesday afternoon, May 10, courtesy of my German professor and colleague, Josh Kavaloski. He is such a kind and warm person, and I'm glad that I will be able to reciprocate by taking him to the airport on Friday the 19th for the summer with his family in Eberbach, Germany. Janine was flying in from London that same afternoon, and she popped into our line just as we were boarding our flight. She was full of enthusiasm for her new life and work in London and her upcoming beach vacation. Our flight to Miami was smooth and on time, but our experience with the U-Save car rental agency was just the opposite. The agency did not have a booth in the car rental corridor; their cars were located several miles outside the airport on an industrial back street; only one agent was serving a line of customers, who expressed their dismay as he was explaining additional fees; and when our car was finally ready, it was dripping from the hosedown it had just received and had stains all over the back seat.

We arrived at Lisa's apartment in the Kendall section of Miami around 10:30 and gave Lisa and Windy warm hugs. Janine stayed with her siblings, and Kersti and I soon drove over the Rickenbacker Causeway to our motel on Key Biscayne. When we checked in, we were given the cottage with the best view of the ocean. We walked beyond the pool to greet the ocean before finally turning out the lights around 12:30 AM.

Thursday was graduation day. Kersti and I picked up Janine and Lisa after their hair was coiffed at Ramses' salon in Coral Gables, and then drove to the university and parked near Lisa's office in the Flipse

Building, off of Route 1. The graduation took place in the basketball arena. We managed to find seats on the lower level, close to where Lisa and the doctoral candidates would be sitting. Just as the music was beginning, Windy arrived along with Anja, Nellie, and Daniel, who had flown to Miami that morning on a 6:00 flight from Newark. The procession began, and soon we identified Lisa, who saw us and waved often beneath her beaming smile. She was joined by her mentor and advisor, Daryl Greenfield. After several greetings, speeches, and a not very memorable commencement speech from a renowned Harvard economics professor and Nobel laureate, the administrators began calling the roll of graduates. When Lisa was announced, you could see Daryl and her on the big screen. She was "hooded" with a colorful sash with the distinctive Miami orange and green colors. She then shook the hand of the university president and graduate dean. We departed from the arena shortly afterwards, leaving behind a thousand or so doctoral and master's students still to be announced.

Outside in the bright, warm sunshine, we found Lisa and Daryl. There were hugs all around, and a number of Lisa's colleagues in the psychology program were there. After photos—our favorite was a shot of the entire family expressing some silliness and joy—we walked over to the student center by the large pond and picked up some salads and chow mein, which we ate outside in the cool shade.

Toward sunset, we drove to Matheson State Park, Lisa's favorite, for a very special graduation dinner for eight at the Red Fish Grill. It was about 8:45 and dark by the time we were seated, but a full moon rose above us in the sky: a good omen for Lisa's future. The dinner was delicious with numerous toasts to Lisa for all her achievements.

Friday was a "chill" day. Kersti and I took a morning swim in the warm ocean and the even warmer pool, which we always passed on the way back to our cottage. We attended a pool party, hosted by Lisa's colleague Ruth in Coral Gables, followed by dinner.

Saturday was the day of Lisa's graduation party at Matheson "Hammock" Park in Coral Gables. That morning, we shopped at Trader Joe's, Target, and Publix and then unloaded everything at Lisa's nearby apartment. We went into action, preparing a Greek salad (me), noodle pesto salad (Janine), and German potato salad (Windy). We chilled the champagne and beer, and then loaded up Lisa's Jetta and our rental Kia and headed to Matheson around 3:30 to set up for our 4:00 start. At first, the wind was blowing so hard, we thought everything might blow away, but it eventually died down, and we enjoyed a beautiful, comfortable late spring evening. Lisa was so happy to bring together the four groups of people who were most special to her and influential in her life and work: her family, her psychology colleagues (Ruth, Mark, Mike, Ashley, Emily, and Brooke), her yoga people (Joan, Jeanette, and their spouses), and her two Brazilian suitors, Marcello and Marcio. Her friends were so gracious and fond of Lisa. She jumped up on the table to thank everyone followed by toasts from Kersti and me. I recalled when Lisa joined us 30 years ago and collaborated with her Mommy on her first performance—demonstrating how to wash a baby girl!

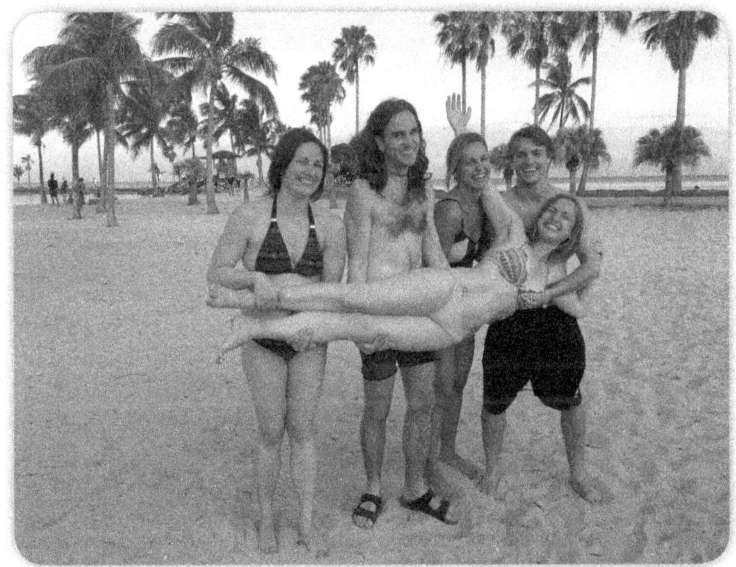

Coral Gables, Florida—more celebrating at Matheson Hammock State Park

Wednesday, May 17: Miami Airport

Our trip to the airport this morning in the early light of day was as quick and smooth as car rental adventure last Wednesday evening was aggravating. I'm sitting at our United gate, and boarding is not for another hour and a half.

The kids returned with us to Silver Sands Saturday after Lisa's party to begin their own beach vacation. Sunday was a relaxing beach day, and we all preferred the Key Biscayne Beach to other options. The resort came alive on Saturday and Sunday with loud Latino music. Sunday was Mother's Day, and after presenting Kersti with my "Top 10 Tips for Mother's Day and Every Day," I rented an umbrella and two lounge chairs, which we pulled up close to the water to muffle the loud Latino music. One downpour caught Kersti on the beach, but later the day turned brighter. Our Cuban attendant collected the beachware a little after 4:00, but by then we had discovered our shady "nook" and nestled there until dinnertime. We ate dinner on the deck—a big salad and heated-up pesto salad with arugula.

Monday featured three highlights, including Lisa's "transition" ceremony in a reception room at the Miami athletic center and a special Mother's Day/graduation dinner. The ceremony was a celebration of the achievements of Psychology Department faculty members and graduate students, especially those who were concluding their time in Miami. Lisa was recognized as one of three students who had presented a talk based on their dissertations. Later she was acknowledged for her contributions to the department and research. Daryl was traveling, so one of her committee members, Rebecca, read a letter from Daryl. Rebecca is a young, shy, nervous professor, and the letter was not one of Daryl's most memorable, but it was still a nice tribute to Lisa as a person and researcher of the highest quality. We enjoyed chatting with several of Lisa's colleagues and faculty members at the reception.

The next stop was the Rusty Pelican, an upscale restaurant on Virginia Key, just across the bridge from the mainland. Lisa reserved a table outside with a magnificent view of the skyline of downtown Miami. It felt as if we were on a cruise with a constant spectacular view. Lisa's roommate, colleague, and good friend Casey joined us after a flight from San Francisco, where she had attended an autism conference. Everyone received a toast: Lisa for her Ph.D. and birthday, Casey for her year-long internship at Duke, Kersti for Mother's Day, Janine for her London experience, Windy for completing his Democracy Now! application, and me for my family support. The lowlight of the evening was definitely the bacon cheesecake dessert—yes, bacon. Lisa blew out the candle and then we all bravely tasted the concoction. Even the waiter admitted that the chef had made a mistake.

The third highlight, perhaps the best of all, was our walk on the beach at Key Biscayne. At times we walked arm in arm, happy to be together. We looked upward and saw the Big Dipper, then outward toward the ocean. I mentioned that this was the same coast and ocean where Kersti and I had met 35 years ago next Tuesday, the 23rd.

Tuesday was another day of transition. Lisa turned 30, and she was thrilled and moved to receive her Snapfish album, capturing her story from birth to present through photos showing her spunk, creativity, curiosity, and joy of living. We piled into our car and drove about 10 miles to the Bill Baggs State Park at the southern tip of Key Biscayne. We continued the birthday celebration at the Lighthouse Restaurant with paella, avocado salad, black bean soup, and pineapple. After lunch, we strolled over to the lighthouse, originally built in 1825 and restored in recent years. Nearby was the restored gatekeeper's cottage, where a park ranger took what will probably be our 2017 family Christmas photo with the lighthouse rising in back of us. Back at our car, an elderly couple asked if we spoke English, and it turned out they were from Montreal. We had a spirited conversation about the joy of traveling, and Windy and Kersti both carried on part of the exchange in French.

We returned to our beach for a final gathering in the nook and a family swim. We frolicked as in years past, and I boosted the three girls up on my shoulders. But time was running out. We all showered, the kids packed their bags, and then it was time to say goodbye. Kersti, Lisa, and I will see Janine in London in July; I will see Lisa when I return to Miami on June 28, and she will see Windy during her visit; but we're not sure when Windy and Janine will see each other the next time. Kersti and I then drove to the airport and dropped off Janine for her flight to Newark and connecting flight to London.

Our cottage seemed empty when we returned. The pool and the compound were also empty. Our mutual feeling was that it was now our time to go after this marvelous, celebratory week. I prepared a big salad, and we hard boiled our four remaining eggs and had our last meal on the deck. The wind was blowing hard, and we could see the white caps on the ocean waves. After dinner, we walked on the beach all the way to Crandon State Park. We waded out into the ocean on several sandbars, feeling part of the elements as we looked back to shore. It was almost dark when we returned to our resort, rinsed our feet, and dipped them into the pool for the last time.

Chapter 32

NEW HAMPSHIRE

May 27-30, 2017

"Peaches was amazing—never a complaint about spending the cool nights in the car and always eager to see us in the morning"

"We knew it was time to go. We will return to New Hampshire for visits in the future, but it is not the right time or place to settle"

Monday, May 29: Memorial Day: Durham

Our long weekend in New Hampshire is drawing to a close on this damp, raw Memorial Day evening. I am sitting on the couch in our comfortable, expertly furnished Airbnb apartment just a two-minute walk from the University of New Hampshire campus. We just returned from campus, where we fed and walked Peaches and then closed the rear door so she can settle in for her final cool night in the car.

We drove north on Saturday on a glorious spring day. Google maps advised us to take the Merritt Parkway (Route 15) up to Hartford, but the old-fashioned, two-lane highway was crowded with holiday travelers, and the trip took longer than anticipated. We arrived in Durham around 3:30 PM, took our first walk on campus along Academic Way, and then drove to Exeter to pick up Cordelia on the way to Pete's house in Rye. Approaching his home in the Liberty Common development, we saw a dumpster in his driveway, plenty of tools and equipment, his front door boarded up, and his house wrapped in new insulation. He has embarked on a major three-phase renovation project, which may cost upwards to $200,000 and include new windows, bathrooms, kitchen, refurbishings of his deck and tool shed, and the felling of a 100-foot pine tree and several maples in back. Pete extended his hearty welcome and quickly fired up the grill and prepared some delicious salmon steaks with rice, broccoli, and salad. Cordelia contributed four small apple pies that she had baked that afternoon. After dinner, we took a brief walk around the neighborhood and then reversed our earlier excursion, dropping Cordelia off in Exeter before taking 108 North directly to Durham.

The beautiful weather continued on Sunday morning. Kersti and I had planned this trip in part to get a feel for the area and townhouse and condo possibilities. We were particularly curious about the expansive Great Bay between Durham and Portsmouth. So we drove along Durham Point Road toward Newmarket, catching occasional glimpses of some magnificent homes whose backyards were the bay, but we were disappointed that the bay close to the shore was murky and full of seagrass, perhaps because of coastal tides. The sun was still shining when we drove into Newmarket, parked, donned our baseball caps, and walked along the Lamprey River. We crossed a wooden bridge with the raging river and waterfall gushing below. A former mill town, Newmarket has converted most of its mills to modern-day apartments and condos. On a small patch of land between the parking lot and riverbank, several adults were tending to their late spring gardens. The town has done a marvelous job, both renovating its old buildings while maintaining its historical, early industrial feel, but we agreed Newmarket was not a place that we could see ourselves settling.

We headed over to Route 4, on the northern side of Great Bay, and traveled east toward Portsmouth. We took Exit 3 and then found our way to the Great Bay National Wildlife Refuge. Our first hike took us on a winding boardwalk, through the woods and over wetlands that would have been impossible to traverse without the boardwalk. We heard one little boy excitedly announce that he was hoping to see crocodiles and snakes! The only wildlife we saw was a solitary turtle, basking on a large branch that was stuck in the water. Even with the steady sound of our feet tromping on the wood, we felt immersed in the environment. Our second trail—the William Furber Ferry Way Trail—had the opposite effect. To approach it, we walked for about a quarter mile along an old, rusted, barb-wired fence, which had been built in 1951 to protect a weapons storage area as part of Pease Air Force Base. It remained operational until 1991, and the following year a coalition of local citizens and environmental organizations mobilized an initiative to convert the base to a wildlife refuge. At the end of the long fence, we followed a grassy path for a while, but when the solid ground became muddy, we turned back.

Returning to Route 4 west, we traveled just a mile or so to Exit 4 for Newington Village. We briefly visited the historic old town, which consisted of a meetinghouse (1712; the oldest in New Hampshire), parsonage (1725), town hall (1872; it housed a schoolhouse on the bottom floor and meeting room on the supper floor), library (1892), and stone school (1922). We paused to read a plaque, acknowledging the oldest town forest in the U.S., dating from 1710.

We returned to Exeter, met Cordelia, and walked into town for a tasty lunch at the Green Bean on Water Street. Outside the window of the restaurant, we watched and listened to the pulsating waters of the Squamscott Falls and River. We then headed east to Rye Beach. The day had turned cloudy and cool, and the ocean breeze was whipping up, so Cordelia retreated to the car along with Peaches, since dogs are banned on the beach from 9:00 AM to 7:00 PM from Memorial Day to Labor Day. The tide was high, and the beach was narrow and not yet tidied from months of vegetative gifts from the sea. We noticed a dead seagull partially buried in the sand. We later drove to Pete's house, less than two miles from the beach, for snacks, drinks, and dinner—grilled chicken breast, Brussels sprouts, mashed potatoes, mashed butternut squash, and fresh strawberries and quarter portions of Cordelia's remaining mini-apple pie from the previous night.

The weather forecast for Memorial Day was not promising, and indeed the day dawned raw and damp, though the promised rain was mostly mist throughout the morning. After breakfast, we walked into town and briefly joined the crowd assembled for the Memorial Day parade and tributes. We then walked along Main Street past the Admissions Office, where we had huddled with Windy and other prospective students and parents five years ago in February in the pouring rain. We stopped by the impressive, spacious student center and studied Hood Hall, home of the career services office, a building in need of significant external renovation. We picked up some salad greens and veggie burgers at the local Hannaford supermarket and had lunch in our apartment.

Cordelia was occupied a good part of the day with her new homemaker and aide, Toni, and thus we did not arrive in Exeter until 3:30 PM. We brought along a store-bought carrot cake and sat at Pete's kitchen table, overlooking his backyard and pool, and enjoyed a traditional German *Kaffee und Kuchen* on this very American holiday. Cordelia decided not to stay at Pete's for dinner, so we bid farewell to him, shuttled Cordelia back to Exeter one final time, and returned to Durham in the light rain for our final dinner of salad, veggie burger, and a rice-tofu-collard heat up that we had brought from home.

Postscript: Wednesday, May 31

We woke up with the first light of day around 4:30 on Tuesday morning, and decided to make an earlier than anticipated departure. We drove a short block to Academic Way to feed and walk Peaches, which we had done each morning of our stay. Peaches was amazing—never a complaint about spending the cool nights in the car and always eager to see us in the morning. The campus was damp and lush and showing a little more life with the Memorial Day weekend behind us. We packed the car and headed east on Route 4 around 7:30 to our favorite beach in Rye off of Wallis Road. It was an early morning dog fest with maybe 20 dogs, many of them unleashed. It was low tide, and we waded out some distance to the edge of the tiny waves. We knew it was time to go. We will return to New Hampshire for visits in the future, but it is not the right time or place to settle.

We had a smooth trip home on our regular 95-495-295-20 (instead of 90)-84-684-287 route, arriving back in showery Morristown by 2:30 PM.

Chapter 33

ROADTRIP: MIAMI TO MORRISTOWN

June 28-30, 2017

"The minutes, miles, and songs kept on rolling along"

Saturday, July 1

On Wednesday, June 28, a little after 9:30 AM, I wrote to the fam on What's App: "I cannot believe what I just did!"

Let me start this travelogue at the beginning, that morning around 4:30 AM, when I woke up, eager to embark on my trip to Miami to help Lisa wrap up her five-year experience in Miami. I beat the alarm by an hour. Daniel, operating the Schindler shuttle, ran into some delays on 287 from a dump truck spill, but after he picked me up, it was smooth sailing to the airport in time for my 8:41 AM flight. For some reason, I couldn't check in, so I asked a United attendant for help. She tried, but couldn't check me in, so she directed me to customer assistance. The lady took one look at the printout and pointed to the time: "It's 8:41 PM!" Ever since I booked the flight in mid-May, I had fixed in my mind an arrival just past noon and a full afternoon and evening to help Lisa sort and pack everything.

But it was not to be. Fortunately, Daniel was not too far from the airport, and he swung back to pick me up. There was a serious accident and five-mile backup on 78, so we opted for 22 and the Springfield exit. It was a slow go, but I arrived home with my 12-hour delay staring me in the face.

Everyone was so accommodating and understanding. Lis was, of course, sad that I was delayed, but forged ahead with her many tasks. Her friend Marcio pitched in to help with the packing. And Daniel was happy to reappear at 6:50 PM to take me back to the airport. I referenced the classic Bill Murray film, "Groundhog Day," as we pulled out of the driveway onto Beechwood Drive.

Everything went smoothly this time. I was in the very last row of the plane, but had a nice chat with a young mom from New Jersey and her adorable three-year-old bilingual son, Danny. I told her that I remembered traveling with my daughters and son when they were Danny's age, but now they were adults. In fact, the daughter whom I was visiting had grown up to specialize in early childhood development and had just completed her Ph.D. with a focus on the cognitive benefits of bilingualism. She was very appreciative and surely will heed my encouragement and advice to keep fostering both languages in her son.

We were scheduled to arrive at 11:54 PM, but the plane pulled up to the gate 20 minutes early, and thus I popped my head into Lisa's passenger window at 11:56, just in time to savor the turn of the clock to midnight and the beginning of my 67th birthday. We sped through the nearly empty roadways of Miami and arrived at Lisa's apartment. She had done a tremendous amount of prep work, and we accomplished a few more things before retiring for a short night.

In the morning, I was up at my regular 6:30 AM time and began quietly organizing and packing some items. Lisa got up around 8:00 and produced three boiled eggs—we split the third one. As the day heated up outside, we made steady progress, packing, discarding stuff, cleaning out the fridge, making multiple trips to the dumpster, sweeping, tightly packing the car, assembling the bike rack, loading the bike onto the car, and even making two delicious, frosty, fruity smoothies. Around 9:30, Lis confidently announced that we might be able to get away by 11:15 or 11:30. We didn't quite make it by that time, but hot, sweaty, satisfied, and eager to begin our journey, we managed to say goodbye to her apartment and pull out of her driveway around 12:30. It took one more hour to find the graduate administrative building on the sprawling campus, so Lisa could drop off her official Ph.D. paperwork. We were northward bound around 1:30, and I slipped the first of my 10 "Dad's mixes," gifts from Windy in recent years. First up and appropriate as we began our journey north was Simon and Garfunkel's "American Tune."

We almost left behind Lisa's ailing orchid, but found a tight space for it up front close to the emergency brake.

To pass the time, we also resurrected our state license plates game. Lis rambled off the 50 states from the song she learned at Torey J; I scribbled down the state abbreviations on the back of a Geico envelope; and we jumped right in. The object of the game was to come closest to the number of state plates that we would see over the next two days. We recorded our original estimates at the beginning of the trip and our revised estimates at the beginning of day two. Here are the results:

	Dad's Estimate	**Lisa's Estimate**	**Actual No.**	**Winner**
Day 1	32	30	34	Dad
Day 2	37	36	34	Lis

So we were both winners: I came closer with my original estimate, and Lisa came closer with her revised estimate. The most unexpected state that we saw was Wyoming. The most expected state that we didn't see was Vermont.

Lisa took the first long leg, up the entire east coast of Florida, and kept going until somewhere in Georgia. I then took over. Mile after mile, we chatted, played my CDs and Lisa's, and did not observe any scenic beauties or wonders. It could have been "Anywhere USA." Our original goal was to drive about 11 or 12 hours to Raleigh, spend the night there, and visit with cousins Sarah and Chris and Aunt Cyndy the next day. But my late arrival in Miami and our resulting later-than-hoped-for departure made a 1:30 or 2:00 AM arrival in Raleigh an overly ambitious goal. We made it to the nondescript town of Florence, South Carolina, attracted by the $1.79 gas sign, and spent the night there. Lisa earlier had treated me to a birthday lunch of a foot-long Black Forest ham and cheese Subway sandwich. I ate six inches in the car for lunch and the remaining six outside at a McDonald's along with Lisa's rice and kale leftover. Clouds were beginning to swirl, and we were fortunate that a heavy downpour did not pelt us until we were back on the road.

I woke up again early on Friday morning and texted Sarah that we had not made it to Raleigh and would not have time to visit. Besides, Chris and she were both working, and Cyndy doesn't remember who we are. Lis treated me to a Subway ham and cheese flat bread breakfast sandwich and herself to a latte from a Starbucks that was located in a nearby hospital. A little after 9:00 AM, we were back on 95 North, heading to Durham for a rendezvous with Lis' dear friend and roommate, Casey. She will be interning for the coming academic year at Duke, counseling autistic-spectrum children from ages 2 to 18. It was hot and muggy when we pulled up in front of the cute Cape Cod-style house that she is renting with two other young professionals. Casey drove us to the West Campus, the heart of the university. It was my visit ever to Duke. Lis and I stood in front of the famous Duke chapel, and Casey snapped a picture of us, after stepping into a small mud hole covered by grass. We drove back to her neighborhood and ate a tasty brunch at Monuts, famous for its homemade donuts. I ate the quiche and salad, the latter of which was particularly good.

Visiting Casey in her new home and bidding her farewell were milestones for Lis. They began the program together nearly five years ago and shared so much of their lives during the past year as roommates. Seeing Casey in a new place will help Lis envision and carry out her own transition in early August in Chicago. Saying goodbye to Casey was bidding farewell to the program, city, and vibe that was Miami.

We began our final leg a little past 1:00 PM with Lis back behind the wheel. We alternated CDs—she admitted to liking about half my songs, whereas my percentage of likes was much less, but it didn't matter. The minutes, miles, and songs kept on rolling along. Each time we passed a border and glimpsed a new state welcome sign—eight times in all—we fist bumped. Every state was a long journey in its own right until we reached Maryland, Delaware, and New Jersey, which gave us confidence that the end of our journey was in sight.

We snacked a bit, but did not stop for dinner. I drove all the way from the Maryland border to Beechwood Drive. By the time we passed into New Jersey, it was dark and approaching 9:00. But we were in the home stretch. I have always preferred 295 to the Turnpike, and we kept a steady pace in between showers. From 295, we picked up 31 and then 202 north, and it felt like we were gliding through the darkness on our way home. We pulled into our driveway at 11:10 PM. The odometer read 1366 miles (2203 km). We took the bike off the rack for safekeeping in the garage, but left most things in the car overnight. We would wait until the morning to bring everything inside, the things that were part of Lisa's life in Miami, now in a holding pattern in New Jersey, and soon to head west to her new life in Chicago.

Chapter 34

GERMANY AND ENGLAND

July 6 – August 7, 2017

"Then Kersti noticed something white between several rocks at the edge of the water: a beautiful, pure white, swan feather. Then she found another and another until she had a collection of five—one for each member of our family"

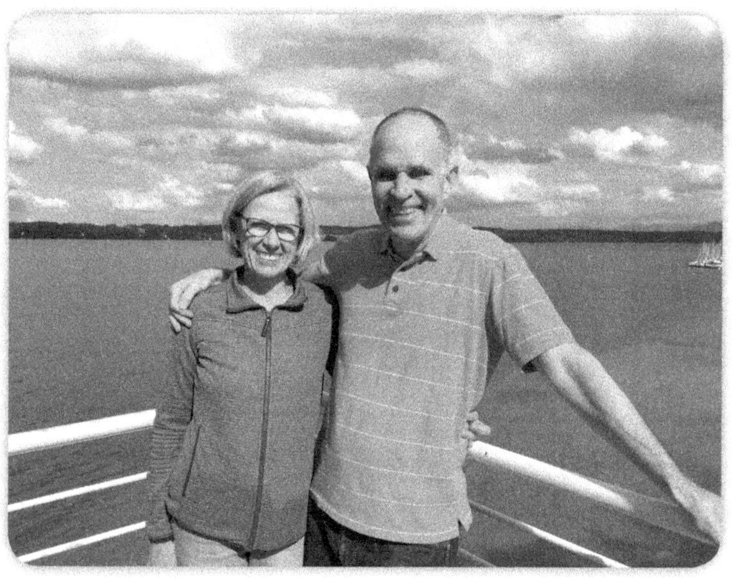

Bernried, Germany—Buchheim Museum of Phantasie

Tuesday, July 11: Solln

Our days in Solln, a quiet suburb with narrow, tree-lined streets that is part of greater Munich, have taken on a comfortable, familiar rhythm. We are enjoying our small, clean, efficient apartment at 15 Festingstrasse, but we are spending most days and eating most meals outside. Each day brings sunshine, some clouds, some passing showers, and brightening skies, and the evenings are cool enough to pull up our comforters. Sometimes my comforter falls off our narrow bed in the night. The pace of Solln is relaxed, even a bit slow, but this gives us a real break from our busy lives at home.

Lisa dropped me at Newark Airport around 3:30 PM on Thursday, July 6. It was the conclusion of our full week together, beginning with my arrival in Miami at the stroke of midnight on my birthday. It was a very special time for us. My United flight to Munich was on time, and I squeezed four films into my short night: "Alone in Berlin" (based on a true story of an older couple that lost their only son in World War II and then tried to undermine the Nazis by posting anti-Nazi messages around the city), "Allied" (another World War II drama starring Brad Pitt ad Marion Cotillard, portraying both a loving wife and a German double agent), "Hidden Figures" (the inspiring true story of the three African-American women who made major contributions to the U.S. space achievements in the 1960s), and "Catching Rye" (a fictional account of two teenagers in search of J.D. Salinger at his home in New Hampshire).

I began the final leg of my journey to Solln by taking the S-Bahn train to the *Hauptbanhof* and then switching to the Wolfratshausen (end stop) train. Solln was the 7th stop, and I stepped out into the bright sunshine at the small station—just two rail lines. There were only two ways to go, and of course, I ignored Kersti's instruction to head toward the "A" sign. I walked up the steps, looking for Sollner Strasse, and when I saw it, I turned left, when I should have continued straight to Diefenbachstrasse. After about 10 minutes, I sensed that I might be on the wrong track, so I asked a nice young man if I was heading toward Diefenbachstrasse. He told me to walk two more blocks and then turn right on Melchiorstrasse. I did just that, but a few minutes later, he pulled up in his car and offered to take me the rest of the way. It was a bit of a ride, so I'm glad he did. We pulled up to the apartment on Festingstrasse just before 10:00.

Kersti was at her sandplay session, about a 10-minute bike ride away, so I sat there on the front step and happily watched the life of this small, typical German suburban town. There was the lady in the flower shop (in actuality, a large, permanent tent) directly across the street. She swept the sidewalk, chatted with customers, and prepared their bouquets. Next door was a fresh produce market, and next to that a shop selling honey and specialty items. Young couples with children in strollers passed by, as did elderly folks, walking gingerly. Young and old Sollners pedaled by on their bikes. The bell of the nearby church, whose *Ziebelturm* (onion tower) I could see above the produce market, announced every quarter hour. A couple of times, I thought I saw a blonde lady on a bike, but it was not Kersti. Finally, around 11:15, I saw her round the corner, and I raced out to the sidewalk to give her a big hug and kiss.

After a light lunch, we headed out on our first of many bike excursions, most of which were 20 kilometers or more. On that Friday afternoon, we rode through the fields and forests of the Fursteriederwald. It was warm and muggy riding through the wheat and cornfields, but the forest was cool and refreshing.

On Saturday, we took our first ride along the Isar, which flows through Munich. We wound our way through the back streets of Solln and arrived at a long, straight, paved pathway down to the Isar, perhaps two kilometers long. The Isar consists of the fairly wide river and a parallel canal. The canal was filled with revelers, many floating along the fairly swift current on log rafts, which had been assembled for the occasion. The patrons were drinking beer, listening to Bavarian country music, dancing, and waving wildly. At several junctures along the canal, there was a mini-waterfall that the raft easily traversed to the great delights of the occupants. We probably saw 10 rafts make their way along the canal.

We rode along the canal path to the next town of Pullach. We paused again to watch some young teens, both boys and girls, jump off a fairly high walk bridge. They then had to swim quickly to the edge because of the strong current.

On the way back, we felt our first drops of rain, and then the torrents began to fall. We waited for about 15 minutes under an evergreen canopy, before venturing back onto the bike path. It was still raining, but soon stopped. We were not at all soaked by the time we returned to our apartment. For dinner, we enjoyed a big fresh salad that we had bought at the produce market that morning.

On Sunday, we explored the other side of the river. We took the same bike path to the Isar, but headed north toward Marienkirche at the center of Munich, intrigued by the sign that it was only 5.3 km away. The path wound along the highway, on occasions through a wooded area, but when we arrived at a busy city intersection, we decided to turn back. Again, we headed south along the Isar, but this time on the east side. This was a much more scenic route than Saturday's. We had good views of the river, rocky and shallow in most places but with a steady current. Most of the path was shaded by trees, so we stayed cool. We picnicked by the river before heading back. We paused for two bottles of *Apfelscharle* (apple seltzer) at one of the local *Biergartens*. That evening, we walked to the Indian restaurant, Siddhartha, and enjoyed lentil and eggplant- mixed vegetable dishes.

On Monday, we returned to the Isar for the third straight day, retracing our route from Saturday along the canal. There were far fewer people on their bikes and sunbathing by the canal than during the busy summer weekend. We decided to curtail this outing, knowing that we had a cross-city bus excursion in the middle of the afternoon. We took two buses to the law office of Kersti's long-time friend, Gina Grundlach, from Bingen. Gina welcomed us warmly, and she and I realized that we had not seen each other for over 30 years. She drove us to her home of 13 years, a western suburb of Munich called Gröbenzell. We toured her three-story townhouse, met her daughter Laura, and marveled at her exotic, semi-tropical backyard garden with two small pools. We drove into town and had dinner at a local *Biergarten*. Gina and Kersti enjoyed reminiscing about their days at the Hildegarde Schule and stories about our six children. Then Gina turned over the keys of her black Peugot to us, generously offering for us to use her car for the next 10 days. It was dark by the time we pulled into an empty spot directly in front of our apartment complex.

With our newfound freedom, we hit the road this morning, driving southwest to the Starnberger See. It is a long, thin lake—Germany's 5th largest though only 12-and-a-half miles long—just 20 minutes from

Solln via the Autobahn. Gina had recommended that we stop in Percha, close to the northern tip on the eastern side of the lake. We drove right through the town, not yet catching a glimpse of the lake. But then we saw it. We turned right, drove down a slight hill, and parked on a narrow street in view of the lake. We immediately found a foot and bicycle path that wound along the lake, through wooded parts, short stone beaches, grassy fields, some boarded up cottages on the left and some magnificent homes on the hill to the right. We retraced our steps, returning to the car to pick up our backpack with our sandwiches. A short distance from the car, we found a secluded beach with lapping waves and some big rocks that made fairly comfortable seats. Then Kersti noticed something white between several rocks at the edge of the water: a beautiful, pure white, swan feather. Then she found another and another until she had a collection of five—one for each member of our family. Later on our walk back to the open public space, she found one more on the wooded part of the path. We wondered how it got there—perhaps dropped magically from the sky.

This evening, we rode our bikes back to the fields where we had biked on Friday afternoon. We crisscrossed the fields, riding along narrow footpaths, passing by walkers and joggers who nicely stepped aside onto the grass for us to pass. We smelled the fresh hay. We looked west across the fields to the setting sun. Then it began to rain, lightly at first, then heavier as we sped our way through the streets of Solln and back to our apartment when it was nearly dark. I hear the pitter patter of the rain and feel the cool night air as I write this.

Thursday, July 13: Solln

Yesterday, we traveled to the *Hauptbahnhof* in the center of Munich via the S-Bahn and then took the tram on a westward route to the Botanical Garden stop. We visited the Klinikum Dritter Orden, a large medical and rehabilitation complex. Our destination was the Franziskuskappelle, the small, unadorned chapel on the second floor where the artist and Kersti's friend, Erich Horndasch, had painted a beautiful backdrop to the pulpit some years ago. Painting a large rectangular panel, he depicted the ancient city of Jerusalem in dark blue and three dark red panels, including Christ on the cross, attended by Mary, and St. Francis caring for the birds and animals. We sat in the back row, quietly thinking, meditating, and praying for our family, our children, and the two unborns we lost in 1984 ad 1990. We dedicated five candles to them.

After lunch on the clinic grounds, we walked across the street to the Munich Botanical Garden. The day was warming up, and it was more pleasant when the roving clouds covered the sun. We walked into the heart of the garden, a large area in the English garden style with may different varieties of perennials and annuals, planted closely together and offering a feast of colors and textures. The flowers swayed in the wind. Later we walked through several landscapes, including an alpine setting, a tropical setting, and German woods. In the middle of our self-guided tour, we paused on a bench and had a good chat with Eric, who decided to stay in the U.S. rather than join us in Germany. Inside the great hall, we stepped into several special indoor biospheres, including a desert, the tropics (so muggy, it was hard to breathe), Africa, and South America.

Back in Solln, we ate dinner at a local *Döner*/kebab place close to the train station. After dinner, as it was growing dark, we decided to take one more walk around our neighborhood. We had an umbrella, because it had begun to drizzle, but then the skies opened up and pelted us with rain. We hurried back past the church and into our cozy apartment room for the night.

Saturday, July 15: Solln

It was chilly and damp this morning, as we walked our half block to the Tengelmann food stores (two small, nearby facilities rather than a larger one) and the local vegetable stand. The day did not hold a lot of promise. But we prepared our sandwiches and headed out in Gina's car to the Starnbarger See. This time, we drove along the western coast through Starnberg to the mid-sized town of Tutzing. We found a free parking lot just beyond the town, and this led to a beautiful path that wound along the lake with numerous benches—we probably sat in about five of them—and pretty views, looking north and south. The day turned warmer, and the sun alternated with the passing clouds. As we were eating lunch, three swans—a father, mother, and probably their child—swam into our view and paddled closer to shore. Were they the same swans that had greeted us and left us such precious treasures a few days ago? We strolled southward along the path, and they appeared to go with us. We paused at another bench in the shade, and amazingly they bent and coiled their necks into a compact position, and all three took a brief afternoon snooze. Then two of them awoke, spread their wings, and flew away, gliding majestically and low over the water.

We decided to drive around the entire lake, and thus we headed south toward Bernried. We noticed a sign for the Buchheim Museum of Phantasie with two large orange wooden giraffe-like figures standing in front. We pulled into the parking lot and then walked along a winding path before we stood at the crest of a hill, overlooking a modern, building-block-like structure with the lake stretching beyond. We immediately noticed several "fantastic" objects: a colorful minibus with dummies at the wheel, and a colorful play helicopter that reminded me of the Budgie story that I used to read to the kids. Inside the museum, we discovered room after room of creative artwork, covering a wide range of media: expressionist paintings from Max Ernst, Max Beckmann, and Lothar Buchheim himself; an interactive kids' art room with circus artifacts; a mock cafe with weird characters seated at tables; and perhaps best of all, the room with the large model of a castle with perhaps 30 or more intricately decorated and detailed rooms, a lifelong creation of the American artist, Herbert Scherreiks (1930-2016), who returned to Germany and lived most of his life there after the war. We were fascinated by Buchheim's creativity, artistry, and creativity from his painting to his sculptures to his collection of African art to his colorful "pip-pap" posters to his novels, which included "Das Boot," which became a major motion picture. Born in 1918, he served in the German marines in World War II on a U-boat and died in Starnberg in

2007. The museum dedicated to his life, art, and German expressionism opened in 2001, and by 2015 over 1.5 million people had visited.

By late afternoon, we completed our drive around the lake, stopping for a casual lakeside dinner at the outdoor cafe in Kempfenhausen, where we had a drink on Wednesday. The water was glistening and the air was fresh and cool as we wrapped up a special day of nature, art, and their interplay.

Wednesday, July 19: Solln

Our stretch of warm, sunny days and cool nights continued through the weekend and early the next week. On Sunday, we took our longest *Ausflug* (excursion) to date, driving south past the Starnberger See about 60 kilometers to Kochelsee. It's a smaller lake than Starnberger See, but more dramatic with steep mountains rising up around half the lake. Our primary destination was the Franz Marc Museum. He was one of the leading German expressionist painters in the first the first 16 years of the new century, a founding member of the *Die Brucke* (The Bridge), a group of painters who assumed the role of bridging the art and culture of the 19th and 20th centuries. He was also a member of the "Blue Group." His paintings are distinctive for their brilliant colors, expressionist shapes and angles, reflections on art and nature, and his appreciation of animals and their free, natural instincts, especially horses. Born in Munich in 1880, he was drafted into the German army and nearly survived the war when in 1916 the government issued an exemption from service for painters and other creative artists. But it came too late: he died with so many others at the Battle of Verdun in France. It was a tragic loss for the German and worldwide artist communities.

We had lunch outdoors at the museum cafe, high above the lake with a view of the nearby mountains. Kersti had an Asian salad with chicken, and I had a big, delicious slice of *Apfelkuchen* accompanied by a mound of fresh cream. We descended the pathway and crossed the street to pick up the boat tour of the Kochelsee. We had to wait for over an hour, but found a bench in the shade close to the lake. As we were now accustomed, a number of swans swam over to us, looking for food bits. With the long wait, I walked back to the car to fetch a bottle of water. Just as I returned, a gust of wind swept away a sandwich bag. Kersti exclaimed, "Get the bag," and I lunged for it, tripping over a small tree stump that I had not seen. I grabbed the bag, but in so doing, I scraped the shin of my lower right leg, and it was dirty and bleeding. Kerstin cleaned my wound with water and a paper towel, and I was able to proceed with the boat tour. It was the regularly scheduled boat, making its way around the lake with six or seven stops. Passengers got on and off at each stop. Seats were scarce, so I sat downstairs at first, but the joined Kersti on the upper deck for a better view of the mountains, forests, marshes, fields, and small towns that decorated the shorelines. On the way home, we considered exiting the Autobahn at Seeshaupt and again driving up the eastern side of Starnberger See on the coastal route, but we headed right back to Solln on the Autobahn. It felt good to come back into our apartment and eat a home-cooked meal and salad.

Monday was a leisurely day of local activity. We shopped at the nearby Tengelman and the vegetable stand in the morning. Kersti had her Monday session with "Frau" in the afternoon, and despite my leg injury, I was mobile and surprised Kersti by waiting for her on the bench at the corner of Whistlerweg ad Melchiorstrasse. After dinner, we took a wonderful bike ride through the Furstenreid Forest at our favorite time of the day, discovering new roads and paths through the deep, dark woods comprised of thousands of spindly pine trees. I couldn't help but recite the final lines of Frost's "Stopping by Woods on a Snowy Evening":

> The woods are lovely, dark and deep
> But I have promises to keep
> And miles to go before I sleep
> And miles to go before I sleep

On Tuesday, we returned to several familiar locations at Starnberger See for a picnic and an afternoon of swimming, reading, and relaxation.

The water was clear and cool, especially after we waded beyond the shallow, rocky area, which we traversed gingerly. We swarm for a short time, but soon returned to the lawn where we had set up our towel and yoga mat. Later in the afternoon, we sat for a short time at the rocky spot where Kersti had collected all the swan feathers; but no swans or feathers were visible this day. We concluded the afternoon with a walk—as it turned out a hike up a steep, winding road and through the dark woods—to the neighboring town of Berg in search of the *Votivchapelle,* a monument to (mad) Konig Ludwig II, who drowned in the lake along with his doctor close to the site of the chapel in 1886 at the age of 41. The chapel was built by his mother and opened on June 13, 1900—14 years to the day after his death.

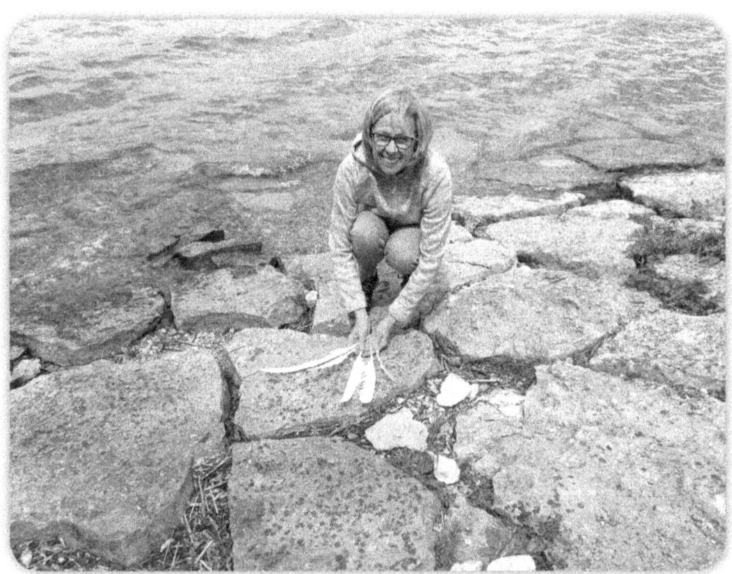

Starnbergersee, Perch, Germany

Monday, July 24: Solln and Bad Reichenhal

We are back in Solln on a cool, damp Monday morning after our long weekend with Omi and Lisa in Bad Reichenhall. Our four days and three nights there were a time of reconnection, recollection, and previewing the future. The days were mostly sunny and comfortable, and the occasional downpours and showers always gave way to clearing skies.

Kersti and I departed from Solln around 10:00 AM and took the Autobahn most of the way toward Salzburg. We encountered a number of *Staus* (traffic jams) as part of the wave of southbound summer vacationers, but we arrived just as Omi was about to sit down for lunch. We initially noticed her green handbag on a table outside the Alipina Kurhotel; she had forgotten it there when she went inside. We joined her for lunch, munching on the sandwiches and veggies we had prepared that morning. After lunch, we settled into our room in the hotel annex. It was a comfortable room with a balcony full of geraniums and views of the steep mountains surrounding Bad Reichenhall. Between the double doors, the old-fashioned locks, old-style sitting chairs, and later the common sitting room and dining hall, we felt we had arrived at a cure resort in the late 19th century.

Around 4:00 PM, we headed to the nearby Austrian border and the short drive to Salzburg Airport to pick up Lisa, who was flying in from London via Dusseldorf. I dropped Omi and Kersti at the small terminal, filled up the tank, and then waited in the free parking area. The day was growing dark and ominous. Fortunately, Lisa's German Wings plane arrived at its rescheduled time, and I was able to watch it make a long, slow turn past the mountains and into the valley carved by the Inn River over the millennia. It arrived just before we were pounded by a deluge. The rain was so strong and the windshield so fogged up that I had to pull over until the rain subsided. We returned to our hotel, happy to have Lis in our midst as she transitioned from London and Scotland to a few days in Germany on route to New Jersey and her new life in Chicago.

The next two days took on a familiar pattern. Kersti and Lisa wanted to engage in some serious hiking and relaxed shopping together; I was still partially hobbled by my leg injury; and I was happy to serve as Omi's morning and afternoon companion. While mother and daughter hiked up one of the nearby trails on Friday morning, Omi and I settled in lounge chairs outside. I did my email and read while she alternated between reading a book about a *Schloss* (castle) that Daniela and she had visited in Salzburg earlier in the week and napping. At 12:00 sharp, we proceeded slowly, for she has become increasingly frail, into the dining room for her three-course full lunch. Lisa and Kersti returned from their hike around 3:00, totally energized and ready for some shopping and *Kaffee und Kuchen* in the *Fussgangerzone* area. I dropped them off and then rejoined them *zu Fuss* (on foot) at 6:00. Once again, a storm seemed imminent, but we sat down at the town's most popular *Biergarten* for a German-style meal and atmosphere. As soon as we ordered, the rain started falling, and fortunately a table was available inside. It was another heavy downpour. But it subsided by the time I walked the steep steps to the hotel garage to fetch and car and then pick up my three companions.

On a cloudy and cool Saturday morning, Kersti and Lisa headed back into town for more shopping, while Omi and I settled indoors. The sun burned through the clouds in the afternoon, so we went in search of another *See* (lake), the nearby Tunnsee. Unfortunately, everyone was out on a sunny Saturday afternoon in mid-July, and parking and access to the lake were both limited. We decided to return to the restaurant in the nearby town of Grossmein, where Kersti and Lisa had had lunch on their way back from their hike. It was quite a challenge for Omi, as we hiked along some streets, a narrow patch adjacent to the train tracks, down 22 steps (we counted them), and across a busy street, but she made it. She then treated herself to a gigantic ice cream-fresh cream—sweet fruit treat, while I enjoyed my daily beer, Kersti a cup of peppermint tea, and Lis a scoop of hazelnut ice cream. It was a beautiful setting in a residential neighborhood with kids riding their bikes, dads and moms pushing their toddlers in strollers, and a wide open green with the mountains rising in the back, some as high as 1700 meters (5200 feet). A second range of mountains in back of the first range, not visible because of the low haze, rose as high as 2200 meters (6700 feet). We left Omi sitting there while we walked briskly back to the car. Kersti got behind the wheel and drove Omi back to the hotel, while Lis and I enjoyed walking along a winding path, past wide open fields and grazing cows, with the late afternoon sun pouring down and the church bells tolling on Saturday evening. It was a special father-daughter time together.

Sunday was our travel day, and we packed our suitcases and bags and departed for the train station in Freilassing a little after 11:00 AM. We accompanied Omi and Lisa to the platform and gave them warm hugs as their train pulled into the station. Getting Omi with all her luggage up the steep steps and onto the train was a challenge, as it was when Lisa disembarked with her in Bingen six hours later.

Kersti and I set off on our westward route, focused again on lakes. We took the back roads through the rolling green hills of Bavaria around the north side of Bavaria's largest lake, the Chiemsee, where Eric had joined us for a week in August 2007. We had lunch on a grassy knoll just above the clear, green-tinted waters and then strolled up and down the pathway. Completing our trip around the lake, we picked up the *Autobahn* at Bernau, close to where we had stayed. There was an enormous *Stau* in the eastbound lanes, but the flow of traffic toward Munich was steady. We exited when we saw the sign for Schliersee, curious about where my Drew professor and friend, Josh Kavaloski, will be vacationing with his wife Marilyn and two small boys, Leo and Teddy, in early August. After about 20 kilometers of driving, we discovered a town on a fairly small, picturesque, family-friendly lake with numerous *Ferienwohnung* (vacation apartments). We had an early dinner at the *Biergarten* right on the lake—goulash soup, two pairs of *Weiner* (four in all), and German potato salad—stuffing, even with one *Weiner* to go. After a walk along the lake and ascending a street with several *Ferienwohnung*, we continued our drive toward Solln, heading first to Wolfratshausen (the final stop on the Solln S-Bahn line) and then to Pullach and Solln. It felt good to return to our familiar, cozy apartment. It began to rain after a short walk and bike ride, and rained fairly steadily throughout the night.

Wednesday, July 26: Solln

The past two days and nights have been cool, windy, and rainy. It's a different season than the mild summer days that we enjoyed our first two weeks. Undeterred by the weather, yesterday we returned to the Starnberger See for the fourth time for a farewell visit, and immersed ourselves in the elements. We pulled the hoods up from our rain jackets, and walked along the lake, most of the time in a pelting rain. Buffeted by the wind, the lake waters were choppy and distinctly green, and little waves splashed upon the shore. We walked north along the coastline to the top of the long, narrow lake, and then looked all the way south to the gray silhouette of the lower Alps. With the rain pouring down, we popped into a restaurant for a coffee, tea, and shared plum tart. The rain let up as we headed back to our car, close to the small beach where Kersti found the swan feathers on our first visit, but the wind kept whipping. It felt good to be dry and warm when we climbed back into our car.

After dinner at a nearby Italian restaurant, Al Caminetto on Diefenbachstrasse, we returned to our apartment to meet with Sabine and Corinne, the sisters who own this *Wohnung*. We discussed with them the possibility of a yearlong rental. They were kind and engaging and interested in our lives, and we made a good impression as potential renters. But this morning after breakfast, Kersti and I talked through all the pros and cons of committing to such long rental, and decided to withdraw from the sisters' consideration. It was the right decision and will give us more flexibility and convenience when we return to Solln, either separately or together.

Friday, July 28: Solln

It's another travel day. For the last time, I am heading off to meet Kersti as she wraps up this phase of her sessions with "Frau." Our bags are packed, and we are saying goodbye to our days in Solln. The rhythm of life here has been relaxing and very good for our peace of mind and relationship.

Yesterday, we took a retrospective bike ride through the fields and down to the Isar. The steady rain of the past few days has created a raging river, which is flowing at a mighty pace, taking limbs and logs with it. Parts of the river were overflowing, and the canal was nearly at capacity. We crossed over the river twice, pausing to stare down at this force of nature. We ate our picnic sandwiches on a big log overlooking the river, and got back on our bikes as it began to rain again.

We'll be heading to the airport after our warm lunch for our 6:30 flight to London. Farewell Solln.

Monday, July 31: London

On this comfortable, mostly sunny Monday morning, we are sitting on the wide brown couch in Janine's apartment (Flat 52) in the Ansell Building on Mile End Road in the Whitechapel section of East London.

We arrived on Friday evening around 11:00 PM (midnight body time) after a 10-hour door-to-door trip from Solln. The trek to Munich Airport was slow and tedious, especially the trip from the *Hauptbahnhof* standing next to a bunch of loud, beer-drinking young soccer fans. We arrived three hours early at the airport; endured a one-hour delay because the push-back vehicle was not yet available; scrambled around Stanstead Airport in search of a National Standard Bus ticket office, because the befuddled young man could not work the ticket machine; and our bus had to exit the Motorway and take the back roads because of an accident and major delay on the M2. But when we pulled up to the Whitechapel bus stop, we saw Janine standing there, welcoming us with her beaming smile and tight hugs. We walked the few blocks to her apartment, took the elevator to the fourth floor, and settled in to the room currently vacated by her roommate, Aurelie.

We debated our mode of transportation for our weekend trip to Canterbury and the coast, surprised that the 11-pound one-way fare had risen to 30 pounds for the "full fare," so Janine reached into her wallet and took advantage of her Zip Car membership. She arranged for a two-day Zip Car rental.

On Saturday morning, Janine and I picked up sporty black VW Golf with its bright, circular, polka-dot insignia on the side and back of the car, waiting for us on a street just a few blocks from her apartment. Janine drove the very first leg back to the apartment to pick up Kersti, and then she turned the keys over to me. Behind the wheel on the right side of the car with my left hand on the stick shift, I got off to a rocky start, first bumping another car with my left mirror and then the front left wheel on a subsequent curb. We pulled over after each incident; they popped the mirror back into place and the tire passed inspection. It was a little dicey on the narrow back streets of London, and I knew that in the first ten minutes of our trip, I already had two strikes against me. Admittedly (silently to myself, but not to my traveling companions), I was a bit nervous, but I just concentrated intently for the remainder of the trip, making sure there was enough room on the left side of the car.

We made good progress on the A2 and M2, heading toward the coast. It was a sunny Saturday morning in late July, the high season with schools out, and after our experience driving the Autobahn in Germany, I was surprised that on the two-lane highway heading toward the Chunnel and the Continent, we did not encounter a single traffic jam. We arrived in Canterbury around noon, parked on a small street outside the center, and walked toward the mighty cathedral. After lunch at an Italian restaurant, we drove to the university to check in to Keynes College. The new construction at the university was a little disorienting, and we were running late, so we did not have time to drop our things in our rooms until later.

It was beginning to rain as we drove just a few miles to Garden Close in the Rough Common development in the small Canterbury suburb of Harbledon, the home of Mike Wilkins and Kalia Yiannakis. We had last visited in 1999, when our girls (13 and 12), Natalie (12), and Eric (6) played in the back yard and later watched episodes of "Friends." Kalia and Mike gave us the warmest greetings at their front door. Mike is now battling advanced prostate cancer, and it is a difficult struggle for them both, but they were in good spirits. Kalia served tiramisu and a raspberry cake from Marks and Spencer for teatime, and we began hours of engaging conversation, covering everything from our kids to Ian Park's daughters to Elvis to world soccer to our three aging Moms to Brexit to Trump. We all piled into Kalia's car for the drive to town and with our umbrella held high, walked through the rainy streets to a Moroccan restaurant. We spent nearly four hours there, eating, drinking, and conversing. Kalia and Mike then accompanied us to Keynes to help us check in, and they did not leave until we had to request a second, made-up room because the first one was not prepared. They are dear friends, and we wish them both well and hope Mike overcomes his current battle.

We had a good night's sleep, waking up to the squawking sounds of sea gulls. They were summoning us to the nearby sea. We joined Janine for a full English breakfast—mushrooms, potatoes, regular sausage, vegetarian sausage, and scrambled eggs—outside next to the duck pond, a landmark from my year at Keynes, but which was now overgrown with vegetation. The former Keynes bar was now the Dolce Vita restaurant, and the D block where I had my room on the third floor was now administrative offices. After breakfast, we strolled over to Eliot College to catch the best view of the cathedral and downtown Canterbury, but we were disappointed that a large tree had spread its wings and now covers most of the view from the dining hall. We had a better view from a nearby slope.

We headed north to the coast at Whitstable, just a seven-mile drive from the university. We first caught a glimpse of the sea as we drove into the quaint town with most shops open on Sunday. We parked close to the promenade and then walked along the shore. There were no sandy beaches, just small rocks, but the views were magnificent and the day remained comfortable as the sun and clouds alternated with each other. We stopped at the Lobster Shack twice for lunch: Kersti ate her lobster roll on the wharf extending into the sea and later Janine had a big basket of fish and chips, as the wind picked up. After lunch, we walked westward along the curving coastline, past small artists' shops and colorful fishermen's huts, small shacks with enough room for a few chairs and one or two single mattresses. Most were boarded up, even in the high season. We paused for teatime at a beachfront restaurant, and later Kersti and Janine picked up scones at the Whitstable Castle, while I watched elderly men on the bowling pitch. We ate our scones on a bench high above the water, which turned blue-green in the late afternoon sun. It was the most magical moment of our visit. We left at 5:30 PM and encountered a traffic jam close to London, but Janine navigated us through the traffic, and we pulled into our Zip Car spot about 20 minutes ahead of schedule.

Bad Reichenhall, German

Wednesday, August 2: London

On this rainy day, our third full day in London, we walked north from Janine's apartment on Cambridge Heath Road to visit the Victoria and Albert Children's Museum close to the Bethnel Green Park and underground stop. On the way we paused at a memorial to the nearly 173 local citizens who suffocated or were crushed to death in the underground in March 1943, responding to a German air raid. It is thought to be the largest single civilian loss of life in the war. At the museum, we saw much happier displays: children's toys, games, and dolls from the past three centuries. Our favorite exhibit was a display of the works and life of the prolific and beloved young adult writer, Michael Morpurgo, whose most famous work, *War Horse*, became a Steven Spielberg film a few years ago. We especially enjoyed the video in which he described his creative process: gaining inspiration from a place and a moment in time or history, imagining, dreaming, and generating ideas, and then allowing the ideas and stories to flow from his head to his hands onto the pages of his orange notebooks. He was born in 1943, was a student at the private King's College in Canterbury, and has lived on a farm in Devon for over 30 years.

We paused for lunch at the nearby Garden Cafe on Old Ford Road and then walked to Victoria Park in the steady rain. It is the largest park in London, commissioned by Queen Victoria in 1845, when she was a young monarch in her twenties. We saw two swans, which noticed us and glided toward us for a friendly greeting and a photo. We returned to the cafe for a tea and an Americano coffee, and then retraced our late morning walk back to the apartment. Soon we will pack for tomorrow's trip to Ambleside in the Lake District.

Monday was sunny and warm, and we took the underground to the Tottenham Court stop and picked up the London City bus tour at the Old Vic Theatre. We sat upstairs in the open air as we toured the main sights of central London: Parliament, the Thames, Big Ben, Westminster Abbey, London Bridge, Trafalgar Square, and St Paul's Cathedral. We got off the bus at Pall Mall and walked through St. James' Park, pausing at a bench, and then proceeding to Buckingham Palace and a further stroll through Green Park. We took a cab to the Donmar Warehouse on Earlham Street, where we met Janine, who arrived on her bike after her day of work. We ate dinner outdoors at a famous fish & chips restaurant, dating from 1871, and then returned to the theatre for a performance of "Committee," which examined the government's investigation of the corruption and mismanagement surrounding the Kids Company charity in Great Britain in 2015. It was an occasional musical with a single set, some strong voices, and a thought-provoking theme, which raised implications for the work of all charities in Britain and elsewhere.

Janine walked with us to a nearby bus stop, which was heading directly to Whitechapel. At one stop, about halfway to our destination, we were excited to see Janine pull up on her bike, look up, and wave at us. We were immediately reminded of the moment in 2008 when we were on the Valencia bus tour at night and saw Lisa on her bike! Janine was faster than the bus, and was waiting for us as we pulled into the stop on Mile End.

On Tuesday, we stayed close to home. Janine ordered some Indian (or Bangladeshi) dishes for our evening meal, and we enjoyed meeting and chatting with her On Purpose colleague, Nadia, who is the daughter of a German father and Filipino mother and resident of London—a "three-culture person," as Nadia described herself. Like Janine, she is in the process of thinking about where she will live and work when the program concludes next April.

Sunday, August 6: Ambleside, Lake District, England

I'm sitting in our room in the Queen's Hotel in the village of Ambleside in the final hours of our long weekend at this quaint town at the top of Windermere Lake in England's renowned lake district. We have enjoyed our four getaway days—especially our two full days here. Windermere is the largest of the lakes in the area—a sliver of a lake, stretching for 10 miles while only a mile wide at its widest point.

We arrived Thursday evening, August 2 around 11:00 PM after a six-and-a-half-hour drive from City Airport in London. Driving along the narrow, rain-swept streets into town, with the lake to our left side but invisible, we were reminded of our drive into Boscastle, treading ever so carefully through the high hedges, in August 1999. It felt good to pull into an overnight parking spot right in front of the hotel.

When we pulled the curtain back on Friday morning, we saw Granny Smith's small grocery store across the street, and we felt like we were in a place where time had stood still. Our hotel was also old with its tall ceilings and creaky and in some places uneven floors. Our Friday breakfast was plentiful with pots of tea, breakfast cereal, and thick omelettes. After breakfast, we explored the town, which came to life with shoppers and tourists at the height of the summer season. We drove toward the town of Windermere, taking a spontaneous left turn up a steep, narrow, winding road until we found a small place to park and a trail. It led back down the mountain, through the woods and fields past grazing cows and sheep with occasional beautiful views of the lake. Kersti decided to continue down to the main road, while Janine and I hiked back to the top to pick up our car. After picking up Kersti, we pulled into the Windermere information center, which included trails, a boat stop, and an adventure park. We took the trail along the lake and paused for a cup of tea and picnic lunch. Clouds alternated with pockets of sun and blue sky, and when a shower passed over us, we just stayed put at our picnic bench like the English. As usual, the shower was a brief one.

After lunch, we drove back to Ambleside to the small port and boarded the lake cruise boat. It took us to the town of Bowness (pronounced "bonus") midway down the eastern side of the lake. It was blustery on board, and we zipped up our jackets. We found a trail along the lake in Bowness, pausing at a bench with a broad view of the lake. Every family passing by greeted us in a friendly manner, and it seemed as if most had a dog, often unleashed. The minutes slipped away, and so we had to rush back into town in time for afternoon tea. We hurried up to a grand "Laura Ashley" hotel high above the lake, but it was too late for tea. Instead, we found an old pub, where Charles Dickens had visited on one or more occasions. I asked for a half pint, but the bartender insisted on giving me two halves to make a whole. We sat outside, sipping on our drinks and imbibing the atmosphere. We returned to the port for our ride back to Ambleside and bundled up for dinner outside at the Wateredge Hotel. Kersti and Janine took the mile walk back to the hotel, while I figured out overnight parking a short walk from the hotel.

After breakfast on Saturday, we went our separate ways. Janine took a four-hour, seven-mile hike from town, through the woods, past waterfalls, and into the open fields. At the peak, she not only had a full view of Windermere Lake, but even a glimpse of the Atlantic some 30 or more miles away. Kersti and I drove to the even smaller village of Rydal, just two miles from Ambleside, and in the pouring rain, we entered Rydal Mount House, home of William Wordsworth for the last 37 years of his life from 1813-1850. It was here that he composed many of his poems, including his most famous, "Daffodils," in 1815. Born in Cockermouth in the northern Lake District in 1770, he was orphaned by age 13, graduated from Cambridge, and began a dramatic new poetic movement, romanticism, when he collaborated with Samuel

Coleridge on the publication of their *Lyrical Ballads* in 1798. He married Mary Hutchinson in 1802, and they had five children, though three died young, including Thomas and Catherine in 1812, just four and six years old. The house gave us a very good impression of the poet's life and work as we moved from his library and sitting room to his bedroom and study upstairs. From his bedroom, he could glimpse the lake and his extensive gardens. Of particular interest was his letter to Queen Victoria in 1843, initially turning down her invitation to be England's poet laureate, because he thought it would be too much work. She assured him that this was not the case; Sir Robert Peel encouraged him to accept; and he did, serving as the only poet laureate In English history not to produce a single poem during his tenure.

Afterwards, we walked along the "coffin route" toward Grasmere. It was mostly level, cutting across the hillside and providing scenic views of Rydal Lake. Later, we walked through the gardens of Rydal Castle with a spectacular garden landscaped in 1907. We wandered along paths by a small stream and waterfall, pausing at a small "bridge house" overlooking the waterfall. Our final stop on our Wordsworth tour was Grasmere, where we found the Wordsworth gravesite with tombstones memorializing William, Mary, his sister Dorothy, daughter Dora, Thomas and Catherine, and William's brother, John, a captain who perished in 1805 when his ship went down in the English Channel.

We returned to Ambleside in mid-afternoon to meet Janine. We stepped into the Bridge House, a tiny, two-story, shoe-like structure that in the 1850s housed a family of six, and then enjoyed afternoon tea at the Giggling Goose beside a stream. We then drove to Wray Castle on the western shore of Windermere Lake and took our final walk along the lake, sometimes gently chasing grazing sheep away from the path. We had a What's App chat with Lisa in Chicago during one of our pauses. We returned to Ambleside and had dinner at one of the Thai restaurants in town, capping off the evening with a drink at a pub just down the street from the hotel.

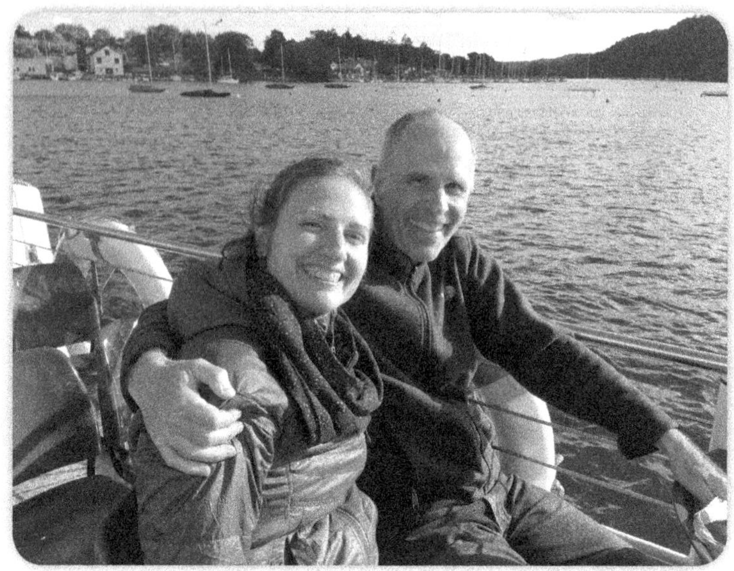

Lake Windemere, Lake District, England

Postscript: August 10: Morristown

The highlight of our trip south on Sunday, August 6 was stopping and glimpsing the Atlantic Ocean close to the small seaside town of Heysham. We walked across a wide grassy heath, battling the strong winds, as we watched the ferry arrive, likely from the Isle of Man. We paused for lunch at the bay before beginning our nearly six-hour trip back to London. We encountered one traffic jam close to London, but managed to pull into the Avis lot at City Airport just a few minutes past our projected arrival time of 7:00 PM. Mathilde thoughtfully prepared a delicious three-course dinner for us with a zucchini-tomato ratatouille, pea soup, and a tuna tart topped off by Janine's salad.

Kersti and I left the apartment around 8:15 Monday morning. We gave Janine and Mathilde big warm hugs, thanking them for their hospitality during our nine days in England. We rolled our suitcases to the Whitechapel Underground station, rode about 11 stops to Earl's Court and switched to the Piccadilly line for another 11 or 12 stops to Heathrow. Our check in and security went smoothly and quickly, and Kersti and I arrived at my United gate more than an hour before boarding. We chatted for a while, and then she said it was time to go to look for her Lufthansa gate. We kissed and hugged, and she shed a slight tear. Our 31 days together, captured in this travelogue, were very good and very special for us.

My flight arrived only 20 minutes late in Newark, despite some turbulent weather on the East Coast. I waited outside for a while on a mild, rainy day, and then was picked up by Michael Pacheco. Peaches jumped off the couch and greeted me when I came through the front door.

Chapter 35

NEW HAMPSHIRE

September 8-10, 2017

"Rye Beach is such a special place. In the late afternoon sunlight, we approached the gentle waves, and even Peaches got her paws wet when one small wave surprised her"

On this peaceful, comfortable Sunday afternoon, I'm sitting in an Adirondack chair, overlooking the small lake in Exeter. Peaches' leash connects her to the chair. Kersti is just a hundred yards from here in her session with her sandplay therapist and colleague, Sally Suggatt. A few minutes ago, a shower nearly chased Peaches and me back to the car, but we are under a protective tree, and the sun came out a little while later.

Our whirlwind visit to New Hampshire has been packed with visits to family and friends and time split between the Atlantic and Lake Winnipesauke. We did not leave until Friday around 4:30 PM, after my German class, and traffic backups in Morristown, Rockland County, Waterbury, and Hartford slowed down our progress. It was dark by 7:30, but by then we were beyond Hartford and making good progress. We arrived in Rye a little after 10:00 PM and at first drove right by Pete's renovated house, because it looked different. In addition, there was an unfamiliar white car in his driveway (his Chinese tenant's), and his outside lights were not yet connected. We had a good chat before turning in to bed.

On Saturday morning, Kersti headed to the beach for a walk amidst the surf, breeze, and salt air, while Pete and I drove to Exeter to pick up Cordelia. Back in Rye, Pete served up a country breakfast of scrambled eggs, sausages, toast, and orange juice. It was a beautiful late summer day, so after breakfast we strolled to the end of Liberty Common and walked along a wooded trail. Cordelia was breathing heavily, so she waited at a big rock until we returned.

We said goodbye to Pete and Cordelia and headed to Rye Beach. The day was sunny and warm, and we sat on the bottom steps leading to the beach club. Peaches sat in the sand in the shade in back of the steps. We were very concerned about Peaches, who has slowed down considerably, no longer eats as heartily or consistently as she once did, and needs to be lifted in and out of the Tiguan. But in these moments, she seemed to connect with the elements, the waves, the ocean air, and the wide-open blue sky.

Around 1:00 PM, we headed northwest toward Laconia to visit Neil and Denise Decker. They have a time-share condo this week, and we were planning to spend three days and two nights with them. But our concerns about Peaches prompted us to cut the visit short by a day. As it turned out, we had enough time to cover a wide range of topics from politics, modern parenting, water filters, old dogs, young people's entitlement, our kids' whereabouts and livelihoods, health foods, Neil's retirement, and Denise's work with slow learning children.

On Sunday morning, the Deckers and we walked down the hill to Weirs Beach and along the boardwalk of Winnipesauke. The sun was shining brightly. We took a close look at a statue of a Native American, which towered over Endicott Rock, a monument to Governor Endicott and the early days of New Hampshire. The male figure was reaching out his hand, and we wondered if he was offering land or peace to the settlers. Some motorboats were passing through a nearby canal into the wider lake, and Neil jokingly suggested that the Native American was requesting a toll. We returned to their condo and ate turkey sandwiches on the deck before departing for our return trip to the coast.

Rye Beach is such a special place. In the late afternoon sunlight, we approached the gentle waves, and even Peaches got her paws wet when one small wave surprised her.

We drove to Exeter, where Kersti had her meeting with Sally, and I studied German vocabulary for my quiz on Monday, wrote a short essay on the graphic novel that we have been reading about the DDR, and began this travelogue. Peaches attracted a number of admirers as she lay by my side. Then Kersti appeared on the walkway with a big smile. We were tempted to stay for a while, but we had a long drive ahead of us. We headed south and west toward the setting sun, marveling at the golden sunshine and first nips of color as the miles passed. Departing from our only stop at the Charlton service area on the Mass Pike, I predicted a 10:47 arrival time at 10 Beechwood Drive. It was my best prediction ever. When we pulled into our driveway, the clock said 10:47. We were glad to be back home a little earlier than planned, and we enjoyed sleeping in our bed and Peaches in her familiar cage.

Chapter 36

GERMANY

March 22 – April 3, 2018

"Our days in Bingen do not yet have a rhythm and may never again achieve that familiar pace and routine"

Monday, March 26: Solln

After the 4th nor'easter of the month dropped another 8 inches of snow on Beechwood Drive on Wednesday, closing Drew once again, I rose around 5:30 on Thursday morning and shoveled the driveway for hopefully the final time during this long winter. I headed to the office early on Thursday to wrap up a bunch of things, then drove to Fairleigh Dickinson University for a lunch meeting with my friends from the Fairleigh Dickinson and College of Saint Elizabeth career centers. Around 2:00, I carried our mailbox, a casualty of the earlier 24" snowfall, over to our neighbor Larry Roscoe's garage, after he said he would be happy to help repair it after our return from Germany. At 3:35, my professor buddy Josh Kavaloski pulled into the driveway in his Passat station wagon, and we were off to the airport. Despite some 4,000 flight cancellations on Wednesday, we boarded our flight on time and pulled away from the gate precisely at the 6:30 departure time.

It was a smooth, uneventful flight. I closed my eyes for 10-15 minutes on two occasions, but the rest of the time watched two films, this year's "best picture," "The Shape of Water" (it was artistic and metaphorical but unrealistic and weird, and I just couldn't suspend my disbelief) and "You Can Call My Name," the coming of age tale of a gay summer romance in Italy between two Americans, a teenager and a 30-something man (it conveyed a nice sense of mood and place, but was thin on plot and meaning). During our long descent into Munich, we seemed stuck for a long time in a thick, endless cloud, emerging just a few hundred feet from the runway in a swirl of snow. And I thought I was escaping the snow! But it was only flurries. We touched down half an hour early at 7:00 AM.

I took the S-Bahn first to the Hauptbahnhof and then on the connecting route to Solln, arriving around 9:30 AM. I pulled my light, not fully packed suitcase along Sollnerstrasse and then Melchiorstrasse, when all of a sudden a woman on a bike called out "Hey!" It was Kersti, heading to her session with Frau, and welcoming me back to Solln. We gave each other a big hug, and then she was on her way, and I covered the final few blocks to our apartment on Randelshofersweg.

Or should I say "cottage" or "cabin?" I walked up the metal, see-through steps and opened the door into a spacious, rustic *Wohnung* with an office/library, full kitchen, eating area, den, main floor bedroom, and upstairs loft with four beds and a crib. Kersti returned for lunch, and we spent the afternoon riding our bikes, picking up a roasted halfchicken from the truck and fresh salad and veggies at our favorite vegetable stand close to Festingstrasse, and later taking a stroll around the neighborhood.

The weather turned bright, sunny, and a little warmer on Saturday and Sunday. We still needed to bundle up on Saturday for our bike ride along the Isar. We encountered some puddles and muddy tracks along the way, but most of the wide paths were dry. Heading north along the Isar toward the city, more and more Müncheners were out in the early spring sunshine, urging the spring on. Crossing a big bridge, we saw a hundred or more swans gathered by the river's rocky shore. We walked our bikes over the rocks for a closer look. We were amazed when occasionally these graceful creatures demonstrated their size and majesty by spreading their wings and indulging in a spray bath. On our way back to the path, Kersti found a small soft white horse with a hearty whinny. After crossing back to the Solln side of the river, we hiked up the steep 200-meter hill to the "Wald" *Biergarten* and kicked off the spring with our first outdoors beer and *Apfelschorle*. On Saturday evening, we rode through the dark streets of Solln to our favorite local restaurant, Siddharta, and celebrated our 35th wedding anniversary with delicious eggplant and lamb-vegetable dishes.

On Sunday, after an early lunch and long talk about Kersti's family constellation the previous weekend, we headed to the nearby fields and forest on our bikes. At first, it was still chilly enough to be wearing our gloves and beanies, but the warming air and our exertion, even at our leisurely pace, enabled us to take them off midway through our excursion. We paused to reflect on the moment and our lives at a bench beside a small sanctuary with Jesus on the cross on this Palm Sunday. We took advantage of the later light, having moved the clocks ahead by an hour on Saturday night, and took a final stroll after dinner.

This morning we walked and took the bus to the small Europcar office to pick up our rental car. Our first car (a Golf) smelled like smoke, so we drove right back and exchanged it for a Huyndai, which was much more accommodating. Now we are packing for our trip tomorrow to Karlsruhe to visit Albert and Irmgard and then on to Bingen.

We have spoken numerous times to Anja in recent days about Mutti's condition and the possibility that there was an opening at St. Martin's assisted-living facility. But there was a mistaken communication, and a room is not yet available. It will be good to be together with Anja and Mutti tomorrow afternoon.

Saturday, March 31: Bingen

The sun is shining this morning as I look out the window across the Nahe to Bingerbrück. Mutti is sleeping in her automatic chair after an exhausting early morning and breakfast. Kersti is trying to do yoga in our cluttered room with our suitcases still open and awaiting repacking. Anja is cleaning up the kitchen. Our days in Bingen do not yet have a rhythm and may never again achieve that familiar pace and routine. It feels like a vigil, as we witness and endure Mutti's slow, steady decline and prepare her for her transition to St. Martin's on Wednesday morning. We learned recently that a double room was available on the 6th floor. She has been here for 46 years, the same time Mom was at 19 Dellwood Avenue. But the circumstances of her moving to Juniper and Mutti to St. Martin's are almost opposite. Mom made the choice to move when she was still very fit and ready and willing to integrate into the elder community. Mutti does not want to go. She is clinging to her life in this familiar place, and unable to accept that St. Martin's will provide the community, infrastructure, and professional support that she desperately needs. If she rallies, she may be able to return here, but this seems unlikely. And Kersti is bearing the brunt of this transition, moving a loved one against her will but necessarily to an institution. It's a different time, different place, different circumstance, and a reverse of generations. But it's Scheidegg revisited. It is very hard for my Kersti and for all of us.

We departed from Solln on Tuesday morning and had a smooth ride across southern Germany with minimal *Staus* (traffic jams). We arrived at Albert's and Irmgard's home in Karlsruhe on a slightly warmer afternoon, and found the daffodils and other flowers a few weeks ahead of those in the Munich area. We enjoyed Irmgard's carrot soup, salad, and her homemade specialty, her cheesecake for an early *Kaffee und Kuchen.* The final leg to Bingen took about an hour and a half. We found Mutti and Anja waiting for us. Mutti was so much frailer than when I last saw her.

On Thursday, Anja joined us for our regular pilgrimage to Biebertal to visit Hans and Rosi. Rosi has also declined and is no longer able to engage in a sustained conversation. Hans was his witty, conversant self, serving a morning *K&K* (a delicious fruity, chocolaty cake) followed by lunch at Tre Penoce, an Italian restaurant in nearby Wetzlar, where Goethe resided for a number of years. We wrapped up back in Bibertal with one final round of *K&K* (cheesecake). We returned to Bingen around 5:30, and bid farewell to Mutti's aide, Sabina. We were able to let her go, because she has been replaced by a delightful, compassionate, (*goldisch*, in Mutti's own words) new aide, Nancy. She is exceptionally mature for her 23 years and brings nurture, warmth, comfort, and a "can-do" attitude each time she visits.

On Friday a little past noon, we met the train from Frankfurt, and Janine emerged from the crowded train, wearing her big backpack and flashing her wide smile. We broke up the afternoon with hot drinks and treats, sitting outside at a busy Rialto on this Good Friday. We had a long Skype call with Lis later in the afternoon, and a nice, brief visit with Ansgar, Bärbel, and Antonia after dinner. Janine is staying with them Friday and Saturday nights. Kersti and I wrapped up the day by walking through the dark, quiet streets of Bingen.

Monday, April 2: Bingen

It was a quiet Easter weekend. On Saturday afternoon, Kersti and I drove over to Angar's house for *Kaffee und Kuchen* with Ansgar, Bärbel, Antonia, and Gina. Ansgar and I then headed upstairs for a "guy talk," covering a wide range of topics from my current work to his running a major business in Ukraine to his retirement plans. For dinner, Janine, Kersti, and I walked into town to the Alte Wache (old police station) restaurant, where I enjoyed a penne pesto dish, Janine a whole trout, and Kersti a chicken salad. Easter Sunday was rainy and cool, and we spent most of the day close to home.

And so we enter head first into this time of transitions. Janine left yesterday morning for Wales, carrying her bulging backpack and giving us big hugs as the Koblenz train pulled into the station. This morning, I drove Anja to the station to begin her long trek—more than 15 hours door to door—from Bingen to Boulder. I am leaving tomorrow morning, and Jörg is flying in from Nice. As I write this, Lisa is wrapping up her abbreviated postdoc at Loyola of Chicago, uncertain about the next step in her career. And the biggest transition of all is Mutti's move to St. Martin's. This apartment will never be or feel the same. The rhythm of her life will change dramatically, though it already was limited to her unsteady movements from her bed to dining table to easy chair. Thank goodness for Nancy, who will be such a big help when the move actually occurs on Wednesday morning at 10:30. It is touching how she sits on the floor beside Mutti, looking up at her with her sparkling eyes, engaging her and making her smile or laugh.

Now let the move happen, and may Mutti make the most of her new community and daily contact with her best friend, Suse, who moved to St. Martin's in January and whom we visited this morning just before lunch time. Her friendship will play an important role in Mutti's adjustment. I hope so much that it goes well on Wednesday

Postscript

On Tuesday morning, I put the finishing touches on my packing, said goodbye to Mutti and Kersti, and drove to the airport. It was a smooth drive with no backups and no wrong turns. I spent almost the entire nearly eight-hour flight on Lufthansa watching films: *Mrs. Brown*, the story of Queen Victoria's long and endearing friendship with John Brown following the death of Prince Albert; *Un Beau Soleil Interieur (Let the Sunshine In*), a lame French relationship film, featuring Juliette Binoche in search of love, as usual; *Beasts of the Southern Wild,* one of my favorites of all time with the amazing Hush Puppy (Quazhene Wallis) in "The Bathtub"; and one more that I don't remember. In Hush Puppy's memorable, moving reflection at the end of the film, she observes, "When I die, the scientists of the future will know that I was a little piece of a big universe, and I lived with my Daddy in the Bathtub." It always brings tears to my eyes.

We encountered some very rocky turbulence over northern Canada, and our landing into drizzly, chilly Newark was unusually hard. But I moved through the accelerated customs process (semi-self-service) and baggage pickup, and found Josh waiting for me exactly 55 minutes—as I had predicted—after touchdown. As we pulled into the driveway, I was relieved that the quick snowstorm, which had closed Drew on Monday, had melted away.

Chapter 37

GERMANY (AND AUSTRIA)

June 28 – July 30, 2018

"I will miss our walks at sunset in the fields, shopping by bike, the gigantic one-euro heads of green and red lettuce, the sounds of the schoolchildren still in school late in July, and our Ausfluge"

Eibsee, Germany

Sunday, July 1: Bingen

Our neighbor, Cathy Yamashita, shuttled us to the airport on Thursday afternoon. We arrived a little after 4:00 PM for our 7:40 flight, which did not take off until nearly 8:30. We arrived on my 68th birthday, which was shorter by six hours because of the time change—six hours when I normally would have been sleeping. After a long wait at Europcar, we finally jumped into a black Jeep—our rental for the entire month—and had a smooth ride to Bingen under mostly sunny skies with low humidity. We dropped our things at Dr. Sieglitz Strasse, finding an unfamiliar quiet and calm in the apartment with no one living there any longer. We summoned our second wind and hiked up, over, and down the hill to St. Martin's assisted-living facility. We found Mutti sitting in her usual designated spot for meals with Nancy by her side. To Mutti's left is a magnificent view of the Rhein and the vineyards across the river in Hessen. Unfortunately, she is stiff and unable to move her head to the left to fully enjoy the view. We rolled her downstairs to the garden and had *Kaffee und Kuchen* (*K&K*), before returning her to the 6th floor for an early dinner and bed. Kersti and I picked up a *Döner* and split it, before concluding our long day after a short night by walking along the Rhein and Nahe toward home. We managed to read in bed until 10:00 PM and slept until 9:00 AM the next morning.

On Saturday, we arrived at the *"Heim"* in late morning and then walked with Mutti down to the Zollamt restaurant directly overlooking the Rhein. We ordered salads for us and *Wiener Schnitzel* and fries for Mutti. The meat was too tough for her—she recently lost her bottom teeth—so she exchanged her meat for my wedge of soft *camembert* cheese. Mutti took a nap after lunch, but we returned for K&K in mid-afternoon and an early dinner. I joined a few of Mutti's 6th-floor colleagues to watch France beat Argentina 4-3 in the World Cup round of 16. The very friendly aide, Klaus Peter, kindly served me a Bitburg and "Hawaii-toast." Kersti and I shared another *Döner*, sitting in the breezy, cool shade of the large patio on the first floor of the *Heim* before heading home for a delicious fresh salad. Kersti was riveted by her "Bergrettung" (mountain rescue) show, and later I watched Uruguay's 2-1 victory over Portugal.

This morning while eating our Sunday egg and toast, we decided to leave earlier tomorrow than originally planned. We will stop in Karlsruhe for a light lunch with Irmgard and Albert and then head on to Munich/Solln. We will have lunch today at the Heim with Mutti's dear friend, Suse, now 93 and in relatively good health, mind, and spirit.

Thursday, July 5: Solln

Our days in Solln have assumed a comfortable, relaxed pace. We sleep in, usually until 7:30, 8:00, or even 8:30 AM, have leisurely meals, do some yoga, shop for food and fresh veggies, read, write, watch World Cup games, and take walks and bike rides through the nearby fields. The weather has been ideal—at times a big muggy, but cool enough to wear our jackets in the morning and pull up our comforters at night.

Monday was a busy, long day. We loaded up our Jeep and then stopped for a quick goodbye to Mutti. It's best when we simply say "*Tschuss*" and don't explain that we will be away for the next few weeks. We set out for Karlsruhe around 10:30 and arrived at Irmgard's and Albert's place a little after noon. Irmgard served a tasty lunch of basil-mozzarella-tomatoes, salad, and pasta with pesto sauce, concluding with homemade strawberry ice cream and fresh strawberries. Irmgard was her usual talkative self on a wide range of topics. We left around 3:00 PM, and we were on the road for another three and a half hours before arriving at our apartment on Randelshofersweg. Kersti drove for over an hour while I napped. We settled quickly into our familiar place. While Kersti picked up a few things from the local Rossman, I emptied the suitcases and organized the clothes on our closet shelves.

On Wednesday afternoon, we drove to another of our favorite sites, the Starnbergersee. We parked in our usual spot and then walked along the path from Berg toward Percha and Starnberg. The wind was whipping up and creating some small waves. We felt a brief sprinkle, but it passed. We paused at a bench and each took a turn with my rubber Tevas, walking on the stony bottom of the lake. The water, which was clear and not too cool, lapped up to our knees. By dinnertime, the full sun and blue sky returned, and we ate our dinner of *Weisswurst*, broccoli, and salad on the narrow deck just outside our door.

Monday, July 8: Solln

This past Friday was a day of cool, soaking rain followed by a better but still stay-at-home day on Saturday, with entertainment provided by four quarter final World Cup games (England 2, Sweden 0; France

2, Uruguay 1; Belgium 2, Brazil 1; and Croatia 4, Russia 3 in penalty kicks after a 2-2 tie). Eager to get out of the house, on Sunday on a warm, sunny day we rode our bikes to the Solln station and took the #7 S-Bahn to the Munich *Hauptbahnhof.* From there we took the *Strassenbahn* to the quaint section of the city called Haidhausen, just east of central Munich after crossing the Isar. It is one of the suburban districts that was developed during the second half of the 19th century. We walked along Kirchstrasse and Preysingstrasse, where we paused for lunch outdoors at a local pub. Kersti had a tasty scalloped potato-leek dish and salad, and I downed two *Wurstchen* and dark bread with my *kleines helles Bier.*

After lunch, we strolled around the neighborhood, admiring the small old houses with windows below our line of vision and finely sculptured gardens in back. A small museum in a typical house from that period was already closed, but a few blocks away we visited the Haidhausen Museum. It was probably more interesting on the outside than the inside, where Kersti read about Hitler's *Putsch* in Haidhausen in 1923, which led to his arrest. We were welcomed inside by two older, friendly ladies, who complained about the heat, but were prepared to do something about it: they treated themselves to cold beers from their small downstairs fridge. In addition to being warm, the museum was musty, but fortunately the upstairs and downstairs exhibits, consisting mostly of old photos and posters, did not take much time. The highlight was the sizeable model of a large wooden structure, which consisted of individual family units on the first and second floors—a precursor to today's apartments and condos.

We headed back to the tram stop and drank a cup of peppermint tea and coffee in a French-style cafe before boarding the tram. We thought about cruising around the city on trams for a while, but without air conditioning, we felt increasingly warm and stuffy. So we returned to the "Hbf" and cruised down the escalator to pick up the #7 S-Bahn back to Solln. It was air conditioned and not crowded, and it felt good to be heading back to our familiar town with tree-lined streets and quietude.

We felt this again when we strolled through the wheat fields after 9:00 PM, watching the sunset and the white, low-lying clouds turn to yellow and then pink before vanishing with the ensuring darkness.

Friday, July 13: Solln

Another week has flown by. We are looking forward to Windy's visit this evening. They are taking the train from Bingen, where they visited Omi the last two days and befriended Nancy. We had good skype conversations with Lisa (now actively pursuing jobs) and Janine (back from a getaway in the Cotswolds in the Midlands with Windy).

On Monday, we enjoyed an *Ausflug* to Andechs and Herrsching near Ammersee, a sister lake to the Starnbergersee. We drove through Starnberg and then west along a winding road and rolling hills. Our first stop was the Kloster Andechs, established in 1455. It is now most famous for its monastery brewery and numerous *Biergartens*. The monks have been observing the Benedictine brewing tradition since 1455. Brewing and bottling still take place locally in Andechs. We walked up the steep cobbled streets all the way to the *Wallfahrtskirche* (Pilgrimmage Church). We were reminded of a busy village square in medieval times, dominated by the church and tower. We paused in the *Versohnungskapelle* (Chapel of Reconciliation), and then embarked on a bit of an adventure: climbing about 100 steps to the tower. At times, we had to kneel on the next step and duck our heads to continue upward. Some steps were so narrow in width that we had to turn our shoes accordingly. Midway, we passed the gigantic church bell. At the top, we were in cramped quarters with only partial views of the surrounding countrywide and lakes. But overall it was a fun excursion.

We continued driving a few more miles west to Herrsching on the Ammersee. We parked and then walked along the promenade. There was a comfortable breeze, and small waves lapped along the shore. It was warm in the sun, but we pulled our light jackets on when the clouds prevailed. We passed numerous eating and drinking establishments and people of all ages. We walked for a while; sat a bench; walked some more; enjoyed a tasty minty drink while lounging on an outdoor couch;

and finally walked some more before returning to our car and heading back to Solln. It was good to get away for the day and also to walk back into our cozy, familiar apartment.

Yesterday evening, in the continuing beautiful weather, we enjoyed dinner at Iberl's, a family-focused *Biergarten* and Kersti's favorite. It was not crowded on a Thursday evening, and small children were frolicking on the adjacent swings and trampolines. Kersti and I shared our dishes—potato pancakes, mushrooms, and salad; and veal burgers and potato/cucumber salad. Both delicious.

On the way home on our bikes, we rode through the golden fields as the sun was setting. We paused and looked out over the tranquil landscape. It is only mid-July, but already some of the wheat has been harvested and the fields have been shorn until the next growing season.

Monday, July 16: Solln

We had an enjoyable long weekend with Windy. They arrived on Friday afternoon after their long train ride from Bingen, where they had spent the past two days visiting Omi and Nancy. Kersti was at her hairdresser close to the train station, so I waited on the platform for Windy to emerge from the southbound Wolfratshausen train. Kersti arrived just in time, having skipped her usual blow dry. Windy was tired but glad to be with us. We walked home along Wolfratshausenstrasse, and Windy was excited to see their spacious upstairs quarters after their more confined sleeping arrangements in Janine's apartment in London and their "pod" in the Cotswolds. For dinner, we walked down Melchiorstrasse to the Siddhartha restaurant and afterwards strolled through the fields.

On Saturday, Kersti and Windy picked up a bike in the city for use throughout Windy's stay. After lunch, we headed out to the Isar for a ride along both sides of the river. It was sunny and warm, and many Muncheners were basking on the rocky beaches. Windy and Kersti wanted to take a swim, so I headed back to the apartment to watch the third place game between Belgium and England. Belgium scored early and late; England dominated the possession time; but they did not have the speed or creativity to score, and Belgium completed the World Cup with its best finish ever. After the game, we ate baked balsamic cauliflower, mixed dinkel noodles with pesto, and field salad and regular salad. We rode through the fields after dinner, witnessing the most spectacular sunset yet, streaks of yellow, orange and pink framing the setting sun.

On Sunday, we headed south on 95 past Starnbergersee and Kochelsee, originally intending to take a hike and cable car ride up another peak. But as the high German Alps rose majestically before us, and the mostly sunny weather was holding, we decided to go for it: to take the gondola to the Zupsptize, the "top of Germany." We missed the 11:15 train, so we strolled around the *Fussgangerzone* in Garmisch to bide our time. When we arrived at the station, we found the train waiting for us and secured some prime seats at the front of the small train. Looking out, I saw the familiar colored, intersecting Olympic rings and the large hall that was likely the central meeting place for the athletes and officials who participated in the 1936 Winter Olympics at Garmisch-Partenkirchen. (Norway finished first with 15 medals/7 gold; Germany second with 6 medals/3 gold; and the U.S. 8th with 4 medals/1 gold.)

The train began its slow, gradual ascent, stopping at several tiny stations, crisscrossing the wide fields with the tall peaks looming more and more grand. At the Eibsee station, we noticed the large Zugspitze gondola shuttling travelers up the steep mountain, and so we took the next trip. We had a front-row view of the mountain as we hurtled skyward, up to the top of the highest peak in Germany: 2,962 meters (9,718 feet). It was not scary, except for one moment when the gondola felt like it was going over an enormous bump: it jerked then settled, as the passengers gasped a bit. We pulled very gingerly into the station at the top and walked outside into the cool air, 20 degrees less than what we had left at the base. Windy noticed that a bunch of people were climbing a fairly challenging, potentially dangerous outcrop that led to the golden cross at the summit of the Zugspitze. He decided to go for it. With his long legs and stretches, hanging on to the ropes, he carefully made his way to the top and documented the ascent with selfies and 360-degree photos. We were in the clouds, and thus the views of the surrounding landscape and countries—Switzerland, Italy, and Austria— were only partial. The best view was of the turquoise Eibsee some 2,000 meters below. Kersti and I munched on a sausage and then Windy joined us for fries with ketchup (our preference) and mayo (Windy's preference). On the descent, we crowded into a packed gondola, which felt more like a New York City subway than an alpine transport, so our views were very limited. Back at Eibsee, after Windy took a swim in the cool lake, we walked along about a portion of the wide, gravel pathway surrounding the lake. The lake shimmered with its rich variety of greens and blues, depending on the water depth. I was reminded of our walk around Jordan Pond on Mount Desert Island in 1999, though this was more spectacular.

To save some time, we took the bus rather than the train back to Garmisch. As we drove in low gear back into town, we looked up a few more times at the magic mountain. Looking up was even more amazing than looking down from on high.

Back in town around 4:15 PM, we decided to drive to Murnau and the Saffelsee, a recommendation from Kersti's sandplay therapist, Frau Wachter, hoping to arrive in time at a lakefront *Biergarten* to watch the France-Croatia final. We didn't find too many choices, passing by a "Beach and Burger" place that appeared not to have a TV, and finally arriving at the family-owned Gastatte Burgstube in Seehausen. It was adjacent to, almost a part of, a large campground. We found a table with a TV with the game in its first minutes. It was not a great view of the game, but it was adequate as we sipped on our *Hefe Weizen*, rosé, and *Apfelschorle* and then ordered salads. France scored first and held a 2-1 lead at halftime, then went up 4-1 before completing its 4-2 triumph. We enjoyed the family atmosphere, the cheerful mother and daughter servers, the home-cooked meals, and the sharing of tables among the largely pro-Croatia crowd. Thunder rumbled outside, and finally the downpour erupted. We left shortly after the final whistle. The ride home was smooth and without any delays or backups. Our second dinner consisted of some pasta and small sweet potato cubes. It was after nine and growing dark when Windy and I took at walk through the fields, admiring the last light of day and the sliver of a moon that appeared in the sky. We had a good talk about health, work, community, and life.

Thursday, July 19: Solln

Monday, July 16 was another beautiful day, and we again headed south on 95, but this time took the first exit at Starnberg. We wanted to show Windy our favorite local beach at the Starnbergersee. We set up our towels in the shade and then waded into the cool water. Kersti and I had our rubber sandals, but Windy braved the rocky lakebed. They went in first, and then we waded in, step by cool step, before Windy splashed us and forced us to dive in. Afterwards, I read a novel that Windy gave me, *Ruby-Fruit Jungle* by Rita Mae Brown (1973), and Windy and Kersti took a stroll along the lake promenade. Suddenly, the sky turned darker and the clouds started swirling, so we quickly packed up and hastened to the car, getting caught in the rain but not drenched. For dinner, we picked up some takeouts from the Halong Bay restaurant, featuring Vietnamese cuisine.

On Tuesday, we packed a picnic lunch and headed back to the bike paths along the Isar. We intended to ride some distance south in the direction of Wolfratshausen, but we got stuck on the western side of the river and the adjacent canal. We kept looking for a bridge and a place to swim. We finally crossed over and saw that the current was quite swift, so we headed back north. Close to the steep walkway to the Waldwirtschaft pub, we found a partially shaded area and spread our towels for our picnic lunch. We had forgotten our rubber sandals, so navigating through the stony river was uncomfortable. The water was chillier than the Starnbergersee. It was too shallow to swim, but Windy walked out toward the center and sat down in the rushing water. After dinner, we loaded the Windy's rental bike in the car and drove it back to the rental place, then stopped for ice cream to celebrate Windy's visit.

Wednesday was getaway day for Windy. During Kersti's morning therapy session, Windy put the finishing touches on their packing, and we then took a farewell walk through the fields. We had another meaningful conversation. It was a very special time together. Around 12:30 PM, we walked our bikes to the Solln station, boarded the S-Bahn, and took it to Marienplatz. We did a little shopping for about half an hour in Kaufhof, but then it was time to say a quick goodbye. Kersti and I wandered through the nearby Viktualienmarkt and downed two delicious *Wurstchen* with sweet mustard in a roll. Upon our return, the apartment felt empty without Windy, but we called up to their loft anyhow.

Today was a "top-10 day" with only a few passing clouds and no rain or even the threat of rain. Outside our window in the morning, we saw three horses and a pony grazing in the adjacent field. After lunch, we drove back to the Starnbergersee for another restful afternoon. Gina joined Kersti for dinner, while I heated up some leftovers and got caught up on my travelogue.

Monday, July 23: Solln

The three grazing horses and pony are very much a focus of our attention both day and night. I was up briefly at 4:00 AM this morning and looked out the window to see the large steed standing and one of the smaller horses crouched on the grass in the dim light. Yesterday, I fed some grass to the large one, but the others were a bit shy and did not respond to my offering.

Sunday was a washout, except for a pause in the evening for a walk to Siddhartha, where Patrick and Sven joined us for an enjoyable evening of family updates and conversation. They are impressive young men—Patrick is owning and co-managing a company of 60 employees, and Sven is an architect with a promising future. Dirk is very busy with his CPA exams and work schedule—up to 100 hours a week—and was unable to join us.

Saturday was the highlight of the weekend. Similar to our *Ausflug* to the Zugspitze and Eibsee with Windy, we combined a tourist site with the discovery of a pristine, off-the-beaten track lake in Austria. Our first stop was the Lindenhof Castle, the smallest but most ornate of Ludwig II's three castles in Bavaria. It was also the castle where he lived most of his final years. (He drowned in the Starnbergersee in 1886.) Built between 1869 and 1878, the castle and surrounding grounds were inspired by Ludwig's admiration of the French "Sun King," Louis XIV and his son, Louis XV. On the English tour, our guide took us through rooms that were filled with gold trim and ornaments and lavish chandeliers and furnishings from Germany, France, and Italy. Ludwig was reclusive and nocturnal, sleeping late into the day and reading and writing deep into the night in his "king-sized" bed, chaise, or lounge chairs. He often ate alone, and meals could be served on either the first or second floor through a small lift. Outside the castle, we walked through some colorful, sculptured gardens and then up a pathway to a small, Moorish, Alhambra-inspired structure where Ludwig occasionally visited to get away from the main edifice.

Leaving Linderhof, we faced a choice: turn left to head back along the winding Alpenstrasse to the Autobahn or right to Plansee. On this trip, the word "*See*" has always been a magnet. So we turned right. Little did we know that the 16 km through forests and rolling fields would bring us to Austria and a beautiful lake. After coffee, tea, and *Apfelstrudel* at the Forelle (Trout) Hotel, we walked through the adjacent campground and discovered a path that led around the entire lake. Often we paused to look out at the colorful water and the reflection of the faint sunlight. We stopped and sat for a while on large boulders beside the rocky beach, and Kersti waded into the water. We returned to our car and drove back to Germany and our home base.

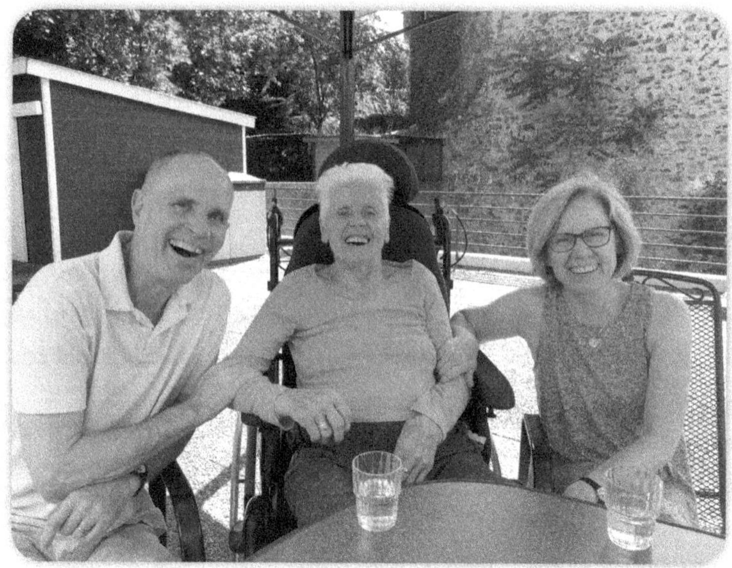

Bingen, Germany—St. Martin's Altenheim

Thursday, July 26: Farewell to Solln

It's our final morning in Solln. Kersti is at her concluding session with Frau Wachter on Whistlerweg. It is quiet in the apartment except for Quincy's occasional barks when other dogs pass by. (Quincy is our hosts' adorable dachshund, which loves to have his belly rubbed.) Our backpacks and suitcases are packed. The last thing to do is clear out our fridge after lunch before we hit the road to Karlsruhe.

It has been a meaningful, restful, spiritual, reflective three and a half weeks in this special place. I will be pleased to turn over the keys of our Jeep Renegade and no longer navigate through these narrow streets with single or double-parked cars. I will not miss the stares of some people and the usual non-greeting when you pass them on the street or in the fields. But I will miss our walks at sunset in the fields, shopping by bike, the gigantic one-euro heads of green and red lettuce, the sounds of the schoolchildren still in school late in July, and our *Ausfluge*—especially to Starnbergersee and the Isar. The weather cleared up on Tuesday and Wednesday, and we made our farewell visits to the *See* on Tuesday afternoon and the Isar on Wednesday afternoon.

I snapped some photos of Kersti bathing in the cool, churning waters of the Isar, and Lis appropriately called her "Little Mommers."

We will have an early dinner in Karlsruhe with Irmgard and Albert, arriving this evening in Bingen. We will visit Mutti tomorrow at the *Heim*, and I will also host Josh, who is taking the train from Eberbach. Janine arrives Friday evening from Leipzig and will join our dinner with Gabi and Wolfgang. We will devote the weekend to visits to Mutti and our special time with Janine, and then begin our long journey home with a wakeup at 3:30 Monday morning for our 6:30 AM flight to Frankfurt.

Auf Wiedersehen Solln.

Tuesday, July 31: Madison

I am back in my office at Drew. I came in early, a little after 7:00 AM, and at 8:15 my car is still the only one in the parking lot. My desktop computer was not working, so I had some time to put the finishing touches on this travelogue.

Our final days in Germany were busy and reflective. Our drive on Thursday afternoon to Karlsruhe took five hours, about an hour and a half longer than normal, because of he many *Staue*. The Autobahn has too many cars and trucks, especially the trucks that are crisscrossing Germany to deliver their goods in the heart of Europe. The temperature rose into the mid-90s. Irmgard and Albert were happy to see us again. She served a light bouillon, cantaloupe, local tomatoes with basil and mozzarella, and salad. We stayed for about three hours, and then headed home to Bingen, arriving around quarter to ten as it was growing dark.

We visited Mutti early on Friday morning during her physical therapy, but then I left to meet Josh back at the apartment. We chatted for a while in the living room, and then set out for a quick tour of Bingen. Because of the heat, we decided not to travel to the ruins of Hildegard's monastery in Disibodenberg or take the ferry to Rudesheim and hike up the hill to the Eibingen monastery. We walked through the grounds of Burg Klopp, catching some excellent views of the Ehrenfels castle, Germania, Rudesheim, and Eibingen. Just as we were approaching the Heim to touch base with Kersti, she came walking out.

It was perfect timing. We sauntered along the Rhein, catching up on our lives in Eberbach, Solln, Bingen, and Morristown, and continued over lunch at the *Biergarten*. After lunch, Josh and I visited the Bingen town museum, featuring its permanent history of Hildegard and her connection to Bingen. We returned to the Heim and had *Kaffee und Kuchen* outside next to the colorful and talkative chickens and roosters that are now part of a small *Tiergarten* that Nancy is overseeing.

We had a fun evening with Gabi, Wolfgang, and Janine. Because of the heat, we decided to get a takeout from a local Italian restaurant—four delicious vegetarian pizzas and a pasta dish for Wolfi. We shared some cold beers and *Radlers* (half beer, half lemon soda). We interrupted our cocktail hour and dinner twice, when Wolfgang and I first drove to pick up the dinner and later to pick up Janine at the station. She had taken the train from Leipzig following her flight to Berlin on Wednesday afternoon. Gabi and Wolfgang are dear, loyal, long-time friends.

On Saturday, we visited Mutti in the morning and afternoon. I brought along the album that Kersti and I had presented to Vati and Mutti at Christmas 1985, as we were awaiting the birth of Janine...or Brian. Mutti showed some interest in some photos, but was no longer sure whom everyone was. The album was fragile, and I made a plan to take it home to revive it in a new album. Janine, Kersti, and I took Mutti to the Rhein promenade, which has always brought her pleasure. Later in the afternoon, during Mutti's early dinner, we were treated to a real St. Martin's cocktail hour with wine and beer served by the gregarious and generous kitchen aide, Klaus Peter.

The weather remained warm and sticky on Sunday. Kersti and I went to the Heim early to take Mutti to the 10:15 church service. It was held in a small, crammed chapel. The highlight of the day was the *Grillfest*, which included a local band playing traditional German music. Mutti was really into the atmosphere; the music brought her back to a time when she was moving around the dance floor. She waved her arms, sometimes holding a knife or the light green napkins. Kersti shot a video of me dancing with her. It was cloudy at first, but the sun broke through, and we moved back into the shade. After our lunch of *Wurst*, potato salad, *Kraut* salad, and noodle salad, we took Mutti back upstairs and said a quick goodbye—no longer a prolonged one. That afternoon, we put the finishing touches on our packing, and then Kersti and Janine cooled off for a few hours in the Bingerbrück pool. Meanwhile, I stumbled upon a brand new album in Vati's bedroom closest, and happily transferred the photos and captions from the decaying album to the new one. We sat down in the dining room for our final dinner consisting of a zucchini omelette, salad, and noodles.

We set our alarms for Monday morning at 3:30, but of course I beat the alarm when I shined the flashlight on the clock at 3:15 AM. We left just past 4:00 and had a smooth ride to the airport. Around Mainz and our Rhein crossing, we saw the first light of the new day. We happily deposited our jeep in the underground Europcar lot; we will not miss driving it either on the Autobahn or the narrow streets of Solln. Janine stayed with us as we patiently waited our turn with the Lufthansa agent, and then we gave her big hugs and wished her well as she headed to her Ryan Air flight back to London. Our 6:30 flight to Hamburg was on time, as was our 9:00 flight to Newark. I passed my time, as usual, watching four films: *Chappaquidick* (so-so), *Charlotte's Web* (cute and familiar; I took my one short nap during it), *I Can Only Imagine* (the story of country music star Brad Millard; a compelling, well-acted story combining writing, healing, good music, perseverance, and forgiveness; Kersti also enjoyed it), and *Love, Simon* (a touching story about a young man coming out with a very appealing performance by Nick Robinson). We landed early, around 11:15 AM, but did not reach the gate until closer to noon. After some back up at the immigration hall, we quickly fetched our suitcases, hailed a taxi, and walked back into our clean, spacious, quiet home by 1:00 PM.

In the middle of the afternoon, we went to Shop Rite to restock our fridge, and then headed over to Juniper to visit Grammy and Cynthia. Mom is so excited about her birthday. She is as energetic and sprightly as, unfortunately, Mutti is stiff and morose. It is hard to believe that their ages are not reversed, given their conditions. It's sad that Mutti no longer has anything to look forward to.

But we move on and look forward. And now we embark on the next chapter in our lives.

Chapter 38

COLORADO

September 19-26, 2018

"On multiple levels, it's a time of reflection, transition, and bold new steps into the future"

"We rushed outside and saw a thick, arching rainbow reaching all the way down to the earth. It was another gift from Norbert"

Near Nederland, Colorado—Caribou Ranch hike

Friday, September 21, Coal Creek Canyon

Janine, Lisa, Kersti, and I are sitting in our lodge on a brisk Friday morning. I just lit our first fire to take some of the chill out of the air. Windy is still sleeping after picking them up at the airport just before 2:00 AM this morning.

Janine, Kersti, and I woke early on Wednesday morning at 10 Beechwood to get the house ready for showings and another open house on Sunday. A driver from Guatemala picked us up at 8:30 AM, and we headed to the airport. We had a good flight to Denver, so smooth that we arrived around 1:50 PM Denver time, half an hour ahead of schedule. We met Lisa at the airport following her morning flight from Laguardia, and later Nellie at the Advantage car rental, where we picked up our Toyota Camry. It has California plates, appropriate for Lisa's pending move to the Bay area.

We managed to cram all of our luggage and five people into the car for our drive to Anja and Rich's place in the hills above Golden. It was muggy and summery, and we drove through a brief shower. We stopped at Whole Foods to stock up on food supplies for the week and then headed to Anja's rental cottage. She rushed out of the house and gave us big warm hugs, thanking us for coming to Colorado to celebrate her marriage. We checked into our lodge, just a few miles from Anja's place, and loved the western decor and spaciousness. Anja and Nellie came over later and brought a delicious carrot-potato soup with salad—perfect for our first evening.

Thursday dawned cloudy and cool. Rich stopped by in his pick-up truck to say hello and check out our premises. Later in the morning, Anja picked us up, and we all piled into her white BMW SUV with Nellie graciously volunteering to ride in the back. The sun began breaking through the clouds, as Anja took us on the winding back roads to Boulder. The sun was shining brightly and the wind was whipping up as we stopped at the spectacular Gross Dam, overlooking the reservoir and dam. We continued our drive into Boulder, descending about 4,000 feet from roughly 9,000 to 5,000. We stopped at several scenic overlooks with broad views of the Boulder plain and later the University of Colorado with its distinctive brick buildings and orange rooftops. When we arrived in bustling Boulder, it was summer again, so we stripped off our sweatshirts and long-sleeve shirts. We ate lunch outdoors at Mad Greens, picked up a few more things at Trader Joe's, visited Daniel at his off-campus apartment, and then headed back to Anja's place along another stunning route. We stopped in Nederland for a drink and a stroll around the distinctly "wild western" town with its old shops, saloon, and eateries. On our final leg back to our mountain retreat, we sometimes took 10 mph double hairpin turns through jagged rock formations and the always present evergreens.

The sun was beginning to fade when Anja drove us to the new house that Rich and she are building. We were able to walk inside and out onto the temporary deck where we witnessed the most amazing view of the mountains and valley. Anja led us through each room, for now just frames, but with so much promise. When Janine walked along the narrow bridge, still lacking a railing, and into the spacious, all-purpose room with its incredible views, she immediately added this to her list of locations for future yoga retreats. Nellie, Lisa, Janine, and I walked down the hill about 15 minutes, arriving back at Anja's place to welcome Jörg, Sonny, and their dog Ben back from their three days of travel in and around Rocky Mountain National Park. We wrapped up the day back at our lodge with a pasta-kale-tomato-red onion dish and a big salad. Kersti and I tried to sleep or slept for a few short hours, before we beat the 12:50 AM alarm, as usual. We quickly pulled on our clothes and headed to the airport to pick up Windy.

Saturday, September 22: Anja and Rich's Wedding Day

Today is a day we will always remember and celebrate. Not only are we attending Anja and Rich's wedding less than two hours from now, but this morning we received word of the offer on our house from Enrique and Lynette Torres. On multiple levels, it's a time of reflection, transition, and bold new steps into the future.

On Friday, we woke up to a splendid day, which was fall in the mountains but still summer when we drove to Nederland in search of a family hike. Nellie joined us, and the four women squeezed into the back seat. Over drinks at the same cafe where we paused on Thursday, Lisa asked a man for hiking recommendations, and he suggested that we take the nearby Caribou Ranch trail. It was only a few miles west of the town. We had lunch at a picnic table in the shade and then headed off on our hike. It was a beautiful trail, which wound through pine-needle woods and meadows in the brilliant sunshine. The younger generation completed a longer loop, while Kersti and I rested on a bench and later lay down on the pine needles close to the trailhead.

We hosted the family for dinner on Friday evening. We joked that this was Anja's bachelorette bash or her rehearsal dinner. Jörg and Sonny joined us; Daniel drove back to the Canyon from Boulder; and even cousin Peter joined us after his direct flight from Zurich. All ten of us managed to sit around the large wooden table for a meal of pasta (pesto and tomato sauce), fried chicken, and salad. The bride was growing tired a little after 9:00 PM, and so we wished everyone a good night.

Early this morning, just before we received word about the house offer, I look out and saw an enormous buck grazing in our yard. Then a second, even larger buck joined him. They were so majestic, so gentle, so relaxed. From time to time, they heard a sound, opened their large fluffy ears, and looked straight at us. It almost seemed like they were the messengers about our house sale. A few minutes later, Kersti checked her email, and we were on our way.

Tuesday, September 25

I am alone in our lodge on another brisk early fall morning under a cloudless blue sky. Janine went for a walk, while Kersti went to Anja's house to pick up some documents related to our home sale, which was finalized on Monday.

The wedding on Saturday afternoon was a perfect event in all respects: the splendid weather, the picturesque backdrop of the mountains, the service, the food, the blend of families and friends, and the marriage ceremony. It was conducted by a freelance pastor named Jen, who spoke of this union with compassion, humor, grace, and familiarity. Anja and Rich were both emotional and spoke personally and intimately of their love, respect, and dedication to each other. Jen included a nice interactive touch, in which she passed around a stone and asked family members and friends to utter one-word gifts for the newlyweds. I later reconstructed the list as best as I could remember and sent it to Anja.

Following the 3:00 PM service, we enjoyed drinks and hors d'oeuvres followed by a delicious buffet dinner at small round tables. Jörg, Sonny, and Peter joined the five of us. The afternoon light grew dim and the air turned cool, and the lodge staff set up tall heaters. Nellie then picked up her guitar, perched high on a bar chair, and sang a variety of songs to close out the evening.

On Sunday morning around 8:40, we headed to the airport with Windy and Lisa. Windy was flying to LaGuardia to get ready for another busy week of teaching and graduate school, while Lis was heading to San Francisco to conduct her apartment search in the San Francisco and San Mateo area. On the way back, Kersti and I stopped at the King Soopers supermarket and picked up food supplies for our final days in the mountains. Janine, Kersti, and I were still not feeling ourselves, so we took it easy the rest of the day, conversing, stoking the wood stove, and preparing a sweet potato-kale-pepper soup for dinner. Nellie joined us for the evening, and played songs on the guitar and piano until past 10:00 PM.

After lunch on Monday, our new foursome took the scenic drive back to Nederland and then west on Route 72 to the Roosevelt National Forest near Ward. The clouds were thickening as we parked close to Brainard Lake (elevation 10,300 feet), and a light rain began falling as we set out for the hike around the small lake. We looked up at the higher surrounding mountains, stretching above the tree line. We heard deep, unexpected rumbles of thunder. The rain grew steadier, and then all of a sudden the sky started pelting us with hailstones. The hail bounced off my bare head. We had to traverse several small rocky inlets before completing the loop and returning to our car. We stopped in Nederland as the sky was clearing for soup and samosas at the Tibetan/Indian restaurant or coffees at the local cafe. Kersti and I were in a gift shop, buying a salt lamp for Anja, when we heard someone shout, "Look at the rainbow!" We rushed outside and saw a thick, arching rainbow reaching all the way down to the earth. It was another gift from Norbert.

Anja joined us for an afternoon debrief and another soup and salad dinner, before we dropped her off a little after 9:00 PM.

Postscript

On Tuesday morning, we took it easy, before eating an early lunch and heading down the mountain to Boulder. Janine visited her friend and roommate from Columbia, Dara, in North Boulder, while Kersti and I drove east to Lafayette to visit my high school classmate, Bobbie Watson. Bobbie married our classmate Eric Anderson after they graduated from college, and they soon moved to Aspen. Their two boys were born in 1979 and 1983, and then Eric was tragically skilled in a drunk driving incident in 1988. Bobbie related the remarkable story of forgiving the driver who killed Eric, and they later went around the state as a duo in an effort to prevent future tragedies. It always feels good to reconnect with classmates and share our life stories.

We had a smooth trip home on Wednesday. We departed from our cabin and then stopped to bid farewell to Jörg and Sonny, as they headed out on the road again, and soon after to Anja and Rich. We dropped off the car at Advantage, took the air train to Terminal B, picked up salads for lunch, and walked to the gate. Our flight left on time and arrived a few minutes early. Janine loaned me her earplugs, so I was able to watch the Mr. Rogers documentary. Kersti's Lyft app wasn't responding, so we took a cab home. We had a nice chat with our driver, who lives in Brooklyn and whose 11-year-old daughter attends a charter school. We pulled into our driveway around 7:00 PM, and it was already growing dark. We walked into the clean, streamlined, ready-to-show house, and it felt different. We will be moving—*moving on*—very soon.

Chapter 39

GERMANY

December 16, 2018 – February 4, 2019

"We sang, clapped, swayed, and joined a collective feeling of good will among people from many different nations... I had a strong feeling that the world would be okay, that peace and civility will prevail over the darker forces"

Wednesday, December 19, Bingen

It's another typical *nasskalt* (damp, cool) early winter day in Bingen. But we are glad to be here in our now warm and festively decorated apartment at 18-22 Dr Sieglitz Strasse. Kersti is at the *Altenheim (*elder home, *Heim* for short) this morning, interviewing candidates to replace Nancy in early February. I had to take an extra walk up over the muddy road and walkway, currently under construction, to St. Martin's, because Kersti wound up with both sets of keys. The moist, chilly air brought tears to my eyes. It felt good when I was back in the apartment and proceeding with the main morning chore: removing the portable seat from the bathtub and cleaning up the entire bathroom in anticipation of baths for Kersti and the arrival of Janine, Lisa, and Nellie this weekend.

We had a whirlwind visit to Brooklyn and Madison on Saturday and Sunday, December 15 and 16. We made good time on our trip south on Route 15, until we encountered the closure of "the Hutch" (Hutchinson Parkway) around New Rochelle. We lost an hour or more, winding through the narrow streets of New Rochelle. At one backup, we noticed two dogs, likely from the same home, racing along the street and darting in and out of traffic. Fortunately, it was moving very slowly. When the dogs came close to our car, Kersti was hoping to corral them with her open door, but the little one—some kind of spaniel—jumped up into her lap, muddy paws, wet fur, and all! The larger one was also vying to hop in, but Kersti pushed the smaller one right out of the car. As we drove ahead, we saw the two racing down another side street in the hope of a rescue.

We had a delightful afternoon with Windy. We dropped off their ski boots for their upcoming holiday ski trip to Park City, Utah with Anja, Daniel, and Rich (we were sorry not to deliver their helmet and googles), and then strolled through the residential streets adjacent to Bedford Avenue. It grew dark—one of the 12 shortest days of the year—and Christmas lights were flicking on. We walked along Cortelyou Avenue, looking for a place to eat, and finally settled on a casual Indian buffet restaurant. We had our choice of 30 or more dishes, and our varied selections were all delicious. We have had numerous meals in Brooklyn with Windy since they moved there, and this was the best. We'll definitely go back.

Our drive through the Battery/Carey Tunnel, across the lower tip of Manhattan, through the Holland Tunnel, south on Route 1 and west on 78/24 was relatively quick, in spite of the predicted holiday "gridlock" on this second to last Saturday before Christmas. We stayed at Hamilton Park overnight, took a swim in our private pool on Sunday morning, joined Mom for Sunday lunch at Juniper, and the spent the afternoon with Rocky, Anita, Alissa, and Michael. It was raining all day, even as Anita and Rocky drove us to the airport.

Our flight was delayed by two hours because of some small mechanical issues within the cabin and some freezing rain, which necessitated a stop at the deicing area. As indicted by our wide range of wakeup times, it seems like we never made up those two hours during our first few days in Germany. But we managed to settle in, visiting Mutti every day and tidying up various rooms and closets in the apartment. It feels good to be here.

Sunday, December 23

It's a quiet evening in the *Wohnung* (apartment) in Bingen I have been battling a cold the last few days, and so I stayed behind when Kersti, Janine, Lisa, and Nellie headed across the river on the ferry to the Rudesheim *Weihnachtsmarkt* (Christmas market). It's the last day of the market, since tomorrow is *Heilige Abend* (Christmas Eve, holy evening), the most sacred day of the German religious calendar. I'm enjoying the task of opening the doors of Mutti's desks and cabinets to discover a rich variety of photos (mostly black and white), cards, letters, and photo calendars that Mutti saved throughout the years. It appears that she saved everything that we ever sent to her.

The family highlights of the last three days were the arrivals of Nellie from New York via Paris because of the two-day Gatwick drone shutdown, Lisa from San Francisco via Dallas and London after a nearly 23-hour odyssey, and Janine from London following a stopover to visit her friend Nina in Köln. On Friday evening, we joined Mutti for a Christmas service and special meal at the *Heim*, and today we enjoyed *Kaffee und Kuchen,* featuring *Plätzchen* (cookies) baked by Janine in her spacious new kitchen in London. I served the cookies on the famous Lenox serving dish with the screwed-in handle, which I had given to Mutti as a house gift during my first visit in December 1982. I was hopeful that she would recall how she always presented the tray, holding her left hand underneath for security, but she did not remember.

The travel highlight of the week was our *Aufflug* (excursion) with Wolfgang and Vera to the Eberbach Kloster, not far from Rüdesheim. It was founded by St Bernard of Clairvaux and 12 Cistercian monks in 1136. In the 12th and 13th centuries, some 150 monks and up to 300 lay brothers studied and made copies of the Bible in the years before the invention of the printing press in nearby Mainz. We walked through the courtyard, chapter house, monastery church, dining hall, wine cellar, and dormitory, marveling on this cool, damp, raw day in late December how they lived in this place of such unrelenting cold. Just prior to our walking tour, Wolfgang and Vera treated us to a delicious lunch in an adjacent restaurant, lit up almost entirely by candles. It was a fun day and a joy to reconnect with one of Kersti's best friends from the Hildegardeschule.

Saturday, December 29

I'm alone again on another cool, cloudy day at the end of December and the conclusion of the year. The sun rarely shines in Germany at this time of the year. We did enjoy some sunshine on Christmas Eve Day. Early in the afternoon, I dropped off Janine, Lisa, and Nellie at the Bingerbrück station, and they took the train to Esslingen to spend two days with Detlef and Frank Schindler and their families. Kersti and I joined Mutti for some live music on the 6th floor, but the familiar Christmas melodies presented by the two trumpeters and two French horn players was uncomfortably loud; so Kersti and I pushed up Mutti's neck ring to cover each ear. She grew tired, so we slipped away and headed to the Bretzenheim section of Mainz for a special Christmas Eve dinner with Gabi and Wolfgang. Gabi went all out, preparing a chestnut soup, salad, pork loin, dumplings with a white sauce, red cabbage, and baked apples for dessert. Everything was delicious, and we chatted and reminisced about our New England and Canada trip in August 1982 and other things until after 10:00 PM.

On December 26, *der zweite Weihnachtstag* (second Christmas Day), we hosted the Ramges for *K&K*. The *Heim* staff prepared a festive table in one of the private rooms. We provided some chocolate and marzipan-filled croissants, which Kersti purchased that morning at the Aral *Tankstelle* (gas station) in Büdesheim, and several pieces of cake leftover from the previous day's festivities. Peter brought Rosi, and Thomas was accompanied by Anna and 11-year-old Moritz. Hans stayed in Biebertal to take a much-needed break from caring for Rosi. She hardly speaks anymore and only recognizes immediate family members. Nellie returned from Stuttgart in mid-afternoon, while Janine and Lisa were spending the afternoon and evening with Ilaria, Janine's friend from her semester at Konstanz in the spring of 2007.

One special moment occurred after our guests left, and we took Mutti up to the 6th floor. She was enthusiastically greeted with open arms by Klaus Peter, and she immediately lifted her arms and broke into a wide grin. In that moment, she felt she was back home.

On Thursday, Nellie, Kersti, and I drove to Karlsruhe for a gourmet lunch with Irmgard and Albert. Janine and Lisa made their way to Irmgard's from Stuttgart. Irmgard served a pumpkin soup, salad, ratatouille, and apricot cake and *Stollen* for dessert. We then headed south on "the 5," arriving in the quiet, dark, chilly town of Oberkirch a little over an hour after leaving Karlsruhe. The town is on the northern edge of the Schwarzwald, but it did not feel like we were close to or in the forest. After dropping off our bags, we drove into town and discovered a delightful center and *Fussgangerzone* (pedestrian zone), brightly decorated for Christmas. After picking up some food and staples at Reve, we had a tasty dinner at a Greek restaurant.

On Friday afternoon and evening, the four girls began their three-day yoga and meditation program at the Art of Living Center in Bad Antogast. I was very content to catch up on my email (glad to have Internet access once again) and the national and international news through CNN. Now I am off for a Saturday stroll into town and a bit of shopping at Reve.

Thursday, January 3, 2019

We arrived back in Bingen on Wednesday afternoon after our final child-niece dropoff: Janine at the train station in Mainz for her journey back to London. Kersti is suffering from a bad cold, so she is resting on the bed while I reflect on the past few days, sitting in my familiar corner chair overlooking Dr. Sieglitz Strasse.

On Sunday morning the 30th, we drove southeast for about 20 minutes to the Art and Living Center in Bad Antogast for the half-day finale of their "Happiness" program. We drove up to a higher elevation along winding roads with vistas of wide green fields, valleys, and forests. I joined the group for a casual lunch in their meeting space, including Timo (owner and CEO of his Like Meat company), his girlfriend Katarina, and his sister Isabel. After lunch, Nellie stayed behind for a massage, while our "original four" walked along the wooded path above the complex. We paused at a stable with five horses and talked about our family. On the return trip, Nellie treated us to *K&K* at a café in Oppenau. We shared large, delicious slices of *Schwarzwalderkirchtorte* (Black Forest cake), cherry cake, apple cake, and chocolate cake.

Early on the morning of the 31st, Kersti and I got up at 4:45 AM and left with Lis around 5:45 for a quick trip to the Karlsruhe train station for her 7:00 train to the Frankfurt airport. There was very little traffic as we sped north on the rain-swept *Autobahn.* As we were conversing at the platform around 6:45, a familiar figure in her winter coat and hat quickly approached us: it was Irmgard, bearing envelopes for Lisa, Janine, and Nellie with some funds to support their travels. The train pulled away at 7:00 sharp, and Lis was on her way for her 24-hour trip home to San Francisco.

That evening, we experienced one of our most meaningful and memorable New Year's Eves ever at the ashram. We arrived early to secure a parking spot, and then Nellie and Janine headed off on a serious hike, while Kersti and I retraced our steps to the horses. Just before dinner, Guru Shri Shri Ravi Shankar appeared, slowly walking down the stairs, followed by his energetic entourage. In their excitement, some people pushed forward to touch him or get a closer look. The special New Year's Eve dinner was mediocre in terms of quality and uncomfortable in terms of the logistics and seating. But the program that followed was by far the highlight of the evening. After dinner, we gathered in the large meeting room, and Timo welcomed us to join his family and friends. Then everyone turned toward the open door and saw the guru entering the ballroom. Some people gave him flowers, cards, or gifts, and he would casually hand them to an aide over his shoulder. He arrived at the large, comfortable chair, settled in, sipped some water, and looked out at the 500+ people. With a twinkle in his eye, he patiently, quietly, deliberately waited to speak. He then shared with us in English his New Year's message of peace, hope, and balance—balance between comfort and challenge, responsibility and inaction, and the slow and rapid movement of time. He spoke with such wisdom, clarity, and inspiration. After he concluded his remarks, several musicians led everyone in Hindi songs. We sang, clapped, swayed, and joined a collective feeling of good will among people from many different nations. The program was being beamed to many countries around the world. When we departed around 10:30 PM, I had a strong feeling that the world would be okay, that peace and civility will prevail over the darker forces. Kersti and I drove back to Oberkirch, while Nellie and Janine rang in the new year with Timo and company. As we approached midnight, I kept looking for a German TV program to celebrate the first moments of the new year, but had to settle for the ball drop at the Arc de Triomphe in Paris.

Just like almost every other day of our trip so far, New Year's Day was damp, cloudy, and chilly. We dropped Nellie off at the train station in nearby Offenburg and enjoyed our final evening with Janine that evening.

Thursday, January 10, Solln

When we left New Hampshire on December 15, we thought we had left winter behind. But while southern New Hampshire is experiencing a mild winter to date, southeastern Germany has been inundated the past week by a major, accumulating, ongoing snowstorm. We were lucky to drive to Solln on Monday, January 7, encountering no *Staus* (traffic jams) and arriving in the daylight after a comfortable four-and-a-half-hour drive. It felt good and familiar to turn the corner onto our small street, Randelshofersweg, and find "Herr" and his adorable dachshund Quincy standing in the street, almost as if they were waiting and looking for us. It was pleasing to carry our suitcases and multiple bags up the steel steps and into our cozy apartment. Herr had thoughtfully put the heat on for us.

The days are passing slowly but comfortably. Kersti has been dealing valiantly with an annoying, uncomfortable sciatic condition, and is currently at a local chiropractor as I write this. The snow has not prevented us from trips on foot or by car to Frau Wachter (therapy), Edeka (food), Rossman (pharmacy), the butcher (*Putinwiener,* turkey hot dogs), and the movie theater to see what is playing. Kersti finished reading *Becoming,* Michelle Obama's memoir, and then turned her

Kindle over to me for the first time to read the same. We are staying apprised of the news via the online *New York Times* and staying in touch with family and friends, now that we are back with an Internet connection.

The days are growing longer now, though we don't notice it, especially dealing with about 20 inches (50 cm) of snow. It was still light when I dropped Kersti off at her chiropractor, but it's dark now. I will leave in 15 minutes to pick her up. I hope we don't miss each other.

The adjacent streets are narrow at all times of the year, but the snow, ice, and especially the unplowed conditions make driving challenging, hazardous, and annoying. I can't believe that in this wealthy section of Munich they have not plowed most roads. When driving, it is often necessary to pull into an open space—if you an even find one—because most roads are now single lanes. Some cars are simply snowed in, compounding the problem. In addition, many Sollners do not shovel the sidewalks in front of their homes, leaving icy, slippery, and dangerous conditions.

Monday, January 21, Solln

After many chilly, gray days, the sun came out this past Saturday, and we finally made it to the Isar. Kersti is still recovering from her sciatic condition, which has limited her mobility, so we drove to the parking area close to the bridge and outdoor pool. It was cold, so we bundled up with scarves, gloves, and inner and outer jackets, but the sun felt *schön warm* at the moment when we stood still, closed our eyes, and faced the sun. We walked over the bridge that we have traversed so often on our bikes and then south along the east bank of the river. The water was at a low level, and at one point we walked out into the river on the dry stone bed. Afterwards, we drove to Pullach and had a tea and coffee at a friendly bistro with a partial view of the Isar River and valley.

On Sunday, we returned to the Isar. The sun was nowhere to be found, and it felt like snow. We drove south through Pullach to Grundwald, a small town that sits high bank overlooking the Isar on the eastern slope. We parked close to the Grundwald *Burg,* a small, oddly shaped yellow castle with a tall rectangular tower. It was closed for renovations. We walked along the street and icy path with the river to our left. The steeply graded woods were thick with thin trees, and even in the winter with their leaves down, they did not offer much of a view of the river. On our way back to the car, it began snowing. We drove back to our apartment for teatime.

We are still in the depths of winter. This morning's temperature is -3° C (26° F), and, as I have to do on many mornings, I had to brush the thin layer of snow off the car and scrape the windshield before delivering Kersti to her acupuncture appointment. I picked up some green and red lettuce at one Edeka location, and some cookies and chips at the other location near Festingstrasse, and then drove home.

Tuesday, January 29, Solln

On Wednesday, the 23rd, we had a change of scenery and a date with Gina in Gröbenzell, northwest of Solln and about 30 kilometers from here. She has battled pneumonia for the past five weeks, but was in good enough health and spirits to take a chilly walk in her neighborhood. We noticed a beautiful blue "ice bird," which flew ahead of us along a small canal, often stopping so we could admire and photograph it. Afterwards, we were treated to Gina's delicious apple cake and *Marmelkuchen.* We talked about our move to New Hampshire, our six children, the 2020 presidential race, and numerous other topics as the afternoon light faded to darkness.

We had visitors early on Friday morning, the 25th. Janine and her former roommate, Mathilde, "ubered" into snowy Solln around 1:30 AM after their delayed flight from London. I was planning to pick them up at the Solln station, but they took an Uber instead from the *Hauptbahnhof* in central Munich. I had stayed up, happy to discover on CNBC (the only English channel) the "Tonight Show" with Jimmy Fallon at 11:30 PM, just as in the U.S., followed by "NBC Nightly News" with Lester Holt. We saw the lights of the car on Randelshofersweg followed by the lifting of the trunk and slam of the doors. I popped outside at the top of the stairs and saw Janine's beaming smile and full backpack, followed by Mathilde. They were spending the short night with us prior to taking the train south to ski at Kitzbühel in Austria. In the morning, Kersti and I enjoyed breakfast with them, featuring eggs from the local farm, fresh German bread, and tea. We dropped them at the Solln station for their S-Bahn ride to the *Ostbahnhof.*

Back in our apartment, as I stepped into the shower, I noticed that Mathilde had left her toiletry bag and a plastic bag with her various cosmetics. I wound up meeting the girls at the *Ostbahnhof* yesterday afternoon on their way back to the airport after their enjoyable ski weekend. Kersti made the arrangements, and I executed the plan, walking briskly to the Solln station and taking the S7 to the *Ostbahnhof,* arriving 20 minutes early. The girls' train pulled in on time, and we enjoyed a cup of coffee or tea in a small station café. They each bought some fresh German bread to take back to London. I had to wait for a while in the chilly afternoon for the Wolfratshausen train, but it finally arrived. It was still light when I turned he key and entered the apartment around 4:30 PM.

We started packing this morning. We will be on the road again this Thursday for our usual soup and salad stop in Karlsruhe followed by our return to Bingen. It will be a busy Friday with appointments with a local real estate agent and a disposal company as we take the first big steps toward selling the apartment. I believe the Wiebe family has been there 46 years—the same as our family's time at 19 Dellwood Avenue in Chatham.

As we slowly pack our suitcases and back packs and manage our food supply in these waning days in Solln, we are reflective. We have spent these wintry days largely confined to our apartment. We have usually walked to the stores and to our therapy appointments, all within 15 minutes, adding a minute or two because of the sidewalks, which are still icy and slippery in spots. We think and talk about the many changes that have occurred in our lives and our children's lives during the past year, inevitably with more to come in 2019. I will miss some aspects of our lives here—the slow pace, the challenging, bracing walks, the fluffy layers of nighttime snow, the red and green salads, my instant morning coffee, strolls through the wide white fields, and quiet times to read and talk. I will not miss the cold, often raw weather, but look forward to our return in April, when we will be able to jump on our bikes and speed through the streets of Solln after the banks of snow and ridges of ice have melted away.

Monday, February 4, Frankfurt

The sun is pouring down n Frankfurt Airport just past noon as we sit at the Lufthansa gate, awaiting our 1:25 PM flight to Newark. Almost every day in Germany was chilly, gray, and overcast, but every time we traveled, the sun helped us on our way. This was true last Thursday, when we wrapped up our time in Solln after Kersti's "finale" with Frau. Nancy's morning text message from Bingen included a warning about snow and an urging that we drive with caution, but we had blue skies and smooth sailing all the way to Karlsruhe. We stopped for our usual *Brotzeit* (literally, bread time) at Irmgard's and Albert's; she served a delicious pepper soup, *Feldsalat* (field salad), and cherry pie and *Marmelkuchen* (marble cake) for dessert. The sun was dipping below the horizon as we departed on our final leg to Bingen. We arrived at the *Wohnung* around 7:30 PM and have quickly settled in.

Friday was a busy and productive day. In the morning, we met with Doreen and her colleague from the local Harman real estate agency, and after a quick tour of the apartment, she suggested a starting asking price of 260 eruos. Doreen was knowledgeable, cordial, and not pushy, and we will likely go with her. We visited Mutti for *K&K*—she always smiles when I reference this special German tradition—and we found her in good spirits. She smiled and laughed often as we chatted with her. She seems much more accepting of her circumstances and home in the *Heim*. At 5:00 PM, we were back in the apartment for a meeting with a young man from a Mainz-based company that helps home sellers dispose of their household items. He was very pleasant and professional as we moved from room to room, and he snapped photos of all the items that we will likely dispense with. We were impressed by his estimate in the 900 euros range, which factors in the company's ability to sell most of the furniture items as income.

On Saturday, we had an enjoyable visit with Gabi and Wolfgang. While Wolf was playing his regular Saturday indoor soccer game, Gabi, her brother's ex-wife Kordula, and Kersti took a walk all the way to and back from he Rochusberg. Back in the apartment, Gabi served her delicious flat apple cake topped by fresh whipped cream. They are very dear, long-term friends, and we look forward to visiting them at their vacation apartment in Austria in May.

Sunday's highlight was the *Heim's* celebration of *Fastnacht/Fasching*. Mutti, Kersti, and I joined Suse at the same spot close to the stage where we sat for the Christmas celebration in December. We enjoyed a kids' dance group, consisting of Snow White and her seven dwarfs, one a cute young blond girl who reminded me of Lisa as she danced across the stage. Other acts included teenage "rockettes," a group of guys in their 20s, 30s, and 40s who impersonated Mexicans, Russians, and women, and individual light-hearted presentations by the *Bischof* (bishop), *Burgermesiter* (mayor), a 50-year female Bingen resident, and even the Chef (boss) Wolfgang, who told stories about Bingen and its residents in rhymed couplets.

Wednesday, February 4, Nyack, New York

It's the final day and leg of our trip. Once again, the sun is shining as I sit in our warm car in front of Dr. Ron's brown house with bright yellow shutters, during Kersti's session. I just walked down to the Hudson, which was frozen in just one small section; most of the wide river was free flowing.

Almost ever aspect of our trip back to New Jersey went smoothly, heading to an on-time arrival at 4:10 in Newark and pick up by Josh Kavaloski exactly 65 minutes later, as planned. The one exception was at the security line in Frankfurt. Unlike at Newark, there was virtually no line, but this actually worked to our disadvantage: we were both stopped because they had so many people with so little to do. I was told that I had been selected for a random in-depth security check, which included digging out all three pairs of shoes from my carefully packed carry-on suitcase. The agent closely examined and bent all six shoes. Meanwhile, Kersti's pre-TSA status got her only as far as the discovery of a small sample of her green powder in a plastic bag. Police were called in, suspecting it might be an explosive. The agent even sniffed it and grimaced at the foul odor. He generously allowed Kersti to take it with her.

On board the flight, we watched films the entire time: I chose the riveting *Bohemian Rhapsody*, the story of Freddie Mercury and Queen; *Ludwig II,* an account of the Bavarian king that helped us to string together his adult life and various castles that we visited; and an encore of *Mamma Mia II* with the wonderful, beautiful, charming, captivating, and talented Lily James in the lead role. Kersti watched *Buddenbooks, Ludwig II*, and *Das Wunder von Bern (The Miracle of Berne*), the story of a young boy, his POW father, and Germany's triumph over Hungary in the 1954 World Cup.

We stayed with Anita on Monday evening, enjoying her turkey dinner and conversation. Rocky was in Connecticut at this annual condo association meeting. Tuesday was a busy day, including a "no-show" breakfast at Drew (my colleague and friend Yasmin Acosta was hoping to move our meeting from 7:30 to 8:30, but I was out of email and phone contact and never saw her message until later), a visit to Overlook Hospital in Summit, where Mom was recovering from her flu, a visit to Sycamore Cottage before and after lunch to chat with former colleagues, lunch in the student center with Josh, our meeting with Joe Grippo at Merrill Lynch to discuss our finances, *K&K* with Barbara Gilford at her home in Morris Township, and finally a kick-off to the barbecue season with the Pachecos, featuring hamburgers, turkey burgers, and the always engaging company of Alissa, Andy, and Michael.

Postcript

Our trip from Nyack to Exeter went smoothly, and we pulled into our parking spot around 2:30. We had a brief moment of panic when our keys to the new lock and door did not work. So we went over to the post office to pick up our heavy bin of mail. By the time we returned, our contractor Ryan had sent the code to the lock box, and we opened the door and stepped into the next phase of our lives.

Chapter 40

SAN FRANCISCO

March 13-18, 2019

"It's the San Francisco vibe"

San Francisco

Friday, March 15

I am sitting on a bench at the Pacific Ocean on our third day of brilliant sunshine and solid blue skies. A guy just sauntered by with a friend and said, "That is a great office, dude." It's the San Francisco vibe. I just strolled through the small, lapping waves with my bare feet. The water is chilly, and the sand is a shade of brown and still wet from the higher tide. I picked up a white grooved shell and two fairly in tact sand dollars on my walk. Sea gulls and geese are squawking and soaring through the sky.

We left Exeter in the dark early on Wednesday morning around 5:45 AM. It was 23°F. Everything went smoothly: our drive to Boston and Revere, just outside Logan Airport; our dropoff at the Comfort Inn; our shuttle to the United terminal; our boarding; and our flight, which arrived a few minutes early. We flew above the clouds most of the way, but in the west above Colorado and the Sierra Nevada of California, we glimpsed majestic, snow-covered mountains.

We took a Lyft to Lisa's A.I.R. office in San Mateo. Our beaming Lisa came out, and we gave her big hugs. She showed us around her office with beautiful views of the skyline of San Francisco, San Francisco Bay, and the long Bay Bridge. She was busy working on multiple proposals, and so she gave us her keys and a recommendation to visit Coyote Point. After a short drive, we walked along a trail close to the Coyote Point Yacht Club and later up a steep, winding path from the narrow beach. The views were spectacular, and the sun felt warm on our faces, but the wind was whipping up, and we were glad that we were able to zip up our in-between season jackets.

We picked up Lis and after her chiropractor appointment, we drove to a nearby Vietnamese restaurant for a multi-dish, tasty dinner, which extended into Thursday's lunch and my pending picnic at the beach. Back at Lisa's apartment at 1062 Page Street in the Haight-Ashbury section of the city, we met her roommate Michelle and her cat Bennie, and concluded our extra-long day on Lisa's bed in her spacious room. She slept in the loft in the small guest room.

On Thursday, Lisa worked at home, including four hours of conference calls. But she was able to join us for half an hour at a local café to reconnect with our friend from our years in Madison, Anne Reinert. We spent more than three hours with Anne, talking about our kids, moves, former jobs, future jobs, travels, politics, and more. Anne graciously invited us to stay with Scott, Maggie (their mid-sized poodle), and her the next time we are in San Francisco, and she also invited our kids and us to spend some days at their cabin in Lake Tahoe, about three hours from San Francisco.

After wrapping up with Anne, we moved Lisa's car to the corner of Haight and Baker Streets, directly across from Buena Vista Park. It's a small, beautiful, lush, hilly park with winding pathways and great views of downtown San Francisco and the shiny red Golden Gate Bridge. After some heat ups at Lisa's apartment, we took the bus northeast toward the northern bay to scout out Kersti's sandplay workshop at the corner of Fillmore and Union and our weekend hotel, the Coventry Inn on Lombard Street. Our bus rides north and south gave us a good sense of the lay of the land. The bus grew more and more crowded, so when we were preparing to hop off at our next step with the bus still moving, I lost my footing and wound up in the lap of a bewildered, mildly annoyed Chinese man. I apologized, and we quickly departed from the bus.

After a warm day, it grew chilly as Lis led us east toward Dolores Park and later along Mission Street for dinner at Kitava, a vegetarian restaurant. On the way back, Lisa treated us to ice cream at a very popular parlor; waiting time: 20 minutes. But the girls' dairy-free, gluten-free chocolate hazel cup and my generous coffee caramel praline scoop in a freshly-made waffle cone were well worth the wait.

We had a meaningful talk with Lisa on our way home and as we were preparing for bed. She is doing important, high-quality work, but still feels somewhat isolated and lonely both in San Mateo and San Francisco. She is still settling in. Her move to the West Coast took a lot of courage.

Sunday, March 17

It's our fifth consecutive beautiful spring day in San Francisco. While Kersti concludes her three-day sandplay workshop, I took the 90-minute guidebook tour of nearby Russian Hill. It is located just south of Lombard Street and the "crookedest street in the world." One highlight was the old thatched-roofed, gabled house in the Bay Area tradition, located at 1019 Vallejo Street. It was built in 1892 by Willis Polk, one of the key architects of the post-1906 earthquake reconstruction, and it was visited by Robert Louis Stevenson and Laura Ingalls Wlder. Just below his own house at 1013 Vallejo, Polk created the zigzagging Beaux Arts-style Vallejo Street steps, known as "the ramps." It winds through a garden lush with hydrangeas, azaleas, palms, magnolias, and overarching pine and cypress trees. A second highlight was Coolbrith Park at the bottom of the stairs and just across Taylor Street. The beautifully landscaped, sloping park commemorates the life of Ina Donna Coolbrith (1841-1928), the first white child to enter California by Beckwourth Pass, traveling in the first covered wagon train that followed that route in September 1852. Later, Coolbrith was a librarian, poet, and supporter of California writers. She was a member of the Native Daughters of the Golden West, and in 1919, she was given the honorary title "loved Laurel-crowned poet of California."

Saturday's walk took me to Fort Mason and Aquatic Park on the northern edge of the city, overlooking San Francisco Bay. Fort Mason, consisting of multiple large barracks with distinctive orange roofs, dates from the Civil War period and was a major supplier of materiel and men during World War II. Dad was in San Francisco prior to his deployment on the *U.S.S. Sturgis* on his way to the Pacific. I wonder if he spent time at Fort Mason or at another barracks in the bustling war-time city. I then followed the wooded path up, around, and down toward the Maritime National Historical Park and Museum, the Municipal Pier, and the Hyde Street Pier. Among the ships moored in Aquatic Park off the Hyde Street Pier is the *S.S. Balcutha*. Built and launched in Glasgow in 1886, it traveled between England and California, rounding Cape Horn some 17 times, often trading California wheat for British coal.

After Kersti's workshop, she and I walked along Fillmore, Lombard, and Chestnut Streets, past drunk roving bands of young men and women, mostly in their twenties and sporting green attire. They were celebrating St. Patrick's Day, one day early. Many were loud, pushy, and obnoxious. We finally settled on a small Indian restaurant, and it was still warm and quiet enough to eat our chicken and lamb rice/quinoa bowls at a small outdoor table.

Postcript

On Sunday evening, Anne and Scott Darling invited us to their beautiful condo at 1259 Francisco Street, which parallels Chestnut and Bay Streets. Anne served mushroom soup, chicken, stir-fried veggies, rice, salad, and fresh fruit for desert. Lis joined us after her day with her Miami buddies, Casey and Dina. After dinner, Anne dropped us back at the Coventry and then took Lisa back to Page Street.

Our flight was not until 1:55 PM on Monday afternoon, so Kersti and I enjoyed a leisurely Monday morning with breakfast at a French-style bistro on Union Street and a walk along the bay heading west from Fort Mason. A playful seal, hunting for breakfast, swooped up and below the surface of the water. We had a grand view of the Golden Gate Bridge.

We had a smooth flight from west to east, from daylight to darkness, from springtime back to winter. I watched *What They Had*, a film about Alzheimer's with Hilary Swank and Blythe Danner, and *It Will Be Chaos*, a moving documentary on refugees fleeing war and strife in Syria and Eritrea. The one frantic moment came at the Comfort Inn parking lot, where I was unable to open the Jetta car door. But a few guys from the parking company helped out, and we were on our way back to Exeter. We arrived a little past midnight. Around 12:10 AM, I looked Kersti in the eyes and wished her a happy 36th wedding anniversary.

Chapter 41

GERMANY AND ENGLAND (AND BRIEFLY, BELGIUM AND FRANCE)

April 8 – May 18, 2019

"It is a beautiful, sacred, peaceful, final resting place"

"I have never before had the opportunity to observe so closely and connect so spiritually with these graceful, gentle creatures"

Solln, Munich, Germany

Wednesday, April 10: Solln

It's a cool, damp day in Solln, a stark contrast to the string of warming sunny days in Exeter. But when I set out on foot on Monday afternoon from 32 Franklin Street to the Exeter train station, it was raining lightly. The station is just over a mile away. I was wearing my brown fleece with my spring jacket on top and my winter gloves still on. Once on board, the slow Amtrak "Downeaster" rolled through the wooded areas of southern New Hampshire and northeastern Massachusetts, along the Merrimack River for one stretch, stopping only at Haverhill and Woburn before pulling into Boston's North Station 70 minutes later. A transit officer directed me down two flights of stairs to the "T" Green Line to Government Square and then the Blue Line to Logan. I hopped on the shuttle bus to Terminal C and another bus to Terminal E and the Icelandair counter. A team of three agents was awaiting me; there was no delay.

We left on time at 9:10 PM and arrived a little early at the Keflavik Airport in Iceland around 6:00 AM following a 4-hour, 50-minute flight. After an hour stopover, highlighted by a colorful Icelandic sunrise, I boarded another plane for the final, nearly four-hour flight to Munich. We touched down around 1:15 PM. After retrieving my luggage, I took the S8 S-Bahn to the *Hauptbahnhof* and the S7 to Solln. From there, I rolled my black suitcase with its aqua ribbon to our apartment on Randelshoferweg, walking in close to 4:00 PM, about 19 hours after locking the door on Franklin Street. It was a long trip, but totally expected and on time. I don't mind spending some extra time to save a sizeable amount of money.

Kersti had provided most of the staples for our 10-day stay here, but I got on my bike and rode to Edeka to pick up a 6-pack of *Hefe Weizen*, milk, cookies, and cereal. It felt good to be back in this familiar place, doing familiar tasks.

Sunday, April 14: Solln

On Saturday, April 13, we ventured into central Munich, prompted by a visit to the Apple store adjacent to Marienplatz, because Kersti accidentally spilled a quarter of a glass of water onto her computer when we were speaking with Janine on Thursday evening. It felt like we were entering a crowded Apple store in the Short Hills mall or anywhere in the U.S. We walked upstairs, and a tech guy briefly explained that we would need to schedule an appointment later in the week (of course, Easter week) and that the potential damage might be very expensive. It sounded like an opening sales pitch. It was just past noon, and we had the entire day and evening in front of us. It was still chilly, but the sun was out, and it was warm enough to eat our lunch and a sample of vegan goulash, provided by the on-stage vegan cooking demo at Marienplatz. We saw a flyer at the information center for the Munich Mass Choir, performing that evening in nearby Haidhausen, so we bought tickets.

We strolled through a park surrounded by 19th-century buildings with no cars in sight, and felt for a few moments what it was like to live in Munich two centuries ago. A visit to the magnificently sculptured Frauenkirche was in the same vein. In the spirit of spontaneity, we jumped on the No. 100 bus, which winds past many of Munich's museums and historical sites. After a short ride, Kersti noticed the Brandhorst Museum and the exhibit by the American artist, Alex Katz, who was born in Brooklyn in 1927. She had researched the exhibit during our stay in January, but the wintry weather had kept us away from the city. We paused for a cup of coffee and tea in the museum bistro, and then thoroughly enjoyed our tour of Katz's work, featuring bright colors, people (often his wife Ada), people in motion (dancers or skaters), and landscapes at night, dawn, or dusk. Often he played with doubles or triples to challenge the viewer's perspective. An upstairs exhibit by another American artist, Cy Twombly (1928-2011), made us wonder how modern abstract expressionist art is even considered art. His "scribbles," while colorful, seemed juvenile and thoughtless, a spontaneous free for all, though we understood there was a creative process at work somewhere—we just didn't know where. The room full of rose paintings of various colors was somewhat more recognizable and appealing.

We took the bus to the *Hauptbahnhof* and then the S-Bahn just a few stops to Rosenheimerplatz. We had burgers, fries, and sweet potato fries at Hans und Gluck, and arrived at the youth center for the concert around 7:20 PM. There was open seating, and we were able to find seats close to the stage with a good view. At 8:00, about 60 or 70 singers in black dresses and trousers with white shirts and teal scarves paraded toward the stage followed by their amazing choir director and performer, Michael Flannagan. An American native who has lived in Munich for many years, he introduced all the songs in clear German and English with the flair and conviction of a southern Baptist preacher. We quickly realized that we this was a gospel concert, sung entirely in English, by white Germans and their black conductor. The African-American spirituals were rousing, and often the crowd clapped in unison. The rendition of Toto's "I Bless the Rains down in Africa" was one of my favorites. Michael frequently picked up the mic and added his own inspiring singing voice. They must have sung nearly 20 songs over nearly two hours without an intermission. It was a memorable day and evening in Munich.

We took the S-Bahn back to the Hauptbahnhof; waited for the S-7 to Wolfratshausen for about 15 minutes; arrived in Solln; and completed our day biking through the cool, dark streets of Solln. I don't think we passed a single car just past 11:00 PM.

On Wednesday evening, I had a snippet of a dream about Norbert. He was standing at a doorway with his usual beaming smile. He was much younger and had a full head of dark hair. He didn't say anything; he was just a familiar and gratifying presence. The next evening, Anja called Kersti and told her that she and Rich were breaking up after just seven months of marriage.

Good Friday, Karfreitag, April 19: Bingerbrück

It is another beautiful spring day at our small *Ferienwohnung* on Heinrich Becker Strasse in Bingerbrück. I just came back from Langenlonsheim, where Kersti and I had a scrumptious brunch hosted by Kordula, Kersti's new friend and Gabi's former sister-in-law.

Thursday was our first full day in town, and it was special and memorable. We visited Mutti around lunchtime and again for *Kaffee und Kuchen* and a Maundy Thursday *Gottesdienst* (church service). She smiled when we arrived, and was pleased to see us, but she was languid and less energetic than during our Christmas, early January, and early February visits.

The highlight of the day was our discovery of and visit to the Jewish cemetery in Bingen. It is literally walled off from the main cemetery clearly by historical design, not by 20th-century ostracism. The Jewish graves are high on the hill overlooking the Burg Klopp and the vineyards where the Nahe meets the Rhein. It is a beautiful, sacred, peaceful, final resting place. Walking up a long, graded path through the woods, we noticed a few very old scattered tombstones in Hebrew, then hundreds more until they were tightly packed together. We unlocked the gate with the large gray memorial key plate, and entered a site where time has stood still. To the left of the entrance were hundreds of memorials with family names, dates, and tributes in clear German. Katz, Rosenblum, Meyer, Nathan, Schiff, Seligman, even Rheinstrom—they were living, working, contributing, patriotic Jews, maybe even proud Germans first. The utter inhumanity and devastation that was perpetrated on them in the 1930s and 1940s are unfathomable. Thankfully, if just a little, almost everyone who was buried here died before the 1930s. As a gesture toward a future of peace and reconciliation while never forgetting the horrid past, we found four or five gravesites from the past 15 years in a sunny, grassy knoll. There is a lot of room for Jews who still live in Germany and choose this holy place for their final rest.

After departing the grounds and securely locking the gate, we walked back down the shaded hill and chatted with Hermann-Josef Gundlach, the *Vorsitzender* (caretaker) of the cemetery. He told us that the cemetery was established in 1570 and gave us some detailed brochures. One lists the names of everyone buried there and another provides a map of all the headstones. Bingen is recognizing and acknowledging the importance and value of its Jewish past.

For old time's sake, we had dinner at Vati's favorite restaurant, Calimero. We were greeted and fondly remembered by the Italian owner, who referred to Kersti on numerous occasions as "Frau Wiebe."

Easter Sunday, April 21: Bingen

On Good Friday evening, we drove to Eliesenhöhe, high above Bingerbrück, to enjoy the magnificent view of Bingen and the Rhein where it curves east and west. We were surprised that there was only one extended family there. The young boys and girls were playing soccer. The women were covered and everyone was speaking Arabic. One lady was taking a photo of the river valley, so I said, "*Schön.*" I asked, "Syrian?," and she replied that indeed they were. She said that her teenage daughter spoke good English and German and called her over. She was delightful. She explained that they were living near Dusseldorf, and we quickly greeted her dad via Skype. They came from Damascus three years ago, and she had already passed her earlier exams in German and was now pursuing her *Abitur.* We felt in these moments a deep sense of human connection, of welcome to these courageous, hard-working people who had escaped their war-torn country and arrived in this place of peace and future prosperity. They did admit that they missed their homeland.

Thursday, April 24: London

Today is a day of rest, relaxation, and getting to know Janine's cozy neighborhood of Lauriston close to Victoria Park in the Borough of Hackney in East London. Janine has a full day of work at Ark.

Yesterday was a long, action-packed day, travelling from Bingen to London close to 16 hours in all with a long break in Köln. On another sunny, slightly chilly morning in Bingerbrück, we loaded up all our luggage—two suitcases, two regular backpacks, Janine's big backpack, assorted carry bags, and our familiar green food bag—into a taxi along with Kersti, while Janine and I walked down the hill and around the bend to the Bingen Hauptbahnhof. The train took off on its journey north along the Rhein, following its bends and passing villages nestled on the banks of the river, as numerous slow-moving river cruises floated by. We changed at Koblenz, witnessing one mean conductor who blocked a frantic woman with her stroller and young son from boarding the train. She was understandably furious. Our train to Köln passed through the flat topography of western Germany and an increasing number of industrial sites. As we approached Köln, the *Dom* appeared, arching high above this city of one million inhabitants.

Shortly after noon, Marianne and Michael Ullrich arrived from Munster. They treated us to lunch at an Italian restaurant, just across the street from the *Dom,* and we caught up on all the family news and geneaologies. Michael said that his family tree stretches back to about 1450. After lunch, we toured the cathedral, which was begun in 1248 and not completed until 1880. I kept wondering how such a glorious, soaring, sky-high structure could be built without the benefits of modern technology, including cranes and electricity. Michael had a simple explanation: "Time." Unlike today, they had all the time in the world and were not in a hurry. Marianne pointed out some hooks that Napoleon's forces had installed for their horses when they converted the cathedral to a stable during France's control of Germany in the early 1800s. We later strolled down to the Rhein and concluded our pleasant and meaningful time together with coffee, tea, and ice cream at an outdoor café. Janine rejoined us after her visit with her friend Nina from Osnabrück and Nina's three-month-old baby.

We bid farewell to Marianne and Michael and boarded a slow-moving "DB" (Deutsche Bahn) train to Brussels. We passed Aachen as raindrops signaled the end of our string of sunny, warm, summer-like days. Soon after, we crossed into Belgium. The train was moving slowly or not moving at all, and at one point we headed back in the direction from which we had come. Janine warned us that we might not make our connecting train to London. We should have had an hour and a half between trains, but when we finally eased into the Brussels-Midi station, we had only 15 minutes to spare. So we scurried through the station and the Belgian and British customs and passport controls. We made it on time and climbed aboard the best train of our journey. The Eurostar felt like we were sitting in the first class section of a major airline. It was dark as we headed southwest through Lille to Calais, and then through the 50-kilometer "Chunnel" in just about 15 minutes at more than 220 km per hour. We had one brief stop at Ebbsfleet in Kent, and I was pleased to see the posting about the next train "calling" at familiar locales: Ashford, Canterbury West, Broadstairs, Ramsgate, and Margate. It all felt very familiar and welcoming.

We arrived just a few minutes late at the impressive St. Pancras station, and then Janine led us to a waiting Uber driver. The evening was chilly in London. We took numerous back roads, turning through narrow, one-way streets in largely residential London, finally arriving at Janine's apartment at 8 Rutland Place around 10:45 PM. She opened her door and welcomed us into her spacious kitchen and living room on the first floor. I lugged the heavy red suitcase up the carpeted stairs to her bedroom, where she invited us to stay. We unpacked as needed, and climbed into bed, sleeping soundly until morning.

Sunday, April 28: London

It's our last full day in London. After another blustery, cool day with occasional brief showers, the sun just came out and chased the clouds away—for the moment. The sun is welcoming the large pot of daises, the pretty purple flowers, and the lavender, basil, parsley, and rosemary that we just planted in Janine's beautiful urban garden. Kersti and Janine just went to see Judi Dench's latest film, *Red Joan*, while I finished up with the gardening and am now catching up on our activities of the last few days.

On Friday morning, while Janine worked at home, Kersti and I took a long, leisurely walk through Victoria Park. Everything was in early spring bloom. We walked past the large pond, along the canal lined with houseboats, past the Chinese pagoda, and back along a winding path decorated with freshly-planted annuals. Around 11:00, Janine led us to the Bethnal Green Underground, and we took it to the Holborn stop, close to her office on King's Way. Kersti and I had a quick early lunch of a falafel sandwich and falafel box while sitting in Bloomsbury Square. Then we proceeded through Russell Square, stopping outside the Faber & Faber Publishers office where T.S. Eliot worked from 1925 to 1965. The building is now part of the University of London, which is spread out around the area. Its tallest building is Senate House on Malet Street, which was the model for George Orwell's Ministry of

Truth building in *1984*. A few blocks beyond Russell Square, we came to Gordon Square, where Virginia Woolf (nee Stephen) lived at No. 46 with her sister Vanessa and brothers Thoby and Adrian from 1904 to 1907; John Maynard Keynes, the famous economist, later lived in the same apartment. Virginia, Vanessa, and Keynes were all members of the Bloomsbury Group, which also included E.M. Forster, art critic Clive Bell (Vanessa's husband), and essayist and cultural critic Lytton Strachey. Our final stop on our afternoon literary tour was Tavistock Square. We paused at the statue of Mahatma Ghandi and at a plaque, recognizing the site of Leonard and Virigina Woolf's townhouse from 1924 to 1939. It was destroyed in the German Blitz in October 1940, a year after the Woolfs had moved to safety in Sussex. One year later, burdened by the destruction of her home, the devastating war, and her ongoing depression, Virginia drowned herself in the river running close to their country estate.

After a cup of tea and coffee at the indoor/outdoor café in Russell Square, we walked to the nearby British Museum. Admission is free; the line at the side entrance was not too long; so we went in. We headed to the third floor to the Iraq/Mesopotamia exhibit, but this museum's incredible portrayal of the history of civilization and the world was a bit overwhelming given our limited time and tiredness.

We made a few wrong turns, winding up at the picturesque Bedford Square, before arriving at Janine's office at 55 King's Way. Her half-day of work had grown to a full day, and, persuaded by a colleague, she welcomed us to Ark's 6th-floor location. We were surprised that it was a totally open, free-flowing work environment—interactive, but potentially distracting. We met Janine's colleague Rebecca, just to her right, and Janine's boss Hannah and chief advocate Liz along with Aaron and a few other people.

Kersti was tired, so Janine and I put her on a bus back to Lauriston and then set off on my second literary tour of the day, utilizing *Literary London* a great guide by Ed Glinert. Janine did a superb job navigating the busy streets of central London with her phone on a Friday afternoon. We walked by or into the following sites:

- St. Bride's Church at Fleet Street and St. Bride's Ave.; Christopher Wren was the architect of the church; Samuel Richardson is buried here; Samuel Pepys was baptized here; Milton lived in a house in the churchyard; and John Dryden wrote his ode, *Alexander's Feast*, for the church
- 32 Cornhill in the Moorgate section—Location of the visit of Anne, Charlotte, and Emily Bronte to their publisher, Smith Elder, in 1848, posing as Acton, Currer, and Ellis Bell
- 85 Moorgate—Location of John Keats' birth on October 31, 1795; he lived there until 1804; now the location of a pub that bears his name
- Bunhill Fields in the Clerkenwell section—this burial ground for some 23,000 people was discontinued in 1852, but it remains open to the public; the monuments to Daniel Defoe and William Blake are prominent; John Bunyan is also buried here

We arrived back at Janine's place around 7:30 PM and had dinner at the fish and chips restaurant, just around the corner from Janine's flat.

Our Saturday literary tour took us to Hampstead Heath via the Overground from the Homerton Station, a 20-minute walk from Janine's apartment. After lunch at the King William IV pub in the center of this delightful village, we set out in search of and located several D.H. Lawrence residences: 1 Elm Row (1923-1924), 32 Well Walk (1917; he came here with wife Frieda after they were evicted from Cornwall because she was suspected of being a German spy); and 30 Willoughby Road (1926, during his last visit to London). We also saw the fictional home of Gordon Comstock at 31 Willoughby; he was the hero of Orwell's novel, *Keep the Aspidistra Flying*, which satirizes society's pre-occupation with money and respectability. Finally, we walked along Keats' Grove with its quaint homes, sometimes brightly colored doors, and lush gardens behind iron gates. We stopped in at the Keats Community Library and Wentworth Place, where Keats lived from 1818 to 1820 and fell in love with Fanny Brawne. We were surprised to find the Keats home and museum closed from November through April. We just missed it by a few days.

We concluded our visit with three cups of tea and three slices of a scone at a local café. We then climbed up to the top of the heath where we had a few of the London skyline. The blustery wind reminded us of our visit to Boscastle in August 1999.

Kersti and I had a quiet evening, while Janine rode her bike for a special two-hour yoga session.

We stayed on foot today, walking through the Victoria Park market, along the canal, and all the way to the flower market on Columbia Road. It was tightly packed with flower vendors on both sides and hundreds of slow-moving people. We bought Janine her flowers and herbs and then had lunch at restaurant close to the canal.

It has been fun exploring a few sections of this amazing city through self-guided tours, literary and otherwise, rather than trying to take it all in through the standard city bus tour or visits to major sites. We have had some quality time with Janine, and it always means a lot to see where our children are living, working, walking, socializing, growing, and contributing to the greater good.

Hampstead Heath, London—visiting Keats' home

Thursday, May 3: Solln

On Tuesday morning, Kersti and I followed online directions over to Morning Lane to find Woolpack House, Kalia Yiannakis' home from 1964 until 1975. A local café owner pointed us in the wrong direction, and we realized it, Kersti decided to head back to Janine's apartment. Soon after, I found Woolpack House, where Lou and I had stayed several times with Kalia and her kind mum, Loucia, during our year in England. I snapped a photo and sent it to Kalia, who with Mike is currently enjoying an Elvis-inspired excursion to Atlanta, Nashville, and, of course, Memphis.

Our one-hour-and-forty-minute flight back to Munich on Tuesday afternoon and evening on Easy Jet was the centerpiece of a door-to-door journey that began at 2:30 PM England time and ended at nearly 11:00 PM German time. A cool rain was falling, but it felt good to climb the steel stairs and open the door into our familiar apartment in Solln.

Tuesday was a day of transition, including the restocking of our fridge and kitchen. I made three trips to Edeka and two to my favorite vegetable stand near Festingstrasse, while Kersti went to Rossman, the butcher, and the post office to mail Janine's computer cord that we had mistakenly packed.

The sun finally came out on Thursday, and we took the S-Bahn into Munich to join the Thomas Mann literary tour, sponsored by Stattreise, the city travel agency. Our tour was led by Natalie, a friendly German literature and history professor. We started at the Königplatz, where Mann's wife, Katja, had grown up in a wealthy Jewish household. Their home was demolished and replaced by a Nazi administrative building in the 1930s. We wound our way through various parts of the city, on foot, by bus, and by tram, stopping at several apartment complexes, including those still standing in Schwabing and Odeonplatz. We concluded at the *Literaturhaus*, where a stuffed, upright, growling bear that once stood tall in Mann's villa was on display.

Mann had a tragic life, full of turmoil and surrounded by suicides: two sisters (Carla and Lulu) and two sons (Klaus and Michael) all took their own lives. Mann lived in Munich from 1891 to 1933, and received the Nobel Prize for Literature in 1929. But he was compelled to escape the growing Nazi menace, settling first in Switzerland, then France, and finally the U.S. in 1939. He taught at Princeton from 1939 to 1942 and then moved to Pacific Palisades, close to Los Angeles, until 1952. During the war, he made anti-Nazi audiotapes, which were flown to England and broadcast regularly on the BBC. He had a triumphant return to Germany in 1949, but never lived there again, residing his final three years in a suburb of Zurich.

Monday, May 6: Solln

On a cool, mostly damp weekend, we spontaneously decided at breakfast on Saturday morning to "get out of town." I rented a car online from Europcar in the Sendling section of Munich, and then rode my bike there—about 15 minutes—to pick up our spiffy Skoda vehicle. I locked my bike at a bike rack near Reve, and then drove back to Solln to pick up Kersti.

We headed south on 95 and then west on 17 toward Füssen. The day was clear enough that we were able to see the snow-capped mountains of the lower Alps as we entered and drove through the Allgäu region. Shortly after Kersti noticed on the map that we were close to Neuschwanstein, Ludwig II's most magnificent castle, it suddenly appeared to our left. This marvel of Romanesque revival architecture was begun in 1869 and opened in 1886. Before reaching Füssen, we stopped at a *Gasthaus* in Waltenhofen, a small town on the Forggensee. It was chilly and windy, but we envisoned having lunch overlooking a large blue-green lake. We ate a typical German lunch—*Spargel, Sauerkraut, Putenschnitzel, Schinken, Kartoffeln, und Salat.* But when we looked out at the *See*, we were disappointed to see that it was almost entirely dried up. We later read that the town floods this part of the lake for vacationers during the summer months, but not until mid-June.

We drove into Füssen and walked around the *historische Altstadt* and up along the cobblestoned walkway to the castle, expanded by Bishop Frederick II of Zollern around 1500. He often received King Maximillian I and his royal entourage at the castle. We admired the seemingly 3-D paintings of windows and gables on the sides of the fortress. Leaving the city, we followed signs to Neuschwanstein and Alpsee, driving slowly and carefully through the crowded touristy area and parking near the Alpsee. Dodging the intermittent showers and bundling up from the chilly air, we embarked on a *Rundfahrt* (round trip) of the lake. We traversed a mostly level forested path close to the pristine waters with small, lapping waves. As we looked back, we could see Neuschwanstein and the distinctive orange-colored Schloss Hohenschwangau, built by Ludwig's father, König Maximillian II, and opened in 1837. We passed only a handful of other hikers and felt we had the lake all to ourselves—just as members of the royal family felt during the 19th century. On the other side of the lake, we hiked up a fairly steep path to circumvent a large outcrop of solid rock. We passed a monument to Königen Marie of Prussia (1825-1889), who reigned with her husband from 1848 to 1864, when her son Ludwig ascended to the throne. I flung a number of stones down toward the lake, waiting for two or three seconds for the "whoshing" sound of the stones breaking the water. Kersti began feeling a blister on her foot, and as the rain began to fall more steadily, we completed our hike. We agreed that it was one of our "top 5" hikes of all time. Two swans bid us farewell at the end.

Our destination on Sunday morning also took us south and west, this time on the 96 to the expansive thermal pool on the outskirts of the spa town of Wörishofen. We took the four-hour package and walked out into a spacious tropical setting with large connected indoor and outdoor pools, lounge chairs, palm trees, pulsating showers, underground eddies, and numerous health-related sections. It was very crowded by mid-morning, and we were not able to find lounge chairs next to each other. It was fun wading through the warm water, participating in a group exercise program, and cruising along the swirling current in the outdoor pool. Our heads felt cold, while our bodies stayed warm. After lunch, we walked through an ice-cold wading pool and then returned to the pool one more time. When we walked outside, it was snowing!

A few exits to the north on 96, we drove into Landsberg, a picturesque town of nearly 30,000 people on the Lech River. We walked across the bridge to the sound of the rushing water, spilling over four levels. At the center of town was a wide *Fussgängerzone* with a number of small *Gasse* (alleys) leading toward the river and parallel canal. We retreated from the *nass kalt* (damp, cool) afternoon with a cup of coffee, a cup of tea, and a pretzel at a busy bakery.

We arrived back in Solln a little after 5:00 PM. I dropped Kersti off; drove back to Europcar; deposited the car; unlocked my bike; and rode it back to our apartment for omelettes and salad on a quiet Sunday evening.

Friday, May 10: Solln

I need to write about the horses. They have graced the field outside three of our windows ever since we returned from England. I have never before had the opportunity to observe so closely and connect so spiritually with these graceful, gentle creatures. They are like a family: the big dark brown male horse with its long brown mane and white mark between its eyes; the sleek light brown mid-sized female; the smaller dark brown horse with white boots and a solid white mark on its nose; and the small, rotund black pony. The amazing thing is how much they mirror each other and relate to each other. Currently, on this cool, cloudy morning, they are all resting on their bottoms in the center of the field. At other times, they congregate under the one tree, especially when the sun comes out and the temperature warms up. Sometimes, standing opposite each other, their tales swat each other when the flies are erupting, or they nibble each other's necks. Whenever the two largest horses are saddled up and taken for rides by the young women who care for them, the other two wait expectantly at the electric fence, watching for their companions' return. In less than two weeks, they have mowed through much of the field, and they are receptive to the long, fresh bunches of grass that I offer to them. They have been communicating with us: it's a message of mindfulness, contemplation, peace, acceptance, mirroring, empathy, and living in the moment. They have been one of Solln's biggest gifts to us.

Wednesday, May 15: Solln

I told Kersti that I did not look forward to another big trip to Bingen, but she felt that we had to go to visit Mutti, retrieve Peaches (the painting), say goodbye to the *Wohnung*, and take one more look in the *Kellar.* We finalized our plans on Friday, reserving a new

Airbnb apartment and our Europcar rental. As I had done the previous weekend, I rode my bike to the Europcar office on Saturday morning, retrieved a mid-sized orange metallic VW "T-Roc," and we were back on the road to Bingen by 9:30 AM. We had a smooth ride on an increasingly brighter and warmer day, taking the 8, 81, and 6 toward Heilbronn rather than Karlsruhe, and then picking up the 61 to Bingen.

We enjoyed our light and airy apartment on Taunusstrasse, just a 10-minute walk from the *Heim* through a small park and cemetery. It had a full dining room, a spacious living room, a well-furnished kitchen, and comfortable bedroom and bed. Our only concern with regard to future visits is that it only accommodates a couple. A sleeper couch would definitely boost usage.

Mutti was pleased to see us. We stayed for *K&K* and through her early dinner. We took her down to the first floor dining area, where we had privacy, and she had good views of the trains, cars, buses, and pedestrians. We kept her engaged through a call with Anja and my usual key words, which brought smiles to her face: *Schwiegermutter, Schwiegersohn*, Petershagen, Tiegenhof, Tiege, *babich (sticky)*, and so on. She even began offering phrases from her English lessons from many years ago, such as "Thank you very much." After Mutti, we had a bite to eat at the Alte Wache restaurant—Kersti had a *Spargel* dish and green tea, and I enjoyed my *Hefe Heizen* and carrot soup.

Sunday was Mother's Day. In the morning, we walked back to the Jewish cemetery for a time of reflection and quietude. Returning to town, we parked at the *Heim* and then walked to the Chinese restaurant for a delicious lunch, occupying the only available table in a cozy corner. We treated ourselves to ice cream cones from Rialto (hazelnut and cookies and cream) and three scoops for Mutti in a cup: hazelnut, banana, and chocolate. She enjoyed the treat, but was not as perky as she was on Saturday, even when we visited Suse. She surely knew that this and our other visits are now short-lived and infrequent. When we said goodbye before dinner, we said we would see her tomorrow, and we had every intention of doing so. But we did not return on Monday morning.

Kersti visited Inge Guha, who lives around the corner from our apartment, on Sunday at 6:00 PM for a round up of family news. On Monday morning, we returned to Dr. Sieglitz Strasse one last time and took some food items and all of Vati's slides from the late 70s to the early 90s—maybe 1,500 or more. Kersti began reviewing them on our drive back to Solln, and we continued on Monday and Tuesday evenings. We saved about 50 slides to look at when we get back home.

Yesterday afternoon around dinnertime, I watched intently as the two larger horses were saddled and taken for a long ride—almost two hours. The mid-sized horse and pony were very concerned about the absence of their companions. The horse kept whinnying and sometimes broke into a run, followed closely by the pony. They were very attentive when their fellow horses reappeared, close to dusk.

As I have done every morning in Solln, this morning I looked out the bathroom and dining area windows on the chilly field to say "*Guten Morgen*" to the horses. But they were gone. No doubt they are saying that we also will soon be gone.

Friday, May 17: Solln

It is the final full day of our trip. After many gray days, the sun is shining, and the temperature is warming up, so we won't need our beanies or gloves. But Kersti is battling a bad cold—fever, sore throat, cough, and congestion—so we will not take a final walk through the fields. Time is moving slowly, and our packing is relaxed and deliberate.

We keep saying our goodbyes. Tuesday was my final session with Dr. Madert, and Wednesday turned out to be Kersti's concluding session with Frau Wachter, because Kersti had to cancel this morning's double session on account of her illness. Yesterday morning, May 16, we said goodbye to Kersti's black bike, which had taken her on many rides through the fields, along the Isar, to town for shopping, and to her sessions on Whistlerweg. I rode it on a 7-kilometer excursion to Gina's legal office in the Laim section of Munich, just off of Fürstenriedstrasse. I pedaled through the cool, gray, increasingly business-oriented streets of Munich with my jacket zipper pulled up high and still wearing my gloves and baseball cap. I chatted briefly with Gina in German, wishing her a happy 60th birthday and reminding her that it was also Lisa's 32nd birthday. I said how sorry we were that Kersti's illness was preventing us from joining her on Thursday evening for a birthday celebration. The sky turned partly sunny, and so I decided to make the return trip on foot—about an hour and 20 minutes. The walk through an outlying section of the city reminded me of my walk in Hackney in search of Kalia's apartment on our final morning in London.

We're ready to go home.

Postscript

Kersti and I had separate flights from Munich, but our departure and arrival times were fairly compatible, in spite of my brief stopover and change of planes in Iceland on Icelandair. She arrived a little after 6:00 PM, and I followed by 6:30. Pete and Cordelia picked us up at Logan. Cordelia was struggling as we slowly made our way to the parking area. We had a smooth ride back to Exeter. It was good to be home for the spring and summer months.

Chapter 42

PENNSYLVANIA, MARYLAND, VIRGINIA, DELAWARE, AND NEW JERSEY

October 31 – November 8, 2019

"The joy of the present moment, and the promise of the future"

Saturday, November 2: Oakland, Maryland

It is cool and clear on this Saturday afternoon as we get ready for Julianne Decker's wedding. We are spending the weekend in this delightful "small cabin" in the woods just south of Oakland, Maryland. This morning I created a small trail with dead braches and small logs, winding up the hill toward the ridge overlooking one of the many valleys in this rolling landscape. During our two days of travel from southern New Hampshire to western Maryland, we wondered at times why Julianne and Adam chose this remote location for their wedding, but we are gratified that they brought their family and friends to this special place.

The trip south on Thursday reminded us more of mid-summer than mid-fall. It rained most of the way. The temperature was in the high seventies, and the air was muggy and mild. We drove right past our familiar Morristown exit and then took 78 West toward Allentown, as we had done so many times on our trips to the Amish country. But we passed by Allentown, finally stopping for the night in Jonestown, Pennsylvania, close to Lebanon. The rain was swirling and the wind was whipping as we pulled up to our small cottage, the so-called "flower box." It was a bare bones facility, and we could have used an extra blanket or two as the temperature plummeted and the air cleared overnight. We ate dinner at a local Chinese restaurant and then walked through the nearly empty town, which had postponed Halloween until Saturday because of the violent weather. We stopped by a small café for coffee and tea and enjoyed the final song or two of Amber Nadine, a young songwriter and singer who reminded us of Nellie both in terms of her music and her appealing personality.

We were on the road by 9:00 on Friday morning. We drove through nearby Hershey and Harrisburg, where Kersti had stayed with families on her trip west to Erie in early January 1981. Unlike Jonestown, which was a bit run down, Hershey's buildings, streets, and small squares were beautifully maintained with the obvious infusions of corporate money. We passed a number of Hershey Company administrative buildings and plants. Harrisburg reminded us of Trenton with many row houses that had seen much better days. The capitol complex was impressive as was the developed waterfront area. We crossed the mighty Susquehanna three times, finally winding our way to 81 South toward the Maryland border.

The highlight of our trip west on Route 70 was driving toward and through the Cumberland Pass. It was one of the major thoroughfares west to Ohio during the early days of America's westward expansion. At the visitor's center, we stopped for lunch, overlooking the vast valley with different shades of golden leaves, some dark, some light. It was too windy and chilly to eat outside. We continued west on I-68 toward Frostburg and then south on Maryland 219 toward Oakland. Turning left from 219, we drove up and down along the narrow roads, happy to see the Friday washes of Amish residents dancing in the wind. We finally spotted our small, nondescript house and drove up a gravel driveway that was covered by brown oak leaves. But inside we found a comfortable, modern, one-bedroom cottage, just two years old. It felt good to be here.

On Friday evening, we joined Neil and Denise along with Julianne and Adam, and Scott and Emily, and lots of their friends at the Mountain State Brewing pub in McHenry, Maryland, close to Accident. It was a bit raucous, but we managed to have good conversations with Neil and Denise. Julianne and Adam were both excited and calm on the eve of their big day.

Now we are off to the wedding at a refurbished barn just a few miles from here.

Monday, November 4: Dasgsboro, Delaware

It's a sunny, quiet afternoon at Jan Wells' townhouse at Seagrass Plantation in Dagsboro, Delaware. Julianne and Adam's wedding on Saturday afternoon was a beautiful affair—outside in the cool wind of late afternoon with the backdrop of solid blue skies and brown corn stalks swaying in the stiff wind. Julianne and Adam have such great chemistry, and they combined emotion, humor, and obvious affection in their vows, embraces, and raised arms in celebration. After a brief chilly reception on the patio, Kersti and I retreated inside and took our seats, honored to be at the Decker "family table." We sat with Denise's brother, Tony, and his lady friend, Claudia, who live in the Manchester area; Denise's sister, Theresa, and her husband; and Denise and Neil themselves. After the traditional introductions of the wedding party and first dances, we proceeded to the buffet table by table. After dinner, Kersti and I enjoyed lots of dancing. (I ignored my right pinky toe, which I had used to break the fall of a framed picture the previous Sunday when Pete and I were carrying the large easy chair to my home study—but I felt it in the days that followed.) Around 9:30, we grew tired of the loud, pounding music and decided to turn over the rest of the celebration to the young people. Kersti snapped a beautiful photo of the brightly lit, shimmering barn at night as we walked toward our car.

There were three highlights in our drive east toward the Delaware coast on Sunday. First, we marveled at the spectacular hills and valleys driving along Route 48 in West Virginia. The landscape was ablaze in colors that were different than those in New England: various shades of gold and red, some light, some darker. At times we saw the highways like ribbons pulled through the valleys and hills for miles ahead. The second memorable moment was our visit with Dave Houseman in Dumfries, Virginia. We were there to console Andrew and him on the loss of their beloved Jeannie this past August. Dave was in relatively good spirits. We laughed and reminisced, and he openly shared the story of Jeannie's courage and positive outlook during her final seven months. Their small bulldog, Cinnamon, and purring cat provided some comfort. As we departed, I reminded Dave of our special friendship, now spanning 64 years. Our final highlight of the long day of travel was crossing the Bay Bridge near Annapolis. With Kersti at the wheel, we drove across the wide bridge, high above the sparking water, as the sun was setting. After dinner at a Mexican restaurant in Delaware, I drove the final leg, arriving at Jan's shortly before 8:00 PM. As always, she extended a very warm welcome. She's another long-time friend, who is "fam."

Saturday, November 9: Exeter

We left on Halloween morning on a rainy, mild day in the middle of fall, and returned yesterday afternoon in the bright, blustery chill that was suggestive of early winter. It was 48 degrees when we walked into the house just past 3:00 PM, glad to be home in the daylight. It was a quick, smooth trip from Madison, lasting just 5 hours and 20 minutes with a few short stops. After sleeping in assorted beds for one night in Pennsylvania, two in Maryland, three in Delaware, and two in New Jersey, we were glad to climb into our cozy, familiar bed on the third floor of 32 Franklin Street.

The final two legs or our trip were as enjoyable and successful as the first two legs. Our days with Jan in Delaware were relaxing and slow-paced with no obligations. We did not need to be anywhere at any particular time. On Monday morning in the bright sunshine, Jan drove us to Bethany Beach. We walked along the boardwalk and sat for a while on a bench gazing out to the sea. I shared with Jan the significance of the Atlantic coast for Kersti and me: we met here in May 1982; spent numerous occasions at the Jersey shore with the kids growing up; and now live just 20 minutes from the northern coast. On the way back to Dagsboro, we stopped for a relaxing hour in a 90-degree indoor pool. On Monday evening we watched "Doubt," a provocative film starring Meryl Streep and Philip Seymour Hoffman. Kersti tried to stay awake, but snoozed on the couch during most of the film.

Tuesday was rainy, so we planned to drive to the bargain cinema in nearby Ocean City, Maryland. Kersti and I saw "Harriet," the story of the Underground Railroad heroine and activist, Harriet Tubman; Cynthia Erivo was sensational in the lead role. Jan had seen "Harriet" the previous week, so she watched "Motherless Brooklyn" at the same time. For dinner, Jan drove us to Northeast Seafood Kitchen in Ocean View, Delaware; we ate half-price scallops, fried chicken, and steak entrees at the bar to avoid the 45-minute wait for a table, even at 5:00 PM.

The sun was shining again on Wednesday. We packed our car once again—increasingly disorganized—and took a final stroll to the bay. The wind was whipping through the tall grasses and creating small caps on the water. We departed by 9:00 AM. About an hour into the trip, driving north on 113, a speeding car honked at us from the left lane; it was Jan, heading to Madison and Mendham to visit and care for her 10 grandchildren. We made good time, arriving at Hamilton Park with plenty of time to spare before the 4:00 PM Holocaust lecture at Drew. There we chatted with Josh Kavaloski and Barbara Gilford, who was so easy to notice in a crowd with her thick white hair. The presenter, 96-year-old Josef Eisinger, told his compelling tale of escaping from Vienna as a 15-year-old teenager on the Kinder Transport. We bought his personally signed book, *Flight and Revenge: Reminiscences of a Motley Youth* (2016).

We were planning to have dinner with Barbara at an Italian restaurant, but she thankfully decided to pick up a baked chicken at Whole Foods and serve us an intimate dinner in her cozy home in Morris Township. Her cute gray poodle, Molly, was so excited to see us, jumping up continuously as we slipped into the house. After dinner, we settled into Barbara's living room beside a roaring fire that I had set up, and Kersti shared with Barbara our plans to visit Liesbeth's graveside in northern Denmark. Barbara, in turn, read us the moving prologue to her own story of searching for her grandmother. This is the mutual theme that Kersti and Barbara will unfold at their Holocaust presentation at Drew on April 1, 2020.

As we pulled open the curtain on November 7, Kersti's birthday dawned cloudy and cool, but I warmed things up with my presentation: the New Hampshire philharmonic season series, the Krystal Ballroom dance lesson, dangling blue earrings, a subscription to "O" magazine, two days plus swims at Hamilton Park, a card, and of course the dinner celebration. We drove to the Pachecos to say "hi," and of course Rocky treated us to a birthday breakfast. They are "fam" through and through. Back at the hotel, we took a leisurely swim and later drove to Chopt in Florham Park for a soup and salad. Later in the afternoon, we had a long chat with Janine and were rushing a bit by the time we left Hamilton Park to drive to Maplewood to pick up Birgit. We forgot my "Ode to Kersti on Your 60th Birthday," so we had to backtrack a few miles, and then we ran into heavy rush-hour traffic on Columbia Turnpike. After all the twists, turns, and delays, and detour to Maplewood to pick up Birgit, we managed to arrive at the new Blossom restaurant on Springfield Avenue in Summit just 15 minutes late. Nellie, Rocky, Anita, Barbara, and Marion were already there, sipping Rocky's wine in bright, open, private space. Driving from New York after a day of teaching and parent conferences, Windy finally arrived bearing gifts. Kersti greeted her special guests, thanking them for their love and friendship. We drank a champagne toast, and I followed with a recitation of my ode with the concluding two couplets:

> So as we pause on this very special day
> And reflect on the past and our future way
> I look deeply into your sweet eyes sky blue
> Feeling blessed to be able to grow old with you

The appetizers kept coming—seaweed salad, spring rolls, sushi, tuna slices, and scallion pancakes—and then the main courses. Our server was engaging, friendly, and attentive. She took a group photo and then capped off the evening with a bowl of ice cream and a single candle signifying the realities of he past, the joy of the present moment, and the promise of the future.

Chapter 43

GERMANY, DENMARK, AND ENGLAND

November 14 – December 12, 2019

"There she was..."

"We were making peace with the harrowing events that ended one life, saved another life, and altered many others' lives"

Klitmoller, Denmark

Monday, November 18: Bingerbrück

It's a quiet, cool, damp, and cloudy morning at our apartment in Bingerbrück with our splendid view of the Rhein, the *Weinberge (vineyards)* across the river in Hessen, Burg Klopp, St. Martin's *Altenheim*, the Dr. Sieglitz Strasse *Wohnung,* and the border of the Jewish cemetery on the high ridge above Bingen. Kersti is in town, visiting Mutti and doing a bit of shopping.

Our trip to Frankfurt from Exeter on Thursday afternoon and evening had a few new twists on the U.S. side of the ocean. We took an Uber to the Newburyport, Massachusetts bus depot and then hopped on the very comfortable C&J bus, which dropped us right in front of Terminal E at Logan Airport. Our Lufthansa flight left on time and arrived a few minutes early after just 6 hours and 20 minutes. I passed the time with three different films: *The Art of Racing in the Rain* (a touching dog film), *After* (a college romance film), and *Yesterday* (a clever and enjoyable film imagining if an Indian immigrant in London had been the writer and performer of all the Beatles songs). We arrived at the Hertz counter before it even opened at 6:00 AM and endured a wait until our car was ready, a somewhat clunky Citroën. It was still dark when we left the airport, but the light of day grew as we headed west and approached Bingerbrück.

We have visited Mutti twice each day, usually late morning and in the afternoon for *Kaffee und Kuchen*. She lights up when she sees us with a deep smile and a sparkle in her eyes. She still recognizes us, and her laughs and smiles express her gratitude. But after a while, she grows tired and languid. We can no longer engage in a sustained or meaningful conversation. But at least her medication keeps her stable, and she no longer suffers from the sadness and weeping that Kersti witnessed during her August visit (August 2-19).

Over the weekend, we had long conversations with our three *Kinder* and also made plans to visit Irmgard and Albert tomorrow, and Hans and Rosi on December 5, the day Janine arrives from London. Later today, we will see Kersti's friend Kordula in Langenlonheim and make a final stop at the *Wohnung* to retrieve a few albums and items. On Thursday morning, we will head north to Munster and then on to Denmark on Saturday.

Sunday, November 24: Klitmöller, Denmark

We arrived at our Airbnb apartment yesterday around 5:45 PM in the darkness. We could hear the wind whipping and the waves crashing along the shore just 300 meters away. Just before dinner, we walked toward the sea and saw enormous dunes rising to our left and right, but Kersti's miner's light was faint, and we could not see where we were going. So we turned back.

We just returned from a blustery morning walk on the beach and dunes on a chilly, gray day. The wide sandy beach is decorated by stones of many different colors, shapes, and sizes. We collected our favorites to leave at Liesbeth's gravesite. Her presence is very strong, especially when we are feeling the same wind and breathing the same sea air that she and Mutti did during the summer of 1945. They are same wind and air, but very different at the same time—a different time and circumstances.

Our days in Bingen were quiet and uneventful with morning and afternoon visits to Mutti on most days. She seemed more languid and less excited to see us than that initial expression of surprise and joy when we first visited on Friday, November 15. At least it has become easier to say goodbye to her. Kersti arranged for an experienced, energetic aide named Erica, who speaks a classic *Bingerdialekt*, to spend two hours a week with Mutti.

We embarked on our 12-day excursion on Thursday morning, November 21. We drove directly to Marianne's and Michael's home in Munster, arriving around 2:30 PM after a drive of less than four hours. Marianne and Michael welcomed us warmly with guava juice and chicken soup. We thought we were staying with them, but because of their limited accommodations—single beds in separate rooms—they generously put us up at a nearby, recently renovated hostel, which was formerly a convent.

On Friday, they treated us to a delicious lunch at an old pub in the *Altstadt*. It was already decked out with Christmas ornaments. After lunch, we walked to Munster's art museum for an exhibit of Joseph Mallord William Turner's (1775-1851) paintings and sketches, focusing primarily on his seascapes and mountain images inspired by his visits to Switzerland and Italy. Michael broke away to ride back home on his bike, while the three of us walked to the *Altenheim* to visit Marianne's 94-year-old sister Ruth. Ruth was a nurse in one of the Danish refugee camps in the summer of 1945, and Marianne was hopeful that she would remember Liesbeth, wife of everyone's favorite Onkel "Brunchen." She listened intently and tried to remember, but the memories were just not forthcoming. She spoke softly and sweetly and was so careful to lift the small bites of the creamy fruitcake to her mouth. We were all amused that she kept calling me Helmut—prompted by her memory either of Mutti's older brother or Ruth's own husband, an old friend whom she married when she was 66. We wrapped up our visit with a light dinner at Marianne's. When we left just past 9:00 PM, Marianne held her hand on her heart and wished us safe travels and good feelings on our journey to Denmark in search of Liesbeth.

On Saturday morning, we were on the road by 8:32 AM. The entire trip, including a number of stops, covered about 800 kilometers (about 500 miles) and spanned around 9 hours. But it all went smoothly with minimal delays, construction, and trucks. The countryside was mostly flat and not very scenic, and the sky was a solid gray for most of the trip. By the time we reached scenic highway 34 heading west toward the Danish coast and traversing inlets and fjords, it was dark. We decided to change rooms and mattresses around 11:30 PM, but then slept fairly soundly until the gray light of morning.

Tuesday, November 26: Mutti's 84th Birthday

It's hard to believe that we have been in Denmark for just 72 hours. The days have been damp and gray, but full of discoveries and light. On Sunday afternoon, we drove about 45 km to Fjerritslev, the site of the camp where Mutti, her brother Helmut, Liesbeth, and Oma Neufeld were interned during the summer of 1945. The camp is long gone, replaced by a brick school, built in 1979 with a large boulder and the statue of a scary eagle in front. We walked around the school and down a wooded path, feeling the essence of the place. Kersti deeply felt the loss that occurred here 74 years ago.

On Monday morning, we drove to east toward Grove, the site of the German cemetery where Liesbeth was reinterred in 1962 along with 1,118 refugees and 175 soldiers. We walked along the soggy grounds past row after row of graves, finally arriving at Liesbeth's row (no. 22) and her numbered site. There she was. It was very moving, as we stood there, offering our reflections and prayers, our small bouquet of flowers and the "blood line" stone that I had found on Sunday morning on the Kiltmöller beach. I glanced at some of the graves. One infant was born 10 days before Liesbeth died, and the tiny person succumbed the day after. But that infant's life and all the lives remembered there had value and meaning.

We continued driving southeast toward Aahuis, Denmark's second largest city. We stopped in Gammel (old) Rye, the home of Annette Jacoksen, author of *Wenn Seufzer Luftballons Waren* (2011; *When Sighs Were Balloons*). Her book recreates life in the German refugee camps in Denmark from the perspective of a 9-year-old girl—she could have been young Annelie—as well as a 14-year-old boy and 22-year-old woman. As we approached Annette's house, she came bounding out in a short-sleeve shirt despite the cool afternoon. We had an immediate connection, prompted by our shared interest in the German refugees. Over lunch of cold cuts and homemade rolls, we talked about our lives and interest in the suffering and resilience of the German refugees. After lunch, Annette showed us several films that she had contributed to as a writer and researcher. I was startled to learn that 80% of the children who were less than one year old perished in 1945 from malnutrition, disease, inadequate supplies, unsanitary conditions, and/or the neglect of Danish doctors. It was already dark when we departed for Klitmöller. Annette stood outside on the road, waving a warm farewell.

Our only excursion today was back to Fjerritslev for an afternoon meeting with the archivists at the local library. We were hoping to take one more walk on the beach after breakfast, but it was raining steadily.

After strolling through the commercial center of the town in the light rain, we had our one Danish meal out at a local restaurant—a burger for me and a falafel *Döner* for Kersti. The three town historians and archivists welcomed us warmly, and they tried so hard to be helpful, but their English and German were unfortunately limited. They did produce a photo of the small internment camp at Klim Strand and a photo of the doctor who operated on Mutti and saved her life. One of the women proudly smiled and said that he had also "borned" her. They showed us aerial images of the campground and hospital (no longer in existence) and the cemetery where Liesbeth was originally buried and lay from 1945 until 1962. We drove to all three places after leaving the library to feel the damp air.

Our final stop was the beach at Klim Strand, where Mutti and her family members had spent some time at a very small camp adjacent to the beach. Mutti once told Kersti that Liesbeth had been seriously ill with typhoid during the spring or summer of 1945, presumably in this camp, before recovering and moving to the larger camp at Fjerritslev. Mutti may have been confined to the camp, unable to walk down to the water, but the camp may have been close enough for her to hear the waves. We parked our car and walked to the edge of the water. I scooped up some sand to bring home for a memorial to Liesbeth and Mutti.

It was still light enough to marvel at the moon-like landscape of the Thy (pronounced "Too") National Park as we drove back to Klitmöller. We called Mutti to wish her a happy 84th birthday. She was laughing and in good spirits. We did not tell her that we were in Denmark or send greetings from Denmark, but maybe she knew intuitively that we were here…that we were making peace with the harrowing events that ended one life, saved another life, and altered many others' lives.

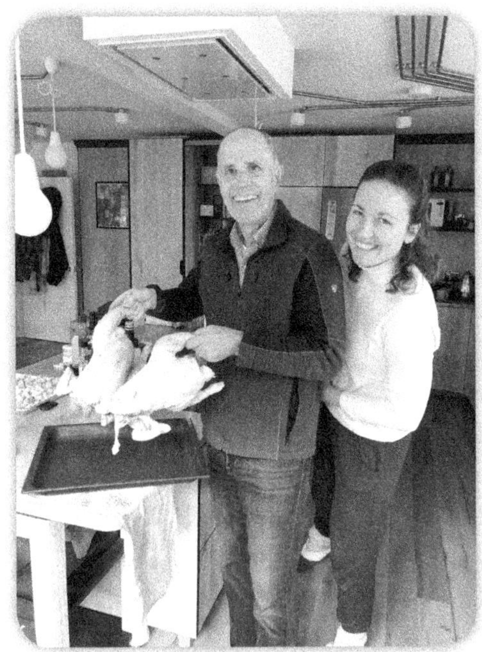

Village of Lauriston, Borough of Hackney, London, England—Thanksgiving in England

Monday, December 2: Heathrow Airport, London

The sun is shining brightly on this cool Monday morning as we await our flight to Frankfurt. From Janine's flat on Rutland Road in the Lauriston section of South Hackney, we took an Uber to the Holborn underground and then 22 stops on the Piccadilly line to Terminals 1, 2, and 3.

This segment of our travels began on a dark, rainy morning in northern Denmark. We drove along narrow, winding roads east toward the Allborg Airport for about an hour and a half. As always, it was a relief to turn over the keys of our rental car, having driven our Citroën a total of 2,244 kilometers (1,391 miles). There was only a scattering of people at the airport at 6:30 in the morning. Five or six personnel attended to just the two of us as we passed through security. The SAS flight left on time and arrived early. We were in thick fog most of the way, until there were breaks of sun looking down on the countryside of eastern England. We took the National Standard Bus from Stanstead to a stop just a few hundred yards from Janine's flat, and then paused for a coffee and tea at Elbows, a café, where we had a nice chat with a local lady, her daughter, and granddaughter. Eventually, Janine came bounding up on her bike, and we gave her big hugs.

Janine went to work on Thursday, so Kersti and I had a leisurely morning. We were very pleased to meet Beks, Janine's cheerful, delightful new roommate from Scotland. In the afternoon, we took two buses to 10-20 Whitechapel Road, the location of Janine's London Interdisciplinary School (LIS) office. Only two colleagues were in the office at the time, but we liked the welcoming, interactive vibe of the office. We then set out and walked along Brick Lane, slick from a recent shower, with many people milling about on their way to pubs and Indian restaurants. We ate a tasty "official" Thanksgiving Indian dinner at Dishoom followed by coffee and tea at a modern café. Janine rode her bike home, while we took the bus, and we unexpectedly made contact on Victoria Park Road, a few blocks from Janine's flat.

On Friday, Janine departed around 9:00 AM for her all-day office Christmas party. The day was sunny and brisk, and Kersti and I took the bus and then the Central Line to the St. Paul's stop to visit the Museum of London. We walked through the history of the city from the first small settlements around 12,000 B.C. to the present. After lunch at the bistro, we were welcomed by the "Beasts of London," the current interactive experience, narrated by a lion and other animals that have roamed the fields, forests, waterways, zoos, pubs, and houses of the island from prehistoric times. Among our favorite of the nine stations was the old apothecary, where scientists and pharmacists were struggling to identify and defeat the bacteria that led to the plague and death of 100,000 Londoners in 1665 and 1666. We also enjoyed watching images of the small dog named Tiny, who scurried about the round space in a pub, catching and devouring the rats before the raucous, admiring pub patrons.

On Friday evening, we began preparations for our official Thanksgiving feast on the following day. We shred the cabbage; peeled the potatoes, sweet potatoes, and three types of squash; quartered the sprouts; cooked the cranberry sauce; and prepared and baked the pumpkin and pecan pies. On Saturday morning, we walked across the street and purchased two beautiful, free-range, five-pound chickens. Waves of people began arriving around 3:00 and they kept coming until well into the evening. Among them were Janine's colleague Marielle and Carlos, yoga friends, On Purpose friends, and even Lisa's friend Aysa from San Francisco. Eight countries were represented: England, Scotland, the U.S., Turkey, Columbia, Holland, Italy, and Germany. On Kersti's and my *Verdauungspazziergang,* we stopped by a Christmas tree market at the edge of Victoria Park and bought a live three-foot tall Christmas tree. We returned, exclaiming "Happy Christmas" to the smiling guests. Later, Janine's friend Ollie led us in a swing dance routine around the kitchen island. It was the perfect Thanksgiving dinner and afternoon/evening—delicious, plentiful, brimming with engaging people, and well paced in Janine's large kitchen and dining area. It surpassed our expectations. The final guests left around 11:30 PM.

Sunday was a day of relaxation, debriefing, packing, and chilling. We bought some cheese, eggs, and greens at the Victoria Park market and later watched three episodes of "The Crown" while Janine attended an engagement party at a pub. For dinner, we enjoyed chicken soup and fresh salad.

This morning, Janine had to leave early for an 8:30 breakfast meeting. We ended the visit the way it began: with big hugs, gratitude for Janine's hospitality, and appreciation for the full life that she is leading in London.

Monday, December 9: Bingerbrück

On this quiet Monday afternoon in Bingerbrück, a few moments ago, I laid out the three suitcases and began packing for our trip home on Thursday. Kersti just ran into town to do a few errands, and I am updating this travelogue with the House of Representatives' Judicial Committee impeachment proceedings on CNN in the background.

The highlights of the past week were our daily visits to Mutti in the *Heim*, our dinner with Gabi and Wolfgang on Wednesday evening, our visit to Hans and Rosi in Bibertal on Thursday, Janine's time with us from Thursday evening until this morning, our hike to the Eibingen *Kloster*, and our visit to the Rudesheim *Weihnachtsmarkt* on a cool, damp Friday evening. We have seen the sun very rarely. Some days Mutti has been conversant, engaged, and funny, such as this morning, when we presented her a soft, cuddly stuffed rabbit, and she called it her "kleiner Mann"; on other days, she was languid and disengaged. Nevertheless, the contrast with Rosi is more pronounced and obvious than ever. Rosi rarely talks now, especially when Hans is prompting the conversation. She never smiles and wears a perpetual frown. During most of our visit, she sat silently on the couch, absorbed in her own isolated world. She was a bit more responsive during the walk that she, Kersti, and I took while Hans attended the funeral of a friend. When a car drove by, she sometimes observed, "*Guck m*al," and she was also drawn to a small, energetic puppy. It's very sad. Hans does so much for her; his only breaks are when she goes to adult day care and is visited by two aides for a few hours each week. We realize how special it is and how fortunate we are that Mutti can still laugh, smile, react, point her finger, and hug her little *Hase*.

On Friday afternoon, Janine, Kersti, and I did not depart for Rudesheim until after visiting Mutti for *Kaffee und Kuchen*. We parked close to the *Fähre* (ferry) and then took it across the river. We were debating whether to walk all the way up to Hildegard's closter, but Janine encouraged us to forge ahead, and we began the ascent. Most of the walk took us along paved roads until the final climb along a fairly steep, rocky, muddy path. We bought some Christmas presents at the gift shop and then stopped by an art exhibit, featuring works celebrating water and the environment. During the descent, a light rain fell. We were tired, wet, and chilly, and when we arrived at the *Weihnactsmarkt*, we had an early dinner at a local restaurant with a hunting lodge theme. Afterwards, we strolled past all the exhibits and booths, pausing to admire the large, life-like manger. Janine drank a cup of *Glühwein;* Kersti and Janine ate three large fried potato pancakes for desert; and Kersti purchased mittens from Norway. It felt good to hurry aboard *the Fähre* without a wait and to arrive in Bingen a few minutes later.

Janine was planning to spend Saturday and Sunday morning in Frankfurt with Eva and her husband Gunner, but she woke up with a bad headache and spent most of the day on the couch. She was much better on Sunday, and she joined us for lunch at the Röthgen café and a visit to Mutti for a holiday program. On Friday, Saturday, and Sunday evenings, we watched films on Netflix: *Marriage Story* with Scarlett Johannson; *Iron Lady* with Meryl Streep as British Prime Minister Margaret Thatcher; and a German Christmas film, which I skipped and Kersti mostly slept through.

During a special moment during our Sunday lunch, Cordelia paid us a surprise and moving visit. Following a number of Christmas songs, we heard the soothing, familiar sounds of the Hawaiian version of "Over the Rainbow." We paused our conversation and listened intently, remembering our dear Cordelia. She is still very much with us.

Postscript: Tuesday, December 17: Exeter

Winter has come to Exeter. It's snowing as I record these final reflections on our trip.

Our last three days in Bingen were fairly routine with visits to the *Heim*, packing, shopping in town, and managing our food supply. One highlight stood out above all: the immediate bond between Mutti and her new baby *Puppe* (doll). Alicia had suggested it, and the doll, known as "Muffin," was a big hit. We loved the way Mutti held her baby, talked to her, lay her down to sleep with her eyes closed, and brought her to her lips for some kisses. After our fourth visit of the year, we had the best feeling yet about Mutti's caregivers (Alicia, Erica, and the caring staff) and her overall acceptance of her situation at this stage of her life. It was easier to say goodbye this time. We did not say a word about flying back to the U.S. We simply kissed her on her soft white hair and said to her "*Bis gleich.*"

Kersti set the alarm for 5:00 AM on Thursday morning, and of course I bet it by 15 minutes. We were loaded up and rolling down the narrow street for the last time by 6:15. We began our trip in the dark on the *Autobahn* and ended it in the dark. During our 10-day car rental, we drove only 527 kilometers (327 miles), but having a car made our trips into town so much easier, especially during the *nasskalt* (wet cool) days of late fall. We made good time to the airport, arriving three and a half hours prior to our scheduled departure. Our Lufthansa flight left a little late and arrived a little late, and we enjoyed the extra legroom of our emergency seats. I watched three films to pass the time: On *Chesil Beach* with Saoire Ronan as a young bride struggling with her sexuality, *Rocketman* featuring the fantastic Taron Egerton, and *German Lessons*, a dark German film about abuse, loyalty, and morality in the final months and aftermath of World War II. We were thrilled to sail through Boston customs in about 10 minutes, and Kersti gave the U.S. Customs interviewer a string of "5's" on the random interview as we awaited our luggage. We gave back the time that we had saved during the delay with our Uber driver at the open Tobin Drawbridge not far from the airport, but 95 North was as smooth as ever. I asked our driver to take the back roads—107, 150, and 108—to Exeter, and the sun had not yet fallen beneath the horizon as we pulled in to 32 Franklin. We looked out our front door a bit later and glimpsed the soothing orange winter welcome-home sky.

Chapter 44

BOULDER, COLORADO

December 23-30, 2019

"The day brightened, and we glimpsed the shimmering, magical white-pink mountains rising above Boulder to the west"

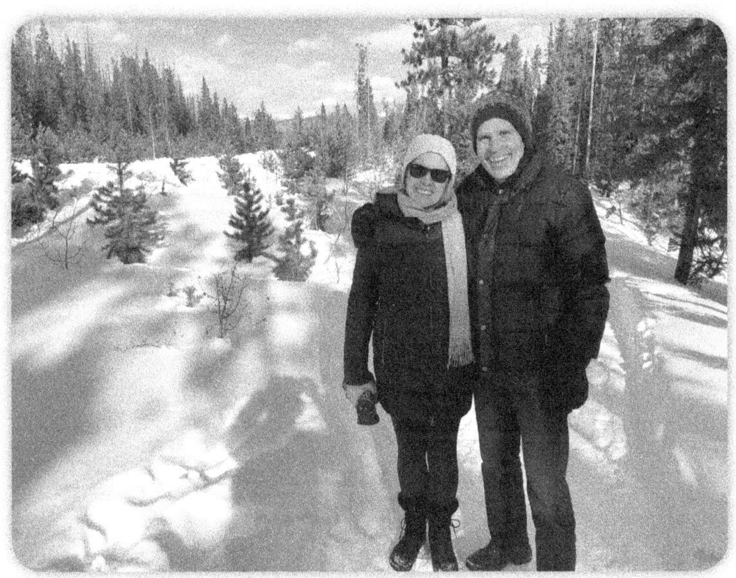

Fraser, Colorado

Saturday, December 28

A light snow continues to fall on this Saturday afternoon at our home for the week at 707 North Street off of 9th Street in Boulder. I'm alone and enjoying the quietude. Janine just left to walk into town to have lunch with her friend Dara, and Kersti, Lisa, and Windy join Nellie and Anja for a trip to one of the chiropractors in town. Kersti and I left Exeter around 7:15 AM on Monday morning for our quick drive to Newburyport, where we picked up the 8:30 C&J bus to Logan Airport. We arrived more than three hours before our 1:45 PM flight.

Kersti likes the secure feeling of being at the airport with plenty of time to spare. We had a smooth flight to balmy Denver, walked just outside Terminal B to a temperature in the low 60s. Anja picked us up and drove us on the loop around Denver and northwest toward Boulder.

We quickly settled into our spacious house with three bedrooms, a loft, a living room, dining area, and kitchen. Anja treated us to a big pot of chicken-squash soup for a tasty, easy dinner. Our abode was a bit rundown, funky, and dusty, but one could call it "quaint." Janine was already in Chicago, awaiting her connecting flight to Denver, while Windy missed their flight from Newark but was able to get on board the next direct flight. In the true spirit and legacy of the Schindler shuttle and our memory of Norbert, Daniel waited the extra hour or two for Windy and delivered them to our house around 10:40 PM.

Lisa and Nellie arrived the following day—Christmas Eve—to complete our family of eight. It did not feel like Christmas, in spite of the small evergreen with a string of lights that Anja gave us. But our candlelit family dinner of salmon, soup, and salad helped to get us in the mood for our evening gift exchange. Our gifts were small but thoughtful and appreciated: books, earrings, Hildegard tea, small jars of granola, an Exeter salt cave gift card, Windy's 14th music CD, and of course digestive biscuits from England.

Daniel kindly loaned us his Jeep Cherokee for the week, and after a video call with Grammy and Cynthia on Christmas afternoon, we hopped in the car with Windy behind the wheel and drove to Anja's apartment in Arvada, about 35-40 minutes south of Boulder. After *Kaffee und Kuchen* and a "cousin walk," we settled in to hear Kersti's story of our recent trip to Denmark in search of Liesbeth. It was after 8:00 PM when we realized how much time had passed. Anja served her pureed vegetable soup alongside the salad that we had brought. It was nearly 10:00 PM when we arrived back in Boulder.

We stayed in Boulder on Thursday, the day after Christmas. Lisa worked at home for nearly five hours; Janine and Windy took a long hike along the nearby Sanitas Trail; the kids rented skis and boots in town, and joined Anja and Nellie for coffee and tea; and Kersti and I had Daniel's tires checked, picked up a few items at Whole Foods, and bided our time at Barnes & Noble. I bought *Rocketman,* the pictorial story of Elton John's rise to stardom and stellar career with lists of songs for each of his 30 albums. It was a fun retrospective of my favorite musician.

Friday was a beautiful, mostly sunny day, and we took advantage of it to head to the mountains. Daniel drove his car with his sister and three cousins, while Kersti and I went with Anja. Our destination was Winter Park, a modest (compared to Vail or Aspen), family-oriented resort about an hour and 40 minutes from Boulder. We drove south along Route 93 for over 25 flat, nondescript miles, and then turned on to Route 40 South and West to begin our ascent into the mountains. The snow from recent storms clung to the endless evergreens, as we twisted and turned our way from about 5,500 feet to nearly 9,000. The mountains glistened against the blue sky. Kersti and I got to work as the ski assistants for the day, depositing the cars and later picking up the kids' bags, "hiking" to the remote overflow parking lot, and loading the kids and equipment at the end of the day at another slope several miles from the main gondola. During the afternoon, Anja took us on a tour of the towns of Winter Park and Fraser, and later we walked along a scenic path in the woods where she sometimes rides her bike in the summer. By the end of the day, just after the lifts shut down at 4:00 PM and the daylight began to fade, the cousins were happily tired. Kersti and I had spent enough time outdoors and handling skis and boots that we almost felt that we had been with them on the slopes. It was dark by the time we were back on the road. We drove through the center of Golden, which was ablaze with so many glittering Christmas lights that keeping our eyes on the road was a challenge. The Thai restaurant that Anja recommended was booked, so we settled for a tasty Lebanese dinner at Amir on the outskirts of Golden.

Monday, December 30

The sun is shining brightly as we put the finishing touches on our packing in preparation for our flights east this afternoon. Early this morning, in the first light of day around 6:45 AM, we drove Lisa to the

Budget car rental, where she picked up her car for her drive to New Mexico for her yoga retreat. The rental guy arrived about 10 minutes late; he was on Colorado or holiday time and did not apologize. On the way outside, I helped him out by flipping the "Closed" sign to "Open." The day brightened, and we glimpsed the shimmering, magical white-pink mountains rising above Boulder to the west.

We stayed in town during our final two days in Boulder. On Friday morning, I swept the walkway leading to the street after two to three powdery inches fell the previous evening. Later in the afternoon, Janine and Lisa watched *Frozen 2,* while Windy did some shopping at the Pearl Street mall. They had a late dinner at a local pub. Meanwhile, Kersti and I were content to have a quiet dinner and a Netflix German film about two sisters who were glassblowers and who challenged the German patriarchal system in the 1890s.

Sunday, December 29 was another bright, mild winter day. Windy went for an early massage and then joined the four of us at the Boulder Dushanbe Teahouse at 1770 13th Street for a special celebration of Kersti's 60th birthday. We also toasted Janine's 34th birthday and the 39th anniversary of Kersti's arrival in the U.S. on December 30, 1980. (I forgot to mention my 70th half-birthday.) The teahouse was originally constructed in its native Tajikistan and later reassembled on this site in downtown Boulder. We arrived at 10:30 AM, concerned that we might have a long wait for a Sunday holiday brunch, but we were quickly seated just as Lis was filming me performing Robert Frost's short poem, "Dust of Snow," one of my favorites:

The way a crow
Shook down on me
The dust of snow
From a hemlock tree
Has given my heart
A change of mood
And saved a part
Of a day I had rued.

We began a leisurely, pleasing repast, featuring special teas and dishes from around the world, including India, Korea, and Indonesia. Our server, Sonofina (?), was superb; as I wrote in my comment, she was kind, engaging, courteous, patient, and knowledgeable. Afterwards, we walked along Pearl Street, looking for some earrings for Windy and other sundry items. Anja and Nellie arrived; Nellie, Janine, and Windy took a long hike along the mountain trail, while Lisa napped; and Anja, Kersti, and I chatted about recent discoveries of our German family history. Daniel joined us for dinner; we rolled the tall breakfast table into the dining area to create a setting for eight; Windy ordered some pizzas; and over dinner, we shared a highlight of the week, most relating to family and our meaningful time together.

Boulder, Colorado—Brunch at the Dushanbe Teahouse

Postscript

By check out time at 11:00 on Monday morning, we were loaded up in two cars and headed over to Daniel's house. He shares it with a bunch of his Phi Delta Phi "brothers" and their delightful, cute, blue-eyed, spunky dog Keystone. (He is not named after the ski resort, but rather the brand of cheap beer.) Daniel and Keystone took us on a tour of the Colorado campus, including stops at the buffalo, the CU mascot, and the amazing sports center, which felt like a five-star resort. Around 1:45 PM, we climbed into Anja's car. Unfortunately, there was not enough space for Nellie. She looked a bit forlorn as we waved and pulled away. She is leaving her job at Sony in mid-January and heading to Berlin and perhaps later to Los Angeles to pursue her musical aspirations. At curbside at the airport, Anja held it together when hugging Windy, Kersti, and me, but she began weeping as she hugged Janine and then turned away with a final farewell. Our presence and family connection were very important to her during her own time of transition. Windy and Janine, and Kersti and I proceeded through separate security points to different gates, but they visited us for a final hug and goodbye before boarding their plane. We arrived in Boston a bit early, relieved that the forecasted snow was only a cold rain. We took an Uber to the parking lot in Newburyport, and I brushed off a layer of frosty snow. The rain continued as we drove north on 95 and then west on 88 toward Exeter. Just as we entered town around 11:30 PM, the rain turned to snow.